45⁰⁰

Race, War, and Surveillance

Race, War, and Surveillance

African Americans and
the United States Government
during World War I

Mark Ellis

Indiana University Press
Bloomington and Indianapolis

This book is a publication of
Indiana University Press
601 North Morton Street
Bloomington, Indiana 47404-3797 USA

http://iupress.indiana.edu

Telephone orders 800-842-6796
Fax orders 812-855-7931
Orders by email iuporder@indiana.edu

The paper used in this publication meets the minimum requirements of American National Standard for Information Sciences—Permanence of Paper for Printed Library Materials, ANSI Z39.48-1984.

Manufactured in the United States of America

Library of Congress Cataloging-in-Publication Data

Ellis, Mark, date
Race, war, and surveillance : African Americans and the United States government during World War I / Mark Ellis.
p. cm.
Includes bibliographical references and index.
ISBN 0-253-33923-5 (alk. paper)
1. World War, 1914–1918—Afro-Americans. 2. World War, 1914–1918—United States. 3. Political persecution—United States—History—20th century. 4. World War, 1914–1918—Participation, Afro-American. I. Title.

D639.N4 E55 2001
940.4′03—dc21

00-047137

1 2 3 4 5 06 05 04 03 02 01

For Sue, Tom, and Sam

Contents

Acknowledgments   *ix*

Introduction   *xi*

One
African Americans and
the War for Democracy, 1917   *1*

Two
The Wilson Administration
and Black Opinion, 1917–1918   *48*

Three
Black Doughboys   *74*

Four
The Surveillance of African-American Leadership   *101*

Five
W. E. B. Du Bois, Joel Spingarn,
and Military Intelligence   *141*

Six
Diplomacy and Demobilization, 1918–1919   *183*

Seven
Conclusion   *228*

Notes   *233*

Selected Bibliography   *305*

Index   *313*

Acknowledgments

This book grew out of my initial research into the causes of the major race riots that took place in the United States during May–October 1919 and the governmental responses those disorders produced. As I investigated the turmoil of American race relations during what James Weldon Johnson called "the Red Summer," it became obvious that critical shifts in African-American political consciousness and the government's position on the "race problem" had occurred during, rather than after, World War I.

For valued advice and assistance in using their collections on this period, I would like to thank the staff of the National Archives, the Library of Congress Manuscript Division, the Moorland-Spingarn Research Center at Howard University (particularly Esme Bhan), the University of Massachusetts Library, the Houghton Library at Harvard University, the Beinecke Rare Book and Manuscript Library at Yale University, the New York Public Library, and Strathclyde University Library (particularly Hamish Good).

This book could not have been completed, alongside self-inflicted administrative burdens, without the support and encouragement of several colleagues, past and present, including Bernard Aspinwall, Tom Devine, Conan Fischer, Graham Cummings, Gordon Jackson, Jay Kleinberg, Tom Tomlinson, and Barrie Walters. The History Department and the Faculty of Arts and Social Sciences at Strathclyde University granted me valuable study leave for a semester. I continue to be grateful to Ted Ranson of Aberdeen University for introducing me to American history in the first place, for overseeing my early work in this field, and for the example that he has set in his commitment to students.

I wish to thank the publishers of the *Journal of American History* (OAH) and the *Journal of Policy History* (Pennsylvania State University Press) for permission to reprint parts of chapter 5.

Above all, I thank my wife and my boys, to whom the book is dedicated.

Introduction

Looking back over half a century, the novelist and poet Arna Bontemps identified 1917 as the year in which "the seeds of the Black Renaissance of the Twenties were planted."[1] It can equally be argued that many elements of the civil rights movement of the 1950s and 1960s began to germinate at the same time. The entry of the United States into World War I, ostensibly in the name of democracy, brought about dramatic changes in African-American life, art, and political consciousness. Twenty months of warfare would also affect the ways in which black people were perceived by white Americans, producing a reactionary backlash in many quarters and a new empathy in others.

In the fifty years that followed the Civil War, the lives of black and white Americans became rigidly separate. One of the most obvious consequences of this separation was the dearth of discursive interaction between the races (outwith philanthropic circles, in which black participants usually chose their words carefully). This, in turn, led to widespread ignorance and persistent indifference on the part of white people of all classes concerning the trials of African-American life, so that much of what the white University of North Carolina sociologist Howard Odum would observe about southern race relations during World War II could have been written equally truthfully twenty-five years earlier:

> There was extraordinary ignorance on the part of the white South concerning the culture, personalities, and general progress of the Negro.
>
> Accordingly, there was extraordinary distance between the white South and the upper brackets of Negro leadership.
>
> There was extraordinary ignorance on the part of the rest of the Nation concerning both the Negro and the South. . . .
>
> There was a considerable trend in the South for the policies and actions of law enforcement officers to coincide with the folkways to keep the Negro in his place. . . .
>
> There was an ever-increasing trend on the part of the Negro to resist the folkways and to get "out of his place."[2]

Given that very few American institutions promoted egalitarian views on race, this gulf is perhaps not surprising. The Republican party did just enough, mostly through patronage and symbolism, to retain most of the existing black vote as elections approached, but otherwise chose not to enlighten the wider electorate on the subject of racial problems.[3] To the Democratic party, black political organization and thought were virtually closed books, in spite of occasional flirtations like that of W. E. B. Du Bois with Woodrow Wilson in 1912 and the racial and ethnic bartering which marked electoral politics in some northern cities. The white reformers and the philanthropists who, influenced by what William A. Link has called a "combination of refined racism and a belief in black progress," sustained the turn-of-the-century campaigns of the American Missionary Association, the Southern Education Board, the Southern Sociological Congress, and the University Race Commission, and the white liberals who would nurture the National Urban League (NUL), the National Association for the Advancement of Colored People (NAACP), and the Commission on Interracial Cooperation during their first years, represented a network of articulate, well-connected, and sometimes wealthy individuals, but they amounted to no more than a hundred or so people at any one time and their impact on wider American opinion in this period was limited.[4] Thus, whereas most blacks took a growing interest in where power lay in America and in the factions competing for control of national and local government, very few whites took any serious interest in, let alone understood, political developments in black America in the first two decades of the twentieth century. African Americans read white daily newspapers as well as their own wide and growing choice of weekly and monthly journals, but hardly any whites read the black press. References to blacks in white newspapers were normally confined to crime reports and demeaning anecdotes or cartoons. The few black public figures of whom white Americans were ordinarily aware were conservative educators and clergymen who enjoyed the approval of white philanthropists and politicians, men in the mold of Booker T. Washington, principal of Tuskegee Institute in Alabama, who died in 1915, but the newer generation of black social workers, economists, political leaders, and journalists, those associated with the Niagara Movement, for instance, forged *their* new critiques and alliances largely beyond the gaze or curiosity of most white Americans. This was despite the burgeoning efforts before World War I of black writers such as Du Bois, Kelly Miller, and Richard R. Wright, Jr., some white Progressive writers, such as Ray Stannard Baker and Mary White Ovington, and some white adherents of the social gospel, such as Edgar Gardner Murphy, Harlan Paul Douglass, and W. D. Weatherford, to provide serious, diverse, and forward-looking analyses of black life in American society.[5] White readers were far more likely to be familiar with the portrait of African Americans as immutable brutes to be found in the works of Thomas Dixon, Jr., an emphatic segregationist.[6]

The opportunities and expectations of African Americans were abridged in numerous ways at the start of the twentieth century—in educational provision and literacy, in health care and life expectancy, in housing and transport facilities, in employment and income, and in voting and representation—but none of these impairments was more virulent and demoralizing than the impunity with which violence, particularly that meted out by mobs, could be inflicted by whites upon blacks, largely in the former slave-holding states. Although lynching was gradually declining in frequency, from a peak of more than one hundred African Americans murdered by mobs in 1900 to an annual average of sixty-five between 1910 and 1919, it was marked at the same time by increasing depravity. Since 1890, lynching had been primarily a symbolic demonstration of white supremacy, and as a consequence the pretence that lynching represented swift communal justice was virtually abandoned; racial killings in the New South commonly involved the mutilation and slow public torture of victims, followed by grisly souvenir-hunting.[7]

The war years were a turning point in this violent tradition—a bloody catharsis at home, as well as abroad—out of which African Americans gained a new generation of leadership and organizations, and the confidence, experiences, and voices with which to confront, if not defeat, racial discrimination.

The link between racial violence and the mounting campaign for equal rights was strong. In May 1909, a conference of African-American radicals and sympathetic whites gathered in New York City to protest against the indifference of America to the devastation in a riot nine months earlier of the black district of Springfield, Ill., and the general discrimination endured by the black population. From this National Negro Conference grew a civil rights group that became the NAACP. Thereafter, until the 1950s, the suppression of lynching and other racial violence was the most important single goal for which the NAACP campaigned—investigating, exposing, and condemning hundreds of atrocities and calling on local law-enforcement officers and state and federal legislators to punish those who took part.[8]

The dominant intellectual and hardest worker within the NAACP was the black sociologist W. E. B. Du Bois. In 1910, soon after the formation of the NAACP, Du Bois became its director of publications and research and editor of its monthly journal, *Crisis,* which he made into the leading organ of the campaign for equal rights and against lynching. Within five years, the circulation of the *Crisis* exceeded thirty thousand; by 1919 it had reached one hundred thousand.[9] From 1903, Du Bois's work had pushed him to the fore among African Americans who questioned the conservative, gradualist leadership of Booker T. Washington and the Tuskegee Machine. Du Bois became the chief propagandist and strategist of the Niagara Movement, formed for "organized determination and aggressive action on the part of men who believe in Negro freedom and growth." For his part, Washington dismissed the movement as "a class of coloured people who make a business of keeping the troubles, the wrongs, and the hardships of the Negro race before the public. Having learned that they are able to make a living out of their troubles, they have grown into the settled habit of advertising their wrongs—partly because they want sympathy and partly because it pays."[10] A few individuals, such as John Hope of Morehouse College in Atlanta, managed to maintain good relations with both sides in the rivalry between the Niagara-ites and the Tuskegee-ites, but the split was deep and bitter. The adherents of each faction scorned and schemed against the other, so that black political activism in the Progressive era was full of intrigue, favoritism, and scandal. After 1910, it became clear that, for all Washington's cunning and financial influence, he was unable to restrain the growing impatience of the African-American population with leaders who dared not give offense to white people and that more outspoken, radical forms of protest were in the ascendant. A year before Washington's death, the white NAACP treasurer and newspaper publisher Oswald Garrison Villard noted, "His name is getting to be anathema among the educated colored people in the country, and he is drifting further in the rear as a real leader."[11] After Washington, there would be no pre-eminent African-American messenger; in his place, a multitude of writers, speakers, and campaigners addressed audiences that were increasingly radical, race-centered, internationalist, and—in the cities—affluent. Du Bois spoke eloquently for a certain kind of integrationism, but there was a range of alternative paths to follow, including socialism and a rekindled nationalism.

One of the issues taken up by the NAACP and other activists, such as William Monroe Trotter of the National Equal Rights League, was the racial segregation of federal employees under President Woodrow Wilson. Although this discrimination had begun earlier, it became much more widespread after 1913, deeply disappointing those African Americans who had joined Du Bois in supporting Wilson in 1912. Equal rights activists found it difficult to bear the Wilson administration's apparent hypocrisy and endless prevarication on racial matters and the Democratic Party's untroubled smothering of Progressive liberalism in a blanket of southern conservatism. Historian Joel Williamson has observed that "the administration as a whole ultimately did not regard race as a vital matter. . . . Race relations was something they handled with the little finger of the left hand—and they preferred to do it quickly, almost summarily."[12] Wilson, a southerner himself, maintained that segregation in the workplace was "distinctly to the advantage of the colored people themselves," and was unable to comprehend suggestions that his government was injuring and alienating a tenth of the population.[13] Links between NAACP officials and progressive members of the government meant that protest could be registered, but segregation was allowed to persist and, as a result, most black leaders and newspapers were hostile toward the administration by the time the United States entered the war.[14]

Most white Americans, particularly in the southern states, shared a common nightmare of black vengefulness, which since the colonial period had powerfully influenced social intercourse, political allegiances, and the legal system. This anxiety had grown after 1890, so that many commentators confessed or noted a permanent sense of floating paranoia about an imminent race war, and by 1910, after twenty years of an unhindered high level of lynching in the South, many black people undoubtedly did want revenge.[15] In 1917–18, in a context of widespread repression of dissent and strident pro-war propaganda and a belief that enemy agents would exploit any divisions in the community, many white people were troubled by the prospect of thousands of black men being drafted, armed, and trained to fight in army camps across the United States. Suspicion and dread welled up to create a "black scare" of unprecedented proportions. The white Georgian sociologist Thomas J. Woofter, reflecting on a lifetime spent studying racial problems, later recalled that the war had revealed some ancient truths about the southern white mentality that were normally submerged, but were always present and potent:

The last thing that would be admitted by the ardent advocate of white supremacy is that some elements in the South have a lurking fear of the

Negro. Their inability to recognize this fear arises from the fact that it is for the most part subconscious. It shows clearly, however, whenever crises appear and its most persistent manifestation is in the uncritical belief of baseless rumors and the speed with which these tall tales spread.

War brings on the type of crisis psychology which is particularly hospitable to rumor. There is something about the Negro in uniform which gives the more ignorant Southerner a first class case of jitters and spawns the most absurd fantasies.

There are stories of what the Negro in uniform will do, stories of what he won't do. There are stories of what the Negro who stays at home will do and won't do.[16]

The possibility that blacks were a weak link in the political, economic, and military cohesion required for total war had occurred to government officials at the very beginning of American mobilization. When the United States entered the war in April 1917, the white press claimed that German agents were spreading anti-war propaganda among blacks, especially in the South. The Wilson administration took such allegations seriously, and for the next four years, six federal government departments and several local agencies maintained a constant watch on the activities of black civilians and soldiers and equal rights organizations and publications. This surveillance was part of a general growth of anti-radical government activity during the war and the post-war red scare.[17] The federal investigative agencies suspected that black protest against lynching and demands for equal rights were the results of pro-German or pacifist propaganda, and that the tone, at the very least, of much of the black press was essentially disloyal. This was accompanied by a recognition that should all-out black opposition to the war arise, involving the non-cooperation of black labor and military personnel, the consequences for domestic order and the war effort could be serious.

The only federal agency with the resources to undertake an immediate large-scale investigation into "Pro-Germanism among the Negroes" was the Bureau of Investigation (BI) of the Justice Department. The Justice Department had ended its investigative dependence on the Secret Service in 1908 by creating its own detective arm, formally named the BI in 1909 when Congress voted new funds for the prosecution of fraud committed against the United States.[18] During its first six years, the BI was one of the weapons of Progressivism, combating customs, postal, and revenue fraud and violations of laws concerning white slavery, immigration, and naturalization.[19]

Introduction

From 1912, the chief of the BI was A. Bruce Bielaski, a Maryland minister's son who had graduated with a degree in law from George Washington University, where a number of the BI's leading figures were later to study.[20]

In 1915, Bielaski's force of 219 agents investigated violations of the neutrality laws, but left suspected German espionage to the State Department and the Treasury Department's Secret Service agents. By the end of 1916, the Department of Justice had spent $64,000 on war-related investigations and the number of BI agents had risen to three hundred. In the first two months of 1917, the number of letters received by the BI containing warnings or allegations about German intrigue increased fourfold, persuading Attorney General Thomas Watt Gregory to allow BI agents a free hand in the investigation of sabotage and espionage, without congressional authorization. Although there were now four hundred BI agents, they could not keep up with the number of incidents and individuals said to be worthy of investigation. (At its peak, in the summer of 1917, this torrent of letters from alarmed citizens would reach a thousand per day, of which an estimated 95 percent turned out to be of no significance.) Gregory told district attorneys, "Complaints of even the most informal or confidential nature are always welcome . . . citizens should feel free to bring their information or suspicions to the attention of the nearest representative of the Department of Justice."[21] The BI was assisted by the volunteer investigators of the American Protective League (APL), which was funded nationwide by business donations. Although the APL was a subordinate auxiliary of the Justice Department, it became barely controllable at times, and was prone to an overzealous "100% Americanism" which trampled on the civil liberties of aliens, union members, and "slackers." It was more of an embarrassment than an asset to the Department of Justice by the end of the war.[22]

In the days immediately prior to the U.S. declaration of war, the Wilson administration was much concerned with the problem of the thousands of non-naturalized Germans and Austrians resident in the United States. Rejecting the suggestion of Secretary of War Newton D. Baker that enemy aliens should only be arrested in connection with specific offenses, Department of Justice officials argued that pre-emptive action was called for. A presidential proclamation was drafted, advising enemy aliens to obey the law, relinquish firearms, and avoid military establishments, and warning that detention and internment awaited potential offenders. District attorneys and U.S. marshals were alerted on March 27 and April 1 to be on the lookout for illegal enemy alien activity and told to acquaint themselves and district judges with correct procedures should the proclamation be issued. Gregory advised the solicitor general, "There are a very large number of German citizens in this country who are dangerous and who are plotting trouble, men from whom we must necessarily expect trouble promptly of a sinister sort." On April 6, Wilson issued the proclamation about aliens, to which the attorney general added succinct advice to German citizens: "Obey the law; keep your mouth shut."[23] The BI in Washington now began to be inundated by complaints from private citizens and reports from BI agents in the field about German intrigue and propaganda, a remarkable number of which concerned the real or imagined attitude of the African-American population.

One other federal agency, the Military Intelligence Branch (MIB) of the General Staff, also came to play a major part in the wartime investigation of alleged black disloyalty. Military intelligence was normally given very low priority in defense planning prior to World War I and it was not envisaged as having any role in domestic surveillance. After the Spanish-American war, in which intelligence was one of the few praiseworthy branches of the United States army, six officers ran the Military Intelligence Division of the General Staff, created under reforms called for by President William McKinley's secretary of war, Elihu Root, before the division was merged in 1908 with the War College Division, giving intelligence officers a teaching role. With the reorganization of the War College Division in 1915, intelligence was given separate status, so that additional congressional appropriations could be secured. Intelligence-gathering, itself, remained superficial, stifled by its inclusion in the War College Division.[24]

In 1916, the General Staff sent twenty-three military attachés abroad, eight of whom observed the French army as the War College Division attempted to learn about trench warfare. The censorship methods of the British Directorate of Military Intelligence also interested the General Staff. At home, intelligence officers were appointed for six territorial divisions of the United States, with special attention devoted to the Mexican border, and some National Guard officers were brought to Washington for intelligence training. Thus, the framework of a new wartime military intelligence agency of the General Staff was created in advance of the declaration of war.[25]

The War Department's eventual recognition of the importance of efficient intelligence work was due largely to the efforts of a Harvard-educated Ohioan, Maj. Ralph Van Deman, who had served in the Military Information Section of the Philippines Department from 1901 to 1903. In 1915, Van Deman joined the War College Division, where he argued that intelligence operations should be stepped up without waiting for higher approval. When the United States abandoned neutrality, Van Deman appealed over the head of the chief of staff to Secretary Baker, who approved Van Deman's proposals, promoted him, and placed him in charge of the newly formed MIB. The MIB was allocated over $1 million during 1917 to enable it to fulfill three distinct functions: "Administration," involving assigning attachés, issuing and compiling maps, codes, and ciphers, and liaising with the Allied intelligence services; "Information," to be obtained by maintaining files on suspect individuals, gathering economic intelligence on enemy countries, and engaging in espionage and counter-espionage; and, finally, "Censorship," of mails, cables, and telegraphs. The secret aspects of this work were to be divided, after the British example, into "positive" intelligence (accumulation and distribution of useful information) and "negative" intelligence ("all necessary measures to negative or thwart the enemy in his attempt to do us harm").[26]

In the spring and summer of 1917, Van Deman became convinced that the security of the United States and the war effort faced internal threats, not only from enemy agents, but also from the anti-war activities of American left-wing radicalism, in the form of unions such as the Industrial Workers of the World, journals such as the *Masses* and *Mother Earth,* and ethnic groups ill-disposed toward the Allied cause, such as German Americans, Irish Americans, and Indian nationalists seeking the overthrow of British rule. As the subversive menace that Van Deman perceived grew, the MIB expanded accordingly: when Van Deman decided that new topics fell within the scope of military intelligence work, he resolved any lack of expertise in the MIB by recruiting newly commissioned officers with specialized knowledge acquired in civilian life, or else sought commissions for specialists who were still civilians. The result was an agency top-heavy with experts, almost incidentally in uniform, who were allowed to concentrate on, and sometimes jealously guard, their own fields, often with little sense of the wider picture. (Although the personnel of military intelligence in Washington at one point reached 282 officers and 1,159 civilians, there were never more than six regular army officers in the MIB at any time.)[27]

In August 1917, when Van Deman, like Bielaski, became convinced that black disloyalty represented a further real threat to national security, he quickly assigned new officers with what were considered to be the right qualifications to gather information on the activities and expression of black civilians and soldiers. Thereafter, the BI and the MIB pursued parallel investigative paths, sometimes collaborating, and their files became part of the Wilson administration's attempt to monitor and influence the changing mood of the African-American population. The MIB filed and cross-referenced almost all its information about African-American organizations, publications, and individuals under the heading "Negro Subversion," while the BI used variations on "German Propaganda amongst the Negroes" whenever a report concerned one or more black people, regardless of whether the subject matter was alleged subversion.[28] One of the many peculiarities of these archives is the chronically inferior quality of the separate data-gathering operations of which they are the record. While historians will continue to find much otherwise unobtainable information about the activities of certain African Americans in this period in the intelligence files, the management of the surveillance process was abysmal from the point of view of generating and analyzing useful intelligence, let alone the formulation of effective and just policies on race relations.

Race, War, and Surveillance

One

African Americans and the War for Democracy, 1917

During the first three years of World War I, the great majority of African Americans supported the United States government's policy of neutrality. Indeed, few groups of Americans regarded the European conflict with greater emotional detachment; the war seemed particularly irrelevant beside the economic and political struggles in which African Americans were engaged at home. Kelly Miller, the influential dean of arts and sciences at Howard University, probably spoke for most members of his race when he wrote in 1915, "This is essentially a white man's war. . . . The American Negro is so far removed from the intimate issues of the European struggle that its effects on him must be secondary and indirect."[1] Nevertheless, some black leaders took a close interest in the war and those who formed a preference hoped that the more effectively publicized Allied cause would be victorious, a view shared generally by progressive American opinion. W. E. B. Du Bois, writing in the NAACP journal, the *Crisis,* saw the war's origins as fundamentally colonial, and he sided with the Allies as the more benign imperialists. Victory for Germany would mean "the triumph of every force calculated to subordinate darker peoples." By the time the United States broke off diplomatic relations with Germany in February 1917, he had arrived at a positive black perspective on the possible effects of warfare on American society, akin to the *New Republic*'s belief that the war could effect a transformation of American democracy and government, and in April he was fully prepared to exhort the eighty thousand readers of the *Crisis* to support the administration's call to arms, despite Woodrow Wilson's lack of concern for black people. Racial discrimination had grown in recent years, but Du Bois argued that war could deliver political and economic gains to the African American citizen, if he would only "put himself into the turmoil and work effectively for a new democracy that shall know no color." Although Du Bois felt intense frustration and anger at recurrent acts of violence committed against blacks by white communities before and after the United States entered the war and the studied indifference of the government, his support for the American war effort did not waver. It sprang partly from his internationalist perspective, which others shared but few articulated so plainly, and his conviction that a "war against war" and a "world organized for peace" were more than mere ideals. He anticipated that as the moral authority of Europe declined the colonized peoples of the world would assert themselves, and that at the same time America would achieve new influence as an international democratic force and this, in turn, would quicken reform within the United States. Du Bois returned repeatedly to this theme: in the spring of 1918, he would offer *Crisis* readers this vision:

> Out of this war will rise, soon or late, an independent China; a self-governing India, an Egypt with representative institutions; an Africa for the Africans and not merely for business exploitation. Out of this war will rise, too, an American Negro, with a right to vote and a right to work and a right to live without insult.[2]

At this stage in his life, Du Bois believed that progress was inevitable and that democracy and equality were bound to be extended to blacks one day. It was his task to accelerate the pace of change, while maintaining the morale and optimism of his readers.[3]

Early in 1917, Du Bois's belief in the potential benefits of war service led him to support a bid to allow black men to train as army officers during the precautionary build-up of the American forces after the election of 1916. The leading advocate of this initiative was his white friend and colleague, Joel E. Spingarn, the chairman of the NAACP. An enthusiastic supporter of the preparedness movement and a leading member of the Home Defense Committee of Dutchess County, N.Y., Spingarn persuaded his neighbor, Assistant Secretary of the Navy Franklin D. Roosevelt, and ex-president Theodore Roosevelt to recommend him for an army commission in March 1917. He was to become one of only three men, out of twenty-five hundred newly commissioned officers, to be immediately promoted to the rank of major, but before entering training camp he fought to ensure that black troops in their segregated regiments would be commanded to as high a level as possible by men of their own race.[4] For this to happen, Spingarn believed, black officer training had to be made palatable to the War Department, and there was no time to make an anti-segregation issue out of it. He reached an understanding in February 1917 with Gen. Leonard Wood, commander of the eastern division of the army, that a separate camp for black officers would be set up if two hundred suitable applicants could be quickly found. For the next three months, Spingarn appealed in pamphlets and speeches for would-be officers to contact him and urged the War Department not to give up on the scheme. By persuading Du Bois that the separate camp made good pragmatic sense, Spingarn also secured the endorsement of the *Crisis.*[5]

For proposing something that necessitated official segregation of members of the educated elite dubbed by Du Bois the "Talented Tenth"—the very section of the black male population that was expected to lead the fight against discrimination—Spingarn and Du Bois drew sharp criticism from a number of black newspapers. The *Cleveland Gazette,* a long-time supporter of the NAACP, was moved to question the sincerity of the association's white philanthropists. The *New York News,* a frequent critic of the association, seeing Booker T. Washington's opponents put forward a segregated program, accused Spingarn of hypocrisy and unconditional surrender "to those associated for the degradation of colored people." The *News* declared that for Spingarn and his friends to call for "this surrender at this critical juncture, fraught with splendid strategic opportunities for the race," revealed only "the silly selfishness of these advocates, and their moral cowardice."[6] Spingarn insisted that, in the face of strong reservations within the army and active opposition from southern white politicians to any suggestion of black officer training, his proposal was the only way to show both the leadership qualities and the patriotism of African Americans to a skeptical administration. Any qualified black man who refused to take advantage of this hard-won opportunity was, he wrote, "biting off his nose to spite his face." Spingarn received vital support from the highest ranking black officer in the army, Lt. Col. Charles A. Young, a close friend of Du Bois. Young told the editor of the *Cleveland Gazette,* Harry C. Smith, that he understood the latter's unease, but it was worth accepting a separate training camp since the alternative was to leave black troops under the command only of white officers: "I admit that a whole loaf is better than half a loaf; but the half beats none at all."[7] Spingarn concentrated on soliciting applications, and one week before the United States declared war he had gathered 230 names, having been particularly successful at Howard University in Washington, D.C., and Hampton Institute in Virginia. Aided by the Washington branch of the NAACP, he continued to press Secretary of War Newton D. Baker and was rewarded with official approval on May 19.[8]

The officers' training camp campaign obscured a more fundamental dilemma which faced black citizens: whether African Americans should feel any obligation at all to fight for the United States. The writer of a letter to the *New York Sun* couched the problem in a tendentious, but frequently echoed, style:

> The first blood shed for America's Independence was by Crispus Attuck [*sic*], a black man, in Boston. A question comes to my mind now, should a black man shoulder a gun and go to war and fight for this country, a country which denies him the rights of citizenship under a flag which offers him no protection, strips him of his manhood by enacting laws which keeps him [*sic*] from the ballot box, disfranchised, segregated, discriminated against, lynched, burned at the stake, Jim Crowed and disarmed[?] If he fight, and fight he must, for what does he fight?[9]

Virtually all African-American newspapers and spokesmen responded to questions of this kind by advising that blacks had no choice but to serve and contribute to the war effort, but the level of enthusiasm with which they pushed this message varied considerably. A few declared that uncritical and selfless service was the only option for loyal citizens, but many others saw participation as basically the means to an end. Roscoe Conkling Simmons, a Republican party regular whose aunt, Margaret Murray, had married Booker T. Washington, put the conservative viewpoint most plainly. His message at this time was that

> the nation faces danger from a foreign foe, treason stalks and skulks up and down our land, in dark councils intrigue is being hatched. . . . [I]n this hour of peril I forget—and you must forget—all thoughts of self or race or creed or politics or color. That, boys, is loyalty.[10]

Not even the *New York Age*, the most influential northern organ of the Tuskegee-ites, went this far. It recognized that blacks might not be as quick to enlist for this war as in the past and that their patriotism had dimmed in recent years, but warned that fulfilling the duties of citizenship was an integral part of claiming one's rights. It seemed to the *Age* that "the Negro has a case in court upon which his life depends and which he cannot afford in any way to jeopardize. He should not let any of his rights go by default.

African Americans and the War for Democracy, 1917

Neither can he afford to weaken his claim to any of those rights by a non-performance of duty."[11] By late March 1917, as war seemed inevitable and National Guard units, including black troops, began to patrol the streets of Washington, D.C., the *Age* was urging its male readers to show their commitment to the United States by volunteering immediately for military service, "despite the strain put on that loyalty by an administration most unfriendly to them." After all, "administrations come and go, but the nation endures for ever."[12]

In the period of transition from American neutrality to belligerency, most African Americans across the country agreed that, although the Wilson administration was deservedly unpopular, they would fight unquestioningly for the flag.[13] Aside from individual feelings of patriotism, they were influenced in this respect by the need to react to two threats. Firstly, it was widely believed that German secret agents were attempting to disrupt the ability of the United States to wage war by fomenting unrest and disloyalty among the black population, particularly in the South. Secondly, a few white politicians attempted to have blacks excluded from military draft legislation. Black leaders reasoned that a section of the population engaged in local and national struggles for equal rights and justice could ill afford to be portrayed either as the willing target of enemy propaganda or as generally unfit for war service.

In the same week that Congress passed the war resolution, stories about German efforts to undermine the loyalty of black citizens were carried in newspapers across the United States. On April 4, 1917, the *New York Tribune* carried what it claimed was "the first information that had been published about the activities of German agents among the negroes of the South." It was reported from Greensboro, N.C., that two Germans, posing as doctors, were concealed at Elm Grove, "a nearby negro settlement, which is thought to be the chief seeding ground for the propaganda of sedition. . . . Absolute social equality has been one of the rewards which the German agents have dangled before the eyes of the black man." Another alleged source of German propaganda was a local Lutheran college. This story was headlined "Germans Plot Negro Uprising in the South—Whites Prepare for Possible Rebellion When War Comes—Kaiser's Agents Tempt the Blacks with Offers of Social Equality" and continued,

As in Ireland, Egypt, South Africa and India, so here in the South secret agents of the Imperial German government have been fomenting revolt

under the pretence of spreading Kultur. They have been insidiously working to bring about a rising of the negroes against the whites.

The black population of the area was alleged to be "showing symptoms of
unusual ill-temper" and whites were talking about the need to revive the
Ku Klux Klan.[14]

The day after the *Tribune* report appeared, the Associated Press put out
a number of stories about newly discovered conspiracies and arrests under
headlines such as "German Negro Plots to Unite Negroes—Kaiser's Agents,
as Preachers and Bible Salesmen, at Work in Gulf States" and "German
Negro Plots Feared in Six States."[15] The federal authorities were said to
know about conspiracies "to incite negroes against the United States government" in Alabama, North Carolina, South Carolina, Florida, Georgia,
Louisiana, and Mississippi. Such treason was reported to be "allied closely"
with the recent migration of southern blacks to northern cities and enemy
agents were also said to be urging migration to Mexico. There were no
reports yet of widespread disaffection among blacks, but white farmers in
Alabama had "formed Ku Klux Klans to meet possible uprisings," and
several Germans had been arrested in Mississippi, where blacks had allegedly been promised "complete franchise freedom and political and social
equality." German agents were said to be adopting various guises, including
those of saloon-keepers, Lutheran priests, and traveling Bible salesmen, in
order to spread unrest. The *Tribune* carried these stories on its front page,
after seeking confirmation from an African-American newspaper editor,
George Harris of the *New York News,* that the Greensboro story was factual
and that "serious trouble" resulting from enemy intrigue had been only
"narrowly avoided" in the South and Southwest. Harris emphasized that
any susceptibility of African Americans to the blandishments of German,
Mexican, or Japanese agents was due only to the intolerable conditions under which they were forced to live. In addition, both Harris and Royal Nash,
the white secretary of the NAACP, assured the *Tribune* that the slow rate at
which blacks were reported to be volunteering for war duty was due only
to the fear that they would be treated badly in the army and that any bitterness they felt toward the Wilson administration was not directed at the
United States as a whole. The *Tribune* nevertheless stuck by its story and
further claimed that "men in the pay of the Imperial Government [had
been] sowing the seeds of discontent among the negroes" in New York City,
before heading south.[16] The *New York Times* announced that the government

had seized a white man and a black man at Birmingham after they had toured Alabama, Louisiana, Georgia, the Carolinas, and Mississippi, "posing as bible salesmen and ministers of the gospel" and urging black people to migrate to Mexico on specially provided trains.[17] In the southern press, these allegations were given an added twist—the *Florence (S.C.) Daily Times* ran the headline "Teutons Try Yankee Trick of Making Negroes Rise in Rebellion against Whites."[18]

The press had been on the alert for signs of aggression from Mexico since the publication of the Zimmerman telegram on March 1, 1917. This message to the Mexican government from the German foreign secretary, offering an alliance if the resumption of unrestricted submarine warfare were to bring the United States into the war, was intercepted and decoded by the British Admiralty before being passed to the government of the United States, which made it public.[19] A certain amount of excitement was occasioned, therefore, by accounts of a Mexican conspiracy to foment a race war in the Southwest. Dubbed the "Plan of San Diego," and already known to the U.S. government for two years, the scheme had been formulated early in 1915 by Mexicans in the San Diego area of southern Texas, between San Antonio and Nuevo Laredo. It supposedly invited Mexicans, Indians, and African Americans to rebel jointly against the United States and establish the independence of Texas, New Mexico, Arizona, Colorado, and California. All male Anglos over the age of sixteen would be killed and Indians would have their ancestral lands returned to them. According to the self-styled Supreme Revolutionary Congress of San Diego,

> When we shall have obtained independence for the Negroes, we shall grant them a banner, which they themselves shall be permitted to select, and we shall aid them in obtaining six states of the American Union, which states border upon those already mentioned, and they may therefore be independent.

Newcomers would not be allowed to join the rebellion, "unless said stranger belong to the Latin, the Negro, or the Japanese race." According to historian James Sandos, the Plan of San Diego is best understood, not as a concerted conspiracy against the United States, but as a movement born of the internal politics of revolutionary Mexico, international anarchism, and economic conditions on the lower Rio Grande. Initially, the reaction of the United States was concern for the stability of U.S.-Mexican relations and protection of the border, but state and federal officials who investigated the plan in 1915 apparently agreed that it was "visionary and ridiculous." It was mentioned briefly in official reports to Washington in 1916, when Gen. John J. Pershing's punitive expedition was active in northern Mexico.[20] Nevertheless, in April 1917, the New York press reported the Plan of San Diego as if it were of recent origin and its execution were imminent. George Harris of the *New York News* claimed to have heard about it by "subterranean channels" and the focus of press reports generally was on the subversive appeal to African Americans and the involvement of Germans, despite the fact that these were marginal aspects of the now-defunct conspiracy.[21]

Reports that the loyalty of African Americans had been undermined by enemy agents or other conspirators were to recur throughout the remaining months of World War I and would persist thereafter. One reason why such stories became firmly entrenched in popular and official minds was that they conformed to the pre-existing view of German agents in America. Since 1915, pro-Allied publicists, preparedness advocates, and the Wilson administration had claimed that American neutrality was being abused by German spies and saboteurs, and that public opinion had been deliberately divided by a campaign of whispering propaganda.[22] In his repeated references to "foreign intrigue," it also became clear that Woodrow Wilson regarded outside attempts to influence ordinary Americans as more heinous crimes than the gathering of official secrets, although that was done, too. He specifically denounced German spies in his war message to Congress in April 1917 and afterward continued to accuse Germany of having "filled our unsuspecting communities with vicious spies and conspirators and sought to corrupt the opinion of our people in their own behalf."[23]

A few white southerners responded by expressing confidence in the docility and contentment of the black population, but they were in a minority. For example, in May 1918, Rep. Edward Pou of North Carolina dismissed the allegations of German intrigue among blacks when the United States had entered the war, preferring to recite a standard southern tribute. During the Civil War, he reminded the House of Representatives,

> The helpless women and children of the South during those four memorable years were left largely to the mercy of the negro race. Be it said to their everlasting credit that in not one instance did they prove treacherous. [Applause] . . . As I stand here now I can see all over the South the vine-clad cabins of this kindly race. They have their faults, but disloyalty is not among those faults. In their homes you will find a burning love of country, a burning love for the flag. From these little homes throughout

the South responding to their country's call the young negro men are answering, "Here; we are ready." [Applause][24]

A less complimentary, but equally hackneyed, testimony to the imperviousness of African Americans to the efforts of German secret agents was offered by the *Montgomery (Ala.) Advertiser.* It did not doubt that German racial intrigue existed, but added that the spies were bound to fail because "the average negro would patiently hear the appeal of a 'German spy' and immediately repeat the full conversation, with embellishments, to his white friends."[25]

The great majority of white southerners appear to have found allegations of racial subversion by the enemy consistent with their own deep-seated prejudices and fears, and the prospect of a race war at home appears to have had a generally cohesive effect on them. The spy scare seemed to confirm not only the guile of the Kaiser's agents but also the gullibility and potential treachery of elements of the black population. The *Macon (Ga.) Telegraph* found the allegations entirely plausible, and even invoked memories of abolitionism, asserting that German spies had succeeded in

planting fruitful seeds of seditious trouble among that small percentage of Southern negroes who, poisoned by too much foolish exploitation by well-meaning philanthropists in the North and East, have come to feel that the negro's destiny in the South is best served by the overthrow in some fashion or other of peculiarly Southern institutions.

And though disaffected blacks might be only a minority, the *Telegraph* considered that "doubtless there are enough of them lending a willing ear to call for prompt and severe treatment."[26]

The suggestion that "peculiarly Southern institutions" such as segregation and disfranchisement were threatened by enemy intrigue in the spring and summer of 1917 led to an upsurge of white chauvinism and a determination to defend the system. This involved a heightened sensitivity to any indications that African Americans might press against the racial boundaries with new vigor. From the colonial period to the New South, white southerners of all classes had exhibited a mixture of contempt, frustration, and apprehension in their dealings with black people, along with rarer moments of affinity and paternalism. Southern hysteria about real and, more often, imagined instances of slave rebellion before 1860 had created lasting anxiety, which persisted after Reconstruction and grew to include fierce resistance to the idea of black political power and wealth. In 1908, the

Michigan-born progressive journalist Ray Stannard Baker had described white southerners as "torn between their feeling of race prejudice and their downright economic needs. Hating and fearing the Negro as a race (though often loving individual Negroes), they want him to work for them; they can't get along without him."[27] By 1910, any black political advances during Reconstruction had been decisively reversed and black economic progress across most of the South had stalled, but racist speakers and writers persisted in playing on the fear of "social equality," accusing blacks of yearning for it and some northern reformers of (usually unintentionally) promoting it.[28] "Social equality" connoted much more than granting blacks and whites simultaneous access to the same juries, schools, housing, transportation, restaurants, and other public facilities. For whites across the United States it had become a conveniently broad, and yet at the same time piercing, euphemism encompassing all forms of familiarity between the races, and especially between black men and white women, ranging from casual conversation to sexual intercourse (with the implied emphasis normally on the latter). Its usage by white Americans usually came in the form of warnings that the boundaries of racial etiquette were not to be tampered with. Any passing mention by a black writer of "social equality" affronted the sensibilities of whites across a spectrum wide enough to encompass extremist demagogues like Sen. Ben Tillman of South Carolina, racial theorists like Lothrop Stoddard, and liberal reformers like Jane Addams and Florence Kelley.[29]

Quite aside from any considerations of national security, therefore, the 1917 racial spy scare seemed to authenticate ancient terrors, and the alleged presence of shadowy, marginal white men attempting to foment rebellion, a common feature of investigations of conspiracies during both slavery and Reconstruction, only made the stories about German agitators more persuasive and sinister.[30] Descriptions in white newspapers of the rewards offered by Germans to blacks to persuade them to rebel, resist the draft, or migrate to the North frequently referred to the lure of "social equality."

From the moment it became clear that there would be a national draft, the prospect of black military enlistment produced frequent outbursts of opposition across the South. These objections cannot simply be attributed to concerns caused by the allegations of German intrigue. In condemning the drafting of blacks, whites expressed widely held southern beliefs about the political and economic need to limit the scope of black citizenship. They also revealed with unusual candor the normally unspoken recognition by whites that, notwithstanding comforting myths about the Civil War and black contentment, the attitudes of African Americans toward whites were basically hostile, and in some cases vengeful, and that arming the sons and grandsons of former slaves might jeopardize white safety and domination. In other words, while they rarely said as much, whites understood perfectly well that the treatment meted out to southern blacks in terms of poor education, limited economic opportunity, the denial of political rights, and the permanent threat and frequent reality of violence amounted to systematic oppression. They could justify each element according to their own beliefs, but could not deny that an alternative system would logically appeal to the freedmen and their descendants. The anxiety provoked by the conjunction of alleged German subversion among blacks and the prospect of a black draft did not simply grow out of a belief system which held that Africans were innately gullible and criminal; it lay in white men's and women's private knowledge of how they would feel if they were black in the same circumstances. Hence, Rep. Richard S. Whaley of South Carolina spoke for many white southerners when he stated that black enlistment "would bring down upon the districts where Negroes far exceed the whites in number a danger far greater than any foe." The populist white supremacist Sen. James K. Vardaman of Mississippi, who opposed American entry into the war, also condemned the proposal to arm "millions of Negroes." He could think of "no greater menace to the South than this." The senior senator from Mississippi, John Sharp Williams, a supporter of Wilson and the war effort (and no friend of Vardaman), accepted that blacks should be included in the draft, but opposed the idea that they should be trained in the South. He thought it would be safer if they were drilled in Cuba. Other southern whites were concerned less about public order than about the boost that black political claims might receive from war service: the *Vicksburg Herald* regretted what it called "the logic of black arms bearing."[31]

The double blow of the spy stories and the growth of white resistance to black war service led to a renewed campaign by African-American leaders to demonstrate that their people could be relied upon. W. E. B. Du Bois was quickest to respond, ridiculing the April 4th report of the *New York Tribune* in that afternoon's edition of the *New York Evening Post*, owned by Oswald Garrison Villard, a fellow director of the NAACP. Du Bois denounced the *Tribune* for printing "a cock and bull story," hurriedly made up by southerners worried about black economic advances and the formation of black regiments. They were, he insisted, simply looking for an excuse to assert their control over the black population, and the "discovery" of an imminent uprising would suit their purposes well. The *Evening Post,* itself, congratulated the *Tribune* on a "superb piece of satire."[32] The *Tribune* story was also denied by President James B. Dudley of Greensboro Agricultural and Technical College, who insisted that recent black migration had nothing to do with German agents, as the *Tribune* had implied, and that the nearby Lutheran Immanuel College, which had sixty-five black students, was blameless.[33] A prominent member of the Colored Missions Board of the Evangelical Lutheran Church also wrote Attorney General Thomas Watt Gregory to point out that the Lutheran schools for African Americans were dominated by black, not white, staff.[34] The *Washington Bee,* the oldest surviving black newspaper in the United States, founded in 1879 and edited by a District of Columbia lawyer, Calvin Chase, argued that the patriotism of the African-American soldier had withstood tests to which no other group in American society had been subjected: "His mother, sister, brother and children are being burned at the stake and yet the American flag is his emblem . . . which he stands ready to defend. In all the battles the Negro soldier has proved his loyalty and today he is the only true American at whom the finger of scorn cannot be pointed." The *Norfolk Journal and Guide* derided the reports of German agents and sympathizers among black people as "too absurd for serious thought."[35] In the following weeks, all cities with large black communities saw well-attended "loyalty meetings" at which blacks expressed overt enthusiasm for the war. Resolutions were endorsed, deploring or denying German intrigue and assuring the local and national authorities that African Americans were as ready as any group to do their bit, regardless of past or present discrimination. Claims that German propagandists had found black sympathizers in southern cotton fields or in northern cities were dismissed. In Norfolk, Va., for example, four thousand black children marched with the Knights of Pythias and brass bands to a rally at which the idea of an imminent black rebellion was branded a "German lie."[36] At a Boston meeting organized by the local branch of the NAACP, the association's field secretary, James Weldon Johnson, declared that "the great mass stands as it has ever stood, loyal to the core. The idea of the colored people being disloyal is absurd." He ascribed the wave of reports about German agitation among blacks to those white southerners who "would like to have the people of the North believe it, so as to excuse themselves for acts of violence they would like to commit."[37]

African Americans and the War for Democracy, 1917

The fear that lynching would suddenly increase in the new crisis of war and espionage was fully justified by the patterns of racial violence in the South over the previous half century. On behalf of the NAACP, Du Bois put out a confidential message to the editors of black newspapers, appealing to them to quash all rumors about enemy agents and black disloyalty. If the rest of the American people began to believe these stories, he predicted,

> the Southern states will be allowed a free hand, under 'military necessity,' to place the Negroes of the South under quasi martial law. Under such regulation, the free movement and free gatherings of colored people would be restrained, and every form of violence and oppression would be excused and justified. The South would see a revival of the Ku Klux Klan, and as long as the war lasted, and perhaps for many years after, the Negro would be held in a state of virtual slavery.[38]

At the very least, Du Bois feared, widespread suspicion of disloyalty could be used by southern congressmen in a determined effort to exclude African Americans from the draft. He returned to this theme in the May 1917 *Crisis*, suggesting that the reports of German subversion were part of a desperate attempt on the part of the "Bourbon South" to create an atmosphere in which the northward migration of labor could be prevented by force. He warned, "Back of the German mask is the grinning skeleton of a Southern slave-driver."[39] James Weldon Johnson also discussed southern anxieties about black enlistment in his weekly newspaper column. He, too, suspected a hidden political agenda:

> Southerners like Congressman Whiley [*sic*] think that if the Negro is in-cluded in the universal service plan, and bears arms, wears the uniform and fights the country's battles it will increase his feelings of equal citi-zenship and strengthen his claim to equal citizenship. And they are quite right in thinking so.[40]

In the hundreds of declarations and assertions of black loyalty which followed American entry into war there emerged a discernible difference in tone and outlook between the statements of those African Americans who took a conservative approach to the achievement of social justice and those who were less patient. The former, generally members of an older generation, insisted that black people had always been utterly loyal to the United States and that, regardless of ill-treatment, they would always put their country first. Those leaders who preferred the policy of "organized determination and aggressive action" laid out by the Niagara Movement after 1905, most of whom were now associated with the NAACP, agreed that blacks would not succumb to German overtures, but at the same time they took care to remind their audiences of the injustices that white America had perpetrated in the past. They advised against allowing African-American compliance with the war effort to be taken for granted and argued that service ought to be rewarded both during and after the war with better treatment of the race by the federal government. Some even implied that the war represented an opportunity to *force* the government into granting the demands of black campaigners in return for a wholehearted commitment to the war.

The most influential call for blacks to render selfless service to their country came from Tuskegee Institute in Alabama. In April 1917, Principal Robert Russa Moton, who had succeeded Booker T. Washington on the latter's death two years earlier, declared that the "few malcontents" who might be "misled by Teuton intrigue" would be sternly dealt with by blacks themselves. The patriotism of the African American—by nature "patient and forgiving, but a brave and loyal fighter"—could not be weakened by "internal misunderstandings" between the races. Moton also released a letter he had sent to Woodrow Wilson assuring the president of the docile loyalty of his people.[41] Hollis B. Frissell, the white principal of Washington's alma mater, Hampton Institute, went even further, urging his alumni to contribute unquestioningly all they could to the war. Like Moton, Frissell did not discount the possibility that there were indeed German agents at work in the South and that "a few [blacks] in their bitterness may have turned to evil counselors," but he called on people to turn a deaf ear to agitators and to report them immediately. Frissell declared that this was no time for "[b]itterness, fear, hatred, narrow jealousies and selfish interests," for, as Washington had taught, "the colored man is going to secure recognition not by demanding his rights, but by deserving them."[42] This was too fainthearted even for Moton; in an unusual gesture he immediately corrected Frissell by pointing out that the rights of citizenship were already long overdue and that black people would secure them "by demanding and deserving them."[43]

A view of war service as expedient was offered by Harry C. Smith, editor of the *Cleveland Gazette,* who predicted that "the war, which every Afro-American looks upon as providential, will do much toward bettering our position, for it will again afford us an opportunity to show the metal of which we are made."[44] John Mitchell, Jr., editor of the *Richmond Planet*, adopted an even more calculating perspective. He hoped for a lengthy American involvement in the war, with heavy casualties, so that the United States would need all the help it could get. When victory was achieved black soldiers would "receive the encomiums of the nation and be welcomed to receive all of the rights and privileges of any other citizens. This can only come from a long and from a bloody war. From a short, quick war, Good Lord deliver us!"[45] West Indian–born Cyril Briggs had a more specific vision of the sort of reward that blacks should seek in return for full participation in the war effort. In the editorial columns of the *Amsterdam News*, he argued that just as the Allies were defending the rights of Belgians and Poles and asserting the principle of national self-determination in Europe, so black republics such as Haiti should be left to themselves "and the colored race in America given equal political and economic rights or be allowed to exercise its talents in nation building in the rich and healthy island of San Domingo or some other quarter of its choice."[46]

Thus, a number of commentators swiftly advised blacks to participate in the war for their own benefit, even though they might find it difficult to feel any real enthusiasm for either the United States or its war aims. These writers stressed that there were social and economic gains to be had, as well as sacrifices to be made. James Weldon Johnson perhaps expressed this cautious optimism most clearly. He hoped that African Americans would be able to don the uniform of the United States and at the same time demand their rights, rather than have to postpone campaigns for the just rewards of service. One of those rights was "the right to fight for one's country; which, after all, is one of the fundamental rights of citizenship," but the black soldier would be fighting "with his eyes wide open . . . , repeating his demand that this nation do its duty." Johnson frankly admitted that,

> even if there can be no sense of patriotism, . . . the bald truth is that the Negro cannot afford to be rated as a disloyal element in this nation. Imagine the results if he should for an instant arouse against himself the sentiment which is now directed against the pro-German element.[47]

In May 1917, the NAACP held a national conference in Washington of branch delegates and members of other organizations. In resolutions written by Du Bois, the conference traced "the real cause of this World War to the despising of the darker races by the dominant groups of men" and colonial rivalries. Lasting peace would result only from "the extension of

Race, War, and Surveillance

the principle of government by the consent of the governed, not simply among the smaller nations of Europe, but among the natives of Asia and Africa, the Western Indies, and the Negroes of the United States." African Americans were urged to play their part in the war in the knowledge that their grievances would not be forgotten: "Absolute loyalty in arms and civil duties need not for a moment lead us to abate our just complaints and just demands."[48]

No matter how much the most visible elements of African-American leadership might proclaim the unswerving loyalty of the race to the United States and predict great changes as a result of war service, the truth was that the wider black population held a very broad range of views on the level of commitment which American belligerency ought to command, and the extent to which they willingly engaged in war-related activities varied accordingly. Theodore Kornweibel, Jr., Gerald R. Gill, and Steven A. Reich have persuasively interpreted a mass of evidence showing that with regard to the declared purposes of the United States in entering the war, many African Americans—perhaps most—were ignorant, or indifferent, or skeptical, or antagonistic, and they were either unimpressed or repelled by the home-front propaganda that accompanied mobilization.[49] Reservations about the war and its relevance were sometimes expressed explicitly, sometimes obliquely; they generally took the form of localized or individual gestures, rather than organized national dissent, and they rarely emerged from a clear ideological position. And yet, taken together, they amount to unequivocal evidence that, along with other sections of the American people, millions of African Americans were not borne along on a patriotic surge in 1917 and 1918. This is not to argue that there existed a hitherto unnoticed mass of black anti-war activists, or that black soldiers did not demonstrate efficiency, initiative, and valor. But it does suggest that many African Americans complied with war regulations and service more because of the penalties involved in non-compliance and dissent than out of a love of country and a sense of duty, and many others engaged in subtle forms of resistance to powerful institutions. After the war, the black commentator George Schuyler asked the largely white readership of the *American Mercury*,

Is it generally known that large numbers of Negroes, though they openly whooped it up for Uncle Sam, would have shed no tears in 1917–18 if the armies of the Kaiser had by some miracle suddenly swooped down upon such fair cities as Memphis, Tenn., Waycross, Ga., or Meridian, Miss.? . . .

African Americans and the War for Democracy, 1917

Any number of intelligent Negroes expressed the opinion under their breath that a good beating would be an excellent thing for the soul of America.[50]

Robin D. G. Kelley's arguments regarding a later period hold true for the era of World War I: far from being passive, long-suffering victims of the racist economic and social structure of the post-Reconstruction South, African Americans found ways to denounce, deflect, and combat white attempts to control their lives.[51] They did not need German agents to point out the hypocrisy and cynicism of sending African Americans overseas to war in the name of democracy. This widespread sense of disillusion was openly confessed by the leading black cleric in Washington, Francis J. Grimké, sickened by the rapturous reception given to Confederate veterans in the capital in June 1917 and saddened by the readiness of American patriots to condemn German tyranny in Europe while ignoring American tyranny in the South:

It is amazing into what spasms of indignation American orators work themselves up when they are speaking on German atrocities; and yet they are moved to no such feelings . . . by the equally atrocious conduct of southern lynchers. . . . These exhibitions of brutality fail to arouse in them even the faintest zephyr of indignation.[52]

Domestic intelligence agencies readily detected this unrest, even if they were incapable of comprehending it. The chief of the Justice Department's Bureau of Investigation (BI), A. Bruce Bielaski, was worried about the problem of black disloyalty from the moment the United States entered the war. He discussed it with other law enforcement officials in Washington and ordered BI field offices to give special attention to tracking down the German agents he believed were trying to "stir up the negroes of this country."[53] Between March and August 1917, the efforts of the BI to monitor "negro activities" set the underlying tone and established the basic surveillance criteria that were to persist beyond the Armistice and throughout the subsequent red scare. However, the powers of the investigators did not grow at the same rate as their desire to act against critics of the government. In the early months of American involvement in the war, although there were numerous arrests in the South in connection with the alleged subversion of black loyalty, prosecutions could only be brought under existing state laws. Until the passage of the Espionage Act of June 15, 1917, which provided stiff penalties for interference with the draft, the BI's special agents could only file reports on such matters and hope for action by local officials under state laws, such as section 3661 of the legal code of Virginia, which provided that "if any person conspire with another to incite the colored population of the state to acts of violence and war against the white population" (or vice-versa), the conspirators were liable to five to ten years' imprisonment.[54] Justice Department officials across the United States found it frustrating not to have clearly defined powers of their own and sought clarification from the attorney general. The U.S. marshal in Asheville, N.C., where a German was nearly lynched, wanted to know what action he could take about reports of Germans inciting black uprisings: "I am, as probably other marshals are, appealed to time and again every day about matters of this kind." The U.S. attorney at Mobile, Ala., believing that he had evidence that certain blacks were persuading their neighbors to leave for Mexico via New Orleans, wanted to do something to defuse local tension: "The white people are very restless and are disposed to be violent. . . . I can keep down mob law, but I would like to know what I can do with some of these [Negro] fellows for an example." The BI gave out what advice it could. Over Bielaski's signature, the attorney who most often dealt with "negro activities," A. H. Pike, advised the Birmingham special agent that, if state statutes did not offer a solution, then section 37 of the federal criminal code, which dealt with conspiracy to defraud or commit offenses against the United States, might be applicable, "although it is realized, of course, that this is stretching this section somewhat." Pike speculated that "a Grand Jury investigation might have a deterrent effect on the instigators of the movement."[55]

Since 1915, several thousand African Americans had migrated from the southern states to the North every month, a phenomenon that came under close scrutiny by the Justice Department when the United States entered the war, in case it should be inspired by German agents. The outbreak of war in 1914 had cut annual immigration from Europe from 1.2 million to 300,000 within a year and this figure continued to fall as the conflict wore on, contributing to a growing labor shortage in northern cities, especially in those industries enjoying war-related demand. At the same time, the predominantly rural economy of the South was contending with successive floods and a spreading boll-weevil infestation which ruined much of the cotton crop of 1915 and 1916 in Louisiana, Mississippi, Georgia, and Florida—states with a combined black population of 4.1 million. Southern farming was by far the most important single economic activity of African

African Americans and the War for Democracy, 1917

Americans—the 1910 census showed that it engaged 55 percent (2.8 million) of the 5.2 million gainfully employed black people in the United States—and the diminishing prospects for black tenants (who made up 75 percent of black farm operators, whereas only 4 percent of white farm operators were tenants) provided an incentive to abandon that way of life if an alternative were to become clear. In addition, black-white relations were dominated by an oppressive climate of violence, in which any black person might be beaten or murdered by a lynch mob anywhere in the South, and particularly in certain counties where lynching had become an extralegal device for intensifying racial oppression. As well as serving as a constant reinforcement of white supremacy and black servility, lynching was undoubtedly a factor in the decision of many southern black people to move to the North. An investigation in southern Georgia showed a direct correlation between migration and the frequency of lynching. As the *Columbia (S.C.) State* put it, "Every Southern lynching is an emigration agent working effectively for Northern employers."[56]

Disheartened, then, by violence, insults, discrimination, denial of basic rights, and crop failures, and becoming more aware of the relatively greater freedom and prosperity to be enjoyed in the North, single black men and women and black families left southern farms in steadily increasing numbers during World War I. Black mobility over short and long distances had been a constant feature of American society since the Civil War, but during 1915 and 1916 such movement began to take on a wholly new character and in some states it became an exodus. Having left their farms, some families remained initially in the South; between 1910 and 1920, 235,000 blacks moved from rural areas to cities in the South Atlantic states. In eastern Tennessee, for example, the black population of industrial towns increased by 54 percent between 1900 and 1920, although the total black population of the state fell by 4.5 percent. However, by far the greatest number of migrants moved to cities in northern states; between 400,000 and 500,000 black people moved northward by train and coastal steamer in 1916 and 1917 and over the next ten years they were joined by another 800,000. As a result of the migration wave of 1916–17, the labor force available to southern landlords became seriously depleted in some sections. For example, an estimated 100,000 black people left Mississippi between 1915 and 1920. Certain southern industries, such as lumber and turpentine in Mississippi and Florida, suffered especially badly and the commercial life of many previously thriving parts of the South experienced a sudden decline. For example, Brunswick, one of the two principal ports of Georgia, lost a thousand stevedores and Jacksonville, one of the leading ports of Florida, lost between six and eight thousand of its citizens. The migrants were seeking more than just economic rewards and freedom from debt; they were also curious and enthusiastic about the prospects which the North seemed to hold out of new social experiences, justice, security, and education.[57]

Southern white reaction to the migration was not uniform. Ultimately, most commentators saw grave consequences for the southern economy and recognized that efforts should be made to encourage blacks to remain in the South by alleviating some of the push factors, if only to allow landlords continued enjoyment of high wartime cotton prices, but some whites openly welcomed the departure of large numbers for other parts of the United States. It would, they argued, both relieve the South to some degree of the "negro problem" and impress the nature of that problem upon the North. When the migration showed no signs of slowing, however, the general southern view became that it was doing serious damage and that measures to prevent it should include banning the dissemination of information among potential migrants about the attractions of northern life.[58] The black press in the North generally welcomed the migration as evidence of the spirit of the race and as a slap in the face for the white people of the South. Some southern black papers, however, maintained that the migrants were mistaken and for several months in 1916 and 1917 urged their readers to stay put. The *Norfolk Journal and Guide,* for example, carried reports and cartoons about the migration in virtually every issue between October 1916 and August 1917, most of which concentrated on the unpleasantness of the climate, labor conditions, and housing in the North and the opportunities which still remained in the South.[59]

The fact that the growth of the migration did not coincide with American entry to the war meant that the BI had few reasons for thinking it might be enemy-inspired, although the white press in South Carolina quoted some federal agents who favored the German conspiracy theory. For one thing, the kind of allegation made to federal agents by southern whites often amounted to no more than repetition of implausible rumors: "Are you aware that the Canadian government has agents in the southland inducing and seducing the negroes to go to Canada to work farms, etc.[?] In case of war, can the U.S. government do without the negro?" The BI could do little with information of this kind, but the volume of such correspondence indicates the level of anxiety that existed in the white population. Forcible attempts were sometimes made to prevent blacks from leaving, but, as the white citizens of lynching-prone Washington County, Miss., discovered, this was futile: by the end of 1917, two hundred homes stood empty near the town of Greenville.[60]

The real targets of southern complaints were therefore often labor agents, commissioned by northern industry, who promised potential migrants jobs and accommodation on their arrival at northern destinations. Some agents were dishonest—in Louisiana, 1,800 black people paid two dollars each to an agent, never to see him again—but most offered a genuine alternative future for the migrants and their families. Among the first employers to recruit through agents were the Pennsylvania and Erie Railroads, followed by steel mills, meat packers, automobile plants, and Connecticut tobacco growers. In Florida, railroad agents arranged mass pickups at Jacksonville, St. Augustine, and Pensacola. Labor agents had to be discreet, because eventually most southern towns placed prohibitive restrictions on their activities. In Jacksonville, for example, labor agents were obliged to pay $1,000 for a license to operate, without which they faced a fine of $600 or sixty days in jail. In Montgomery, Ala., the penalty for operating without a license was $100 or six months' hard labor. The toughest rules of all applied in Macon County, Ga., where labor agents were required to put up $25,000 and be recommended by ten local ministers, ten manufacturers, and ten businessmen. These regulations were so onerous that agents preferred to operate covertly, and their methods consequently contributed to the suspicion that enemy agitators were behind the migration.[61]

The BI had looked into black migration in 1916 at the request of the Wilson administration, after claims that African Americans were being "colonized" in northern cities to improve the Republican vote in the federal elections. Despite investigations based in Birmingham, Macon, Atlanta, Norfolk, Baltimore, Jacksonville, Memphis, Louisville, Fayetteville, N.C., and other cities, no prosecutions resulted.[62] In 1917, some BI field offices passed to the Justice Department in Washington recurring complaints about labor agents, particularly those with possible relevance to sedition. In identifying with the concerns of leading political and commercial interests of the area, they were behaving in a way that was common among BI special agents, many of whom were natives of the cities or districts in which they worked and had often been previously employed as local law enforcement officers. In June 1917, the Birmingham BI office reported that labor agents were telling blacks that if they went north they would not be drafted.

In Cincinnati, the BI reported that seven hundred blacks had arrived on free train tickets and speculated that Germans in the city might be encouraging migration. The San Antonio BI office sent Washington descriptions of three labor agents said by the Texas State Council of Defense to be "inciting labor troubles . . . by displaying large rolls of money to negro laborers after night." The council had resolved "to prosecute all such offenders and disturbers of public peace and welfare."[63]

However, while they submitted dozens of reports, BI agents avoided actual intervention to prevent migration. For example, the Birmingham office ignored a plea by the labor superintendent of the Tennessee Coal, Iron, and Railroad Company for the government to prevent, "if possible, the further exodus of negroes to northern cities and states." The company alleged that at meetings of the Mount Pilgrim Missionary Baptist Association, "the negro ministers were preaching 'Go North.'" The Birmingham agent-in-charge reported,

> There does not appear to have been anything done at these meetings to constitute a breach of *Federal Law,* and the matter was therefore given no further consideration, as it is not the purpose of this office to become involved in any discussion of matters between master and servant, unless so instructed.

In Florida, parts of which had been especially badly hit by the migration, BI agents took a similar stance.[64]

The BI was obliged to take allegations linking the migration to Mexico and the Plan of San Diego more seriously, particularly as they formed the basis of the stories published in the *New York Tribune* and the *New York Times* in the first week of April. From the end of March, reports were received by the BI in Washington of German or Mexican agents in the South urging black men to join a German army in Mexico. The first of these reports told of two men posing as representatives of a Wisconsin orphanage addressing audiences at York, Ala. Bielaski had them traced to Blockton, Ala., where one was arrested and searched. Nothing incriminating was found, but the two men were kept under surveillance.[65] Further reports about Mexican intrigue began to arrive in early April from BI agents in Alabama, Texas, and Mississippi. Near Jackson, Miss., three men were said to be "offering the negroes all sorts of inducements to go to Mexico to join the germans [*sic*] there."[66] In Dallas, Tex., a BI agent attempted unsuccessfully to trace two Mexicans alleged to be advising blacks to cross the border. The next day, two black drunks were "badly beaten by a crowd of *American* [*sic*] citizens" after being accused of recruiting for the Mexican army. They were jailed for vagrancy. Similar reports of blacks being urged to leave rural Texas to join the Mexican army were sent from San Antonio and Austin. In Memphis, a party of 150 migrants, having gathered at a railroad station en route to Chicago, were delayed while rumors that they were on their way to join a "Mexican-German" army were investigated.[67] The veracity of all the allegations of Mexican-German intrigue directed at African Americans in the South in April 1917 is impossible to judge with certainty, but no hard evidence was established, no agitators were prosecuted, and few, if any, blacks apparently defected. By the end of April the scare had petered out, but it was a significant phase in the racial spy-mania, since it showed how easily a few facts, half-truths, and groundless rumors could gain credibility. It also demonstrated the readiness of white southerners to believe the worst of black people, and it helped to ensure that American entry into the war would spark a racist witch-hunt lasting for the next three years.

Many blacks who moved from the South to northern cities were encouraged to do so by what they read in "The World's Greatest Weekly," the *Chicago Defender*, edited and owned by Robert S. Abbott. Abbott was born on a sea island near Savannah, Ga., in 1869, and graduated from Hampton Institute and the Kent College of Law in Chicago. He founded the *Defender* in 1905 and built it up, with city and national editions, by sensational reporting and uncompromising attacks on the treatment of blacks. In April 1917, he claimed a circulation of sixty-seven thousand, much of which was in the South, especially Kentucky, Tennessee, and the Gulf states, where the *Defender* was often distributed by Pullman car porters and copies were usually shared by several readers. Abbott approved of the northward migration, both as a form of protest and as a means of self-help, and he encouraged people to travel in groups. Every wartime issue of the *Defender* advertised jobs in the North, alongside stirring exhortations to join the "flight from Egypt . . . to Canaan." For southern blacks, one of the most powerful attractions of the *Defender* was that it denounced lynchings and other crimes committed by whites in terms which its readers could not have used publicly themselves, and in this respect it also contributed to the readiness of many to leave the South. It was therefore fiercely resented by white southerners. Two of the *Defender*'s agents in the South were killed and others were harassed. Sale of the paper was banned in many places, including Hattiesburg, Miss., which once witnessed the departure of a single group of 147 blacks, including three ministers and their congregations.[68]

The BI had vetted the *Defender* in the past for possible violations of postal regulations, but from April 1917 it began a sustained persecution of Abbott as a result of increasing complaints from influential southerners. On April 9, a New Orleans BI agent attended a branch meeting of the American Protective League (APL), a nationwide volunteer vigilance group, at which the *Defender* was denounced by the city's mayor for "inciting the negroes against the white people in the South." The APL in New Orleans asked Louisiana's U.S. senators to work for the suppression of the paper in the South, as a result of which Sen. Joseph E. Ransdell approached Bruce Bielaski, who ordered the Chicago BI office to investigate.[69] A black "special employee," John E. Hawkins, was hired for three days to cover the *Defender* and recent allegations that Mexican agitators were at work in the city's "black belt." Hawkins found nothing on the Mexican matter, but on the *Defender* he reported that the "better element" of black Chicagoans disapproved of it, that Abbott was "somewhat of an egotist," and that his paper was "inflammatory and working to the detriment of the Negro Race." He also suspected that the *Defender* had the backing of newspaper magnate William Randolph Hearst. Hawkins brought Abbott in to be interviewed at the BI office, where he denied any Hearst connection, defended his editorial policy, and affirmed his loyalty to the United States, stating that his latest edition was "urging the colored man to enlist as it is not only his bound duty but by doing so he will drive away prejudice and increase his value in all directions." The BI agent investigating the *Defender* concluded that "Abbott in his zeal for the betterment of his people may have overstepped the bounds of propriety," but had not broken the law. As a precaution, the BI obtained a finance house's confidential credit report on Abbott, which established that his lifestyle was modest, that he had "a clear commercial record," and that he paid his bills promptly.[70]

White complaints about the *Defender* were growing, however, and in the South this antipathy was shared by federal agents. In Jacksonville, Fla., an agent declared that if the paper were to spread unhindered throughout the South, it would "create a spirit of unrest and possible disloyalty to the Government of the United States on the part of the negroes." He suspected that in encouraging migration the paper "may have only a political purpose as its goal, [but] it seems possible that there may be back of this particular organ some pro-*German* plan of creating a home problem to engage the attention of this country." Another Florida agent also found the *Defender* "a disturbing element among the negroes at this time."[71] In July, Durand Whipple, chairman of the Arkansas State Council of Defense, writing to the founder and chairman of the APL, made one of the most outspoken and paranoid denunciations of the *Defender.* He attributed "a very perceptible difference in the hitherto respectful demeanor of the colored people" of Little Rock to the effects of enemy propaganda which had been

> very vigorously carried on by German influences in order to upset the racial situation, and to drive away the Agricultural labor of the South.
>
> It is more than a coincidence that in many homes in this city where the household servants have hitherto been well-behaved, we have been finding copies of the *'Chicago Defender.'*

The migration of blacks, he wrote, had become "a serious national problem. . . . Whether this is part of the German propaganda or not, no more insidious and ingenious plan could be adopted for crippling the South and its resources, as well as necessitating very comprehensive steps to be taken for domestic defense." Whipple demanded efforts "to curb the activities of this paper, or . . . exclude it from the mails."[72]

Whipple's reference to the attitudes of household servants was to be repeated in many letters about racial relations addressed, or forwarded, to the Justice Department. Many white Americans were apparently confident that the mood of the entire black population could be judged on the basis of their domestic staff's account of something recently overheard, as in this example from Mississippi in March 1917: "Only yesterday our cook told my daughter that 'they are saying why should niggers fight for the United States, for they cannot vote, and if Germany gets the United States niggers will be treated better.'" Another black Mississippian was supposed to have said, "Those Germans are mighty good religious people and they don't believe in hanging, and they also came over and fought here to free the negroes, while the English helped to keep them in slavery." After speaking to his tenants in Lynchburg and Appomattox Counties, a Virginia landowner concluded that someone was "putting the idea into their silly heads that social equality will follow German occupation," while in Kentucky the black community was said to have similar illusions about Japan.[73]

Another common allegation was that Germans were occupying jobs which gave them special opportunities for contact with, and influence over, black people. An Atlanta businessman who corresponded frequently with the White House complained to the president's secretary, Joseph P. Tumulty, that a common German trick was to establish a grocery store or a "blind tiger" liquor store within a black community. His assertions condensed many elements of the black scare of the spring and summer of 1917:

> [The Germans'] design is apparently to create insurrection and disorder in the South, in conjunction with military demonstrations from Mexico which would draw Southern troops to the Borders, believing that they could seriously impair the South's agricultural production and insure scarcity of food and cotton both at home and abroad.
>
> The patriotism and loyalty of the Darkie of the Old School . . . is unquestioned, but the moral attitudes of the modern Negro, induced by the tenets of an educational system the limitations of which he has not yet been able to comprehend, and swayed by a superstition and ignorance which renders him incapable of discerning the motives of his alien mentors, has [sic] created a situation of serious import.[74]

In June 1917, the New Orleans BI office reported that the German-born owner of a "negro bar-room" at Baton Rouge was showing customers a map detailing "what portion of the United States the Germans were going to conquer and advising these negroes against registration," while in Norfolk, Va., a German running the black film theater was suspected of being an enemy propagandist. Another popular disguise for German agents, reported the BI offices in Chicago and Indianapolis, was that of a priest.[75] To support the idea that this kind of cultivation of black people was having an effect, BI agents reported claims that blacks were expressing their admiration for the Kaiser and confidence that they would be treated better once Germany had won the war. In Alabama, the BI tried to track down a "negro selling songs and ballads about the Kaiser being a mighty man" and reported an allegation that blacks believed the absence of Venus from the evening sky was due to the Kaiser having prayed for its removal. In New Orleans, agents interrogated a black man, "inclined to be a 'bad nigger,' " for having allegedly said "that if he could get a square deal he would join the Kaiser's army tomorrow and shoot American people down."[76] Even overtly loyal acts could be suspect. When black women complained about being denied employment in the Charleston navy yard, on the grounds that segregated space could not be found for them, the local BI agent believed their protest had been "inspired by German influence."[77]

Such accounts, official and non-official, of black disaffection in the face of war service are basically unreliable and are almost certainly distorted by combinations of hearsay, prejudice, and the desire of those providing the information to be taken seriously. However, the BI also accumulated persuasive hard evidence that it was not uncommon for African Americans in the South to find the prospect of going overseas to fight for the United States in the name of democracy utterly repellent. In April 1917, a circular was picked up at Friar's Point, Miss.:

> Young men and negro boys[,] what have we to fight for in this country? Nothing. Some of our well educated negroes are touring the country urging our young race to be killed up like sheep, for nothing. If we fight in this war time we fight for nothing. Rather than fight I would rather commit self death.
> Signed by a Negro Educator.
> Stick to your bush and fight not[,] for we will only be a breastwork or a shield for the white race. After war we get nothing.[78]

An anonymous letter to the government was intercepted by the postmaster in Greenville, S.C., in July:

> You white folk are going to war to fight for your rights. You all seems to want us to go. If we was to fight for our rights we would have a war among ourselves. The Germans has not done us any harm and they cannot treat us any meaner than you all has. Beware when you train 50,000 or 60,000 of the Negro race. It going to victory. Somewhere the Germans are fighting for they rights. You all are planning same thing. When we get trained we are going to do the same. So Beware. Sign by the Black Nation.[79]

Despite failing to identify the authors of such material, the BI believed its existence showed the impact of German agitation. If it ever occurred to BI agents that black people might have formed reservations about the war without any external pressure, and that a refusal to fight could be an independent response to the glaring shortcomings of American democracy, none felt comfortable about suggesting this in a report to his division superintendent or to Washington. BI agents shared the basic beliefs and values of their white peers, and certainly their views on African-American life and consciousness were never original.

In their direct dealings with African Americans, many BI agents felt more at home preserving the peace as conventional lawmen than detecting disloyalty. In one such case, in September 1917, a black farmer was arrested by the sheriff of Leon County, in a part of eastern Texas with a tradition of overreaction to signs of black unrest. The farmer, Sam Doyle, was said by another black man, Lige Price, and a white man, Bud Barnett, to have opposed the draft and to have claimed that the Mexican army would soon be over to "clean up the whites." The sheriff appealed to the Justice Department for help, adding that black farmers were hoarding food for the Mexican invaders said to be waiting until American troops set sail for France. The San Antonio BI office sent an agent from Waco to help the sheriff, because "the white people are excited and he fears that they will kill a 'lot of niggers' if *Federal officials* do not make an investigation." On reaching the area, the agent discovered a civil dispute, rather than sedition: "Sam was suspected of improper relations with *Lige's* wife," and "*Bud Barnett* has had it in for Sam because he suspects Sam of stealing his hogs."[80] Even the most unlikely-looking complaint by a white person about the disloyalty of a black person, sent to the White House, the president, the government, the Secret Service, or the Department of Justice, could find its way to Bielaski and then to the appropriate BI field office. In sparsely populated states, this often meant long, futile journeys for the agents concerned. In August 1917, an agent sent to Key West, at the southernmost tip of the Florida strait, concluded that a white woman's allegations about her black employees grew out her having "just overheard some darkies on the farm 'engaging in big talk', which is characteristic of the southern negro." A clipping from the *Cincinnati Post* resulted in a West Virginia agent traveling from Wheeling to the other end of the state only to discover that the shooting of a mining contractor who tried to prevent a black man from giving a pro-German speech to miners was "only a drunken row and no such speech was made," while in Alabama an agent found time to report a carefree interlude during a wasted trip to Cautopa: "At 9.00 o'clock I had completed the investigation but there being no train until 12.45 I passed the time shooting turtles on the creek."[81]

Black citizens who wrote to the government in the early months of the war offering support and pledging the loyalty of their race received polite replies from Bielaski, but agents in the field rarely noted overt patriotism on the part of blacks, unless it was particularly unexpected. An Oklahoma City agent, sent to cover a black anti-war rally in April 1917, reported approvingly that it was, in fact, quite the opposite, and a Jacksonville agent who attended a patriotic meeting concluded, "there does not appear to be the slightest foundation for the wholesale reports of possible disloyalty on the part of the negroes in this community."[82]

The constant possibility of major violence was an undercurrent in many, if not most, southern BI reports on racial matters, but actual outbreaks were relatively rare. Apart from deaths in race rioting, there were thirty-six lynchings in 1917; this was the decade's lowest annual figure for mob murders of blacks, despite the fact that the black spy scare immediately preceded and overlapped the period of May through September, the months in which most lynchings normally occurred. However, it cannot be assumed from this that the allegations did not contribute significantly to vigilante activity by whites; lynching remained a constant threat to the safety of black southerners in the early months of the war. In several instances, deaths were only narrowly averted following allegations of black disloyalty, and there was a high level of war-induced racial tension.[83] In May 1917, the sheriff of Hampton County, S.C., called for federal assistance in dealing with what he said was an imminent black uprising, after a "suspicious shipment [of] ammunition." All was calm when a BI agent arrived and the sheriff admitted he called for help only because "he feared a lynching of one or more negroes unless he appeased the crowd by [the] statement that he had put the matter up to the United States authorities."[84] The white hysteria confronting the sheriff was not rare, but his appeal for federal aid was unusual and may have been due as much to local law as to local conditions. Law enforcement officers in South Carolina attempted to avoid lynchings whenever possible, because it was one of the few states that allowed victims' families to sue counties in which they occurred if officials could be shown to have been negligent.[85]

Whites were especially panicky in the early months of the war in those rural areas where they were in a minority. African Americans made up more than half the population in over three hundred southern counties, and conspiracies could be read into any unusual activity, such as the sudden withdrawal of funds from a bank by blacks at Fort Towson, Okla., or the formation of a farmers' union at Cisco, Tex. Anything faintly mystical could also arouse suspicion, such as the "German prayer" said to have been found on cotton workers in Arkansas, the first third of which was part of John, chapter 1, in German, while the rest was reckoned to be coded instructions to disloyal blacks.[86] Near San Antonio, blacks were said to be forming marauding bands, while in rural Louisiana they were "holding secret meetings and storing away guns and ammunition." In Alexandria, La., a BI agent described local white people as "patriotic citizens who are amply able to take care of any set of negroes who might 'start anything,' " while the white citizens of Lake Village, Ark., outnumbered ten to one by African Americans, formed a special home guard in case the seditious speeches believed to have been made in a black fraternal lodge should lead to unrest. Some of these responses reveal the pre-emptive mentality which would cause a local pogrom at Elaine, Ark., in October 1919. From Crystal Springs, in Copiah County, Miss., where lynchings were common, a white man wrote to tell President Wilson, "We do not want to be awakened by a 'Black Uprising', unless we are PREPARED FOR IT." From the same state, a BI agent reported that in Sharkey County, where blacks were sixteen times more numerous than whites, "the white people there are not going to take any chances if trouble starts; they are simply going to murder or massacre the negros until the trouble is quieted." Although Sharkey County, in the Mississippi-Yazoo Delta, was relatively law-abiding, recording only one lynching between the end of Reconstruction and World War II, mob murder in Mississippi was typified by such expediency and lack of interest in the victims' guilt, particularly during and just after the war. This part of the state exhibited most starkly the racial inequalities of the Deep South: almost all the tenant farmers were black, poor, and exploited, and when the war raised cotton prices, the planters simply forced tenants to take on new debts. Racial control was paramount and, as Neil McMillen has shown, most of Mississippi's lynchings took place in counties where blacks were in a clear majority, such as Sharkey County's neighbors, Washington County (thirteen lynchings) and Yazoo County (eleven).[87] In a scurrilous volume published in 1918, *The Truth about Lynching and the Negro in the South,* a southern writer defended lynchings in black-majority counties: "Is it any wonder that the white man thinks it necessary to strike terror into the soul of the possible or incipient Negro criminal by any method that may cause him to stand in fear of an immediate and dreadful death?"[88]

Several times in the previous thirty years, the fear of black uprisings had produced localized searches for networks of conspirators and serious violence in the South. To some extent, this was a periodic reaction to the prevalence of secret fraternal societies among the freedmen and their male descendants which fueled white paranoia. In 1892, several black members of the ex-carpetbagger Albion W. Tourgée's National Citizens Rights Association were gunned down in clashes in Mississippi, and the massacre of a white family near Statesboro, Ga., in 1904, for which two men were burned to death, was said to be part of a wider conspiracy and local blacks were terrorized as a result.[89] In 1917, a wave of overreaction to rumors once again swept across white communities in the South. A BI agent in Richmond, Va., found the white population in a "hysterical condition" over the suspicious activities of black residents, and on other occasions when disorder threatened, federal agents only narrowly deterred serious violence by their presence. While investigating an alleged black conspiracy near Cocoa, Fla., an agent dispersed a white mob by persuading the leading rabble-rouser that, rather than proceed with immediate lynchings, "it might be as well to know first who the leaders were and that we should lay low till that was discovered."[90]

At times, the motives of mobs appear to have had less to do with the war than with localized jealousies or grudges. Just as there is evidence that many German Americans in the Midwest were subjected to assaults such as tarring and feathering for reasons that had as much to with their political associations and wealth as their ethnicity, so prominent African Americans might be humiliated by vigilantes for similar reasons, as happened to an African-American doctor in Vicksburg, Miss., in July 1918.[91]

Three months after the United States entered the war, the fears of many observers, from W. E. B. Du Bois to BI agents in the field, that the increasingly volatile racial atmosphere would give way to large-scale violence were realized. The outbreak did not come in the Deep South and it was not directly related to allegations of black involvement in pro-German intrigue, but it was undoubtedly caused in part by the suspicions and intergroup tensions which the war had intensified. On July 2, 1917, one of the bloodiest and most sadistic race riots in American history began at East St. Louis, on the southwestern border of Illinois. In a context of bitter industrial relations and evenly balanced political rivalries, union organizers and Democratic politicians in the city had charged that white workers were being cynically outmaneuvered by the deliberate importation of southern blacks to supply employers with non-union labor and the Republican party with extra votes. Between April and June, migrants had been accused of causing the failure of recent strikes (although they constituted a minority of the strikebreakers), particularly at the Aluminum Ore Company, which had hired almost five hundred blacks. In May, the Central Trades and Labor Union (CTLU) demanded "drastic action . . . to get rid of" newly arrived black workers. Ill feeling was heightened further by the invention of a black crime wave by the local press. A foretaste of the July riot came on May 28, when, following a stormy meeting of the CTLU, Mayor Fred Mollman, and the city council, blacks were beaten on the streets until Gov. Frank O. Lowden sent National Guardsmen to restore order.[92]

In addition to labor disputes, the circumstances of the 1916 election had caused lasting bitterness in the city. Allegations that the Republican party was illegally persuading blacks to move north to vote were given wide currency in pro-Democratic newspapers in East St. Louis and the U.S. attorney, a Democrat, promised that prosecutions would ensue.[93] Although Wilson had carried Illinois in 1912 with 400,000 votes, the combined vote in the state for the split Republican tickets of Taft and Roosevelt had been 640,000, making it a borderline state in 1916. The significant black support which Wilson had gained in 1912 had largely evaporated by 1916 and the prospect of an enlarged black vote in Illinois and other midwestern states because of migration concerned the Democrats. In his election-eve message to his campaign supporters, Wilson declared that although votes could no longer be bought in America, there were still "conscienceless agents of sinister forces working in opposition to progressive principles and popular government." The government had already announced a major investigation into allegations of vote fraud involving black migrants. It was run from Indianapolis by Assistant Attorney General Frank C. Dailey, who was given carte blanche and the full cooperation of district attorneys and federal agents in Ohio, Indiana, and Illinois. It was alleged that in eighteen months, three hundred thousand blacks had been "colonized" in the three states to tip the electoral balance. The Justice Department put the number of blacks who had left the South in the four months before the election, alone, at around sixty thousand and stated that a proportion had already registered to vote in violation of the election laws of the states in which they now resided. The anti-Wilson *Chicago Tribune* retorted that there was only one offense

> more likely to shock the sensibilities of the present Department of Justice. . . . It would be unspeakable to vote them in the South, where they have been colonized for somewhat more than eighteen months. However, we congratulate the head of Mr. Wilson's Department of Justice, Mr. Gregory of Texas, on his opportune discovery and we suggest that he let us hear of the measures he has taken to assure the free vote of the several million colored Americans not yet free in the colonized North.[94]

The well-publicized efforts to track down operators of the alleged colonization scheme were plainly made to benefit the Democrats at the polls; Dailey's investigation produced no meaningful evidence and the BI failed to find any corresponding conspiracy in the South. Shortly after the 1916 election, in which Illinois and Indiana went Republican, as usual, the gathering of information on this aspect of migration was discontinued.[95]

As elsewhere, specific allegations of vote fraud in East St. Louis were ostentatiously investigated by the BI. Although a majority of the votes cast in the city had been for Wilson and other Democrats, the allegations were widely believed, so that black migrants were now characterized as a threat to democracy, as well as jobs and public safety.[96] It was against this political and economic background that a virtually uncontrolled attack on the black population of East St. Louis was launched. After the unrest in the city in May, blacks had armed themselves for self-protection, and on the night of Sunday, July 1, 1917, when at least one carload of whites drove through a black district, shooting into the mostly wooden houses, their shots were returned. A police patrol car was also fired upon by black residents, who may have failed to recognize it, and two detectives in the car were killed. A journalist riding with the detectives filed a dramatic account of the shooting, evidence of which was to be seen in the bullet-ridden patrol car, left outside the downtown police station. On July 2, after a meeting at the Labor Temple, white workers marched on the black residential district, attacking men, women, and children on sidewalks and streetcars as they went. Fires were started systematically, destroying over two hundred homes. Members of the Illinois National Guard did little to stop the assaults and fire-raising, while the police did even less. At least thirty-nine blacks died, including several women and children, in brutal assaults on mainly unresisting, unarmed people. In addition, eight whites died, some of them killed accidentally by other whites. Eventually, after a day and a night of rioting, National Guard reinforcements restored order.[97]

Immediately after the riot, BI chief Bielaski responded to hints in some early newspaper reports that German intrigue had been behind the outbreak, by ordering the St. Louis office to investigate this suggestion "as confidentially as possible."[98] The BI agents found from the start that their attempts to identify causes of the riot were complicated by sharp divisions between the big employers on the one hand and the city government and labor leaders on the other. Each side blamed the other for what had happened. Initially, the investigators were satisfied with the union and city hall

version, which was that the riot was simply "the outgrowth of trouble brewing for some time due to the negroes taking the white men [*sic*] jobs and
robberies on the part of the negroes." Large numbers of blacks were said
to have been enticed from the South by the employers, via labor agents, in
order to provide cheap labor and break strikes. These ingredients, combined with a sensationally reported black crime wave and charges of vote
fraud involving the migrants, were presented by BI agents as a plausible
recipe for a race riot. When the agents reported they had been "unable to
find any German influence back of any of these disturbances, but did find
that it is merely a race riot," the Justice Department readily accepted this
analysis and its implication that there were no grounds for a federal investigation. This easy explanation was endorsed by Mayor Mollman and the
East St. Louis police.[99] However, the employers resented being portrayed as
calculating men whose profitable manipulations of the labor market had
led to the riot, and immediately attempted to shift blame away from themselves and black residents and onto the unions and local politicians.[100]

The sickening details of the East St. Louis riot horrified Americans in
all parts of the country. The murders were contrasted repeatedly with the
supposed war aim of preserving democracy, and there were numerous calls
for federal action. On July 20, Justice Department attorney William Herron
identified two statutes under which the government could legally and con-
stitutionally intervene in East St. Louis: section 19 of the U.S. penal code,
allowing prosecution for conspiracy to violate rights and privileges guaranteed by the Constitution and federal laws, and the 1866 Civil Rights Act,
entitling "all persons born in the United States . . . [to] full and equal
benefit of all laws." Herron advised that

> if evidence can be procured showing that either the state, the County, or
> the municipal authorities failed to perform the duties required of them
> by the Illinois law in relation to these people because they were Negroes,
> there is a basis for a [federal] grand jury investigation and such an inves-
> tigation should be had.

(Herron's interpretation of the law was more liberal than that of earlier
Justice Department lawyers. In 1910, the department had concluded that
the federal government could do little to protect the civil rights of African
Americans, except when people were being prevented from living or carrying on a business in a particular place, and even this power was by no
means certain.)[101]

The next day, Bielaski wrote personally to ask the special-agent-in-charge at St. Louis, E. J. Brennan, whether his investigation into the riot thus far had been thorough enough "to make reasonably certain" that there had been no German intrigue behind it. He also asked if Brennan was sure that there had been no violation of any federal statute. Thus far, Bielaski stated, no violations had come to light, but he stressed that he wanted to "make certain that further investigation would not reveal facts on which [the] Federal Government might act."[102] The following Monday, Brennan had a "lengthy conference" with Charles Karch, the U.S. attorney for the Eastern District of Illinois, who afterward recommended to Attorney General Thomas Watt Gregory a grand jury investigation headed by Judge Kenesaw Mountain Landis, on the basis of the statutes identified by Herron. Karch thought that "the violence against the negroes and the consequent denial of their constitutional prerogatives and immunities, were directly due to state action." On the same day, however, Woodrow Wilson made it plain to his attorney general that he was not keen on the idea of a federal investigation into the riot: "we cannot under the existing law extend our jurisdiction, as much as we would like to."[103]

Meanwhile, representatives of the large employers at East St. Louis had descended on Hinton G. Clabaugh, the superintendent of the BI's Central Division, based in Chicago. The president of the Missouri Malleable Iron Company, F. E. Hulson, who had been attracted by the cheap land and low tax assessments in East St. Louis, and an East St. Louis attorney, Dan McGlynn, were taken to see Clabaugh by an army intelligence officer on July 21. They had come to Chicago principally to see the commanding officer of the Illinois National Guard, Gen. Thomas H. Barry. The outcome of their visit demonstrated the pronounced bias of senior BI personnel toward big business and against organized labor, and showed how easy it was for businessmen to enlist the help of the Justice Department and National Guard units to protect their interests by invoking the war effort.[104] Troops had been sent to East St. Louis in April 1917, under Maj. R. W. Cavanaugh, to protect industrial plants affected by strikes, particularly the Aluminum Ore Company. That the purpose of this force was to defend property and not people became clear when Cavanaugh had refused Mayor Mollman's appeal for help to quell the brief outbreak of racial violence at the end of May. The extra troops sent by Governor Lowden on that occasion had been withdrawn by June 20, leaving the original unit to continue guarding factories and protecting strike-breakers. When the major riot of July 2 began,

Cavanaugh's men were called on to help only as a last resort when units arriving from other cities fell short of the number expected.[105] What the employers now sought after the riot was a guarantee of continued protection for their factories and the support of the Justice Department. They had secured an undertaking that the troops would not be withdrawn before more permanent arrangements could be made, but General Barry wanted the BI to assist his officers. Hulson and McGlynn told Clabaugh "most emphatically that the recent trouble was not caused by the negroes at all, but by the labor element there, who bitterly resent negro employees being brought into that district," and claimed that another riot was being planned, "compared to which the recent riot will sink into insignificance." Furthermore, "the Mayor, Chief of Police, etc. or anyone else in that vicinity could not be trusted to either do their duty or cooperate with the industries." The lives of the managers of both the Aluminum Ore Company and the Armour meatpacking plant were said to have been threatened, "along with more or less open threats to destroy the property of the Aluminum Ore Co. as well as the packing plants." Having given their version of events, the employers pledged to cooperate fully with the Justice Department in the essentially anti-union alliance they were proposing and drew the BI's attention to the allegedly crucial production of aluminum at East St. Louis for aircraft parts.[106]

After receiving Clabaugh's account of the meeting, Bielaski told Brennan in St. Louis to confer with Major Cavanaugh and "give special attention" to the Aluminum Ore Company. Probably aware of the lack of enthusiasm in the White House for the distraction and political complication which a federal investigation would represent, Bielaski also now advised Brennan that there was "very little if any justification apparently for Federal action in [the] general situation"—a view which Brennan readily came to endorse. Brennan met with Cavanaugh on July 24 for another "lengthy conference," attended by the assistant manager of Aluminum Ore, who gave a summary of recent union activity. Brennan also sent an agent to East St. Louis each day "with a view of endeavoring every way possible to secure evidence of any violations of the federal laws," but only Illinois laws appeared to have been breached and these violations were being investigated by state officials. This report reached Washington on July 27.[107] That day, apparently acting on the latest information, the attorney general told the president that, despite "a complete investigation" by the district attorney and the BI, and a "good deal of thought[,] . . . no facts have been presented to us which would justify Federal action, though it is conceivable that a condition which would justify it may develop later on." Wilson lost no time in informing St. Louis congressman Leonidas C. Dyer "in candor" that the administration had found no grounds for federal action beyond giving "aid to the state authorities in their efforts to restore tranquility and guard against further outbreak." Gregory informed the district attorney in even more definite terms that the Justice Department was no longer interested. Brennan's investigation was wound up and he passed further information about the riot to the East St. Louis police.[108]

One of Brennan's agents had crossed the Eads bridge into East St. Louis on five consecutive days, ostensibly to look for evidence of violations of federal statutes. However, far from "endeavoring every way possible" to do this, as he claimed, he spoke only to industrialists and their lawyers or the district attorney. Not once did he interview a black person, a union leader, an elected city official, a policeman, or a member of the National Guard about the riot, or, if he did, he did not see fit to report the conversation, nor was he instructed to speak to such people. From the industrial managers and the district attorney, the BI got the standard business explanation of the riot: that it was all the fault of the unions. At the Armour plant, the general superintendent introduced the agent to a foreman who denounced two union leaders, including Charles Lehman, an official of the Aluminum Ore Employees Protective Association, as "agitators of strikes" and "strong Union men" and implied that they had instigated the riot. All the employers conceded that large numbers of black workers had come to the city over the previous year and that they had been employed during strikes for lower wages than white workers, but none would admit to having actually "imported" labor for this purpose, or that the employers might bear some responsibility for the deterioration of race relations.[109] The BI's efforts seem deliberately inadequate and partial when compared to the vigorous on-the-spot investigation conducted in less than a week by W. E. B. Du Bois and Martha Gruening, a white social worker and *Crisis* employee. They hired local assistants and interviewed victims and a wide range of other key individuals, producing a biting twenty-page report in the September *Crisis* in which the context and events of the riot were vividly described and illustrated.[110]

It is abundantly clear that the partial work carried out by the BI in East St. Louis, on which the Wilson administration claimed to base its eventual decision not to conduct a federal investigation, did not constitute a proper examination of either the causes of the riot or the extent to which the riot had led to the breaking of federal laws. The Justice Department was only interested in establishing the role of organized labor in wartime violence and the disruption of industrial production. Apart from making cursory checks on the possible influence of German agitators or the syndicalist Industrial Workers of the World, the BI allowed itself to be used by the East St. Louis employers to focus attention on the dangers of growing industrial union power during the war. The last people to be considered in the BI's reports were the hundreds of African-American victims left dead, injured, or grieving and the thousands made homeless. It is equally clear that the Wilson administration did not want to be drawn into a divisive and complex problem at the same time as it was finalizing its plans for waging war. And yet it is very likely that had a disturbance of similar proportions broken out in a city like East St. Louis involving different parties—a battle growing out of an industrial dispute, say, in which labor and capital were pitted directly against each other, or between supporters and opponents of the war, or a riot in which hundreds of German Americans were the victims—then the government would have immediately seen a clear relevance to the war effort and intervened. As it was, the fact that blacks were the sufferers provided two reasons why federal intervention did not occur: firstly, the Democratic administration preferred at all times to steer clear of the race question— Woodrow Wilson, in particular, was uncomfortable with private or public discussion of the subject—and, secondly, the government continued to believe that black sentiment about the war was neither especially volatile nor especially important.

In fact, the riot was a pivotal moment in the response of black Americans to World War I and the whole issue of equal rights campaigns, and the government's eventual recognition of the change it marked sparked a massive expansion of the surveillance of the African-American population and its leadership. In the first three months of the American belligerency, the approach of almost all black leaders had been to maintain an upbeat and patriotic message, but the ferocity of the assault on the black population of East St. Louis caused a sudden revision of this outlook in public meetings across the country. In Chicago, for example, the BI feared a wave of violent black protest after a speech at the headquarters of the Negro Fellowship League by the city's leading black lawyer, Ferdinand L. Barnett, husband of the anti-lynching campaigner Ida B. Wells-Barnett. Barnett warned that events in East St. Louis could soon be repeated in Chicago and advised his audience to "[a]rm yourselves with guns and pistols. . . . Don't buy an arse-nal but get enough guns to protect yourselves. . . . And when trouble starts let us not hesitate to call upon our Negro militiamen to defend us. . . . And let no black man permit a policeman to come and get those guns." Con-demning the failure of the state of Illinois to quell the rioting, he declared, "We are going to rectify this in some way. The 10,000,000 of our race will not stand for this massacre." Another speaker at the rally put the number of black deaths in the riot at two hundred and hoped that "God would de-mand 100,000 white lives in the war for each Negro slaughtered in East St. Louis. I love my race better than my country. This country under Woodrow Wilson is asking us to carry the flag of democracy to Europe. God for-bid that we take across the Atlantic any of the democracy of East St. Louis." Resolutions were passed for Ida Wells to take to Governor Lowden at Springfield.[111] BI Division Superintendent Clabaugh advised Bielaski that Chicago's German-born chief of police regarded Barnett as "rabidly pro-German . . . , in fact [he] speaks German almost as well as the chief him-self." He warned that blacks had recently bought large numbers of cut-price guns and that Barnett and others could "very easily cause a great deal of trouble if they are not careful." Bielaski instructed Clabaugh to "make a thorough investigation of the activities of Barnett as far as possible, and if it develops that he is amenable to federal law take prompt action." BI agents subsequently failed to find a single black person willing to admit to having heard Barnett speak, and no action was taken.[112] This probably suited the Justice Department, which must have recognized that, in the absence of federal action against the East St. Louis rioters, the prosecution of individu-als for protesting against the riot could not easily be defended, even under the terms of the Espionage Act.

The failure of the highest levels of government to condemn the riot and the lack of a full federal investigation had very damaging long-term effects on black morale, which were most clearly shown in the changing tone of African-American journalism. Repeated contrasts were drawn between the high moral principles which the government claimed for its war policy and the lack of concern it was showing for the plight of ten million of its own people. The owner-editor of the *Norfolk Journal and Guide*, P. B. Young, stated that unless it took "prompt and vigorous action . . . , the United States government should renounce its purposes for entering the world war and stand convicted among the nations of the earth as the greatest hypo-crite of all times." In the *Baltimore Afro-American*, J. H. Murphy declared that

American war aims now meant nothing to black people: "Thru their tears they cannot see the difference between German Frightfulness and American Frightfulness so long as the blood of women and children is shed needlessly." Hubert Harrison, an influential Harlem radical, asked in his new magazine, the *Voice,* how African Americans could be expected to believe in American democratic ideals when, just before the Fourth of July, "the white people, who are denouncing the Germans as Huns and barbarians, break loose in an orgy of unprovoked and villainous barbarism which neither Germans nor any other people have ever equalled." In the *Chicago Defender,* Robert Abbott condemned the failure of the troops to defend black people during the riot: "they acted like children. . . . If this is the way they intend to represent the government, Germany has already won the war."[113]

The white press in the South was divided. Those that took a conservative view, such as the *Atlanta Constitution,* the *Norfolk Ledger-Dispatch,* and the *Norfolk Virginian-Pilot,* blamed the riot on migration, suggesting that blacks would now recognize that it was time to return to the South and taking satisfaction in the proof that northerners were not as charitable as they sometimes claimed. Those papers that took a more progressive view, such as the *Houston Post,* the *Dallas Morning News,* the *Galveston Daily News,* and the *Savannah Morning News,* argued that the attractiveness of southern life for black people had to be improved by urgent action in areas such as education, sanitation, and the legal system. In the North, many white editors, such as the *Outlook*'s Lyman Abbott, a Brooklyn Congregationalist minister and advocate of Booker T. Washington's gradualism, drew parallels between the riot and the worst of the alleged German atrocities in Belgium and warned of the dangers of both northern self-righteousness and weak city government. Some journals, such as the *Survey,* initially explained the riot in purely economic terms, as a predictable result of labor competition, while others, such as Oswald Garrison Villard's *New York Evening Post,* insisted that black people should be free to live and work anywhere they wished.[114] Only one white newspaper, the *Christian Science Monitor,* gave significant coverage to the idea that German plotting was involved. It printed the assertion of a white native of St. Louis that race and labor friction had been only incidental to the disturbances: "rather, that they were due to a deep laid conspiracy to involve the Nation in serious internal complications, and thus divert the thought of the public and the activities of the Federal Government, from external affairs." The migration of southern blacks had been "outside the natural order of things, and consistent with the effort of a few months to tamper with the loyalty of the southern Negro, and with other uncovered plots of a similar nature."[115] This report was noted by other papers, but not given much credence. However, the *Lexington Herald* later claimed that the German government used photographs and descriptions of the devastation at East St. Louis and of lynchings as anti-American propaganda in parts of Russia.[116]

Several African-American delegations traveled to Washington to appeal to Wilson for action, but they received no satisfaction. A week after the East St. Louis riot, a group from Baltimore managed to see Vice-President Thomas R. Marshall and Speaker of the House of Representatives Champ Clark (D-Mo.), both of whom made encouraging noises about a federal investigation, but Wilson would not admit them to the Oval Office, for fear of encouraging further civil rights protest and because of his reluctance to commit himself to any action in the realm of race. Wilson's secretary, Joseph P. Tumulty, had passed him the request for an audience with the note, "I am afraid that if you see this delegation the fire will be rekindled and that a greater impetus will be given to an agitation which is already contagious in its effects."[117] Wilson explained to Sen. Joseph French of Maryland, who had tried to obtain an interview for the delegation, that he was too busy and made typically evasive noises, without once mentioning events at East St. Louis: "Knowing their errand and wishing in every way possible to promote the safety and welfare of our colored fellow-citizens, I am sure that I should listen to their representations with entire sympathy. . . . " He stated that "through the Department of Justice, through the Department of Labor, and through every other channel open to me, I am doing and will do my utmost to safeguard the interests of the colored people who are, of course, as much entitled to our protection and support as any other citizens of the United States." The Baltimore delegation was "only partially cheered" by this.[118] On August 2, another delegation called at the White House to protest racial violence in general and the East St. Louis riot in particular. Among its leading members were James Weldon Johnson, W. E. B. Du Bois, radical Harlem ministers George Frazier Miller and Adam Clayton Powell, Sr., the cosmetics entrepreneur Madame C. J. Walker, and the Tuskegee-ite editor of the *New York Age*, Fred R. Moore. They called for lynching to be made a federal offense, either by legislation or by constitutional amendment, and, in a typically Du Boisian sentence, declared, "No nation that seeks to fight the battles of civilization can afford to march in blood-smeared garments." This group was also obliged to leave its petition with Joseph Tumulty.[119]

One of the few national figures to speak out promptly about East St. Louis was a former occupant of the White House. On July 6, at a Carnegie Hall reception for the mission of the Kerensky government in Russia, Theodore Roosevelt condemned the riot as "an appalling outbreak of savagery," and called on the government to "use with ruthless sternness every instrumentality at their command to punish murder whether committed by whites against blacks or blacks against whites." He was followed on the platform by American Federation of Labor president Samuel Gompers, who deplored the riot but accused the importers of black labor of trying to "undermine the working conditions of white men in the North," comparing the "luring of these colored men to East St. Louis" to "the behavior of the brutal, reactionary and tyrannous forces that existed in Old Russia." This attempt to excuse both the union leaders who had increased the tension and the white workers in the mob provoked Roosevelt into an immediate rejoinder, most of which he yelled into Gompers's face:

> I am not willing that a meeting called for the purpose of commemorating the birth of freedom in Russia shall be made the vehicle for an apology, implied or otherwise, for the unspeakable brutalities committed upon colored men and women and children recently in East St. Louis.
>
> Justice with me is not a mere form of words. How in the name of Heaven can we consistently praise Russia for doing democratic and undiscriminating justice to the men within her borders if we seem, even by implication, to tolerate apology for the criminal atrocities committed within one of our own states?[120]

Black leaders were pleased by this outburst—Adam Clayton Powell and the congregation of Harlem's Abyssinian Baptist Church congratulated Roosevelt and hoped that he would be president again—but no other white politician approached his passionate sincerity on the subject.[121]

In Congress, Republicans William Rodenberg, from East St. Louis, and Leonidas C. Dyer successfully promoted a resolution calling for a congressional investigation of the riot. One of Illinois's U.S. senators, William Yates Sherman, supported the resolution, but the other, Hamilton J. Lewis, expressed misgivings about letting blacks get the idea that the government was "behind them."[122] The resulting special committee of four congressmen held four weeks of hearings, but was given little assistance by the Justice Department. Its ten-thousand-word report was a powerful, if anecdotal, indictment of the politicians and policemen of East St. Louis and the Illinois state militia and included a call for wide-ranging prosecutions, but it was not published until a year after the riot and it did nothing to spark further federal action.[123]

The NAACP staged the most effective and widely reported protest, a silent parade, at the suggestion of Oswald Garrison Villard, whose mother, Fanny Garrison Villard, had organized a similar protest march three years earlier for fifteen hundred black-clad women pacifists and suffragettes. On July 28, 1917, over eight thousand black people of all ages marched to muffled drums down 5th Avenue in New York, watched by a crowd of twenty thousand, bearing banners reading "Mr. President, Why Not Make AMERICA Safe for Democracy?" and "Your Hands Are Full of Blood." The police seized one banner, deemed to be in "bad taste": an enlarged *New York Evening Mail* cartoon of a black mother and two children pleading by the ruins of East St. Louis with a stern-faced Wilson, shown holding a speech on world democracy.[124]

For many African Americans, the riot became the critical moment in their personal deliberations on whether they should regard the war as an irrelevance and an imposition, or as an opportunity and a test. Despite the mounting propaganda of war mobilization in the summer of 1917, the riot and the government's inaction destroyed the faith of many individuals in the possibility of the United States ever permitting black people to enjoy full citizenship, equal rights, and dignity. Hubert Harrison issued a warning:

> Let there be no mistake. Whatever the Negroes may be compelled by law to do and say, the resentment of their hearts will not die down. UNBE-KNOWN TO THE WHITE PEOPLE OF THIS LAND A TEMPER IS BEING DEVELOPED AMONG NEGROES WHICH THE AMERICAN PEOPLE WILL HAVE TO RECKON WITH.[125]

A pattern of bitter protest began to be noted by the Justice Department as possible evidence of general black disaffection. There was a suggestion of orchestrated sabotage: in East St. Louis, a spate of fires in the stockyards were investigated by BI agents in case they were evidence of "a desire for revenge among the negroes."[126] There were also fears of widespread racial violence, this time initiated by blacks. The government began receiving copies of a leaflet declaring

'GET OFF THE EARTH'
'You Japs, Chinese, Hindus an' 'Niggers'!'
No We Won't:—You Stop Shovin'.

Around the edges, it read, "A mild rebuke to 'Pale face' greed, avarice and rapacity, FIRST SHOT in the initial skirmish, inaugurating a War of Races unless colored people are treated better." Black people had never let the United States down, it continued, yet now they were reduced to "a kind of quasi-citizenship." White imperialism had "gobbled up practically the entire earth's surface, exterminated or subjugated the natives, seized, exploited their land and resources, and denied all colored races rights and citizenship; ALL in the name of Christianity, Civilization and Religion." Now, "dark-skinned people the world over" sought "a re-apportionment—a redistribution of the earth's surface."[127] The first copy received by the Justice Department was forwarded by the chief inspector of the Post Office Department, after being referred to a local postmaster by the editor of the *Lexington Herald.* The *Herald* had received several of the leaflets and strongly suspected that they were produced with "an ulterior motive different from that apparently indicated."[128] Within a week, BI agents around the country were sending in further copies received by other papers, including the *Galveston Tribune,* the *Lynchburg News,* the *Buffalo Evening Times,* the *Houston Press,* and the *Houston Chronicle.* Only the Galveston agent suspected that the leaflet might be specifically a response to the East St. Louis riot.[129]

Having been informed that the post office in Springfield was handling the leaflet in large numbers, Chief Bielaski instructed the local BI agent, T. W. Quinlan, to find the person responsible, since it came "fairly close to violating the Espionage Act." It was traced to Dr. James E. Henderson, a black physician, who had been sending it occasionally to newspapers and individuals across the United States for two years, but had increased his output sharply in August 1917, when he sent out several hundred. Black newspapers had also received the leaflet; the *Baltimore Afro-American* agreed with its sentiments, but disliked the reference to "a War of Races." Quinlan reported that Henderson was "a perfectly loyal citizen," with "no intention of creating any trouble"; he was just "a little bit 'off'" when it came to the treatment of his people." Henderson had promised that he would not mail any more leaflets and Quinlan thought it could be left at that.[130] The U.S. attorney at Springfield thought otherwise: Henderson was arrested by a U.S. marshal on September 19 and charged with attempting to incite race riots and interfering with the drafting of black troops by distributing inflammatory materials. When he was released on a $2000 bond, he left Springfield—the city directories do not list him after 1917—and he was ultimately not prosecuted. As with many other individuals charged and bailed under the Espionage Act, the government found the threat of prosecution was sufficient to eliminate further dissent.[131]

Black newspaper editors carried a number of very outspoken contributions from their readers on the East St. Louis riot during July and August 1917. In a long and bitter open letter to Woodrow Wilson, Professor D. J. Jordan of Greensboro, N.C., advised the president, "by your acts you have told your fellow countrymen that you do not regard the Negro as human . . . , the country in its treatment of Negroes has taken its cue from its president." Jordan warned Wilson not to discount the possibility of Germany "raising and equipping an army of a million disaffected Americans in the very heart of the nation."[132] This letter appeared in the black press without interference, but another angry plea caused the *Richmond Planet* to be temporarily barred from the mails by the Richmond postmaster—an early indication to the black press of the Post Office Department's new powers of censorship. While insisting that he loved the American flag, Uzziah Miner, formerly editor of the *Howard University Journal* and now an employee of the War Department, wrote to the *Planet* that he was "completely disgusted with America's hypocrisy and insincerity. . . . I fail to see how I can conscientiously volunteer to fight for a 'World Democracy' while I am denied the fruits and blessings of a Democracy at home." Unless Wilson were to speak out like Roosevelt and the Justice Department took action against the East St. Louis rioters, Miner would regard himself as a "disgrace to my race and my country" if he volunteered: "Democracy, like charity, should begin at home and spread abroad." Since Miner had written against volunteering, rather than submission to the draft, this was not technically a breach of title 1, section 3, of the Espionage Act, although it could have been interpreted as encouraging military insubordination. The editor of the *Richmond Planet*, John Mitchell, succeeded in legal proceedings to get the mail bar lifted—a "victory of the colored press," declared the *Baltimore Afro-American*—allowing other black newspapers to carry and discuss Miner's letter. Borrowing a phrase from James Weldon Johnson's recent delegation to the White House, the *Norfolk Journal and Guide* agreed with Miner that "this country should set its own house in order before going to fight the battles of civilization 'marching in bloodsoaked clothes.' "[133] Both D. J. Jordan's open letter to Wilson and Uzziah Miner's letter to the *Richmond Planet* were noted by the domestic intelligence agencies of the federal government; Jordan's was referred to the BI and Miner's letter was discussed by the Military Intelligence Branch of the War Department's General Staff.[134]

Six weeks after the East St. Louis riot, a new tragedy made wartime race relations a vivid issue once again. On the night of August 23, 1917, after a series of provocations by white civilians and police, a hundred members of the 3rd Battalion of the 24th Infantry, one of the four black regular army regiments, marched from Camp Logan into nearby Houston, firing indiscriminately at white people. The affray left sixteen whites and four blacks dead and led to the largest court-martial in American military history— which, itself, was in sharp contrast to the lax way in which the East St. Louis rioters were treated. The eventual execution of thirteen members of the 24th Infantry in December 1917, with no review or opportunity to appeal, and with the prospect of several more executions thereafter, was to produce a level of outrage among African Americans that severely tested the government's ability to placate blacks and manipulate black opinion.[135]

In April 1917, when the wartime emergency began, the Wilson administration had not anticipated a deterioration of race relations, but by the end of August it was a subject that could not be ignored. Moreover, five months into American belligerency, African Americans resumed open discussion about whether the United States was entitled to their support, in the aftermath of the East St. Louis riot and the Houston mutiny. The broad pro-war consensus among the black leadership was crumbling and frequent reports were being received in Washington about black disenchantment at the grassroots. Certainly there was no evidence that war had generated a new interracial solidarity; if anything, white hostility and black resentment had deepened since the United States abandoned neutrality. The heightened suspicion with which whites regarded African Americans was shared by government agencies, and senior figures in the administration were beginning to become alarmed. The government resorted to two measures in the fall of 1917, just as the draft registration and induction of black men accelerated, which were intended to contain racial strife within the army and equal rights protest by civilians. One initiative, the cooptation of black personnel into the War Department and the creation of a steady dialogue with black leaders, was evidence of a logical, clear-headed approach in the upper echelons of the administration; the second, the massive expansion of intelligence-gathering on the African-American population, was more an expression of the repressive instincts, racial prejudice, and enabling ignorance of the surveillance bureaucracy during World War I.

Both responses had the same goal: to counteract the mood captured in the report of a BI agent in Mobile, Ala., where black residents had allegedly concluded that the war was "the white people's war and the negroes had nothing to do with it, that the white[s] elected Wilson and he had got them in the war and now let Wilson and the white[s] fight it out."[136]

Two

The Wilson Administration and Black Opinion, 1917–1918

By the beginning of September 1917, several events taken together had convinced the director of the Military Intelligence Branch (MIB), Col. Ralph Van Deman, of the need to recruit experts on what the agency came quickly to call "Negro Subversion." The vehement protests following the riot at East St. Louis had seemed to fundamentally question black support for the war effort. Then, on August 2, the office of the counselor of the State Department sent the MIB a Secret Service report reminiscent of those filed by the BI on German propaganda among African Americans in the first few months of the war. The president of the Harlem Neighborhood Organization was claiming that property worth over $500,000 had recently been bought in Harlem, ostensibly by blacks, but in fact with German money. She identified two men, including the well-known real estate businessman Philip A. Payton, as having negotiated the purchases for Wall Street brokers Kuhn, Loeb and Company, the financiers of Ambassador von Bernstorff's earlier propaganda campaign. German agents in Harlem were also said to be operating from a furniture store at 5th Avenue and 135th Street. The Secret Service reported that around the time America entered the war, blacks in Harlem had feted a "distinguished German," who had said, "previous to his departure for Mexico, . . . that they owed nothing to the United States Government and contrasted the treatment of the negroes by the whites of this country with the kindness he claimed they would receive if the Germans were in control." There were further rumors to the effect that "some kind of Mexican plot is being hatched" with the cooperation of blacks.[1] This appears to have been the first report to find its way into MIB files under the heading "Negro Subversion," and its State Department origins may have persuaded Van Deman of its special importance, even though it had a distinctly second-hand air about it.

A few weeks later, part of the 24th Infantry mutinied, forcing the War Department to explicitly confront the issue of race. Van Deman, who had hitherto been content to let the BI handle the question of African-American loyalty, now began to see the combating of "Negro Subversion" as an essential component of military counterintelligence in the United States.[2]

Shortly before the Houston riot, one of Van Deman's typically well-connected recruits, Maj. Herbert Parsons, had begun to make tentative inquiries into the problem of racial tension. A former U.S. congressman from New York (1905–11), Parsons was a leading progressive Republican and had managed Charles Evans Hughes's presidential campaign in 1916; as such, his transfer from the Signal Corps had been a coup for the MIB. In mid-August, soon after he transferred, he was contacted by Cornell University sociology professor Jeremiah W. Jenks, who, like many patriotic academics, had come to Washington to work for the war effort. Jenks, with whom Parsons was acquainted, had received information about the temper of African Americans from a black former student, Hallie E. Queen, who now taught in the District of Columbia.[3] Queen and another woman had been sent by Howard University's Red Cross Auxiliary to investigate conditions in East St. Louis and distribute funds collected in Washington for those affected by the riot. Afterward, she wrote about the plight of the black community and testified before the House Rules Committee in favor of Rep. Leonidas C. Dyer's anti-lynching bill. Parsons met her on August 23 and found her eager to help the government improve African-American morale. Her East St. Louis trip had convinced her that black migration was causing massive problems and that more social work was needed. She recommended that black regiments be sent overseas quickly, to allay fears that they were going to be prevented from participating fully in the war, and she claimed to be on the trail of a German spy in Washington who had ingratiated himself with the black community.[4] Parsons sought the views of fellow New York progressive Joel Spingarn, chairman of the board of directors of the NAACP since 1914. Spingarn had just joined the army, and nine months later he would occupy Parsons's position in the MIB, albeit with a very different agenda. Parsons reported that Queen was "quite fearful of trouble" among blacks and asked Spingarn to consult "responsible colored people in regard to this. . . . Whatever you do, please do not indicate that there is any apprehension on the part of the Government, or that anybody connected with it is making inquiry."[5]

Spingarn immediately assured Parsons that the NAACP's own journal, the *Crisis*, was utterly loyal. He also forwarded a "Memorandum on the

Race, War, and Surveillance

Loyalty of the American Negro in the Present War," written "by two of the ablest and most responsible colored men in the country," one of whom was almost certainly W. E. B. Du Bois; the other was probably James Weldon Johnson, now the NAACP's acting secretary. Parsons probably recognized the authorship of the memorandum; he was a contemporary of Du Bois's at Harvard and knew Johnson through Republican party circles.[6] Spingarn stated that a long talk with the authors had convinced him that, "while isolated attempts in the interests of pro-German dissension may have been made, they are hardly worth considering, and in no way help to understand the unrest—(I might almost say despair)—of the American Negro today." The memorandum acknowledged that lynching, race riots, and growing stories of racism in the army gave blacks every reason to be dissatisfied, but argued that the government could do much to placate its black critics if it would just recognize their concerns:

> [If] the War Department will give early and definite assurance that Negro troops are to be used as soldiers in the same way as white men, and that the draft law is not to be made a method for a kind of enslavement of colored labor, and if also the President of the United States can be induced to give some assurance that he does not sympathize with lynching and mob rule in the case of colored victims, it is certain that the country can count upon the loyalty of its colored citizens to the very end.[7]

This was all very well, Parsons implied in reply, so long as black people could be shown to be enduring their plight with restraint until the government acted, but, he warned Spingarn, "The Houston shooting has complicated the matter."[8]

Van Deman sent the memorandum, with Spingarn's comments, to the chief of staff, Gen. Hugh L. Scott, who knew about the interest of African Americans in the role they were to play in the war because of the earlier efforts by Spingarn and Du Bois to ensure that black men would be trained and commissioned as army officers.[9] The separate black officer training camp was established at Fort Des Moines, Iowa, in June 1917 with an intake of 1,250 men, drawn from both the non-commissioned ranks of regular regiments and from the students and recent graduates of black colleges, of whom 639 received commissions in October.[10] During the war a total of 1200 African American officers were commissioned, most of whom served in France with distinction, despite persistent attempts by white officers to undermine their authority or belittle their achievements. One of the reasons why they were so easily picked on is that they were so few in number, just 0.7 percent of the army's officers, even though the 360,000 black soldiers represented 13 percent of the men enlisted by the United States.[11]

Despite the blatant segregation it entailed, the black officer training camp boosted African-American enthusiasm for the war effort, but another episode relating to black promotion in the army was to have the opposite effect. In the summer of 1917, black leaders charged that the early retirement on medical grounds of Lt. Col. Charles Young, the senior black army officer, was a ploy to get rid of him. Their protests about the medical findings were ill founded, but their suspicion that there was a high-level determination to prevent Young or any other black man holding a senior command was correct. A member of the 10th Cavalry, Young had been the third black graduate of West Point, in 1889, and was one of the most talented men of his generation, with a growing reputation as both a soldier and a diplomat. As a colonel in the regular army, he expected to be automatically promoted to the rank of brigadier general for the duration of the war. In May 1917 he was ordered to undergo tests in San Francisco, where army doctors diagnosed "nephritis, high blood pressure, sclerotic arteries, [and] hypertrophy [of the] left ventricle." Young claimed to feel perfectly fit and the promotion board seemed initially willing to overlook the medical report.[12] However, his case became a political matter in late June, when the senior U.S. senator from Mississippi, John Sharp Williams, spoke with and wrote Woodrow Wilson about the refusal of a white Mississippian officer, Lt. Albert Dockery, to serve under Young. Other senators forwarded similar protests by white 10th Cavalry officers to Secretary of War Newton D. Baker. At first, Wilson assumed that the removal of Young was all that was required, but while that was plainly part of what Williams wanted, he also sought Dockery's transfer out of a black regiment. Williams's dealings with Wilson about Young and Dockery reek of two southern patricians, with indistinguishable views on racial hierarchy and segregation, covertly and smoothly looking after the interests of a young white constituent by pulling strings. Williams returned the letters he had exchanged with the president to the White House, so that Wilson could "read them and destroy them if you choose," while Wilson wrote a "personal and private" letter to Baker sympathizing with Dockery, a "Southerner [who] finds it not only distasteful but practically impossible to serve under a colored commander." Wilson asked Baker to assign a northern officer to replace Dockery: "it has got on his nerves that he . . . remains an officer in a negro regiment."[13] Baker was clearly offended by the whole affair, and the wheedling tone of Wilson's letters suggests that the president knew he was embarrassing the secretary of war. Baker complied to the extent of keeping Young away from his regiment while his medical tests were evaluated, but he declined to interfere with Dockery's posting, telling Acting Chief of Staff Gen. Tasker H. Bliss, "He should either do his duty or resign." Wilson, however, was determined that no black officer should occupy a senior rank in the army. Although Baker advised the president that Young's health seemed to rule out "any present likelihood of his early return to the 10th Cavalry," Wilson went considerably further than this in his assurance to Williams on June 29 that "the lieutenant colonel referred to will not in fact have command because he is in ill health and likely when he gets better himself to be transferred to some other service." With Wilson's approval, Young was removed from the active list.[14]

The truth was that Young was indeed medically unfit for warfare. He had had high blood pressure since 1910, and when he died in Liberia in January 1922 the cause was given as "acute exacerbation of a long-standing complaint"—nephritis.[15] It is equally certain, however, that Young's illness proved highly convenient to Wilson and the military establishment, who would otherwise have been obliged to grant him an automatic promotion or else hold him back explicitly on the grounds of race. Wilson assured Robert Russa Moton of Tuskegee Institute on July 9 that Young was not being discriminated against and allowed Moton to release his letter, but most African Americans assumed that the medical reports on Young were spurious and that his unwilling retirement was proof of the government's determination that black men should not serve as senior officers. After going to great lengths to prove his strength, Young was permitted to train National Guardsmen in his home state of Ohio, but the resentment caused by his treatment lingered throughout the war and there were persistent attempts by equal rights activists to have him returned to active duty.[16] Young's experience became a symbol of the limits placed by the Wilson administration on the advancement of even the most talented black people, and it seemed to say that loyalty was going to be required, but not rewarded.

It is quite clear that in the fall of 1917 opportunities were missed to begin a radical adjustment in the relationship among the government, equal rights activists, and the wider African-American population. If the consistent advice of key individuals within the NAACP and other activists had been followed up effectively by the presidency, the Justice Department, and the War Department in the wake of the East St. Louis riot, the forced retirement of Charles Young, and the Houston mutiny, then the legacy of World War I in the area of race might have been different. The Wilson administration might have developed a coherent policy for improving race relations, the army might have treated the question of the command and deployment of black troops much more seriously, the level of racial violence in the civilian population might have been confronted by federal and local government, and the African-American war experience might have been one of striding toward greater equality and fuller citizenship. As it was, officials almost always approached racial issues by looking for ways to keep the lid on protest, rather than considering its causes and remedies. The administration did not pretend that African Americans had no grounds for complaint about their lack of political and economic rights, but it tried to avoid these issues by repeating two untruths. Firstly, the government asserted that it had very little power or duty to effect improvements in American racial equality and that, in any case, the war effort required that such considerations be treated as non-urgent. Secondly, the government insisted that in its dealings with black people it was not prejudiced. In fact, the president himself and most of his appointees were racists for whom the concerns of African Americans were always secondary to the interests of white people (even though the secretary of war and some middle-ranking bureaucrats were exceptions and were inclined to be as fair as circumstances and policy allowed).

By September 1917, the mood of the African-American population led Van Deman to begin corresponding regularly about "Negro Subversion" with Chief Bielaski of the BI, who reciprocated with copies of BI and APL reports. When certain cases interested him, Van Deman asked Bielaski for further information or ordered his own investigations by the intelligence officers stationed in large army training camps, embarkation ports, and major cities.[17] On September 11, 1917, Van Deman wrote to his senior intelligence officer in New York City, Maj. Nicholas Biddle, a banker and Astor estate trustee who had previously run New York's thuggish bomb squad as a special deputy police commissioner: "As you know, the negro question is more than tense just now, and it behooves us to find out all we can as to conditions." Biddle made only cursory inquiries and concluded that while a few black newspapers had printed "articles that are almost treasonable" and some orators were rather too outspoken, few African Americans were really disloyal. There had been some battles between black men and the police in the San Juan Hill district of New York in May, but that was nothing new.[18] Van Deman was certain that the situation was more alarming. After corresponding with and meeting Robert Russa Moton, and having followed up the latter's suspicions about "a society of colored anarchists" in New York, Van Deman warned Assistant Secretary of War Felix Frankfurter on September 26 that many blacks might genuinely prefer to solve the problem of their place in American society by violence, "providing only that the time was propitious and the colored population was able to carry out their plans."[19]

It is probable, therefore, that the MIB played a part in the Wilson administration's decision to make its most important African-American appointment, that of Emmett J. Scott, who became a special assistant to the secretary of war on October 5, 1917. The official version was that Scott's post was created after a rare conference on racial tension between Woodrow Wilson, Newton D. Baker, and Robert Russa Moton, but Van Deman's warning about a black rebellion almost certainly influenced Baker's thinking, in particular.[20] A Texan with a background in journalism and business, Scott had been Booker T. Washington's secretary from 1897 to the latter's death in 1915. He had hoped to succeed Washington as principal of Tuskegee, but remained to serve the college under Moton. He had been an active participant in Washington's behind-the-scenes manipulations of black politics and rivalries, and gained a reputation as an energetic "black and tan" Republican under Roosevelt and Taft.[21] While Scott's appointment to advise Newton D. Baker on the involvement of African Americans in the war effort was publicly welcomed by all shades of black opinion, radical activists distrusted him to a greater or lesser extent—and with good reason, for at one time or another he had thwarted or defamed most of Tuskegee's critics.

Ironically, one of those critics probably helped to convince Baker of the wisdom of creating a visible black administrative presence in the War Department. In mid-September, on the day after the NAACP had agreed on the need for a representative in Washington "to look after the military situation in general as it affects colored people," W. E. B. Du Bois requested an interview with the secretary of war.[22] The two men had a lengthy meeting, in which they stated their respective positions on race, the war, and military service. The NAACP had played an important part in persuading the War Department to create the officers' training camp, and in the wake of the Houston mutiny Du Bois sought a commitment to lasting fairness on the part of the administration and tried to drive home a consistent NAACP argument: that many forms of racial discrimination interfered with the war effort and all action to redress injustice was therefore worthwhile. After listing specific grievances about the recruitment and training of black men, Du Bois reminded Baker that

> Negroes are human beings, that they have deep seated and long con-tinued grievances against this country; that while the great mass of them are loyal and willing to fight for their country despite this, it certainly will not increase their loyalty or the spirit in which they enter this war if they continue to meet discrimination which borders upon insult or wrong.
>
> I realize that it is not the business of the Secretary of War to settle the Negro problem, and that his work is to raise an army according to law; but I respectfully suggest that the best way to raise an army is to settle at least so much of the Negro problem as interferes with the effective train-ing and use of Negro troops.

Baker replied that he would "have Negroes treated justly and as soldiers" and that black officer cadets would be commissioned.[23] Du Bois later re-wrote this as a spikier exchange, in which Baker relied on the formula that Du Bois had anticipated—that the government "was not trying by this war to settle the Negro problem"—to which Du Bois retorted, "True, but you are trying to settle as much of it as interferes with winning the war."[24] His-torian Paul Koistinen has observed that in relation to economic mobiliza-tion Baker "shared, perhaps even exceeded, Wilson's reluctance to take steps that might permanently expand the size and role of the state"; he was also widely known to prefer a narrow interpretation of his responsibilities with regard to black troops and race relations. He had told Emmett Scott two days before the meeting with Du Bois, "there is no intention on the part of the War Department to undertake at this time to settle the so-called race question"—but the meeting with Du Bois may well have confirmed to him the extent to which small concessions, including the appointment of a black assistant with no executive power, could assist the mobilization.[25]

As soon as he took up his new post, Scott invited Du Bois to help him keep the War Department informed about African-American needs and opinions and told him that Baker had "spoken most appreciatively of your interview with him."[26] Du Bois and other black leaders hoped initially that Scott, despite his accommodationist background and talent for inoffensive-ness, would make a difference and exert a positive influence on government policy, but the plans Scott outlined to Baker on his first day at work were vague and uninspired: "it shall be my purpose to seek, on an extended scale, to popularize the war among the 10,000,000 Colored people of the nation, and to nullify all false and unpatriotic impressions that pro-Germans have sought to make upon Colored Americans in various sections of the country."[27]

Early attempts by the NAACP to lobby, through Scott, for the deployment of more black physicians in the army and to establish the "status and progress" of the 24th Infantry courts-martial were quickly rebuffed by the War Department—it was revealed that he had no power to pursue either issue further. From the start, then, he was little more than a War Department public relations official—making speeches, issuing press releases, and renewing links with Tuskegee loyalists in the black press. He was well regarded by his superiors, but his cautious approach was counterproductive in terms of black public opinion; too often, he was slow to react or delayed the release of information for bureaucratic reasons, with the result that he generated more misgivings than trust among those he sought to influence. After a month in his post, Scott left Washington to spend two weeks at Tuskegee, during which his office mishandled a controversy arising from the fears of equal rights activists and the black press that the army intended to use black troops primarily as laborers, amid growing complaints about their treatment in training camps.[28] On November 9, Scott advised Baker to issue a statement denying that black draftees would be discriminated against. One of Scott's new subordinates, William H. Davis, a black civil servant transferred from the Department of Commerce, drafted a statement which Scott edited before it was finally signed by Baker on November 30. It was released to the press on December 5, although Scott had sent a copy to Du Bois on December 1. The secretary of war insisted that there would be no discrimination, but reiterated the now-standard formula about there being "no intention on the part of the War Department to undertake at this time to settle the so-called Race Question." Cooperation was needed, "if the German propagandists who want to make discord by stirring up sensitive feelings are simply not [to be] allowed to do their work." Race relations were improving, "marred, it is true, here and there by such incidents as that at Houston and that at East St. Louis, which grew out of sad misunderstandings, and were perhaps contributed to, in at least one of these instances, by the malicious activities of people who would rejoice to see any embarrassment come to us as a sign of weakness against our enemy."[29] The strategy backfired. Although Du Bois and the NAACP's other main campaigner on this issue, treasurer Oswald Garrison Villard, had been encouraged by the commissioning of black officers, they now realized the grim existence and lowly function that awaited the great majority of black draftees. Further reassurances were given by Baker and Scott, but these blatant attempts to flatter and deceive, and the sudden execution of thirteen of the Houston mutineers later in December, led Du Bois and other black radicals to lose faith steadily in both Scott's influence and the War Department's sincerity.[30] Scott continued to keep Du Bois informed about his work, but the results were far from spectacular and Du Bois's letters to Scott became notably brusque.[31]

In the MIB, meanwhile, Herbert Parsons had begun to use Hallie E. Queen as an informant, despite a warning passed on by Joel Spingarn that her "imagination is at times lurid, sometimes prompting her to confuse fact and fancy"—a judgment that proved to be entirely correct.[32] Her first tangible contribution to military intelligence was a collage of short articles on racial discrimination from various issues of the *Crisis,* which she described as "an extremely radical paper with about 100,000 circulation." Around the clippings, she wrote comments about the dire results of such journalism. In late September, she told Parsons: "A development of paramount importance makes it necessary that I see you at once." At their meeting, which Jenks also attended, and in subsequent letters, she claimed that a German doctor might be agitating among blacks in New York and named several potential black informants. She added that the editor of the *Boston Guardian,* William Monroe Trotter, was a "radical colored man who might make trouble," which was undeniably true, but also common knowledge. When Parsons and another MIB officer met two of Queen's would-be sleuths, both proved to be more keen than useful.[33]

Of much greater significance to the "Negro Subversion" work of military intelligence was the MIB's recruitment in early September of its only long-term black agent, Walter Howard Loving, who was to provide continuity and regular insights until his departure in August 1919. Loving was born in Virginia in 1872 and educated in the District of Columbia. He joined the 24th Infantry in 1893 and rapidly gained recognition as an outstanding military musician, before being honorably discharged as a second lieutenant in Manila in 1901. He was recommissioned in the Philippine Constabulary, reaching the rank of major, turned the constabulary band into an outstanding exponent of American martial music, and made famous performances across the United States. He was obliged to retire during the process of Filipinization in 1916 and moved to Los Angeles, where he had wealthy relatives. In March 1917, he unsuccessfully sought a further army commission in the hope of commanding African-American volunteers. It is reasonable to assume, given Van Deman's recruitment methods and the fact that his intelligence postings in Manila coincided with Loving's service in the Philippine Constabulary, that their paths crossed there and that Van Deman remembered Loving when searching for a suitable "Negro Subversion" specialist. In Loving, he acquired a black man who was perceptive, industrious, military-minded, and, conveniently, without known alliances in black political circles.[34] When he left military intelligence in 1919, Major Loving was described by Van Deman's successor as "one of the best types of 'white man's negro'"—an accolade that Loving would have resented strongly. In his correspondence with NAACP secretary Roy Nash, prior to joining the MIB, Loving referred to the Association's program as "such a glorious cause," and he may have been an inactive member. In one of his later reports he felt obliged to remind his superiors where he stood: "I am most loyal to the race with which I am identified." However, Loving also had a strong sense of duty to the United States in time of war. While he found blatant discrimination and racial prejudice as painful as any black person, he also promised Van Deman, "my twenty-five years of military training would be able to govern me under any circumstances." He had no hesitation in condemning needlessly provocative acts on the part of white officialdom, but he also believed that in a national crisis African-American criticism of the government should be muted and that situations likely to result in racial tension were best avoided. He therefore reacted swiftly on his own initiative when he felt that black editors and activists were crossing the boundary between defense of the race and disloyalty to the United States, and, while his reports were normally thoughtful and measured, his manner in pursuit of those he regarded as trouble-makers could occasionally become overbearing and self-important.[35]

Although Loving was recognized as the MIB's expert on "Negro Subversion," and often directed the work of white officers, including Parsons, he was subjected to the same racial segregation as other black civil servants under Wilson (including Emmett Scott). Loving was given an office with his own telephonist and documents safe in a separate building from the rest of the MIB, which was still housed in the War College. During the first months of his intelligence work, he reported direct to Van Deman, who dealt personally with his requests and comments regarding government policy. The first raw information he was given consisted of the MIB's copies of BI material on racial matters. On the strength of one of these reports, he was sent to Chicago to look into allegations that blacks in the suburb of Glencoe were collecting arms and ammunition in preparation for another riot on the scale of East St. Louis, but the "plot" turned out to be no more than the drilling of an authorized home guard unit. Thereafter, he rarely relied on BI reports for leads.[36]

Loving felt free to give Van Deman his opinion on all aspects of government policy which affected African Americans. He applauded the decision to appoint Emmett J. Scott to the War Department and told Van Deman that it would be welcomed by all black people, with the exception of William Monroe Trotter, whose views were colored by the bitter feuding between Trotter and Booker T. Washington during the final decade of the latter's life.[37] Loving had a low opinion of the sensationalism of Hallie Queen's work for the MIB, and of those she recommended as potential informants, perhaps regarding them as a challenge to his position. He was quick to ridicule the call by one of Queen's protégés for the urgent investigation of Philip Payton, two months after the latter's death. Loving told Van Deman, "I call your attention to the above facts that you may see that I am investigating the investigators as well as other matters which come to my attention. It is absolutely necessary to have persons associated with you who can be trusted to the last word."[38] Hallie Queen tried to retaliate through Jeremiah Jenks, who gave Parsons her evaluation of Loving in mid-November 1917:

> While she has an excellent opinion of the honesty and trustworthiness of the man under whom you are working, she feels that he is not very keen and that he is likely to miss the point of a good many things that may occur in connection with the work on which she is engaged. . . . The fact that he is a good musician does not especially qualify him, of course, for the other work.

Parsons shot back that his opinion of Loving was higher than Queen's—"At any rate he focusses his mind on specifics more than she does." Queen had kept Parsons waiting weeks for a promised report and he thought she was probably "put out" because her informants were not being used. Parsons deferred to Loving constantly on the subject of "Negro Subversion," without complaint, suggesting both Parsons's generosity and Loving's authority.[39]

On November 23, 1917, Loving reported that with the help of Robert R. Church, Jr., of Memphis, Tenn., a wealthy black member of the Republican national committee, great progress had been made in the establishment of a nationwide organization of black volunteers. This was not a black version of the APL, but a loosely organized alliance of pro-war influential African Americans who would be able to report to Loving or Church on the changing mood of people in their own areas and head off anything which might be construed as disloyal or "pro-German." Church had secured promises of assistance from leading black people in every large southern city and Loving told Van Deman that he expected soon to have extended this "information chain" from coast to coast and that "quick and wonderful results" could be anticipated. In spite of the confidence of both Loving and Van Deman in the monitoring scheme, it never developed into the pro-active network they had envisaged, but Church's southern contacts were to prove valuable in Loving's other efforts to generate patriotic feeling among African Americans and counteract the embittering effects of continued lynching and rumors of ill-treatment of black troops.[40]

Loving planned to stage a presidential-style speaking tour across the country, visiting cities where the ground had been prepared by Church's contacts, to bolster black loyalty and demonstrate it to the white population. He had hoped to start the tour before the end of 1917, but was forced to delay by a succession of incidents in November and early December, culminating in the particularly brutal lynching of Ligon Scott at Dyersburg, Tenn., which drew the headline "Tennessee Lynching Outrivals Worst German Atrocities" from one black newspaper. Racial violence, and lynching in particular, appeared to increase more sharply in Tennessee during the war than any other state, with a steady sequence of outrages being committed. Since June 1917, black newspapers had carried photographs of the severed head of alleged murderer Ell Persons, who was burned to death before a crowd of several hundred at Memphis on May 18. Person's ears, nose, and lower lip had been severed by souvenir-hunters before his head was thrown into Beale Street, the center of Memphis's black community; for months afterward, white stores in the city sold twenty-five-cent postcards showing the head. James Weldon Johnson had spent ten days investigating the lynching for the NAACP, assisted by Robert Church, with little success.[41]

The Wilson Administration and Black Opinion, 1917–1918

Loving realized that while lynching was nothing new, each mob murder of a black—and a hundred or so occurred between the American declaration of war and the Armistice—weakened the argument that black citizens had a duty to participate in the war. He also knew that outbreaks of extreme racialist behavior by white Americans were far more damaging to fragile black patriotism than any German propaganda could ever be. He protested to Van Deman that the work of himself and others, "seeking and preaching loyalty among the negroes in all sections of the country," was being continually undone by lynching and asked why the government could not reassure black people that it would take some action to ensure the prosecution of mob members.[42] During his two years in military intelligence, Loving's work consisted of constant fire-fighting; no sooner had he responded to one crisis than another cause for bitter complaint by African Americans would arise. He nevertheless attempted to develop schemes for improving relations between the government and the black population.

Loving was having difficulty finding the right person to front his tour. At first, he favored the noted Washington educator Nannie Burroughs, despite her role in organizing a series of well-attended protest and prayer meetings after the East St. Louis riot and her association with Hallie Queen, with whom she had testified in support of the Dyer bill. The BI had monitored the activities of Burroughs and her associates between late August and early October and her mail had been intercepted (but not opened), allowing a BI agent to record details of her correspondents and the messages on postcards. Loving saw Burroughs's BI file, but found nothing sinister in it, and visited her school, where her staff were full of praise for her. Another inquiry concluded that she was of "blameless character." By mid-December, Loving had satisfied himself that she was trustworthy and had begun to discuss the tour with her. However, in the same week, he chanced upon a speaker who he realized would do a much better job.[43] On a routine trip in Virginia, following up reports of unrest among black troops at Camp Lee and German agitation at Hampton, Loving learned that the well-known orator Roscoe Conkling Simmons was due to appear at Richmond on December 11. Born in Mississippi, Simmons was a vote-catcher for the Republican party and a former protégé of the politicians Mark Hanna and Medill McCormick. He could be relied on to give a rousing speech on any subject at the drop of a hat.[44] Loving arrived in Richmond, as he put it, "just in time to prevent what might have resulted in a race riot." The evening papers were full of that morning's execution at San Antonio of thirteen members of the 24th Infantry, which had been carried out without prior announcement, leave to appeal, or referral to the secretary of war. Sensing the tension, Loving intercepted Simmons at the railway station and "explained to him just what good service he could render the government at this critical moment." They proceeded to the meeting, where Simmons waved aside loud demands that the executions be condemned, and launched instead into a stirring declaration of the undying loyalty of the African-American citizen to "the flag that set him free." As soon as the crowd of fifteen hundred seemed to have been won over, Loving had the orchestra strike up *The Star-Spangled Banner*, transforming a bitter anti-Wilson protest meeting into a patriotic celebration. Loving told Van Deman afterward, "He is the man that we need to send forth to allay the feeling of unease among the negroes all over the country."[45] Van Deman was sufficiently impressed to send Loving's account of the meeting to Newton D. Baker and later visited him to discuss Loving's scheme. Baker plainly gave the go-ahead, for two days later Loving began sending Simmons special-delivery letters containing outlines of what to say in his next few speeches. Military intelligence began to pay Simmons's expenses and Loving met him in Washington to plan their tour together.[46] Simmons made his first speech as an agent of the MIB on January 1, 1918, to a segregated audience at Marshall, Tex., and was described in publicity leaflets prepared by Loving as "traveling in the interest of Tuskegee and Hampton Institutes." It was a good start and it allowed Loving to compile further advertisements out of favorable Texan press commentary and ringing phrases from Simmons's address. He sent them to the leading black citizens of the cities they were to visit and to the black press, including the *Chicago Defender*, which headed its editorial page with an extract from the Marshall speech:

> When the war is over and the smoke is cleared away, we shall see a new nation, baptized with the fire of suffering; one people with their faces set toward the future; one law for all and all for the law; honor on the throne; kings gone down; the harp of peace in the musician's hand; Ethiopia leading the hymn of a newer and grander republic: 'My Lord is Riding All the Time.'[47]

Loving arranged to join Simmons in Memphis, but on arriving in the city he found the African-American community organizing protest, rather than patriotic, meetings following the murder of a black man in a dispute on a streetcar. According to an eyewitness found by Loving, the victim had intervened to stop a white man forcibly ejecting a black woman from a seat reserved for white passengers. A crowd of whites had quickly gathered and while the black man was held by two policemen he was stabbed. No arrests were made, other than that of the woman passenger, who was fined $25 for disturbing the peace.[48] On Robert Church's advice, Loving postponed the Memphis rally and amended the itinerary so that the next stop would be Jackson, Miss., on January 13, with subsequent visits to New Orleans, Tuskegee, Atlanta, Nashville, and finally Memphis, all timed to coincide with various local gatherings to ensure maximum audiences for Simmons. Church traveled ahead to see to the necessary preparations. At New Orleans, Atlanta, and Memphis, Simmons was to be the principal speaker and in each place his subject was "My Country and My Flag."[49] Heavy snow forced the cancellation of the Atlanta speech, but otherwise, Loving reported to Van Deman, the tour was a tremendous success in the South. Loving clearly felt his organizing abilities were being tested and took care to stress every positive aspect, to the extent that he exaggerated the tour's impact considerably. He reported that Simmons had attracted "the largest crowd ever gathered in New Orleans" when he spoke there at the Pythian Temple and an extra meeting had had to be arranged. In fact, while a large crowd certainly assembled in the building, the people had come, not to see Simmons, but to celebrate a successful fund-raising drive by the Knights of Pythias. Although the leading local newspaper featured the meeting prominently, Simmons's contribution was not mentioned. Loving drew special attention to the fact that his rallies were attended by blacks and whites, including mayors and other local officials. At Tuskegee, where Simmons had "untold effect on the large audience which greeted him," Loving described how "white as well as colored cheered him to the limit." At every stop, he claimed, the interest generated by Church's contacts led to calls for brief special appearances by Simmons at local clubs.[50]

Looking back on the southern dates after his return to Washington, D.C., Loving declared that

> no plan could have been organized to have brought the races closer together than the one formulated. . . . I would that words would permit me to express the sentiments of the colored people all over the United States. . . . And as I sat beneath the trembling voice of the speaker and listened to the words of eloquence and pleading which fell from his lips, I saw prominent white men nod and bow their heads, and grey-haired women weep.

Loving had clearly been affected by six weeks of close contact with Simmons—at no other time were his reports so florid.[51]

Van Deman passed Loving's observations on the early effects of the Simmons tour to the secretary of war's office, where they were described as "interesting."[52] From Memphis, Loving took Simmons westward on an additional sweep including speeches at Little Rock, Oklahoma City, Los Angeles, San Francisco, and Oakland, before returning to the East by way of Colorado Springs, Denver, Kansas City, Mo., and St Louis. Along the way, Loving planned to visit the 24th Infantry battalion stationed at Deming, N.M., to conduct inquiries of his own.[53] They reached the west coast on January 27, and over the next few days Simmons addressed several audiences of between two and six thousand, according to Loving, in Los Angeles and Pasadena. City officials attended the rallies and the Los Angeles chamber of commerce booked Simmons for a return visit in May. Loving constantly assured Van Deman of the tremendous effect the tour was having on black patriotism and its wider recognition, noting that Simmons was asked to make extra speeches wherever they stopped. Again, however, the local press seems to have been oblivious to this excitement.[54] On the return journey, Loving reported that Simmons continued to attract large crowds despite heavy rains, and had received a number of threatening letters, "supposedly from Germans, warning him to cease his tirade against the German people, and to stop trying to fool the people of his race to war against the German people for a nation which does not recognize them as citizens nor give them protection."[55] In his final assessment of the tour, Loving gave Van Deman the credit for hiring Simmons and suggested that as a result black and white Americans were now "linked together with solidarity in one common cause to make the world safe for Democracy." He thought Van Deman ought to be promoted in recognition of what the tour had achieved.[56]

If Loving believed his own reports, he was deluding himself. Simmons's speeches were probably received well—he was a reliable and infectious tub-thumper—but they were part of a mass of official and quasi-official jingoistic propaganda which Americans, black and white, had encountered on an almost daily basis for eight months. There was nothing new to be said about patriotism or loyalty; on the other hand, there were plenty of hard questions to be asked about the sincerity of the country's commitment to democracy. To African Americans, these unanswered questions and the daily realities of insults and potential physical danger weighed more heavily than Simmons's easy sermonizing. Most black publicists simply ignored Simmons, but some expressed explicit dissent. Floyd Delos Francis, secretary general of the Negro American Alliance, a small but vocal organization based in Atlantic City, N.J., cautioned African Americans against allowing themselves to be "swept away on a tide of false optimism" fueled by "machine-made opinion. While being filled with enthusiasm by hired enthusiasts it is well for [us] to pause, face the facts squarely and use [our] common sense." And the undeniable fact still confronting black people was that they enjoyed fewer rights in their native land than did enemy aliens.[57] This charge, in particular, was reiterated by many commentators and groups. For instance, in March 1918, the State Negro Civic League of Louisiana demanded that blacks be given the "privileges granted to 'aliens and enemies', which should and ought to be granted unto those who are truly Americans. . . . There are no hyphens nor 'slackers' among us."[58]

During the latter months of 1917 and throughout 1918, the MIB continued to exchange information with the BI on "Negro Subversion," as hundreds of reports were logged by the two agencies. BI agents had continued to note allegations of black disloyalty and German agitation, just as they had in the first six months or so of American belligerency. Few of these reports consisted more of facts than of hearsay and misconstruction, but their sheer volume is evidence of the perceived scale of the problem and the fact that domestic intelligence agents believed African Americans constituted a group to which they were expected to devote attention. Although the frequency of BI reports fell in 1918, the Department of Justice remained concerned about the threat to law and order posed by racial unrest and most BI offices habitually reported the mood of the local black population. The MIB's interest in racial matters grew throughout the war, as the War Department continued to collect data on African-American civilians and soldiers centrally, committing increased resources to the tracking of "Negro Subversion," and locally, through intelligence officers in cities and army camps across the United States and in Europe.

Well into 1918, Germany's agents were still reported to be spreading propaganda among blacks in the South, disrupting cotton picking, and interfering with the draft by telling blacks that Germany was their friend. As before, government agents reported local white fears about nighttime covens of rebellious blacks meeting in various places, including Mineral, Va., Kansas City, Mo., and Campbello, S.C.[59] Any unrecognized white men seen talking to a black person could spark an investigation, especially if it was suggested that they were "men of rather German accent." Whites who were hard to rank socially or ethnically were particularly suspect. For example, the Charleston military intelligence officer reported rumors about a Turk or Syrian touring the state in the company of a German Jew, agitating among blacks. Most of the pro-German propaganda among blacks in the Southeast, he reported, was carried on by "peddlers, fortune-tellers . . . and transients."[60]

In the popular and official imagination, German preachers continued to be the most popular vehicles of propaganda directed toward blacks. The officer commanding the Home Guard in Miami, Fla., predicted a race riot unless a certain German priest could be prevented from "preaching the doctrine of pacifism [to black people]," while in North Carolina racial prejudice and anti-Catholicism were combined in allegations about a German Catholic school "where negro children are afforded so substantial an equality with white children, that the colored people continually boast of this equality."[61] Sometimes, African Americans initiated the denunciations. In Baltimore, where the black middle class was divided into socially competitive groups, a foreigner who gave music lessons to one clique was denounced by the leading hostess of another as a German propagandist, "who because of drink etc. has lost cast [sic] among his own people."[62]

A number of reports featured charismatic anti-war black churchmen, such as the two ministers said to be touring near Washington in February 1918, preaching on "the Glory of Peace and the Horrors of War." Particular attention was paid to the Rev. Charles Harrison Mason of the Church of God in Christ, based in Memphis, who claimed fifteen thousand followers in four hundred churches across the South, as well as congregations in northern cities such as Pittsburgh, Philadelphia, and New York. He had broken away from the Baptist Church in 1895 in order to found a more mystical pentecostal church, modeled on a Los Angeles holiness sect. Mason's advice to his followers was to ignore the war, which resulted in the frequent harassment and occasional arrest of him and his ministers in parts of the South. A Mississippi BI agent made much of press reports that the Church of God in Christ had built a $10,000 brick church at Lexington, Miss., and that Mason's home in Memphis was worth $25,000, the implication being that he must have had German backing. After Mason asserted that he was a conscientious objector and that he was obliged to call on his followers to follow suit, the inspector of the Mississippi draft exemption board attempted to have Mason prosecuted for interference with the draft, but no action ensued. The *Baltimore Afro-American* concluded that the allegations were, like "many other such rumors about Negroes and others in these war times, 'much ado about nothing.'"[63] Another pacifist black church, the Church of God and Saints of Christ, was also subjected to government pressure. Founded by William S. Crowdy, a black cook on the Santa Fe Railroad, the sect originated in revelations granted to Crowdy in which black people were identified as descendants of the lost tribes of Israel. Crowdy's followers observed the Jewish calendar, feasts such as Passover, and Old Testament rites, including circumcision and animal sacrifice, and the church maintained an industrial and agricultural commune at Belleville, Va. When members of its two-hundred-strong Philadelphia congregation declined to be drafted, its publications and membership lists were seized by military intelligence.[64]

The chances of lynch mobs gathering when blacks were accused of pro-German intrigue in the South remained high. At Gainesville, Fla., near to where five blacks, including two women, had been hung in August 1916 for assisting in the escape of the alleged murderer of a policeman and a physician, fears of a recurrence of violence were aroused by reports of pro-Germanism among the black population. In Birmingham, Ala., a black man was rescued by law officers from a lynch mob after he had been accused of advising soldiers to desert and join the German army once they got to France. In 1918, many white southerners still believed that black migration could be explained in terms of a German plot. There were even press reports that German plots in northeastern Texas had led to Klan-style nightriding by white men to drive black tenants from the land.[65]

In July 1918, the MIB followed up reports that the previous year's rioting at East St. Louis was about to be repeated, following further importation of black labor. Thorough investigation revealed no such danger, but in a comment that was extraordinary, given the race of the victims in the 1917 riot, an agent of the MIB's Plant Protection section in St. Louis attributed the relative calm to the breaking of "the lawless spirit of the vicious negro leaders" and restrictions on their access to firearms.[66]

Another allegation common in the early months of the war that was revived in 1918 was that blacks were looking forward to enjoying distinct new advantages after a German victory. The statement attributed to a cook in West Virginia was typical: "When the Germans get hold of the Government they have promised the blacks to take the property and wealth of the whites and give it to them, this considering they have never had a show for a square deal." Several whites supposedly responsible for implanting such ideas in the minds of blacks were arrested. According to military intelligence, one was a German from New York who had rowed down the Mississippi River to Osceola, Ark., spreading the word that "all negroes withholding their support from the American Government would be given large tracts of land now owned by the Americans." In South Carolina, two supposed agitators were arrested in May 1918 for saying that "the niggers had no business in this war. It was not their war and the Germans did not wish war on them; that the Germans were not killing the niggers over in France and they did not want to kill them; they had nothing against them and only wanted to help them." In New York City, an Austrian insurance collector was arrested in April 1918 for allegedly advising blacks to side with the Kaiser's army in the coming invasion of the United States, because Germany would reward them with the establishment of an independent black state, "under the benevolent protection of the Prussian eagle."[67]

When black public speakers were reported to be promising their audiences "social equality" in the event of a German victory, such claims were said to originate with German propagandists. Preachers in Baltimore and in Norfolk, Va., were reported by the MIB and the BI to be making frequent references to the forthcoming "social equality," and a white woman in San Antonio, Tex., complained to the BI that a pro-German black speaker had declared that "very soon the negroes could get all the white women they wanted." In October 1917, an MIB officer was perturbed to hear of three recent instances of black men behaving with unusual familiarity toward white women in the District of Columbia. After being called down for their "presumption," the blacks were said to have replied "that the white women were high and mighty now, but they would not be so superior in a short time, as conditions would be very much altered shortly." Virtually identical stories were to circulate in the South during World War II.[68] This abiding fascination with miscegenation also underlay the Justice Department's investigation of the activities of a Dutch anthropologist, Herman Moens, whose photographic studies of black female anatomy and affair with a Washington schoolteacher caused a scandal which overshadowed initial suspicions that he was a German spy.[69]

The District of Columbia was always a fertile source of hearsay, although it was rarely so diverting as the gossip about Herman Moens. Many of the investigations into the sources of "Negro Subversion" grew out of, or were inspired by, supposed conditions in Washington, partly because the capital's black population was the most easily observed. Racial segregation was entrenched in Washington, but the city and the government could not function without thousands of black domestic servants, hotel staff, and messengers, the majority of whom lived in the district. There were many points of contact, therefore, and in the prevailing wartime atmosphere of secrecy and conspiracy dozens of rumors and half-truths were passed on directly to BI agents or military intelligence officers by government officials, their families, and their servants. Frequently, reports began with an explanation that the information being submitted had originated with one of the writer's acquaintances or employees, or with a newsvendor. For instance, in November 1917, a BI agent reported that an official in the Department of Agriculture had told him that his black maid had said that a local grocer was advising blacks not to fight for the United States. Another white Washingtonian's servant was supposed to have told her of a meeting called ostensibly to form a servants' union, "but in reality for the discussion of religious and pacifist questions and pro-German views." In April 1918, Van Deman thought it worth informing the BI that the cook employed by House of Representatives Speaker Champ Clark had told Clark's wife, "Just wait a little longer and you white people will be crawling on your knees to try and get us to do your work." This outburst was said to have been provoked by Mrs. Clark's refusal to give the cook the use of her car. Toward the end of the war, Van Deman's successor, Brig. Gen. Marlborough Churchill, would be informing senior government officials, "As is generally known, the German propaganda among the negroes of Washington, DC, . . . is the most serious of any part of the country."[70] Both the BI and the MIB found black informants easy to come by in Washington, and these informants became adept at sending in reports of the kind that seemed to be required—dotted with lumps of wartime journalese, such as "Teutonic plotters" and "rabid pro-German." Under conditions of secrecy and amid waves of public excitement about enemy subversion, the reports submitted by confidential informants were unlikely to be objective. Partly chosen in the first place for their close contacts with suspected individuals or organizations, some informants felt the need to send in damning reports in order to prove their own loyalty. Others were keen to prove their continuing usefulness by finding new individuals about whom to raise doubts. Sometimes, however, conflicting emotions surfaced: informants knew that to portray African-American communities as riddled with treacherous elements would be false, but they also appeared to enjoy being the sources of otherwise unobtainable information.

Hallie E. Queen continued to send the MIB her reports, mostly describing rumors circulating in Washington about the fate of soldiers from the city, and often ridiculing the reports of other informants. She was also capable of constructing foul conspiracies out of the most mundane information. On a trip to New York City in February 1918, she announced that she had discovered "a colony of negroes of German citizenship" in Upper Harlem, "evidently from the African colonies," and reckoned they had recently jumped ship in New York for subversive purposes.[71]

Walter Loving tried to remain aloof from meaningless snooping and maintained a broad outlook on American race relations. Nevertheless, when he set out on his tour with Simmons in January 1918, he left behind a fierce row in Washington over his methods. In December 1917, he had heard that a black teacher of German at the district's Dunbar High School was making pro-German remarks. His information came from a pupil, a minister, and teachers who had been Loving's classmates at Dunbar in 1892. Having interviewed the allegedly disloyal teacher, Georgiana Simpson, in the presence of the principal, Loving concluded that, while she was not a German agent, she was openly sympathetic to Germany, and that she might have affected the loyalty of thirty to forty children and their families. He told her that if she did not control herself she would lose her job, whereupon she complained to the Department of Justice that she had been threatened by a government official and the District of Columbia school board began an inquiry. In response to the allegations against the teacher, the *Baltimore Afro-American* defended the loyalty of the black population of the capital in general and added, in one of very few public comments on his work for the MIB, "Evidently the retired Major Loving has found it necessary to have something to report in order to keep his position and his pay." Loving told Van Deman that, whether or not he had exceeded his authority, if he was not backed up he would resign from the MIB. Van Deman decided that Loving was blameless and by the time he returned from the Simmons tour the heat had gone out of the affair.[72] The incident affected more than Loving's local standing, however. In February 1918, Hallie Queen, who taught part-time at Dunbar High School and had been unable to keep her intelligence work confidential, found herself "harassed constantly by gossip." When she asked the chief of staff for "an open statement" to the effect that she had nothing to do with the allegations against Miss Simpson, Van Deman promised that Loving would see her principal to exonerate her.[73]

In March 1918, Loving had a notable success when he neatly pre-empted the plans of equal rights groups to capitalize on the return to Washington, D.C., of the body of Corporal Larmon J. Brown, one of the thirteen soldiers executed by the army in Texas on December 11, 1917, for their roles in the Houston riot four months earlier. Before the coffin arrived, Loving visited Brown's mother to ask that no mention be made at her son's funeral of "the unfortunate affair at Houston." She agreed, not only to this request, but also to take the body to her family's home in Maryland for burial and to ignore all attempts to turn the service into a protest meeting. Loving then spoke to her minister about his address and also attended the funeral. As a result, what could have been the occasion of a bitter demonstration passed off virtually unnoticed.[74]

Soon afterward, Loving moved his base to Harlem and began spending only short periods in Washington. Van Deman supplied him with a glowing letter of introduction to the MIB's New York office, informing Biddle that he could "put every possible confidence in Loving and rely upon his work in every possible way," and thereafter Biddle rarely interfered in Loving's work, although there were occasions when he might have made more use of him.[75] Loving's work was now divided between advising the MIB and, through it, the rest of the War Department on the morale of black troops, and attempting to influence the attitude of the black civilian population toward the war. By now, his insistence that black patience was not endless, particularly in regard to lynching, appears to have been accepted by many senior military intelligence officers, who recognized that it was not sufficient simply to instruct African Americans to be loyal; there had to be some indication that their complaints were being heard. In December 1917, Loving had pleaded with the War Department, "Is there not some way by which we may reassure the colored people [of the South] that the government will take all steps to bring to justice the perpetrators of this awful crime?"[76] By the spring of 1918, his repeated warnings that German agents could easily cause racial strife unless conditions for African Americans improved had begun to sink in. The MIB's "Counter Espionage Situation Summary" for the War Department and other bureaus for the week ending May 18 commented, "Every lynching, or other unlawful act against the negroes tends to assist [enemy propagandists'] labors."[77]

Mounting black unrest was also starting to worry the director of the Committee on Public Information (CPI), George Creel. During the first year of American belligerency, the CPI had produced rousing films for African Americans, titled "Our Colored Fighters" and "Colored Americans," and created a program of speakers especially for black audiences. But despite these and other efforts on the part of the government, equal rights agitation seemed to be increasing, rather than abating, as the war progressed. In March 1918, Creel confided in Van Deman, "From some source or other a very definite drive is being made to disorganize and disaffect the colored population." Creel's note followed the receipt by Wilson's cabinet of a forceful protest by 116 black citizens of Atlanta, in which lynching was denounced as "worse than Prussianism." The petitioners could not understand the administration's "long sphinx-like silence" on lynching and warned that it might "be construed as tacit approval and active tolerance." For the moment, Creel asked only for Van Deman's help in finding the origins of this discontent; it did not apparently occur to Creel that lynching on its own might be the most significant cause.[78] In April 1918, Creel was stung into taking action himself by a vicious attack on his management of the CPI, especially in relation to black loyalty, by the National Committee of Patriotic Societies (NCPS), representing forty-two zealous organizations. The CPI was accused of churning out "tons of 'highbrow' material printed in such unattractive form that no one will read it." It was time for the government to "interpret the war in terms easily appreciated by the mass of the people"—a call, in other words, for the unadorned denunciation of everything to do with Germany, German culture, and anyone who was lukewarm on American belligerency. Furthermore, careful investigation in the South by the executive secretary of the NCPS had allegedly uncovered ever-increasing German influence among blacks and "that no intelligent campaign is being carried on to combat it." The NCPS wanted the government's propaganda work entrusted to less fastidious people than the CPI (such as the organizers of the NCPS): "We have had our full quota of hate-less days and pussyfooting nights. . . . What we need in Washington at the present time is a group of men who understand human nature."[79] Creel responded by feeding a number of stories to the press highlighting the enormous danger posed by the Kaiser's agents in their work among southern blacks. These press releases repeated promises allegedly made by spies about "social equality" and black advancement taken from the files of the MIB and the BI. The trouble, according to the CPI's writers, was that blacks had "no idea of the tyranny with which Teutonism is synonymous. They have that feeling for the unknown that is often characteristic of the ignorant, and this has been worked on by the enemies of civilization." The American public was assured that the CPI would be taking immediate steps to "enlighten the Negroes."[80] In June 1918, Creel helped to convene a group of black editors and spokesmen in Washington, and a week later the CPI put out a special speech, "Four Minute Men Bulletin No. 33," in which speakers were instructed to urge African Americans to reject German propaganda and be loyal and law-abiding, so that the result of the war would be "a wonderful amalgamation of the races within America."[81]

George Creel seemed genuinely to believe that blandishments of this sort would suffice and that black enthusiasm could be fired by rhetoric alone. Other officials, however, listened to black advisers within the government machinery, such as Walter Loving, and on the outside, such as Robert Moton, and believed that equal rights protest could be dampened only by a mixture of intimidation and bribery. The government knew that the black population was embittered and cynical about the war for democracy; it also knew that any attempt to extend genuinely significant rights to African Americans would provoke a white backlash. Thus, during the last twelve months of the war, the Wilson administration tried to contain the race issue by alternately flattering and thwarting African-American ambitions, without making any major concessions. For example, in order to divert attention from the Justice Department's refusal to sanction a federal investigation of the East St. Louis riot and the War Department's removal of Col. Charles Young from active service, the government allowed the appointment of Emmett Scott to an apparently important position and the commissioning of a few hundred junior black officers. In reality, by the end of 1918, the ill-treatment of black men in uniform and the harrying of black leaders and publications demonstrated that the rights of non-white individuals were of little consequence to the administration. All that mattered was the compliance of the mass of African Americans with the draft and other wartime measures and, if possible, a level of interracial strife that was no higher than normal.

Three

Black Doughboys

Arrangements for drafting and deploying the 357,000 African Americans who served in the United States Army during World War I were only gradually arrived at by the War Department in the summer of 1917.[1] Although senior officers and bureaucrats made no suggestion that the long-standing policy of assigning the races to separate regiments be revised, they debated the actual function of black troops, where best to train them, and whether black officers should be entrusted with commanding them in battle. The formulation of a policy was accelerated and influenced by the Houston mutiny by members of the 24th Infantry. The day after the Houston riot, Acting Chief of Staff Tasker H. Bliss advocated a delayed draft for blacks, followed by minimal weapons-training as near to their homes as possible and rapid transportation to France for labor service in rear areas. He rejected other suggestions, including the concentration of black men in two southern camps, which he regarded as too dangerous, and the provision of basic training for blacks in eight northern camps and weapons-training in France, which was deemed too complicated.[2] Secretary of War Newton D. Baker agreed with Bliss, but he maintained in public statements that blacks and whites would be similarly trained and deployed—that they would be sent to all sixteen army training camps and that as many as possible would be used for combat.[3] In the end, 80 percent of the black soldiers who reached France wound up in supply or labor regiments—unloading ships, building roads, and reburying the dead. Only two combat divisions were formed—the 92nd, consisting of drafted men, and the 93rd, created from a mixture of National Guard units and draftees. American lack of faith in black combat troops was demonstrated further when, before reaching full strength, the 93rd Division was placed under French command in partial fulfillment of Pershing's obligations to the Allies.[4]

The Wilson administration was well aware of white southern anxiety at the prospect of large-scale black enlistment even before the Houston riot, having been warned by the chairman of the House Military Affairs

Committee about probable reactions to the president's call for "universal liability to service."[5] Between 1906 and 1917, a number of bills had been introduced into Congress by southerners seeking to exclude blacks from the army, prompted initially by the brief riot in 1906 at Brownsville, Tex., involving members of the 25th Infantry, and later as part of a general campaign of denigration of the race. In the debate prior to the passage of the National Defense Act of 1916, Sen. James K. Vardaman of Mississippi, a progressive in many respects but also a radical racist, declared that "a negro may become an obedient effective piece of machinery, but he is devoid of the initiative [*sic*] and therefore could not be relied upon in an emergency."[6] Early in August 1917, a South Carolinian delegation consisting of Gov. Richard I. Manning, Sen. Ben Tillman, and Sen. Ellison Smith visited the War Department to protest against a proposal to train black Puerto Ricans in the Palmetto State. They claimed that "the Puerto Rican Negroes did not understand the Southern method of dealing with the race, and trouble may ensue."[7] The Houston riot produced a further wave of complaints about the presence of African-American troops in the South. The *Columbia (S.C.)State* called for all the training of black men to be restricted to the North: "Why risk the outbreak of unpleasantness in the South when it is not necessary and when the one great object is to raise, equip, and train an army with celerity?"[8] Even some liberal northerners agreed; the *New Republic,* a New York weekly normally sympathetic to the equal rights campaign, claimed to understand the peculiar unease of the South at the aggregation of "large numbers of lusty young blacks accustomed to no other discipline than that of the plantation."[9]

Few publications objected for as long or as rabidly as *K. Lamity's Harpoon,* a racist sheet published in San Antonio, Tex., which blustered for months about the "negro characteristic of running amuck when least expected," and denounced those who favored inclusion of blacks in the army as a "gabble of saphead white negrophiles and coon-chasers." Since black people lacked "that spirit of absolute obedience to their superiors, which is the first requisite of a first class soldier," the most useful contribution they could make in wartime was on southern farms. The *Harpoon,* with which Woodrow Wilson's friend Col. Edward House was associated, warned that the black man now expected the government "to enlist him, arm him, train him, and finally turn him out a first class hand at rioting, and shooting up civilian towns."[10] In the event, most white southerners conceded the necessity of the black draft, not least because of the requirement under the Selective

Service Act of May 18, 1917, that each state provide fit men in proportion to its total population. Any reluctance to draft blacks would mean calling up more whites and this, observed the *Montgomery Advertiser,* would be "most unjust."[11]

In their analyses of the issue of black war service, government agents were as fond of incorporating racial stereotypes as any other commentators. In August 1917, a naval intelligence officer predicted outbreaks of racial violence should the draft apply only to white men, and advised the Office of Naval Intelligence that blacks ought to be included, despite alleged physiological grounds for exempting them:

> A negroes [*sic*] feet are naturally flat, just as is his nose. . . . If large num-
> bers of white men are taken for military service and the bulk of the ne-
> groes are left behind, simply because their feet are flat, nothing but
> trouble and the most serious sort of trouble may be expected at some
> later time not only in this country [i.e., Florida] but a great many sections
> of the South.[12]

When the draft actually began, blacks found themselves not merely in-cluded, but more likely than whites to be immediately inducted. Of the 23.8 million American men who registered for the draft in 1917–18, 2.3 million (9.6%) were black. In the first wave, draft boards examined just over one million blacks, of whom 557,000 (52.6%) were found to be of Class I status—liable to immediate call-up—whereas of the 9.5 million whites ex-amined, only 3.1 million (32.5%) were put in Class I. Moreover, while 36 percent of the Class I blacks in the first draft were called into immediate service, this applied to only 24 percent of the Class I whites. It is clear that before the army admitted black troops by draft, many able-bodied whites had already volunteered, thereby contributing to their states' quotas, but racial discrimination was undoubtedly a factor that persuaded draft boards to grant disproportionately more exemptions or reduced status to white men than to blacks on the grounds that they had dependents or were physi-cally unfit. Some boards ingeniously justified designating southern black men with dependents as Class I because army pay was equal to, or ex-ceeded, their normal monetary earnings, meaning that their dependents would be better off with the men in uniform. By the end of the war, five southern states, Florida, Georgia, Louisiana, Mississippi, and South Caro-lina, had drafted more blacks than whites.[13]

African Americans also disproportionately evaded the draft. Over a hundred thousand eligible black men failed to register for the draft, or, having registered, did not report when called up. The delinquency and desertion rate of black registrants (9.81%) was almost three times that of whites (3.47%). States with significant black populations showed wide differences in the rate of evasion, perhaps reflecting the varying efficiency of local draft boards and the mobility of the black population. For instance, in Florida, where 39,013 blacks registered for the draft, 8,319 (21.32%) were reported as deserters, whereas in South Carolina, where 74,265 registered, only 4,589 (6.18%) deserted.[14] Any man failing to register or present himself for examination invited arrest, since the War Department offered a fifty-dollar reward for each delinquent delivered to an army camp, the money being subsequently deducted from his pay. This scheme was far more commonly used against blacks than whites and was exploited by some southern sheriffs and draft boards, who deliberately withheld information from blacks so as to claim rewards. In Virginia, BI agents found evidence that for fraudulent reasons black railroad workers were being prevented from registering at the proper time. Something similar apparently happened near Camp Wheeler, in southern Georgia, which received 1,256 black delinquents and only 31 whites in a six-month period in 1918, implying that the number of blacks not complying with the draft in Georgia was forty times more than the number of whites, whereas in fact it was just twice as great.[15]

During the second half of 1917, BI agents spent thousands of hours hunting down men whose draft boards had declared them delinquent, always noting in reports to Washington when the subjects were black. In some parts of the South, notably Texas, black youths were rounded up on suspicion of having lied about their ages, and men who were obviously mentally or physically unfit were jailed before being considered for exemption. At Beaumont, Tex., a one-armed man was indicted for failing to register and told that his excuse—patent disability—was "not satisfactory." At Houston, a man with brain damage was forced to register in jail. Northern agents tended to be more tolerant—in Pittsburgh, for instance, a BI agent took no action against a black deserter who seemed "mentally unbalanced"—but there were also exceptions in the South. An elderly black man living near Alvin, N.C., who appeared genuinely culpable, having advised young men to hide during the draft and emerge as saboteurs once whites had departed for France, was merely reprimanded by a BI agent.[16]

As well as assisting in the detection and arrest of deserters, BI agents pursued those alleged to be encouraging black opposition to the draft.

Some agents were quick to sense conspiracy; others were less alarmist. At Cincinnati, agents suspected that an excursion for black workers on the first day of registration, June 5, 1917, was part of a plot to undermine the draft. When the grand master of the Masonic Lodge of Texas (Colored) announced that no dues would be collected from drafted Masons and no benefits paid to their dependents if they were killed in action, a BI agent reckoned this was "calculated to restrict enlistment in the army and navy." In northeastern Texas, unconfirmed reports in August and October described armed blacks preparing to resist the draft. The alleged ringleader, a preacher from Corsicana described by a BI agent as having "the face of the lowest type of criminal" and being "nothing more nor less than a brute," was violently arrested, jailed, and fined. At Newport, Ark., the Rev. J. H. Ellis was jailed for ninety-six days, charged with treason, and beaten up on his release in November 1917. The Rev. W. T. Sims suffered the worst fate of all, being lynched at York, S.C., in August 1917, allegedly for opposing the draft.[17]

Plainly, maladministration of the draft, illiteracy, and residential mobility accounted for much apparent delinquency, but the level of evasion in some counties makes it equally clear that many African Americans deliberately refused to cooperate. For instance, in March 1918, near Lexington, Miss., where the pacifist minister Charles Harrison Mason of the Church of God in Christ was influential, only 39 out of 123 black registrants reported for examination, four of whom later deserted. To fill the gap, the Holmes County draft board summoned 63 more black men, of whom only 31 reported; subsequent call-up notices to a further 43 men yielded just six more potential soldiers. Evasion on this scale suggests collective, if informal, opposition to the draft, rather than simply individual resistance. Conscious decisions were being taken either to support the war effort and comply with the draft, or to reject the call and avoid induction.[18] In addition, a small number of black men claimed religious objector status, for which they were sometimes imprisoned. Ammon Hennacy, a white peace campaigner held in the Atlanta Penitentiary for distributing anti-war leaflets, recalled seeing among his fellow inmates "[t]wo Negro objectors from some Holiness sect in the Carolinas [who] would not mix with us. I sent some candy to them but they did not respond. We were not religious and I suppose we shocked them."[19]

A black regular army officer, Lt. Osceola E. McKaine of the 367th Infantry, conceded the reality of black reluctance to join the army, but attributed it to the slogan with which the government was mobilizing for war: "To Make the World Safe for Democracy." According to McKaine, "In his mind [the black man] confuses the principles of democratic government with the Democratic Party, and his bellicose enthusiasm suffers in consequence of his confusion." James Weldon Johnson of the NAACP thought the average black draftee's coolness toward military service was captured concisely in the overheard quip, "The Germans ain't done nothing to me, and if they have, I forgive 'em."[20]

An indication of the War Department's refusal to acknowledge any connection between the duty of African Americans to serve in the army and their rights as citizens came in Gen. C. C. Ballou's order to black soldiers to avoid social contact with white people in the vicinity of Camp Funston, Kans. In March 1918, a medical sergeant of the 92nd Division (composed of the 365th, 366th, 367th and 368th Infantry Regiments) protested when refused admission to a theater in nearby Manhattan. A few days later, Ballou issued Bulletin No. 35, drafted by Col. Allen J. Greer, a white Georgian, reminding all officers and men that "no useful purpose is to be served by such acts as will cause the 'color question' to be raised." It was "not a question of legal rights, but a question of policy." To avoid conflict, the men should "refrain from going where their presence will be resented" and "place the general interest of the division above personal pride and gratification." The order was accompanied by a threat: "White men made the division, and they can break it just as easily if it becomes a troublemaker."[21] Up to this point, Ballou, formerly commander of the black officers' training camp at Fort Des Moines, Iowa, had received favorable coverage in the black press, but Bulletin No. 35 discredited him and the rest of the army in the eyes of the African-American population. Walter Loving found it extremely damaging and reported that blacks now expected unrestrained racist behavior from all white officers. The MIB collected several examples of black anger, including a letter to the *New York World* by the Harlem Democrat boss, Ferdinand Q. Morton, predicting that the "almost treasonable" order would "do more harm than the work of 10,000 German propagandists." From his Brooklyn pulpit, the Rev. George Frazier Miller declared, "The poison gas disseminated in the truckling attitude enjoined in this bulletin is just as deadly an attack upon the morale of the division as that of the German bombs." The *New York News* demanded Ballou's dismissal—he could not "send brow-beaten civil outcasts and social pariahs against the German legions with a hope of success." In a similar vein, the *Chicago Defender* warned,

"Soldiers who go to do and die take heavy steps when their hearts feel the scorn and bear the contempt of their commander."[22]

The publicity given to Bulletin No. 35 alarmed intelligence officers in other training camps. The MIB officer at Camp Sherman, Ohio, feared its effects on the morale of the 317th Engineers (Colored), given "the extreme emotional temperament of the African and that his primitive nature is easily excited to passionate partisanship, rendering it extremely difficult to handle any question that may arise involving the race issue." In particular, the threat to dissolve the 92nd Division had produced "the very thing that it was aimed to quell."[23] In his defense, Ballou asserted that the War Department regarded the black division as experimental and he was determined that it should succeed. He had supported his men when their rights were invaded (indeed, he prosecuted the theater manager, who was fined ten dollars), but he would always "counsel avoidance of that invasion when there is nothing to be gained by it." He implied that his task was being made harder by sinister attempts to foment racial discord. "It was no mere coincidence," he told Emmett Scott, "that the East St. Louis atrocities occurred in a city filled largely with German sympathizers. . . . There is little doubt that the same influence egged on both blacks and whites at Houston."[24]

The treatment of black troops was a matter of constant interest and debate among African Americans and their willingness to enlist was undoubtedly hindered by apprehension at what the army had in store for them. It was repeatedly rumored in black communities across the United States that the War Department planned to use black units as shock troops to soak up the first waves of German attacks and draw the fire of enemy machine-gunners during Allied offensives.[25] For example, in April 1918, leaflets were found in San Antonio warning black men that they were bound for the forward trenches, and from other areas of the country came further reports of this prediction's currency among black civilians, including servants in white households. These rumors were bolstered by claims that the government was concealing the true extent of black casualties in the spring and summer of 1918. The BI and the MIB assumed that these scares were planted in the minds of African Americans by German spies, and both agencies made unsuccessful attempts to trace each story to an original subversive source. Officials seemed unable to grasp the alternative explanation: that members of a racial minority that enjoyed few civil rights and endured the most menial forms of labor, the most inadequate housing, the worst transport, the poorest health and educational provision, and the least protection under the law had concluded, without outside prompting, that once in uniform they would probably, in the words of an old man in Georgetown, La., "be rushed 'across the pond' for 'cannon fodder.' "[26]

The MIB received equally troubling reports that potential black soldiers were being advised to desert to the German army and that Germany was their true friend. In January 1918, Germans in Norfolk, Va., were said to have told black residents that there had been twenty thousand desertions after black troops had gone to France and that the men were now fighting in the German lines. In February, a Washington, D.C., BI agent reported that a drunken black soldier was overheard in a store telling civilians that blacks who had fled to the German lines were being treated much better than in the American army, and that men at Camp Lee, Va., had been approached by German spies. The BI agent believed this was more than "simply booze talk." Two days later, in a subtle variation, an informant in Washington reported to Capt. Harry Taylor of the Morale Section that two itinerant black ministers had been giving local congregations the ingenious advice that, "if they went to War, the Germans would never fire on them in battle, because the Germans love them so, and for that reason, while it is alright to be patriotic, if they enlisted they would be taking uniforms etc. that other people could use."[27]

The overwhelming majority of black Americans were not disloyal to the United States during the war, but they harbored a basic distrust of the segregationist federal government—a fact that black leaders who cooperated with the Wilson administration were to discover as their personal popularity waned. By the spring of 1918, the cumulative effect of the East St. Louis riot, the swiftness of the Houston executions, the treatment of Charles Young, the insult contained in Bulletin No. 35, and the steady increase in lynchings during the war, all of which the government appeared either to condone or to ignore, contributed to the basic plausibility of growing fears that black men were to be sacrificed in the war for democracy and that the race could expect to be given little credit afterward.

When wild accounts surfaced, especially in New York and Washington, of ghastly African-American casualties, the domestic intelligence agencies acted quickly to counteract them. In March 1918, Raymond B. Fosdick, the New York Democrat who chaired the Commission on Training Camp Activities, informed Third Assistant Secretary of War Frederick P. Keppel, to whom racial matters were often referred, that residents of Harlem were "tremendously upset" by rumors not only that black soldiers were being abused by white American officers, but also that the Germans had begun to torture black prisoners. The proof was said to lie concealed at Columbia Hospital, in the form of two hundred men with no eyes or arms, whose captors had returned them mutilated to the American lines, whence they had been quietly shipped home. Fosdick urged that swift action be taken to contradict these stories. Accounts of tortured prisoners would have been especially alarming in Harlem, since the only black combat regiment in France at this time was the 369th Infantry, which consisted largely of the 15th Regiment of the New York National Guard, formed in Harlem in 1916. In March 1918, it had moved into the Argonne Sector with French regiments.[28]

Keppel, commenting that the rumors were "evidently carefully distributed," alerted Emmett Scott and MIB director Van Deman. Scott used the Committee on Public Information to issue denials to the New York press about discrimination in the army and the existence of black invalids at Columbia Hospital, and gave assurances that black and white POWs were not treated differently. Van Deman alerted BI Chief Bielaski and Maj. Nicholas Biddle, the senior New York MIB officer, and ordered Walter Loving, who was already in Harlem, to "take whatever steps you think best to counteract this vicious propaganda."[29] Loving's typically direct response was to organize a hospital tour in mid-April for several influential Harlem residents, including James Anderson of the *Amsterdam News,* George W. Harris of the *New York News,* and real estate dealer John E. Nail. The *Amsterdam News* reported that they saw all parts of the hospital, except the contagious diseases wards, which "of course they were not over-anxious to visit," and interviewed the few black soldiers undergoing treatment, finding no evidence to support the rumors which had "drenched" Harlem for weeks. Loving then spoke to religious leaders on the importance of countering gossip.[30] In June 1918, an American Protective League agent informed the BI that although the mutilation rumors were no longer believed, a possible source had been discovered by a Harlem police sergeant: the nightly open-air oratory of Marcus Garvey. Street meetings were still Garvey's most regular form of broadcast—he had yet to launch the *Negro World* and could not afford to hire halls. His habit of moving on whenever police officers edged close enough to hear him only heightened official distrust.[31]

In the summer of 1918, the mutilation scare reached Washington. Regular informant Hallie E. Queen warned the MIB that a black officer's wife had been wrongly told by several people that he was undergoing treatment for wounds at Walter Reed Hospital. Another rumor described the 1st Separate (Colored) Battalion of the D.C. National Guard, now part of the 372nd Regiment, as having been "cut to pieces." In June, the *Baltimore Afro-American* reported that the battalion's B Company had been "shot to pieces in a recent engagement on the French front," that its black commanding officer had been killed, and that forty severely wounded men were en route to hospitals in the United States. In fact, the 372nd, created in January 1918 and sent to France in March, did not move into the front line until September. It was true that the long-serving commanding officer of the 1st Separate Battalion, Col. James E. Walker, was dead, but he had succumbed to tuberculosis at Fort Bayard, N.Mex., after the regiment had sailed without him.[32]

When a clumsy attempt at counterpropaganda by Queen only gave further credibility to the stories, Walter Loving intervened to place denials in the local black press. He and civilian agents then called on houses in black districts in Washington to repeat the message. Loving believed that black morale in the capital was not especially bad, but noted that government officials were disconcerted by an "air of independence" among black domestic staff, caused by a labor shortage. He recalled that black opinion in Washington had been successfully managed when the Houston rioters were executed six months before, and he could not imagine "a more trying time than that." He told the MIB director he was "confident that we have the situation well in hand, and that the government is needlessly alarmed."[33] Nevertheless, black fears were bolstered in July 1918 by press dispatches from Amsterdam which quoted the semi-official German news agency, the Wolff Bureau, on the subject of heavy American losses in France. At first glance, descriptions of disastrous advances by American and French Senegalese troops gave the impression that black Americans were among the dead: "Dense masses of blacks and Americans were hurled against the German lines. They paid for it in some hundred thousands of killed negroes and Americans." An intelligence officer at Camp Grant, Ill., urged the director of military intelligence to have such press reports suppressed, because any black soldiers reading them would believe they were now doomed. A member of the Savannah, Ga., draft board also warned the army in August 1918 that allowing blacks to read stories emanating from Berlin would cause draft evasion and mutiny. He was especially worried lest stories about black front-line casualties circulate among the five thousand black draftees about to assemble at the city's main railroad station.[34] In

September 1918, further groundless stories about black casualties swept through Washington. In a renewal of what Queen called a " 'whispering propaganda', which gains intensity with every fresh drive," the celebrated Washington-based composer and bandmaster Lt. James Reese Europe was said to be lying blinded in a New York hospital.[35] (In fact, Europe came through the war unscathed, only to be murdered a year later during a rehearsal by one of his own musicians.)

In August 1918, Los Angeles was rife with "wild rumors that colored regiments in France had been totally annihilated" and that local men were among the dead. In the absence of a properly staffed MIB office, BI agents had denials printed in the black press, under headlines such as "Jesse Kimbrough Lives." When a black woman in the city received an unconfirmed report that her son had been killed, a BI agent retraced the story through the conversations of six other women, to show how swiftly rumors could spread. Another resident had received a letter alleging that the mid-Atlantic sinking of a ship carrying black troops to France had been covered up. (In fact a ship carrying part of the 369th Infantry did suffer a collision, a breakdown, and a fire, but it eventually reached France.) In common with other federal bodies, the Justice Department regarded such tales as "very much in the form of German propaganda."[36]

Despite their efforts, the intelligence agencies failed to demonstrate any connection between these alarming accounts of the sufferings of black soldiers and the subversive efforts of German agents or sympathizers. The latter may well have spread lies designed to alarm particular groups, but it is equally likely that the rumors which agents encountered sprang from daily discussion among the friends and relatives of servicemen of worrying events about which there was little reliable new information. Black Americans were generally much less interested in the wider war aims of the United States than they were in the welfare and valor of their own soldiers, many of whom served in regiments with strong connections to particular localities, and entire communities could be affected by tragic news from the front. Black civilians also took a close interest in how soldiers were being treated in training camps, from which there was a constant stream of reports of ill-treatment and racial friction.

The War Department clearly regarded the camps to which black draftees were assigned as riot zones waiting to explode. The Brownsville riot was still a vivid memory and the Houston shootings had raised the possibility that the army might have to deal with recurrent racial conflict during the war. Moreover, the mutineers at Brownsville and Houston had belonged to regular regiments with fine records. If normally disciplined troops could be provoked into attacking southern white communities, how much more dangerous, the army asked, would it be to induct, train, and arm thousands of increasingly race-conscious young black male civilians, particularly in camps which also housed white recruits? One of the army's conclusions following the Houston riot was that "the tendency of the Negro soldier, with fire arms in his possession, unless he is properly handled by officers who know the race, is to become arrogant, overbearing, abusive and a menace to the community in which he happens to be stationed."[37] Misgivings of this kind also troubled the District of Columbia provost marshal. "Owing to the unsettled condition of the country at large, and of Washington in particular, especially in connection with the negro question," he recommended that the 1st Separate Battalion of the D.C. National Guard, which had hitherto been guarding the White House and other federal buildings, "be ordered elsewhere" and replaced by white regulars.[38]

In the event, no repetition of the Houston riot occurred, but more than once serious disorder was only narrowly averted, and the fear of enemy involvement was constant. According to Hallie Queen, "Teutonic plotters" were at work around the camps, agitating among black soldiers—the "same insidious propaganda" that produced the black casualty rumors. She realized life was unpleasant for black soldiers, but the "propaganda system" was making men resent what they might otherwise have "understood and endured."[39] In October 1917, the MIB investigated the possibility that enemy agitation lay behind an affray near Camp Meade, Md., before deciding that it was merely a brief skirmish between black soldiers and local whites, who were '"not particularly strong for the negro race."[40] A more serious lapse occurred a few days later in South Carolina, involving men of the 15th New York National Guard, to whom local Jim Crow laws were anathema. When a rumor spread that two soldiers from Camp Wadsworth had been lynched, a column of forty men marched on nearby Spartanburg, only halting when their commanding officer intervened. On the advice of Emmett Scott, the regiment was sent north to Camp Mills, on Long Island.[41] In November 1917, the 9th Battalion of the Ohio National Guard was also moved from Camp Sheridan, Ala., after several men set off to rescue a soldier they believed was about to be lynched for brushing against a white woman on a street car in Montgomery. They were stopped by military police.[42] In December, the MIB director warned the chief of staff that men of the 24th

Infantry, now stationed at Camp Furlong, N.Mex., had said that if the Houston mutineers were convicted by court-martial, they would wreck nearby Columbus, seize machine guns, and join Pancho Villa in Mexico. This was no mean threat, since Villa had raided the town in 1916.[43] In fact, no trouble occurred when the "Guilty" verdicts were announced.

Perhaps the nearest thing to a repetition of Houston happened at Newport News, Va., in September 1918, when two black soldiers from Camp Alexander were charged with theft, resisting arrest—during which one soldier had a police club broken over his head—and incitement to riot. Around one hundred black army and naval personnel converged on the police station, believing the men were badly injured. When stones were thrown, police fired into the crowd, wounding at least seven. The rioters, who fired no shots, were dispersed by police reserves and the provost guard.[44]

The most serious and bloody clashes were the several that took place between black and white soldiers inside the training camps. These were usually investigated by officers of the MIB's Morale Section, which in October 1918 became the separate Morale Branch. The Morale Section gradually became convinced that blacks were deliberately seeking confrontations, and that this, rather than race prejudice, which military intelligence officers tended to either share or excuse, was the main cause of conflict. The first camp riot was at Camp Mills, N.Y., in October 1917, when men of the 15th New York fought the 167th Alabama Infantry. Officers of both regiments played down the affair, the southerners allowing that their men might have engaged in "a little kidding," but claiming that they respected the uniform, regardless of the wearer. The 15th New York were moved again, to Camp Merritt, N.J., where the horror of southern white officers at the prospect of sharing their barracks with black officers almost caused another riot. The intelligence officer at the Hoboken embarkation port, Maj. L. B. Dunham, a Massachusetts-born lawyer and former deputy police commissioner of New York City, thought the 15th was "a pretty poor outfit" when it sailed as part of the 369th Infantry in December 1917, but added that no black officer should have been "subjected to insult and humiliation."[45] Trouble broke out next at a stevedore camp attached to Camp Hill, Va., in March 1918. Following an alleged insult, a white store clerk struck a black soldier, who returned with two hundred comrades who stoned the store until white guards arrived and ordered them to halt. When the black men scattered, the guards fired, killing two men and seriously wounding a third. The dead men's commanding officer thought the shooting unnecessary and was critical of the guard commander. A BI agent from Newport News failed to discover any evidence of outside agitation, but he eased the tension by arresting the store clerk for draft evasion.[46]

In August 1918, the Morale Section investigated reports that two black sentries had been killed by white soldiers at Camp Meade. In fact, no one had been killed, but a riot *had* occurred, involving black draftees and white regulars of the 17th Infantry, a largely southern regiment, and at least one white soldier had been sentenced to three years' hard labor as a result. The camp intelligence officer found that the 17th were "a hard lot," with "little respect for anyone," but that no "serious undercurrent of race prejudice" existed.[47] Race clearly did play a part, however, in the August 1918 riot at Camp Merritt, which began in one of the few unsegregated YMCA huts. Five blacks from Kentucky writing letters in the hut were beaten and ejected by whites of the 155th Infantry from Mississippi. A white guard detachment, sent to stop the trouble spreading, shot up the black barracks, killing one man and wounding three others. As a result, blacks were confined to barracks. The Hoboken intelligence officer tried to investigate, but found the situation "extremely touchy." He condemned the carping of "professional Southerners," whom his father, a South Carolinian, had told him were mostly low-class whites: "they do not hold the kindly, though, perhaps, feudalistic sentiments toward the negroes that is found among most of the former slave-owners." He attributed racial violence to increasing black-white economic competition, although he realized that the MIB might find this explanation "somewhat fantastic." The Morale Section's new race specialist, Capt. James E. Cutler, replied that, on the contrary, it was worth considering. In the end, the only detailed account of the riot was sent by a YMCA secretary to Emmett Scott.[48] The official inquiry into the Camp Merritt shootings was a whitewash. When Walter Loving visited the camp in November, the only guard so far tried on a charge of firing without orders had been acquitted. In January 1919, the Hoboken intelligence officer reported that so little evidence was gathered that all thirteen guards were acquitted and charges against their corporal were dropped.[49] The last serious camp riot was at Camp Lee, Va., in October 1918. Two blacks and one white were shot, while several others suffered lesser injuries, and at one point it seemed the civilian population around Petersburg might become involved.[50]

The conditions blacks faced in training camps, especially those housing labor battalions, were indeed rotten. They got the worst sanitation, medical attention, clothing, shelter, and food, and were 19 percent more likely to fall ill than white soldiers. The southern camps were the hardest, especially Camp Gordon, Ga., to which only southern blacks were sent. As a result, many men were found to be unfit when they were due to sail to France. White sergeants in these camps were selected for their experience in handling black labor, and white officers made no attempt to hide their disappointment at having to train blacks.[51] Few, however, went as far as Capt. Eugene C. Rowan of Mississippi, who was arrested for refusing to draw up his white soldiers for inspection alongside blacks at Camp Pike, Ark. He complained to Sen. James K. Vardaman, "This will kill enthusiasm for the war." Vardaman appealed to Newton D. Baker on Rowan's behalf: "Race prejudice, such as is manifest in the instant case, is that hereditary sense of prejudice which seeks to preserve the purity and integrity of the white race in America. Without it, America would have had a mongrel population instead of the viril [*sic*], vigorous white race which we have to-day." Rowan escaped punishment, but was discharged.[52]

When blacks disobeyed orders, in contrast, they were punished severely. In July 1918, B company of the 328th Labor Battalion downed tools after cutting wood for several days without rations in the Pisgah National Forest in North Carolina. Two white officers, with one gun and eighteen bullets, faced three hundred disgruntled draftees. Excuses were later made for the officers' incompetence, and the Camp Jackson, S.C., intelligence officer claimed that the trouble had been brewing for weeks and that the black NCOs were ineffectual. At the subsequent court-martial, the testimony of the black men was dismissed as "a mass of lies" and three soldiers were sentenced to death for mutiny, later commuted to ten years in prison.[53]

Walter Loving found many black draftees deeply dismayed by the realization that they were simply uniformed laborers. He blamed unrest at several training camps on War Department suggestions in November 1917 that blacks would be rushed to France to dig trenches. Loving told Van Deman, "Whether or not it is the intention of the government to send these troops post haste to dig trenches, it is certainly unwise to release this information to the Associated Press for publication."[54] In December 1917, a BI agent in Pittsburgh reported that a black minister visiting Camp Lee had found men in labor regiments angry at being given overalls instead of uniforms, and clubs instead of rifles. Loving visited the camp a few days later and confirmed the ill feeling, reporting that when asked to name his regiment, a man told him, "Well, day says we'se trench diggers."[55]

White Americans, meanwhile, were treated to newspaper and magazine articles with titles such as "Mobilizing Rastus" and "Bush Germans Better Watch That 'Chocolate Front'" which portrayed simple, loyal black soldiers submitting cheerfully to military discipline and looking forward to action. Journalists and newsreel cameramen were invited to inspect the best-equipped and most harmonious camps, such as Camp Upton, N.Y., described as "a camp where real Americanism is not a hollow mockery and where racial amity and good will reign."[56] The MIB was well aware, however, that such an atmosphere might change rapidly if the men felt they were being unfairly treated. When rumors circulated among the 367th Infantry at Camp Upton that all pay would stop once they reached France, the MIB director advised the camp intelligence officer that "too much effort cannot be expended" in correcting this falsehood. Attempts were made, without success, to trace the source of the story in New York City.[57] What the MIB feared most was a mass demonstration of the kind of bitterness to which Pvt. Sidney Wilson of the 368th Infantry gave vent in correspondence from Camp Meade in the spring of 1918. Wilson, who was aged twenty-two and from the Binghamton district of Memphis, sent an unsigned letter to the Washington correspondent of the *Memphis Commercial Appeal*:

Dear Sir,
I am glad to have the opotunity of writting to you just to exspress my throught. I will say to you speakin in regards of the niggers from Memphis, we is enjoying the soldier life fine, so I am fosted to say that you is a line Mother Fucker, an dont think the boys from Memphis is the onlyest one said that. We is goin to straiten up this country, just as soon as we get some amonation. We have our guns all ready.
Read it with care.
We wont to let you know that you white son of bitches can fose us to come to war, but if we get what we want we aint goin to war. We have dicided to ourselves that we would do what little fighting we is goin to do in this country an not France. You all can put guns in the nigroes hands, but you all will be sorry after it is done we think. We have not forgot how you all treated us, so if you all does arm us—look out, because that all we want, and we bet when we gets through with you all, you wont be quite so anshous to draft the nigroes in any more, because that show is a ly. Say white man, dont you think we want to see our peoples as well as iny boty else? Some of your coular can see they people ever week. If you son bithes dont let the nigros go to see thay peoples, we will settle the det with you white folks when we get armed. We would rather a dog to wait on us that these docters at this horsepitle.

So you all wills as you all pledges. We will be dam if you all dont regret you ever seen a nigro soldier. We have been wanting to get guns in our hands for a long time—ever since you lynched that niger at Binghamton —an we is about to get them at last.[58]

The lynching to which Wilson referred was the burning of Ell Persons at Memphis in May 1917. The letter was passed to MIB, where it was thought at first to be "the work of an enemy agent or someone who for political reasons objects to the arming of colored troops," and then mistakenly forwarded to Camp Dix, N.J. The white commanding officer of the only black unit at Camp Dix, the 350th Field Artillery, who claimed particular familiarity with black people, asserted that it was written by a white man, since it was "a very poor imitation in dialect as well as manner of expression."[59]

A few weeks later, Wilson wrote to the chairman and examining physician of his draft board in Shelby County, Tenn., signing the letter "Captin G H Hill, Company Commander, 368th Infantry, Camp Mead."

Dear Sir,

It afoads to the soldiers boys wich you have sint so far away from home a great deal of pledger to write you a few lines to let you know that you low-down Mother Fuckers can put a gun in our hands, but who is able to take it out? We may go to France but I want to let you know that it will not be over with untill we straiten up this state. We feel like we have nothing to do with this war, so if you all thinks it, just wait until Uncle Sam puts a gun in the niggers hands and you will be sorry of it, because we is show goin to come back and fight and whip out the United States, because we have colored luetinan up here and thay is planing against this country everday. So all we wants now is the amanation, then you all can look out, for we is coming.[60]

This letter was handed to the Justice Department, which forwarded it to military intelligence. There was no Captain Hill in the 368th Infantry, but the Morale Section suggested to the Camp Meade intelligence officer that "a little energy and ingenuity will result in the apprehension of the guilty man, and that the matter is well worth the effort." The four men from Binghamton in the camp were put in the same platoon for field message training which included writing down distinctively spelled words from the letters, and Wilson was quickly picked out. He denied writing the letters, but, on the additional evidence of a handwriting expert, was convicted by court-martial of obstructing the draft, disgracing the army, and prejudicing good order and discipline. He was sentenced to ten years hard labor, dishonorably discharged, and lost all pay due.[61]

Throughout the summer and fall of 1918, the MIB received reports that black draftees were unhappy at a total of twenty training camps in the U.S.[62] These complaints were usually addressed to Emmett Scott, who passed them to the MIB to be read by Cutler. Further evidence was provided by Walter Loving, who visited eleven camps in September and October, and Charles H. Williams, a black field worker for the Committee on the Welfare of the Negro Troops, who visited all twenty camps.[63] The committee, an offshoot of the General Wartime Commission of the Federal Council of Churches, concluded on the basis of Williams's reports that the conditions endured by black troops made it "more difficult to sustain among the colored people as a whole an adequate recognition of our democratic ideals in the war and the largest devotion to our cause."[64] Cutler presented his own assessment of the black attitude toward military service in a special bulletin, "The Negro Problem in the Army," which he distributed to camp intelligence officers in October 1918. It was not based on personal experience—Cutler appears to have operated solely from within the capital; rather, it was a series of facile assumptions. For all his scholarly reputation in the field of race relations, which rested on a now-outdated book on lynching, he was either unwilling or unable to do more than juxtapose several commonly held prejudices about blacks with some tired observations about army life. He admitted that blacks were relatively badly provided for in the army, that their promotion prospects were poor, and that their commanders were often inadequate. His chief point was that since the black man lacked the self-discipline of the white man, the experience of army life was inevitably a greater shock to him. His "habitual easy-going docility may prove either an asset or a liability according to how he is handled. Army life puts more snap and ginger into him than he ever dreamt of." Until he joined up, the black man was "seldom so accustomed to personal cleanliness or general sanitation. The mere requirement of having to take a bath may seem an intolerable burden." The history of blacks in the U.S. Army, he claimed, was one of

> splendid soldiers on the fighting line and poor soldiers in the barracks. . . . The very instinct to dramatize a situation which makes him usually salute with more flourish and gusto than a white soldier, will stimulate him to remarkable bravery on the fighting line or will put him completely at odds in camp over a fancied or real grievance.

Since "the act of writing letters, if he can write at all, is a mental and physical strain" and because he indulged in "extraordinarily little reading of newspapers," the black soldier was gullible, isolated, and susceptible to the approaches of enemy agents. Cutler's conclusion was that segregation was right, but that "colored troops should have every possible chance, within their domain, that white troops have in theirs. In a word, Separation *but* Equal Opportunity."[65]

In a further note to camp intelligence officers, Cutler raised the issue of black soldiers' sexual behavior. After wondering how much of a problem there was with prostitution, the corruption of young black women near camps, and the regulation of female visitors to the soldiers, he seemed to speculate about the possibility of allowing supervised prostitution: "Would selected young colored women, acting under police authority as 'welfare workers', near large camps, be able to bring about any considerable improvement in conditions?"[66]

As part of its attempt to keep African-American troops in political quarantine, the MIB kept a close watch on the one group of black civilians regularly present in the camps—the secretaries of the Young Men's Christian Association. From May 1918, the Colored Branch of the YMCA was monitored at the urging of William Gilman Low, the seventy-four-year-old Brooklyn lawyer who ran the YMCA's own Intelligence Division (YMCAID). Although Low's doubts about the Colored Branch were not shared by other senior YMCA officials, his reports meshed with the general MIB view that educated blacks, including social workers, were more committed to the campaign for equal rights than to the war. However, the MIB and the new Morale Branch of the General Staff were also alert to the political implications of harassing civilians on the basis of hearsay and were reluctant to act without firm evidence.

When it was announced that the draft would apply to all men between the ages of twenty-one and thirty-one, the War Work Council of the YMCA had resolved that "the same thing done for white soldiers will be done for colored soldiers."[67] In the event, almost all huts were segregated and the allocation of resources was unequal. In the United States, around three hundred black YMCA secretaries worked in training camps, but they were hampered by paltry facilities, and in some camps black soldiers were hardly provided for at all. For a time, white soldiers at Camp Greene, N.C., had five "Y" buildings, while the ten thousand blacks had none.[68] Provision was especially unequal in France, where only 87 of the 7,850 "Y" workers who served were black and the number never exceeded 75 at any one time. Of the 1,350 American women in the YMCA with the American Expeditionary Forces (AEF), nineteen were black, but only three arrived in Europe before the Armistice.[69]

Many soldiers were thus cut off from civilian black life—something which both the MIB and the YMCAID were keen to perpetuate. When Camp Devens, Mass., received twenty-five hundred black soldiers in April 1918, and was awaiting three thousand more, the camp YMCAID agent feared they might be tainted by equal rights agitation from nearby Boston.[70] A civilian MIB agent, who may have been black, drew up a list of local black groups and journals, and "the colored leaders, both sincere and mercinary [sic], and the self-appointed white champions who make it a part of their concern to solve the race problem." Significantly, this agent thought that local equal rights activism would do less lasting damage to military morale than Ballou's Bulletin No. 35.[71] The MIB rejected a YMCAID suggestion that black visitors to Camp Devens be made to report to the white YMCA office, since the same thing would have to be asked of white visitors.[72] Low nevertheless removed a black secretary, Robert B. De Frantz, a member of the War Work Council and an assistant to Dr. Jesse E. Moorland, international secretary of the Colored Men's Branch. Low accused De Frantz of

> an attempt to stir up race feelings in Camp Devens. . . . He tried to get us to put a colored Building Secretary over white assistants and threatened us if we did not do it to make a 'stink to heaven' with Melville [sic] Trotter and other Equal Rights white agitators in Boston. We called the bluff in this case but he could easily make trouble.[73]

The camp MIB officer agreed that De Frantz was "not the right type of man to use" but any further investigation ended when the black troops departed and De Frantz was recalled to Washington.[74]

The YMCAID also pursued the *Crisis,* after the May 1918 issue reprinted an article from the *Baltimore Afro-American* by William Pickens, dean of Morgan College, on racial discrimination at Camp Lee, especially in YMCA facilities. Pickens found that forty thousand whites shared eleven "Y" buildings, while seven thousand blacks had one. Calling for an investigation of the *Crisis,* the YMCAID agent at Camp Lee reported that "some of this stuff may be the natural expression of the black man in his present situation," but "never has it come out so openly in its appeal to race prejudice as in this current issue." The black "Y" secretaries were said to have "fallen for its insidious influence."[75] The MIB's initial response was to try to ban the magazine from training camps, but after Walter Loving questioned "such drastic measures," especially in view of the recent MIB posting of the NAACP chairman, Joel Spingarn, the order was rescinded.[76]

Low persisted, however, announcing in June that through contact with "all its agents throughout the country with reference to negro agitation in and about the camps," the YMCAID had evidence that "systematic attempts may have been made to lay the foundations of future trouble." The Morale Section agreed that the "negro question" was a "tremendous problem," but tried to dissuade him. In an apparent reference to the intentions of Joel Spingarn, Low was advised that the MIB would soon have an "entire section devoted to nothing else." Undeterred, Low continued to compile examples of "colored agitation," maintaining that De Frantz's influence on other black secretaries made them all "rather cocky" and condemning another black secretary's "very poor judgement."[77] When he visited Emmett Scott to discuss these matters, intelligence officers were appalled at the prospect that the work of the YMCAID might become public knowledge. The MIB was always sensitive to anything that might lead to criticism of the Wilson administration for racial discrimination; it also maintained a basic mistrust of all prominent blacks—organizers, editors, educators, and government officials alike—believing that their paramount loyalties were to their race. Although Emmett Scott was identified with Tuskegee-ite conservatism, he plainly had his own agenda within the War Department. Rather than let Scott discover the extent of YMCAID and MIB surveillance and harassment of black YMCA staff, the MIB told Low, "We will be very glad indeed to receive any reports you are in a position to send us, and we trust that your conversation with Mr. Scott will not cause you to direct reports elsewhere at the expense of [military intelligence]." He was reminded that Emmett Scott was "not in any way connected" with the MIB.[78]

In July 1918, the MIB and the YMCAID collaborated in the surveillance of Kelly Miller of Howard University. A speech given by Miller to the 10th Cavalry at Fort Huachuca, Ariz., was denounced as "ill-advised and untimely" by the camp intelligence officer. He claimed that Miller, on a tour sponsored by the YMCA's Colored Men's Branch, had urged the men to be loyal to the United States because of the political gains they might receive at the end of the war, rather than out of patriotism. Fortunately, the officer thought, few understood the speech, because

Miller used large words and talked rather rapidly. . . . Had this address been delivered to an audience intellectually able to grasp its true significance, I am of the opinion that great injustice would have been done the colored race for it would have fomented discord and loosened discipline.[79]

Low supplied the MIB with a list of all Miller's future YMCA engagements and the Texas branches promised to provide "dates, programs, character of speech, financial supply, etc." of events involving him. In August, the Howard University YMCAID agent reported that Miller had no plans for further speeches to the troops.[80]

In mid-August, Low made further sweeping allegations about "racial disturbance" caused by Robert De Frantz and another secretary, Gerard M. Lew, at Camps Devens, Lee, Dix, and Greene. Low was dissatisfied with Jesse Moorland's suggestion that "De Frantz and Lew should be told to use greater care in the future, to avoid giving offense." The MIB ordered camp intelligence officers to secure evidence on which De Frantz and Lew could be dismissed, advising "extreme caution . . . because of the influence which these men had in the activities of the YMCA among colored people." The Camp Devens officer expressed concern about "negro subversion," but reported nothing new, except the arrival of a new "Y" secretary, "a mulatto of unusual mentality, and thoroughly loyal." The Camp Lee officer reported that Lew's work had been good, but that "his remarks were such as to cause ill-feeling between white and colored." The Camp Dix officer could add nothing, and his counterpart at Camp Greene, where Lew had been assigned on August 1, apparently did not reply. By the end of the summer of 1918, therefore, when most black regiments had sailed for France, the MIB had failed to substantiate Low's claim that the outspokenness of black YMCA secretaries in the training camps represented disloyal agitation. Attention was switched, therefore, to the activities of "Y" workers with the AEF.[81]

In April 1919, Moorland could boast that "not a single colored secretary has been returned from overseas on account of inefficiency."[82] However, one woman worker, Helen Noble Curtis, only narrowly escaped repatriation in November 1918, for fostering, in the words of army intelligence, "notions of complete social recognition, and other objectionable matter calculated to make trouble."[83] Her case demonstrated the hostility of the YMCA toward black control of black facilities and the wariness of the U.S. Army about allowing educated black civilians close contact with the troops. The Paris headquarters of the YMCA in France had asked for six black women workers early in 1918, a request endorsed in Washington by Emmett Scott. Three women were sent, the first of whom, Curtis, was to impress military intelligence as a possible "instrument of German propaganda." Described as "African" on her intelligence record, but in fact born in New Orleans, she was the widow of James L. Curtis, a New York lawyer and active Democrat who had campaigned for Wilson in 1912. He had been rewarded in 1915 with a post traditionally reserved for a black political appointee, that of U.S. minister and consul to Liberia—where he died in October 1917. On arriving in France, Helen Curtis worked in YMCA huts in supply sectors and rear areas.[84] She was joined by Kathryn M. Johnson of Chicago, later associate editor of the *Half-Century Magazine,* and Addie W. Hunton, a schoolteacher from Norfolk, Va., whose Canadian-born husband, the late William A. Hunton, was the first non-white secretary of the International Committee of the YMCA.[85] In their later account of "Y" work in France, Johnson and Hunton were scathing about the army's attitude toward black troops. During the war, however, only Curtis spoke out.

Black observers who visited the troops in the months after the Armistice praised the three women, especially Curtis, and found cordial relations between black and white YMCA staff.[86] However, in October 1918 senior officers in the AEF, the MIB, and the YMCAID were convinced that any good she was doing in organizing entertainments and outings for men on furlough was being undone by the damage she was doing to their morale by filling them with ideas of "social equality." The YMCA classified its black workers as disciples either of Booker T. Washington, "the better type for overseas work," or of W. E. B. Du Bois, "the disturbing faction," and Helen Curtis clearly belonged to the latter. In September 1918, a "Y" official had returned to the United States with serious, if sweeping, complaints about her by white secretaries and army officers. She was said to have made uninhibited verbal attacks on American racial discrimination in front of soldiers, declaring that it was "a white man's war" of no interest to blacks, except insofar as the race now had trained soldiers who would prove useful "when the time came to assert their rights." The commanding general at the base port where Curtis worked demanded her immediate repatriation after she had "made herself objectionable by utterances calculated to make negro soldiers discontented."[87] The MIB in Washington agreed and contacted Low, who promised to recommend that she "be watched after her return, and that she should not be used in Y work or any other work of a public character." However, Curtis's removal was canceled when the Women's Overseas Section of the Paris YMCA reported at the end of October that she was now reformed into an "invaluable worker" and ought to be allowed to stay. G-2, the AEF intelligence branch, concluded after further investigation that she could remain, but would be watched, "so that should further difficulties concerning her arise, prompt action may be taken."[88]

In early November, regular MIB informant Hallie Queen reported that the Paris YMCA had requested ten more black women workers. In one of her more cogent reports, she suggested that if pro-Germanism existed at all among blacks, it might have been caused by the conditions endured by their soldiers:

> [S]uch conditions, together with their very unhealthful attendant rumors, could be greatly alleviated by the sending of more colored workers to France, after some selection. This would apply especially to the YMCA huts and canteens. Hundreds of American White women are working in the Y's and canteens overseas. There are practically no colored women. The sending of a few of undoubted loyalty would relieve the point of social racial friction, and put an end to the ugly propaganda rumor that is rapidly gaining force and credence.

She noted that "there will, of course, have to be greater care used in the selection of female personnel" than in the past. Another civilian agent of the MIB established, however, that following the Curtis controversy there was "no possibility of these girls being sent across now."[89] In fact, a contingent of black women was sent to France in 1919, but the official outrage provoked by Curtis's airing of what were commonplace utterances among African Americans about the war undoubtedly played a part in keeping down the number of black YMCA workers with the AEF—and this became part of the African-American indictment of Wilson's war for democracy.

By the end of the war, military intelligence had no evidential basis for any action against the subversive elements allegedly lurking within the Colored Men's Branch of the YMCA. Nevertheless, goaded by Low, who thought he alone within the YMCA could see the danger, the MIB turned on the foremost black official, Jesse Moorland. In mid-October, Low recalled his July meeting with Moorland about De Frantz and Lew; Moorland's "attitude was not that of one who wished to face the matter and assist." He "seemed to wish to keep the thing to himself and to forgive and forget," giving "the impression that he did not much blame De Frantz" for promoting equal rights. Moorland was "not doing his part to help face and eradicate this evil," and had even "gathered several of the Du Bois type of Negro about him." Moorland and his associates would "bear watching," Low thought, especially if a repatriated Curtis were to contact him to "try to start something." On the strength of this, Capt. James E. Cutler, now working in the newly formed Morale Branch of the General Staff, recommended that "a close watch be kept of the activities of Dr. Moreland [sic] and of his associates De Frantz and Lew, to determine whether they are working for the best interests of the government and of the YMCA and what their influence is upon the colored soldiers and civilian population." Hallie Queen found no evidence that Moorland was "pro-German," but claimed that certain secretaries might have concealed their disloyalty when applying to the YMCA and that enemy influence might have hastened their appointment. Her ambiguous reports bolstered fears that racial strife in France and America might follow the war because plotters had disaffected black soldiers. Black YMCA staff in France were ordered to look out for signs of "pro-Germanism" among their colleagues and the troops.[90]

At the end of 1918, the YMCAID was disbanded, but Low made a final effort to get rid of the international secretary of the Colored Men's Branch. Repeating his criticisms of the branch, he claimed that Moorland was "somewhat under the influence of the Dubois [sic] faction and for that reason not likely to be entirely sympathetic to our point of view." He stressed the need for discretion, lest surveillance of Moorland cause a public row. The MIB used a civilian agent to sound out William Knowles Cooper, international secretary of the YMCA in New York, and the Rev. John R. Hawkins, director of the Colored YMCA in Washington and a prominent member of the Committee on the Welfare of Negro Troops of the Federal Council of Churches. Both were satisfied that Moorland was loyal and that if any pro-German staff had been hired, "such sentiments were well-concealed." Cooper conceded, however, that if reports about the outspokenness of black YMCA staff were true, Moorland should be replaced.[91]

Jesse Moorland's career hinged on the outcome of an internal War Department debate between MI-4, the counterespionage division or Negative Branch of military intelligence, and the new Morale Branch. The Negative Branch was the most anti-radical section of the War Department; the Morale Branch was equally conservative, but it was much more alert to the political implications of military decisions and made greater efforts to discover trends in civilian opinion. In a report to Third Assistant Secretary of War Frederick P. Keppel in mid-January 1919, the Negative Branch office dealing with "counter-espionage within the military establishment" summarized its view of the YMCA Colored Men's Branch. Its analysis stemmed less from a genuine belief that the branch was riddled with pro-Germanism than from a white supremacist reaction, heightened by the war, against any strong black opposition to official racial discrimination.

> The whole question in which [De Frantz and Lew] are involved is a very delicate one as it ties with the entire problem of Negro subversion and race agitation in which the so-called Du Bois school of thinking is the chief trouble-maker. This type of thinking, which originates in Boston, advocates general equality between the races and is antagonistic to the interests of the white race when they conflict with those of the colored, and has caused considerable trouble among negro troops both in this country and in France.[92]

Moorland's alleged sympathy with this attitude and his defense of like-minded staff showed he was not a "proper person for the position which he now holds." Likewise, De Frantz and Lew were deemed by the Negative Branch to "belong to a trouble-making faction and should not be in positions in charge of negro work."[93] However, a fortnight later, Cutler visited Keppel's office on behalf of the Morale Branch to argue that the War Department should not press for the dismissal of the men. He pointed out that the allegations against them were all months old and that Moorland had kept De Frantz and Lew away from training camps after the complaints. His advice was accepted and the case was closed.[94] Cutler was not suggesting that Moorland's critics were prejudiced, nor was he dissenting from the antipathy of military intelligence toward equal rights protest. However, he feared growing black anger at systematic racial discrimination and realized that for the government to hound officials of a highly regarded welfare organization amid celebration of the Allied victory would smack of vindictiveness and would generate further ill will unnecessarily.

The attitudes of black Americans toward the society of which they were a part had been hardening prior to the United States entering the European war. The high moral tone adopted by Woodrow Wilson in his enunciation of the principle for which American neutrality had ostensibly been abandoned—the preservation of democracy—had the effect of accelerating and sharpening black critical discussion of nationwide racial discrimination, especially since the government itself seemed fully committed to the maintenance of white supremacy. The peculiar social, economic, and political position occupied by black people was encapsulated in the sight of black men being drafted into segregated regiments to fight for freedoms which most of them could not enjoy, and was made even more unbearable by the discovery that these men were being ill-treated while in uniform. During the war, legislative limitations on expression and the labeling of sincere complaint as disloyalty meant that protest was muted about conditions in the army. After the war, however, blacks were determined to draw attention to the wider debt they felt they were owed by the United States; they demanded that the government take action against lynching, segregation, and disfranchisement.

Four

The Surveillance of African-American Leadership

For most of 1917, Justice Department and War Department investigations of "pro-Germanism among the Negroes" were largely confined to localized instances of black protest, allegations of enemy subversion, and the military implications of civil unrest. Not until the spring of 1918 did the BI and the MIB become routinely engaged in investigating and, in a limited way, analyzing the range of publications, organizations, personalities, and ideologies permeating the politics of the equal rights movement. During the first year of American involvement in the war, the task of tracking and containing printed black protest fell mainly to the Post Office Department, the power of which was markedly increased by the Espionage Act of June 15, 1917. In title 12, section 5, the act empowered the postmaster general to exclude from the mails material that discouraged draft registration and anything that advocated treason, insurrection, or forcible resistance to any law of the United States.[1]

Postmaster General Albert Sidney Burleson, described in 1918 by fellow Texan Col. Edward House as "the most belligerent member of the Cabinet," used the Espionage Act to exclude from the mails a variety of journals that criticized the Allies, American involvement in the war, or the Wilson administration. Once an issue of a journal had been banned from the mails, all subsequent issues could be denied second-class mailing, since to retain this privilege a periodical had to be "regularly issued at stated intervals." The Post Office argued that if a journal had been banned once, then continuity of publication could no longer be shown—an argument that the courts allowed. The Post Office could also simply revoke a journal's second-class mailing privileges at its own discretion, which could have much the same practical effect as banning the journal from the mails altogether.[2]

Socialist publications, in particular, were interfered with in a way that suggested prejudice on the part of postal officials, and repeated appeals to Burleson to take a more reasonable view of criticism of the government were ignored.[3] In August 1917, for example, the trial lawyer Clarence Darrow and the civil libertarian Roger Baldwin asked Burleson to lift the ban on a dozen pacifist and socialist journals. Although Darrow employed what Baldwin called "all his folksy talents of persuasion," Burleson was unmoved. Woodrow Wilson assured Darrow that he would try to get Burleson to handle the question of distribution of socialist literature "in conformity with law and good sense," but the postmaster general, who believed his department's wartime role was to "keep the minds of the American people from being poisoned by treacherous and seditious matter," would not relent and Wilson rarely reopened the issue.[4]

Burleson's narrow-mindedness was, if anything, exceeded by that of the bureaucrat who carried out Post Office policy on a daily basis, the department's solicitor, William H. Lamar. Until the passage of the Espionage Act, Lamar had dealt with mundane legal matters which arose in relation to the Post Office's peacetime role. He was quite unsuited for the task of applying so imprecise a law as the Espionage Act to a wide range of publications in a variety of languages, except insofar as he was eager to enact Burleson's repressive instincts. On June 16, 1917, Burleson had asked postal employees to forward any material that might be in breach of the Espionage Act to his office, where Lamar would pronounce on its mailability.[5] When sending in such material, Post Office officials frequently took advantage of Lamar's lack of objectivity, peppering their recommendations that particular journals should be excluded from the mails with prejudiced remarks about their publishers and readerships.

Writing in the February 1918 issue of the *Forum,* Lamar revealed the logic with which he assessed the acceptability or otherwise of the material submitted to him. In the first place, he was convinced that there existed "an organized propaganda to discredit and obstruct in every way the prosecution of the war" and that those involved had responded to the passage of the Espionage Act by contriving to "subtly guard their utterances in the attempt to evade criminal liability for their acts"—in other words, they had been careful not to break the letter of the law. However, that would not protect them from the attentions of the Post Office Department, which took into account "a variety of considerations, some of which may be extraneous to the material." Lamar asked, "Isn't it not only sensible but fair to take into consideration the known attitude of the writers when searching for the 'intent' behind the comment?" He argued that words which might be unobjectionable when uttered by someone of proven loyalty could be taken to mean something quite different when employed by an opponent of the war or the Allies.[6] Thus, the Post Office felt entitled to exclude a dissenting journal from the mails for printing Thomas Jefferson's opinion that Ireland ought to be a republic.[7]

In most cases, the courts could be relied upon to take the side of the Post Office, and when they did not, Lamar saw to it that the success of his opponents was short-lived. When the National Civil Liberties Bureau (later the American Civil Liberties Union) published a pamphlet containing passages from a court ruling that overturned one of Lamar's decisions, he declared the pamphlet non-mailable.[8] He derided those who clung to "an exaggerated sentimentalism, a misapplied reverence for legal axioms"— what was needed was not so much a strict evaluation of material in relation to the Espionage Act as careful "application of the old adage of reading between the lines."[9]

The passage of a second Espionage Act, usually known as the Sedition Act, in May 1918 further strengthened the government's control over what was published about the war by explicitly inhibiting freedom of expression. The Sedition Act provided for $10,000 fines and imprisonment of up to twenty years for those who

> when the United States is at war, shall wilfully utter, print, write, or publish any disloyal, profane, scurrilous, or abusive language about the form of government of the United States, or the Constitution of the United States, or the military or naval forces of the United States, or the flag . . . or the uniform of the Army or the Navy of the United States, or any language intended to bring the form of government . . . or the Constitution . . . or the military or naval forces . . . of the United States into contempt, scorn, contumely, or disrepute. . . . [10]

A further amendment permitted the postmaster general to stop mail deliveries to anyone who violated the act.[11]

Burleson's officials made enthusiastic use of their new powers. For example, the September 14, 1918, issue of the *Nation* was declared non-mailable because of criticisms it contained of the pro-war president of the American Federation of Labor, Samuel Gompers. The journal's owner and, coincidentally, treasurer of the NAACP, Oswald Garrison Villard, traveled to Washington and managed to persuade Woodrow Wilson, with whom he had had close pre-war contact, to tell Burleson to release the *Nation,* but first he had to endure an exasperating interview with the Post Office solicitor. According to Villard, Lamar said, "You know I am not working in the dark on this censorship thing. I know exactly what I am after. I am after three things and only three things—pro-Germanism, pacifism, and 'high-browism.'" What such bogus precision meant was that while editors had to be careful about anything they printed about the war and the government, they also had to worry about how the Post Office might interpret it in the light of a journal's supposed leanings. Later, Will Hays, the Republican post-war postmaster general, would justly denounce his predecessor's methods as "bureaucratic censorship which in its nature becomes a matter of opinion, prejudice, or caprice."[12]

Administrative control of the censorship of international mails was also largely assumed by the Post Office Department. During the war, the Censorship Board established nineteen stations and substations, in which a Post Office official chaired a "Postal Censorship Committee" on which sat representatives of the chief cable censor, military intelligence, naval intelligence, and the War Trade Board. Apart from these agents, the workforce of the stations was made up of Post Office employees. Mail was supposed to be examined only for military or naval information, banking or trade matters, and the use of codes.[13] Other correspondence was not meant to be interfered with, but letters to and from black Americans which commented on race relations were frequently intercepted.

The black press in the United States was expanding during the war years, with over two hundred weekly newspapers and half a dozen monthly magazines, ranging from conservative and religious exponents of the gradualist philosophy of Booker T. Washington to more radical publications with more aggressive approaches, such as that inspired by the Niagara movement.[14] The most influential journal in 1917–18 was probably the NAACP's monthly magazine, the *Crisis,* in which W. E. B. Du Bois advocated a persistent and vigorous campaign for equal rights. Among those who followed Du Bois's lead and had a significant regional influence was P. B. Young, editor and proprietor of the *Norfolk Journal and Guide,* whose outlook changed from one of encouraging potential black migrants to make the best of the conditions they found in the South in 1916–17, to urging them to insist on better treatment during the war.[15] More outspoken and less avowedly pragmatic were men like William Monroe Trotter, editor of the *Boston Guardian,* who did not trust the white liberals who lionized Du Bois, and A. Philip Randolph and Chandler Owen of the *Messenger,* who were active members of the Socialist Party in New York City.[16]

The Surveillance of African-American Leadership

The very existence of the black press, let alone its changing tone, had gone largely ignored by white Americans before the war. Among the few whites who commented on it was the pro-Wilson journalist Ray Stannard Baker, who for a decade had taken a close interest in the internal politics of black protest. Baker remarked on "an increasing impatience and boldness of tone" and issued a warning:

> The utter ignorance of the great mass of white Americans as to what is really going on among the colored people of the country is appalling—and dangerous. We forget that there are 10,000,000 of them, one-tenth of our population, and that their strides toward self-consciousness in the last twenty years have been marvelous. We have known next to nothing about the constructive developments among them and have not wanted to know; we have preferred to consider the Negro and all his affairs as beneath notice.[17]

This indifference would have persisted, but for the alarm that began in April 1917 with allegations that there had been widespread and successful attempts by German agents to subvert black loyalty.

It would be an exaggeration, however, to claim that the Post Office regarded the black press as a prime concern during the war. It was much more convinced of the need to control the distribution and content of German-language newspapers and socialist-pacifist publications, like the *Masses,* edited by Max Eastman and John Reed.[18] It was not until the red scare of 1919 that Lamar was repeatedly called upon to pronounce on the mailability of black newspapers and magazines, but black editors were well aware in 1917 and 1918 that they risked prosecution when they published material likely to incur official displeasure, and they were frequently reminded that the provisions of the Espionage Act were no idle threat. Although no black journals were permanently barred from the mails during the war, a few were held briefly while their acceptability was determined and one issue of one newspaper, the May 29, 1918, issue of the *Amsterdam News,* a New York weekly, was declared non-mailable.

The *Amsterdam News* had been established by a West Indian chemist, Dr. P. M. H. Savory, in 1911 and catered mainly to New York's West Indian community.[19] Its city editor was Cyril V. Briggs, a native of the British Leeward Islands, who later published and edited the radical magazine *Crusader* and organized the African Blood Brotherhood, which for a while attracted several future members of the Communist Party. Described by one of his followers as "a revolutionary nationalist," Briggs's preferred solution at this time to the problem of racial friction in the United States was the establishment of an independent black republic within the territory of the United States or in the Caribbean. He variously suggested that this might best be situated in California, Idaho, Nevada, Oregon, or Washington or on the island of Santo Domingo. During the war, he put the case for his scheme by drawing parallels with the importance being placed by the Allies on the independence and right to self-determination of European ethnic groups like the Serbs.[20] According to the editor of the *Amsterdam News*, James H. Anderson, and the managing editor, Edward Warren, the May 29 issue was put out in Warren's absence by a junior editor (i.e., Briggs) and the editorials prepared on this occasion "were so at variance with the usual policy of the paper that the printer called up the office to ascertain if they really wished the editorials published in the form they were given to him." He was told to go ahead by the author of the editorials.[21] In the first piece, Briggs made his usual comparison between the Wilson administration's apparent concern for the rights of Europeans and its indifference to the rights of millions of Americans. Blacks knew all about the war aims of the government, he wrote, but would rather know what its intentions were toward its own citizens:

> If the Coloured people have not been so very enthusiastic over the prosecution of the war it is because they have yet to hear themselves included along with the Serbs and Poles in the President's splendid demands that "henceforth security of life, worship, and industrial and social development should be guaranteed to all peoples."

Since lynching showed no signs of declining, Briggs asked,

> Are our women and children to be murdered at home while our men folk are giving up their lives in the Nation's service abroad? Must Coloured men go over seas to fight German Prussianism when Cracker Prussianism is rampant and of more immediate menace here at home? Is lynching to be the reward of our loyalty, and service at home and courage on the battlefield?[22]

In the next editorial, Briggs congratulated army sergeant James Thomas on having told an audience at Harlem's Lafayette Theater, in a speech on behalf of the Red Cross, that "the real Negro" would "no longer be satisfied to bite his tongue and hide his resentment in connection with the grievous

wrongs suffered by his Race at the hands of American fiends who seem
bent on out-Prussianising the Prussians!" Briggs noted that most statements
by blacks on patriotism were "marked by a pernicious attempt to lull into
false security by the indiscriminate making of rosy, but unauthorized, promises of future justice and 'security of life.'" Thomas's speech, on the other
hand,

> contained no attempt to cater to Caucasian susceptibilities or to play with
> Ethiopian credulity. . . . He gave warning that the time for toleration of
> ill-treatment and injustice is past, that the patriotic white American must
> act soon or see the Negro himself act, "FOR IF IT IS WORTH SACRI-
> FICING LIFE FOR DEMOCRACY FOR OTHERS OVER THERE, IT IS
> WORTH SACRIFICING LIFE FOR DEMOCRACY FOR OURSELVES
> OVER HERE."[23]

An intelligence officer at the military embarkation port at Hoboken, N.J.,
thought these editorials worth noting and that "the motives of the editor
might bear scrutiny," but otherwise Briggs's liberties with the leader page
of the *Amsterdam News* would probably have gone unnoticed, had not the
Postal Censorship station at Key West, Fla., examined a copy of the paper
that was on its way to a subscriber in Cuba.[24] The Post Office reader found
the editorials

> decidedly discordant and out of harmony with present purposes of the
> government, as they seek to incite the negro, and spread the idea that it
> is not worth while for the negro to sacrifice himself for a democracy which
> it says does nothing toward improving the conditions and liberties of the
> colored race.[25]

The Key West censors seized every copy of the May 29 *Amsterdam News*
that they could locate and distributed them among the chief cable censor,
the MIB, the Office of Naval Intelligence, the War Trade Board, and the
State Department. Post Office Solicitor Lamar was also furnished with a
copy and duly declared it non-mailable under the Espionage Act.[26] This was
a minor blow to the operations of the *Amsterdam News*, because Lamar took
a month to arrive at his decision, during which publishing was not interrupted and street sales in New York were unaffected. The only loss had been
those issues which the Post Office was able to remove from the mails after
the report from Postal Censorship. However, the episode unnerved the editors of the paper. Visited by an American Protective League (APL) agent,

they insisted that the offending editorials had "slipped into the paper through accident." The agent concluded that "the paper's experience with the Federal Government . . . had made them particularly careful not to overstep the law" and that they were "doing their best to be loyal." Cyril Briggs's resignation from the *Amsterdam News* a year later, ostensibly to concentrate on editing the *Crusader,* was also a belated protest at management interference with his editorials.[27]

The only black editor successfully prosecuted under the Espionage Act was G. W. Bouldin, of the *San Antonio Inquirer,* in a case which demonstrated both the extent to which a sense of proportion was lost in the application of this law and the inefficiency of the federal legal machinery. On November 24, 1917, during the final week of the month-long courts-martial of sixty-three members of the 24th Infantry for their part in the Houston riot, the *Inquirer* carried an article by C. L. Threadgill-Dennis in which she directly addressed the soldiers. She recalled that the final provocations, so far as the Camp Logan mutineers were concerned, had been the pistol-whipping by a white police officer of a black private who intervened during the violent and wrongful arrest of a black woman, and the subsequent police assault on a black provost guard who asked why the private had been beaten. Threadgill-Dennis assured the men now on trial at Fort Sam Houston, near San Antonio, that all women of their race held them in high esteem:

> We would rather see you shot by the highest tribunal of the United States Army because you dared to protect a Negro woman from the insult of a southern brute in the form of a policeman, than to have you forced to go to Europe to fight for a liberty you cannot enjoy. Negro women regret that you mutinied, and we are sorry that you spilt innocent blood, but we are not sorry that five southern policemen's bones now bleech [*sic*] in the graves of Houston, Tex.[28]

The attention of the Justice Department was drawn to this article by a San Antonio BI agent and Bouldin was charged with having made "an unlawful attempt to cause insubordination." His case was not heard until January 1919, when the U.S. district attorney was assisted in the prosecution by a BI agent. Bouldin denied the charge, but was found guilty; he immediately appealed and the two-year prison sentence was deferred. On December 11, 1919, over two years after the appearance of the offending article and over

The Surveillance of African-American Leadership

a year after the end of the war, the conviction was affirmed by the U.S. Circuit Court of Appeals, which ordered that Bouldin should serve his two years in the federal penitentiary at Fort Leavenworth, Kans.[29]

The *Messenger* magazine, described by its editors, A. Philip Randolph and Chandler Owen, as "The Only Magazine of Scientific Radicalism in the World Published by Negroes," first appeared in November 1917. Born within ten days of each other in April, 1889, Randolph and Owen had both moved to New York from the South—Randolph from Florida in 1911 and Owen from North Carolina, via Virginia, in 1913. They met in 1915, finding a common interest in sociology, and the following year joined the Socialist Party and gave up their part-time college studies for street-corner oratory and political meetings. From January to August 1917 they edited the *Hotel Messenger* for the Headwaiters and Sidewaiters Society of Greater New York, until falling foul of the union's president for exposing the corrupt way in which the waiters' pecking order operated. Two months later, they launched their own well-written and neatly laid out magazine with the shortened title of *Messenger.*[30]

The *Messenger* was born in the midst of Morris Hillquit's attempt to be elected mayor of New York City on the anti-war Socialist ticket. (Hillquit finished third, but the Socialist share of the vote, 21.7 percent, was five times higher than normal.)[31] Only three issues of the *Messenger* were produced during the war, but each devoted large sections to critical discussions of American belligerency. Those who profited financially from the war were condemned in each issue, while anti-war stalwarts, such as Sen. Robert La Follette of Wisconsin, were repeatedly applauded.[32] The editors of the *Messenger* agreed with W. E. B. Du Bois that the war had its roots in Africa, for there were to be found "the tools of the capitalists—undeveloped resources and undeveloped peoples—cheap lands and labor," but, unlike Du Bois, they did not believe that this increased the obligation on African Americans to fight in France. The *Messenger*'s advice to Du Bois and his ilk in November 1917 was that they should "volunteer to go to France, if they are so eager to fight to make the world safe for democracy. We would rather make Georgia safe for the Negro." Randolph and Owen identified a "New Patriotism. . . . The new patriotism is consistent. It does not condemn massacres and lynchings in Germany and condone them in its own country. . . . The new patriotism cannot hate a man because he is born or lives on the other side of a strip of water or an imaginary line." They also stated that the 24th

Infantry's Houston rioters deserved clemency.[33] In the next issue, that of January 1918, they condemned the swift execution of thirteen of the soldiers, asserting that it was

> not calculated to stimulate the very low smoldering patriotism which is still left in the Negroes.
>
> We also wish to call the attention of this country to the bold misrepresentation of Negro leaders about the Negro's patriotism. Every ninety out of a hundred Negroes felt before the execution that it was very questionable whether they had any country to fight for. Since that execution, with large and extensive contact, we have not found a Negro man or woman whose position is not passively against the country, or certainly indifferent to its appeals.[34]

The first two issues of the *Messenger* did not attract the hostile government attention which Randolph and Owen might have expected; efforts to detect "negro subversion" were focused on men and women with higher profiles, such as Du Bois and Ida B. Wells-Barnett. Randoph and Owen only began to be harassed by federal officials after the third issue of the *Messenger* appeared, in July 1918. The offending article, "Pro-Germanism among the Negroes," was not remarkable in itself, but its title was guaranteed to catch the official eye. The article mentioned a recent occasion when a government intelligence agent—possibly Walter Loving, who was then working in New York—interrupted a NAACP meeting to warn the audience that blacks "were under suspicion of having been affected by German propaganda." The *Messenger* retorted that ill-treatment of black people in America was a far more effective cause of discontent than any German propaganda:

> The only legitimate connection between this unrest and Germanism is the extensive government advertisement that we are fighting "to make the world safe for democracy," "to carry democracy to Germany;" that we are conscripting the Negro into the military and industrial establishments to achieve this end for white democracy four thousand miles away, while the Negro at home, though bearing the burden in every way, is denied economic, political, educational and civil democracy. And this, despite his loyalty and patriotism in the land of the free and the home of the brave![35]

On Sunday, August 4, 1918, Randolph and Owen were in Cleveland, Ohio, in the middle of a lecture tour promoting socialism and the *Messenger.* That evening, BI agent W. Sawken noticed a large meeting on a street corner and found it being addressed by black and white socialists. While Randolph and Owen spoke, two white Cleveland socialists sold the July issue of the *Messenger*, which a member of the audience showed to Sawken. Since the contents "seemed open to criticism," Sawken bought himself a copy for fifteen cents and at the end of the meeting arrested Randolph, Owen, and one of the white socialists. The editors were jailed overnight and on Monday morning were interrogated as to the purpose of their visit to Cleveland, their interest in socialism, and the source of their funds. They gave full answers and explained that their expenses had been paid by the Cleveland branch of the Socialist Party. They were then asked about their draft status. Randolph had documents to show that he had registered for the draft in New York City and that he had been given the low classification of 4-A, because of a dependent wife and children.[36] (In fact, Randolph had no children and he relied on his wife's beautician business for his own financial support.[37]) Owen, who was single, admitted to Sawken that he had been classified 1-A by his local draft board in New York, had been examined, and was waiting for orders to join up. The BI office in New York immediately checked Owen's status and replied the next day that his draft board wanted him for the August quota and that he "should be kept under surveillance." The BI's agent-in-charge at Cleveland, Bliss Morton, suggested that the New York draft board forward Owen's induction papers to Cleveland so that they could put him in the army there and then, but this proved impossible.[38]

Sawken and Morton discussed the case with Assistant U.S. Attorney F. B. Kavanagh, who agreed that a warrant should be obtained for the formal arrest of Randolph, Owen, and the two white socialists who had been selling copies of the magazine at the street-corner meeting, under title 1, section 3, of the Espionage Act, and that meanwhile they should be kept in jail. The warrants were served on August 6, charging that the four men did "[u]nlawfully, knowingly and feloniously, the United States being then and there at war with the Imperial German Government, wilfully print and cause to be printed, publish and cause to be published and circulated, in certain language intended to incite, provoke and incur resistance to the United States and to promote the cause of its enemies," the article on "Pro-Germanism among the Negroes."[39]

Randolph and Owen appeared in court before a U.S. commissioner and were represented by Seymour Stedman, a leading socialist lawyer from Chicago. They pleaded not guilty, raised the thousand-dollar bail from socialist friends, and left for Chicago. According to Randolph's later account, the commissioner was baffled by the case: "He couldn't believe we were old enough, or, being black, smart enough, to write that red-hot stuff in the *Messenger*. There was no doubt, he said, that the white Socialists were using us, that they had written the stuff for us."[40] They completed the rest of their tour as planned, addressing meetings in Chicago, Milwaukee, Washington, D.C., and Boston before returning to New York City. As Owen's draft board had requested, their movements were monitored throughout by the BI. Although Owen claimed in April 1919 that he and Randolph were still under bond on the Espionage Act indictment, they were never brought to trial and the case was eventually dismissed.[41] Why they were not tried is not clear, but Randolph's biographer may have the answer when he notes that the Justice Department wanted to keep acquittals under the Espionage Act to the absolute minimum. The "Pro-Germanism among the Negroes" article was not the most outspoken piece of black wartime journalism—indeed, an efficient prosecution could have found far more indictable passages elsewhere in the *Messenger*—and the government side had not given the impression at the initial hearing that the chances of a successful prosecution were good. Another explanation that has been offered for the failure to prosecute—that the Justice Department wanted the trial to proceed, but Woodrow Wilson was opposed—may be discounted.[42] The names of A. Philip Randolph and Chandler Owen would have meant nothing to the president.

Production of the *Messenger* had been hampered from the start by lack of funds, printing strikes, and paper shortages. According to Randolph, a few days after the editors returned to New York they suffered another blow—the withdrawal of second-class mailing privileges, or, as Randolph later put it, "Burleson threw the Messenger out of the mails."[43] In fact, there is no evidence in the records of the Post Office Department that the *Messenger's* mailing privileges were interfered with until the July 1919 issue was held up for a week by the New York City postmaster, pending Lamar's decision as to its mailability. It was declared mailable, but second-class privileges were denied to it and subsequent issues.[44] Randolph may have confused the Post Office's reaction to the July 1918 issue with that to the issue of July 1919; alternatively, he may have been overdramatizing his and Owen's experiences at the hands of the government and seeking to explain the non-appearance of the *Messenger* between July 1918 and February 1919.

The event which undoubtedly contributed most to the 1918–19 hibernation of the *Messenger* was the drafting of Chandler Owen in August. He served for four months in a southern army camp, returning to New York in January 1919. Randolph was informed in October 1918 that he too would be called up, for the November quota, but he was saved by the Armistice. Owen was not proud of having submitted to the draft in spite of his anti-war views. He did not write about his military career in the *Messenger* and he endured a certain amount of ribbing from fellow socialists. In April 1919, he wrote to the NAACP's Mary White Ovington, who had shown a benevolent interest in the *Messenger,* criticizing what he saw as W. E. B. Du Bois's cooperation with the Wilson administration in return for a passport to travel to France and refuting Du Bois's remark in the April 1919 *Crisis* about anti-war blacks. Du Bois had written, "There has been talk and talk and talk. But not one of those Negroes has been arrested even as a conscientious objector." Owen pointed out that he and Randolph had been arrested at Cleveland the previous August. Ovington rejected Owen's criticism of Du Bois, but thanked him for calling her attention to his arrest, adding, "I have never fully understood, however, what you did after you left Cleveland, August 6. Did you go to camp and wear the uniform? Perhaps you have written this up and I have failed to see it. If so, please call my attention where I can find the matter."[45] Owen did not respond.

Robert S. Abbott's *Chicago Defender,* the most forthright black weekly newspaper in the United States, continued to disturb those government officials who encountered it. After having been accused in 1917 of promoting disloyalty by encouraging migration to the North, the *Defender* continued to highlight injustice and racial violence, especially in the South. Abbott condemned segregation and described lynchings in the most lurid detail. When referring to the war, however, he was always careful not to contravene the Espionage Act, realizing after his questioning at the BI office in Chicago in April 1917 that the Justice Department would waste no time in prosecuting him if he gave it an excuse. Abbott had no qualms about contrasting the reality of life for black people in America with the worldwide democracy to which their country was now committed, but he skillfully avoided direct criticism of the government or the war effort, arguing that the war should certainly be fought and that black men ought to do their share of the fighting. Every other week's issue of the *Defender* carried a selection of ringing phrases from Roscoe Conkling Simmons's latest exhortation to blacks to be selflessly loyal and defend the flag in the certainty that after the war they would be treated better.[46]

No amount of pro-war rhetoric could make the *Chicago Defender* acceptable to whites in the South, where BI agents continued to report that the paper was disruptive and offensive. In December 1917, the Tucson, Ariz., agent complained to Division Superintendent Hinton Clabaugh (based in Chicago) about a description in the December 8 issue of the burning to death of Lation (or Ligon) Scott at Dyersburg, Tenn., which he thought might be "German propaganda." The *Defender* had declared, "Not in the barbarous days of Belgium's rule in Africa nor the days of the half-civilized people who lived thousands of years before Christ had such barbarism been witnessed." Tucson's chief of police had denounced the *Defender* and stated that "practically every colored resident of Tucson had received a copy." The agent suspected German intrigue.[47]

In response, Clabaugh detailed Chicago BI agent B. D. Adsit to conduct yet another investigation. Once again, a marked difference emerged between the attitudes of many northern agents and the majority of southern agents toward black political protest. Adsit visited the *Defender* offices and, like all other officials who took the trouble to do so, came away impressed by Abbott's straightforwardness. He reported that the paper was "carefully edited, and, since the war began . . . [had been] loyal to the core"; there was not "the slightest evidence of German influence." Also, the dispatch of 210 copies of the December 8 issue to Arizona—sixty each to newsagents in Tucson and Phoenix and the other ninety to subscribers—"was absolutely normal, removing all doubt of German propaganda influence in its [Tucson] office, or at Chicago."[48]

In May 1918, Adsit was told to take yet another look at Abbott following a complaint from an agent in Arkansas about a pessimistic *Defender* editorial about the treatment of black troops. The agent observed that the writer had used

> a lot of nice sentences here and there and paints nice pictures to cover up the real intent of the article. . . . I hope there will be some way to keep it away from ignorant negroes; I don't mean to intimate by that negroes who do not read, but negroes who do read but have what the poet Pope said 'a little learning is a dangerous thing etc.'[49]

Adsit paid "a casual visit" to the *Defender* offices and found that there was nothing new to report about the paper, other than that the weekly circulation had gone up from 92,000 to 120,000 in the previous six months.[50]

The APL continued to find the *Defender* objectionable in the South. In September 1918, an APL operative in Mobile, Ala., warned that the paper contained articles "which cannot but cause actions which will arouse resentment on the part of the white people in this section." Blacks in Mobile were said to be discussing what improvements they could expect to see in their conditions after the war, and, while the precise source of this talk could not be found, the APL man suspected that the *Defender* had a lot to do with it. It was difficult to be certain, because "[a]nyone who knows negro characteristics knows how difficult it is to secure any reliable information from [the] ordinary darkey regarding propaganda."[51]

In April 1918, a Chicago military intelligence agent summarized complaints received by the BI about the *Defender*, beginning with the investigation of Abbott a year earlier and noting subsequent occasions on which he had come close to breaching the Espionage Act. It was even suggested that Abbott might have violated that section of the U.S. Penal Code which dealt with incitement to commit arson, murder, and assassination. The only notable absence from this review of the BI's *Defender* file was Adsit's report of December 22, 1917, which cleared Abbott of any offense. The MIB agent either ignored this or was not shown it.[52] The MIB digest was forwarded to the War Department in Washington with a copy of a letter purporting to be from "A Citizen's Committee of Patriotic Negro Citizens," in which the *Defender* was denounced as the cause of unnecessary racial friction, for which it "should be severely reprimanded . . . not only for the benefit of the country but of the ignorant people of our race."[53] Maj. Walter Loving left for Chicago even before the digest of the BI file was formally passed on to him for investigation. He called on Robert Abbott, whose paper, because of the size of its readership, Loving reckoned to be "the most dangerous of all Negro journals," and left him in no doubt that government officials were waiting for him to give them grounds for a prosecution. Abbott now knew that "the eye of the government [was] centered upon his paper, and caution should be his guide." Abbott evidently regarded Loving's visit as more of a friendly tip-off than a stern warning. He thanked Loving for taking an interest in his welfare, promised to keep their dealings confidential, and assured him that the *Defender* had always supported the war effort and that only southern whites had leveled criticism at the paper. He had told his writers to moderate their tone, as he was aware of the extent to which the administration was controlled by southerners. He would, from now on, "be extremely precautious." Loving sent Abbott's letter to the director of military intelligence with the comment: "The tone of this reply is all that we can expect, if the writer lives up to it, and I shall endeavor to try to see that he does." True to his word, Abbott's next edition carried an editorial recommending that blacks leave the fight for rights until after "the greater task of winning this war is over."[54]

Beginning in August 1917, the Chicago postmaster sent two copies of each issue of the *Defender* to the Post Office solicitor.[55] The paper did not provoke real concern in Lamar's office until the postmaster at Denison, Tex., wrote to Lamar on June 8, 1918, asking whether the *Defender* was mailable. In the postmaster's view, it was

> not directly a fling at the government, but it is a species of rank race hatred which shows the signs of German conspiracy, and also demonstrates the malicious tendencies of anti-Americanism at a time when we need to be a harmonious and united people.
>
> It is precisely this form of public print that stirs in the negro's revolutionary mind not only the seditious thought but the seditious act.[56]

Post Office official C. E. Boles now advised Lamar that

> The fomenting of race hatred among the negroes at this time is extremely unfortunate and flavors strongly of German propaganda. It would be extremely difficult, however, for this Department to get at the root of the matter and the evidence of disloyal intent on the part of the publishers.[57]

Boles suggested that Lamar write to Abbott, advising him that there was "nothing more pleasing to the Imperial German Government and nothing more effective to aid the Imperial German Government than to stir up hatred and strife between the white and black races."[58] (Lamar declined, or neglected, to follow this suggestion.) A fortnight later, the postmaster at Belcher, La., complained to Lamar that every issue of the *Defender* contained "a lible [*sic*] on the South." The encouragement that it gave to blacks to leave the South was disrupting agriculture and was, therefore, "a menace to the whole Nation."[59]

Burleson also began to take an interest in the mailability of the *Defender* after Sen. John Sharp Williams of Mississippi sent him a formal protest by a group of white Mississippians at the continued circulation of the paper. Williams had looked over recent editions of the paper and expected that his own indignation would be shared by Burleson, as it was "a tissue of lies, all intended to create race disturbance and trouble." The white citizens of Madison County, Miss., had also resolved that the *Defender* tended to "revive sectional issues and create race antagonism, both of which we deplore, and the publication and circulation of such matter is in the nature of German Propaganda."[60] Lamar's assistant, James A. Horton, who liaised between the Post Office solicitor and the Justice Department, referred the Mississippi complaint to an official who found the *Defender*'s criticism of an African American opponent of black migration "objectionable since it tends to . . . encourage negro emigration from sections of the country where their labor is needed and . . . keep alive and intensify racial prejudices and animosities." However, even Lamar could see that this was a tenuous claim, and Burleson had to tell Williams that although the *Defender* would be monitored, there were currently insufficient grounds for declaring it nonmailable.[61]

In July 1918, the Translation Bureau of the Post Office in New York, which had been created by the Trading with the Enemy Act of 1917 and was primarily responsible for monitoring foreign-language publications, took it upon itself to scan the African-American press. The bureau began to pass intensely critical evaluations of the *Defender* to the assistant U.S. district attorney in New York City, in an unsuccessful attempt to initiate a prosecution. *Defender* writers were said to "lose no chance to rub in the germs of dissatisfaction," and tortured arguments were used to accuse the paper of actually causing the racial discrimination and violence against which it campaigned. The Justice Department was advised in August,

> This violent negro paper not only puts the attainment of their own objects, that is to say treatment which includes their being allowed to mix as freely as they choose among white people, ahead of the stirring [*sic*] of the war, but they apparently put this object ahead even of the safety of their own race. Surely they must realize that by the constant stirring up of the fires of race prejudice they are doing what is in their power to make lynching more, rather than less, frequent. Surely the frequency of lynching interferes with the war and thus, take it as you will, from whatever point of view, these papers [i.e., recent issues of the *Defender*] are obstructionists.[62]

The most vituperative comments came from Translation Bureau official Robert Adger Bowen, a former literary editor who was later to assume the role of Post Office expert on the black press and whose post-war perusals of mostly New York publications were to form the central part of the government's claim that African Americans were swept along on the supposed Bolshevik tide which produced the red scare of 1919. Bowen admitted that he could find nothing illegal in the *Defender*, but he wanted to alert officials in other departments to the "obstreperous negro spirit that is not the best way about for the negro to help settle his 'problem.'" He was scornful of black attempts to "ape the white man" and equated black editors with "the Irish of the discontented kind—they are always emphasizing their grievances and making grievances where they might evade them."[63]

Walter Loving's dealings with Robert Abbott began as a result of a Justice Department report, but on some occasions the MIB acted alone against the press. In the summer of 1918, the officer in charge of the St. Louis field office, Capt. Roy F. Britton, took a keen interest in the editorial policy of the *St. Louis Argus*, edited by J. E. Mitchell. In May, Britton submitted an editorial from the *Argus* which he considered to be "rather dangerous and insidious propaganda." He regarded the *Argus*'s combined appeal to its readers to buy Liberty Bonds *and* support the anti-lynching bill introduced by St. Louis congressman Leonidas C. Dyer as a disguised attempt at seditious agitation. Mitchell's editorial had noted that blacks were being told that they should show restraint because their demands would be met after the war, while manufacturers and industrial workers were already enjoying greatly increased profits and incomes and were not expected to be so patient.[64] The *Argus* believed blacks should get as much as they could out of the war immediately:

> Now is the time to protest. Now is the time to complain. Now is the time to contend for legal rights that are being denied us, and now is the time to let the world know that we are not satisfied.
>
> These are momentous times. Men of our race are called up to give their lives along with other men.
>
> Our women are called upon to make the same sacrifice as other women, that the country's honor may be upheld. This is right and just. Then why should we be denied even equal justice before the law of the land without protest? Why should we be unjustly discriminated against without protest?
>
> We cannot hold our peace. We should not hold our peace, but should cry aloud until we get relief, using all legitimate, legal, and patriotic means.[65]

This kind of expression had been common a year earlier, when the United States entered the war, but by the spring of 1918 few editors were still brave or sanguine enough to write in such emphatic terms. Britton summoned Herbert Meadows, the city editor of the *Argus*, and warned him against printing anything that might provoke discontent or opposition to military service. Meadows replied that the paper was thoroughly loyal, but Britton was not convinced. As a result, a few days after interviewing Robert Abbott about the tenor of the *Chicago Defender,* Walter Loving was told by Van Deman to use his "best energies towards securing a change of the tone and character" of editorials in the *St. Louis Argus.*[66] Loving wrote to Mitchell from New York, informing him that he had incurred the MIB's displeasure and asking him what he proposed to do about it. Mitchell thanked Loving "for the kindly advice" and stated that the *Argus* had only the best interests of African Americans at heart. They needed better leadership and his editorials were no more than "a plea for our people to awake from their slumber. They could not be advised otherwise." Was it disloyal of him to expose injustice? Loving replied sympathetically, explaining that he enjoyed "the privilege and distinction of being a member of the same race whose honor and dignity you endeavor to safeguard and uphold," but he was, "first of all, a true American" who placed his country above all things. He assured Mitchell that officials of the government in Washington were "daily acquainted with facts of the real grievances of the American negro." He acknowledged that it was "the prerogative and duty of every colored newspaper in the United States to champion the cause of the race," but he wished the *Argus* would do it "in a way so as not to cause unrest and alarm among its patrons and readers. . . . It is not always what you say that offends, but it is the way you say it." He hoped that Mitchell would "not invite action on the part of the government to suppress [the *Argus*] or hold the same up in the mails."[67] The letter revealed something of Loving's personal dilemma and complex character. He knew that the editors he was cajoling and sometimes intimidating were not pro-German and that even their most bitter editorials were legitimate and representative, but he also took his role within the MIB seriously and gave the General Staff thoughtful advice on racial matters of a kind that it was getting from no one else, even Emmett Scott. Loving was trying to bring about adjustments in the tone of black protest so that it would not be misconstrued and suppressed, while at the same time trying to minimize the grosser insensitivities of the government —virtually impossible objectives in the dual contexts of fundamental racial discrimination and increasing race consciousness, and yet Loving appears to have had some small, but tangible, effect on both of his audiences. Certainly, Loving's threat made an impression on J. E. Mitchell: throughout May 1918, Captain Britton had complained about the *Argus* and argued that it contravened the new Sedition Act; in June, he had no complaints, and when he mentioned the *Argus* in July and August it was to note that it was much improved.[68]

The one newspaper about which pro-German allegations could be made with any plausibility was the *Washington Eagle,* but this related largely to events during the period of American neutrality. The *Eagle* was edited by J. Finley Wilson, the Tennessee-born Grand Exalted Ruler of the Elks fraternal order and an influential figure in black Republican politics. During the summer of 1918, the BI's file of "radicalism" articles and cartoons from the black press included several clippings from June and July issues of the *Eagle* on lynching and segregation, such as James B. Davidson's drawing of a black man representing "All of Us" weighed down by "Mob Violence," "Jim Crowism," and "Disfranchisement," and a ball and chain marked "Race Hatred." Although the man's pockets are stuffed with Liberty Bonds, he finds the tree of "Opportunity" fenced off.[69] In May 1917, Wilson had admitted in an interview at the Department of Justice building that he had written a number of pro-German articles during the summer of 1915 and claimed he had been genuinely in sympathy with Germany at the time. He had also taken articles during this period from a man called Martin, who was involved with what Wilson called the "Laborers Peace Council Movement."[70] Labor's National Peace Council, an anti-war trade union offering generous strike pay to members, was organized in 1915 by Franz von Rintelen, one of Berlin's most active agents in the United States, with access to $500,000 through the German ambassador's privy councilor, Dr. H. F. Albert. It caused a small amount of disruption in ports and munitions factories before the United States entered the war.[71] J. Finley Wilson's admission that he had carried pro-German articles supplied by von Rintelen's organization raises the distinct possibility that the *Washington Eagle* was for a time financed by German money. By the time the United States entered the war, however, Wilson was claiming that his attitude had completely changed and that he now supported the Allies.[72] Certainly the wartime content of the *Eagle* did not attract as much adverse comment from federal agents as other papers and at no stage was the paper threatened with prosecution or interfered with by the Post Office.

The wartime gatherings of the National Equal Rights League (NERL) were closely watched by government agencies. The driving force behind the organization was its executive secretary, William Monroe Trotter, the Harvard-educated editor of the *Boston Guardian.* The NERL lacked the white philanthropic and socialist support enjoyed by the NAACP, and had an altogether brasher approach to civil rights agitation. It took a consistently firm anti-segregationist line and Trotter frequently charged the NAACP with an excessive willingness to compromise. During Booker T. Washington's lifetime, Trotter had been implacably opposed to Tuskegee-ite gradualism and his continuing disdain for Washington's associates was fully reciprocated.[73] He particularly resented the appointment of Emmett Scott to the post of special assistant to the secretary of war.

During the war, the NERL cooperated with a new organization, the Liberty League, formed by the West Indian–born New York writer and lecturer Hubert H. Harrison on June 12, 1917. The following day, Harrison traveled to Boston to forge links with Trotter, and together they planned a "race congress," to be held in Washington under the title of the National Liberty Congress.[74] Its purpose would be to press for the suppression of lynching and the inclusion of African Americans in the worldwide democracy for which the United States was fighting. At the Liberty League's first meeting, in a New York church, one of the speakers was Marcus Garvey, the Jamaican founder of the Universal Negro Improvement Association, who had been in the United States for a little over a year. Garvey's address had enhanced his growing reputation and given a much-needed boost to his mission; within three years, Harrison would be working for Garvey.[75]

By September 1917, when the NERL held its Tenth Annual Convention in New York, the militant statements issued by its president, Byron Gunner, had already earned the disapproval of the Department of Justice. Gunner had declared it was time to "'roundabout' and confront and combat the forces of evil that sorely oppress us." These included the Democratic administration: "The party in power has its iron heel on our necks."[76] Chief Bielaski found such statements "decidedly in opposition to the Government," and a Cincinnati BI agent reckoned that they "had a tendency to incite the negroes against the white people."[77]

At the convention, over a hundred delegates resolved that U.S. involvement in the European war could only be justified if the government was prepared to guarantee "freedom and equality of rights to all the citizens of the United States regardless of the incidents of race or color over which they have no control." Specific demands were made for the eradication of lynching, peonage, disfranchisement, and segregated public transport, amid open skepticism about the sincerity of Woodrow Wilson's commitment to democracy. The convention also hosted a concurrent two-day "Na-

tional Race Congress" in which members of other organizations were encouraged to participate, suggesting that Trotter still hoped to build a broad
radical coalition that would reduce his own isolation and reputation as a
maverick.[78]

During the remainder of 1917, the Liberty League organized in New
York, petitioned the U.S. Congress, and advertised itself through Harrison's
irregularly published magazine, the *Voice*. Although the National Liberty
Congress planned for December was postponed until the summer of 1918,
a nationwide publicity campaign was launched to attract delegates. Deliberately, the event was not described as being held under the auspices of any
particular organization.[79] In June 1918, Trotter chose not to attend a conference of black editors sponsored by the Committee on Public Information (CPI), which was due to finish just three days before the National
Liberty Congress began, and he ignored a request from the MIB to postpone his own gathering so as not to overshadow the editors' conference.
The Northeastern Department military intelligence officer called Trotter
and Allen Whaley, his national organizer, into the Boston MIB office and
warned them that a bitter protest meeting in Washington would give great
heart to German propagandists and might even be manipulated by them
to their advantage. Trotter protested that the conference would be meeting
simply to condemn lynching and demand some of the democracy that black
troops were fighting for in France. He rejected any suggestion that German
agents might influence his plans, saying, "If there was any German money
available, the convention would be very much larger than it will be." He
said he would be "on the look out" for enemy propaganda, and promised
to let the MIB know if he found any.[80]

The National Liberty Congress met from June 24 to 29, 1918, at an African Methodist Episcopal church in Washington, attended by 115 delegates
from twenty-nine states and the District of Columbia. The MIB monitored
the proceedings through a black reporter and acquired a list of the names
and addresses of 111 of the delegates. This list was entrusted to Thomas
Jesse Jones, the Welsh-born Negro Education specialist in the Bureau of
Education of the Interior Department. A former professor at Hampton Institute and also a Phelps-Stokes Fund researcher, Jones was a leading advocate of the philanthropy-led approach to industrial education for African
Americans and was regarded by many black radicals, particularly Du Bois,
with deep suspicion. Jones picked out the names he recognized and marked

thirteen of them as "Loyal." Another twenty-five he marked as "Questionable," including Trotter, Harrison, Whaley, and J. Finley Wilson.[81]

The various speeches delivered during the week constantly related the issue of equal rights to the fact of the war, but they contained no remotely pro-German statements. In keeping with the original idea behind the calling of a race congress, repeated references were made to the incongruity of the ill-treatment of African Americans and the war aims of the government. A black lawyer from Oklahoma, whom Jones had marked down as "Loyal," informed the audience that he had three sons serving in the army in France and ended, "We are going to win this war, but when we win I want the black fingers that are pulling triggers to kill the Hun to be able to make a cross on the ballot in Oklahoma." Hubert Harrison drew an ironic international parallel when he remarked, "They say that the Federal Government cannot protect us here, but they can go over to Serbia, a small place scarcely on the map and re-establish government."[82]

BI agent J. G. C. Corcoran was in no doubt as to the aims of the National Liberty Congress. It had been called

> for the sole purpose of drawing up ridiculous resolutions which later will be presented to Congress with the knowledge that Congress will not pass these bills, so as to lay before the colored people the fact that Congress refused to recognize their legislation. This would give them an opening to get in their pro-German propaganda and activities.[83]

Corcoran was correct in his assumption that the U.S. congress would take little notice of Trotter's demands. Two congressmen with large black constituencies, Martin B. Madden of Chicago and Leonidas C. Dyer of St. Louis, addressed the delegates, and a petition was sent to Capitol Hill calling for an end to the segregation of black federal employees, a guarantee that they would receive equal wages and promotion, an end to segregation on federally controlled public transport (which in time of war included the railroads), and the enforcement of the 13th, 14th, and 15th Amendments, so that there would be "no involuntary servitude, no denial of the equal protection of law, no denial of the exercise of the suffrage because of race, color or previous condition." Finally, Trotter and his supporters called for legislation to make "mob murders . . . a crime against the Federal Government." The petition was read into the record by a congressman from Massachusetts, but otherwise ignored.[84]

BI Chief Bielaski was less interested in what was said at the sessions of the National Liberty Congress than in a report that Hubert Harrison was accompanied throughout by two white men. A black informant, Arthur U. Craig, was put on Harrison's trail, while the District of Columbia police commissioner, R. W. Pullman, promised Corcoran the services of another "high class colored informant," if required. Craig, a Dunbar High School teacher who was temporarily working for the Food Administration, made what Corcoran later described as "a violent investigation to ascertain who these two white men were," posing first as a representative of the CPI and then as a delegate to the conference. (He appeared on the MIB list of delegates as "A. V. Craig," but was awarded neither "Loyal" nor "Questionable" status by Jones.) Craig failed to identify the mysterious white men who attended the daily sessions of the congress, but he quoted Harrison as having said that he was being paid by them. Craig also noted that during one of the sessions the entrance of Herman Moens, the so-called "Dutch Darwin," whom Craig was already investigating for the BI, caused Harrison to "flush and seem greatly excited." After the delegates had left Washington, Corcoran and Craig were keen to pursue the matter of the National Liberty Congress and its origins "to the point where the german [sic] interests are working." Under Bielaski's signature, Corcoran asked the New York BI office to gather information on Harrison and his two white friends, adding, for good measure, that Harrison was connected with virtually every facet of the German propaganda among blacks that had been alleged since April 1917.[85]

In September 1918, another informant, John E. Bowles, an employee of the Bureau of Mines, was briefed to cover the National Equal Rights League's Eleventh Annual Convention in Chicago. As instructed, he got to know one of Harrison's Washington contacts, Joseph Stewart, whose law office was described by Corcoran as "a base for *german* [sic] *propaganda* among the negroes of this city." Bowles ventured that Stewart was "a sly old fox [who] has got to be fed with a long handle spoon." Although Bowles secured a letter of introduction to Harrison from Stewart, he was not in the end selected to cover the NERL convention because Corcoran's superiors feared that he might "not 'shoot square.'" Arthur Craig, who Corcoran asserted was "commonly known to be a $1.00 man," was hired again.[86] Craig spent five days in Chicago, incurring fifty dollars in expenses, and filed a brief account of the convention a week after his return. He had been unable to enter the daily sessions, as only thirty delegates had turned up—too few to allow him to wander in unnoticed—so he attended only the public evening meetings. He heard Ida Wells-Barnett denounce the executions of the Houston rioters and a speech by an Irish nationalist whom she had invited along. Trotter's address was unremarkable and Hubert Harrison did not appear. The only item of interest and future significance was the announcement that the NERL was planning to organize another conference, at which a delegation would be elected to travel to the post-war peace negotiations, to draw attention to the imperfections of American democracy.[87]

A few weeks later, the difficulty that white officials often had in distinguishing among the different black political groupings was exemplified by Corcoran's assumption that when a body called the National Race Congress attracted six hundred delegates in Washington on October 1, 2 and 3, 1918, this was an unexpectedly swift return by Trotter and an offshoot of the NERL. In fact, the National Race Congress (NRC) was a different organization entirely, founded in Washington in 1915 and led by the Rev. William H. Jernagin, a Mississippi-born son of former slaves. Although Jernagin was described as a "rock the boat type" by Craig, the NRC's leadership of clergymen, academics, and other professionals was more conservative and affluent than that of the NERL.[88] Woodrow Wilson plainly found the NRC more palatable than the NERL, for although he had expressed some misgivings about Jernagin a year earlier, he agreed to meet the NRC delegation that called at the White House on October 3, 1918. According to the NRC's own account of the meeting, the delegation presented their grievances in language so "chaste, lucid, sympathetic, positive, forceful and replete" that Wilson "was moved to tears." Be that as it may, he was not so overcome as to be swayed from one of his standard evasions, in which he

> assured the delegation that the spokesman had interpreted his spirit and that he would do everything that was in his power to righten all wrongs complained of and would hasten as fast as he could the kind and sort of democracy that he stood for and that the spokesman mentioned.[89]

One of the most eloquent protests that attracted government attention during the war was made by Kelly Miller of Howard University. In August 1917 he sent Woodrow Wilson a twenty-three-page letter, later published as *The Disgrace of Democracy,* condemning the refusal of the United States government to protect African Americans against racial violence or defend their civil rights, in spite of their willingness to serve their country. Miller told the president of their disappointment that he had "preserved a lukewarm aloofness from the tangled issues of this problem."[90] On several occasions during the following year, BI and MIB agents suggested that *The Disgrace of Democracy* constituted disloyal propaganda. In February 1918, a Washington BI agent bought a copy at a newsstand in Alexandria, Va., and extracted several questionable passages: "The white people of this country are not good enough to govern the Negro. . . . The vainglorious boast of Anglo-Saxon superiority will no longer avail to justify these outrages. . . . Reproach is to be cast upon your contention for democratization of the world, in the face of its lamentable failure at home." The agent concluded that Miller's words could have "but one effect, that of further stimulating the propaganda among the Negroes of this country, which has formed the subject of so many reports previously made."[91] Chief Bielaski passed the report to Van Deman, who told Walter Loving to follow it up. Having already interviewed Miller about the pamphlet in November 1917, and "kept a keen eye" on him since, Loving had been allowed to read many of Miller's subsequent articles prior to publication and followed the accounts of his many speeches across the country, but had found nothing objectionable to report. Loving now returned to Howard University to explain the latest complaints to Miller, who claimed he had been quoted out of context and that neither from the White House, where receipt of *The Disgrace of Democracy* had been acknowledged by Wilson's secretary, nor from the Senate, where it was read into the record, had he heard any adverse comment. He said he had offered his services to the government as soon as the United States declared war, had helped to create the training camp for black officers, and had crossed the country giving patriotic speeches to black soldiers. He told Loving, "I confess that I am somewhat surprised and disappointed on finding myself under surveillance by the Intelligence Department of the government." Nevertheless, he thanked Loving for his openness and for showing him the comments of the BI. Loving told Van Deman afterward that he was sure Miller had "been made to see his mistake," that he was "now endeavoring to make amends for the same," and that Loving would continue watching him to make sure. Although the tenor of Miller's speeches to black troops in Texas was to cause the MIB some alarm in July 1918, Loving's verdict was accepted by the War Department.[92]

The Justice Department was determined to persist in its active investigation of Miller. Between August 1918 and January 1919, the Boston BI office tried to trap him into violating the Espionage Act after a tip that *The Disgrace of Democracy* was being distributed in the city's black districts by people whose motives were "not in keeping with patriotic sentiments today." A BI agent obtained a copy from leading black lawyer William H. Lewis, a Harvard-educated Tuskegee-ite, who believed that Miller was unlikely to be involved in disloyal propaganda.[93] After reading it, the agent concluded that although Miller may have only wanted

> to put the negro question before the American Government in a manner which the general public might understand, . . . [it] must find willing readers amongst our enemies, who would be interested to start propaganda through the aid and under cover of the negro question.[94]

The fact that the pamphlet was available through the mails was, according to the agent, "clearly a breach of the Espionage Act." In order to "substantiate these facts," he wrote to Miller, giving his home address rather than the BI office, asking for five further copies of *The Disgrace of Democracy*, and posing as a would-be distributor. When they arrived, the agent consulted the chief clerk of the Post Office Inspection Department, who sent it to Washington. Despite requesting a prompt decision on whether Miller had committed an offense, the Boston BI office had to wait until January 1919 before Lamar announced that no action was to be taken.[95]

The U.S. government's real fear so far as black pressure groups were concerned during the war was openly articulated during the Justice Department's discussions about Kelly Miller's *Disgrace of Democracy*. The degree of credibility accorded by government officials to reports which spoke of direct cooperation between malcontent blacks and German agents fluctuated throughout the war, and it probably rose during periods when they were receiving a large number of reports about enemy espionage activity generally. One panicky, knee-jerk assumption typical of many middle-ranking officials (and many anxious citizens) was that demands by blacks for better treatment were the result of direct German subversion or, at least, evidence of an embedded black sympathy with enemies of the United States. Black dissent, it was argued, had to be curbed immediately and, if necessary, harshly. This view was common in BI field offices and district attorneys' offices. Another view, less paranoid but no less uncomplimentary to African Americans, was that they had simply decided to screw as many concessions out of the government as they could at a time when the United States was under pressure. This view tended to dominate among senior civil servants in Washington. For example, in February 1918, the U.S. attorney at Wilmington, N.C., sent Bielaski a copy of *The Disgrace of Democracy*, which he conceded did not appear to violate the law, but which he suspected might have been distributed in the South "as a means of creating dissatisfaction with the Government" on behalf of pro-German interests.[96] In reply, a BI lawyer assured him that there was no known pro-Germanism behind Miller's pamphlet, nor, as far as the BI's investigations had shown, behind any other such material:

> This investigation, so far as it has been carried, would indicate that the negroes are not really endeavoring to disseminate any pro-German views, but are taking advantage of the present existing conditions to force Federal legislation to prevent lynchings, and also for recognition of themselves upon the same plane as the whites.[97]

The most substantial equal rights organization investigated by the government during the war, and the one which provoked the greatest level of indignation on the part of white southerners, was the National Association for the Advancement of Colored People. The interest of the Department of Justice in the activities of the NAACP reached a peak in the spring of 1918, but on several earlier occasions Bielaski and his assistants contemplated a full-scale investigation.

The earliest Justice Department inquiry during the war into the activities of the NAACP was initiated not by government agents but by a white citizen. In April 1917, the BI's agent in Memphis was contacted via the U.S. district attorney by Bolton Smith, a white real estate dealer and self-styled expert on southern racial problems and the author of a number of pamphlets on the subject. Smith believed black loyalty had been seriously undermined by lynching and, as chairman of the Tennessee Law and Order League, he campaigned for the eradication of mob violence in that state. He was a conservative interracialist of the kind that was emerging in several southern states, seeking black-white cooperation for specific purposes, without advocating any other significant concessions in the area of equal rights and firmly upholding the principle of segregation.[98] Smith would later correspond courteously about race relations with NAACP directors, while simultaneously denouncing the association to patrician southern racists such as Sen. John Sharp Williams.[99] Smith reported that in 1915 he had learned "in a casual way . . . that two young German women were employed on the staff of the 'Crisis'" and that these women "were furiously pro-German, as was to be expected." Smith suggested that these women had conceived the original plot of "the German tampering with the negro." The Memphis agent forwarded Smith's potentially explosive allegation to the New York City BI office and to Washington, adding his own observation that the Memphis BI office kept picking up rumors "concerning an effort to spread German propaganda among the negroes and the best information I have been able to secure is that some of the more intelligent negroes are back of it."[100] A New York agent dispatched to the *Crisis* office on Fifth Avenue to check on Smith's story was assured by Augustus Dill, the general manager, that the journal employed no white people and that it was an utterly loyal publication. This the BI seems to have accepted, for the time being; no routine monitoring of the NAACP was instituted. W. E. B. Du Bois, understandably, regarded the agent's visit as a piece of crude intimidation with its origin in the heart of the Justice Department, but the BI was only following normal bureaucratic procedures and the incident would not have occurred at all but for the mischief and egotism of Bolton Smith.[101]

The Post Office Department began to keep a more systematic watch on the *Crisis* after the East St. Louis riot. In September 1917, Post Office Solicitor W. H. Lamar told the New York City postmaster to send in two copies of all subsequent issues of the magazine.[102] The following month, the BI also noted the impact of the NAACP as protests over East St. Louis continued. After a well-attended "Negro Silent Protest Parade" in Providence, R.I., on October 14, 1917, modeled on the New York City parade of July 28, BI officials in Washington decided it was time to "ascertain just what influences were behind this movement." The Providence agent was told to find out whether it was "a purely local affair," or whether "the movement was fostered by outside influences." He reported that the only "outside influence" he could find was the NAACP.[103]

The BI and the MIB renewed their interest in the NAACP and the *Crisis* in April 1918, and were to maintain it for the rest of the war. This lengthy investigative effort, which ensured continuing government suspicion of the motives of the NAACP for some years to come, originated in the Southwest. After the Houston riot of August 23, 1917, the entire 24th Infantry had been disarmed and ordered to Columbus, N.M., where it was kept under close watch. The two battalions cleared of involvement in the rioting were then sent to camps in Arizona while the initial inquiry took place, before being reunited at Columbus in November 1917. The alarm of white residents of Columbus at the reconcentration of the regiment led the local postmaster to submit for investigation an NAACP leaflet, which he assumed had been dropped by a soldier.[104] The War Department had the leaflet circulated around the southern department of the army, where it was seized upon by the newly appointed commanding officer of the 24th Infantry, Col. Wilson Chase. He insisted that his regiment had behaved well at Columbus, but warned that the influence of the black press, and particularly of the *Crisis*, was dangerous, especially in wartime. He recommended that the NAACP be prosecuted for distributing seditious literature and accused it and other "unpatriotic negro associations" of attempting "to influence the colored people against the white." Summing up for the southern department, a few days after he had authorized the executions of thirteen of the Houston rioters, Maj. Gen. John Ruckman endorsed Chase's comments and predicted that, if NAACP literature was not suppressed, "open mutiny" would be unavoidable.[105]

These recommendations were submitted on January 10, 1918, to the Justice Department, where John Lord O'Brian, one of the attorney general's special assistants in charge of prosecutions under the Espionage Act, took particular interest in the case. He may also have read the January *Crisis*, which contained a bitter protest from Du Bois, prompted by the Houston rioters' executions, in which he denounced the inhumanity of America toward its black people.[106] O'Brian agreed with the War Department's growing belief that the *Crisis* and other black publications, including the *Chicago Defender*, were "objectionable." He believed they were "calculated to stir up the animosity and, thereby, the disloyalty of colored soldiers," but he doubted the wisdom of trying to have them directly suppressed. He favored the prosecution of local distributors of seditious literature, but inquiries revealed that those publications to which the army objected were reaching black soldiers through the mails by subscription, shifting the focus once again to the Post Office.[107]

Postal officials around the country began to make strong complaints about the *Crisis* in the early months of 1918, and eventually, in May, orders were drafted for Lamar's signature declaring both the January and May issues non-mailable under the Espionage Act. The April issue was almost excluded for carrying a fictional dialogue showing how hard it was for many blacks to identify with the American war effort. This item had incensed the official who drew up the orders: "In view of the past record of this paper, . . . the intent of the publisher of the "Crisis" is to keep the negroes from enlisting or otherwise helping in the prosecution of the war." Lamar resisted the temptation to sign the exclusion orders, possibly because the Justice Department may have preferred the option of a prosecution through the federal courts to the normally temporary restrictions available to the Post Office. Whatever the reason, Lamar was content for the time being to leave the question of the *Crisis* to the attorney general's office.[108]

The BI attorney who took over the investigation of the *Crisis* in the summer of 1918, A. H. Pike, clearly wanted to do more than exclude the *Crisis* from the mails. He was convinced that it was a dangerously disloyal and seditious publication, especially when circulated in the South, and actively sought enough evidence to warrant a prosecution under the Espionage Act. After the Columbus complaint, there had been a steady flow of reports from all over the United States alleging that the *Crisis* was the cause of growing tension. In December 1917, the Chicago BI office had passed on a complaint that the *Crisis* was "endeavoring to agitate the negroes" over the Houston affair. Extra grounds for suspicion were said to be that the *Crisis* used white investigators, the implication being that these might be enemy agitators.[109] In April 1918, complaints about the *Crisis* intensified. A Florida BI agent, hinting at the sense of foreboding felt by many white southerners at the deterioration of race relations, submitted a copy of the magazine to the Justice Department because "it seemed as if it might have something to do with the negro unrest found to exist but without [the BI] having been able to find out a cause."[110] The concerns of white citizens of Texas, North Carolina, and Kentucky were also passed on to the BI in Washington by its field agents, the Department of Labor, and U.S. senators. A. H. Pike took all of these complaints seriously.[111]

On instructions from the Justice Department, Earl B. Barnes, the assistant U.S. Attorney in New York City, asked Charles Studin, the NAACP's legal adviser and a board member, to meet him on May 1, 1918. Barnes pointed out those articles in recent issues of the *Crisis* to which the government objected, explaining that the administration "proposes to take steps to prevent propaganda of this kind." This is more likely to have been a reference to the forthcoming Sedition Act than a direct threat to the *Crisis*. Barnes asked to be put on the *Crisis* mailing list and for copies of all the issues published since the U.S. entered the war. Briefed for the meeting by Du Bois, Studin attempted to convince Barnes of the loyalty of the NAACP and its support for the war effort by showing him various pro-war articles from the *Crisis* and friendly letters to Du Bois from Secretary of War Baker. Barnes nevertheless insisted that Du Bois must be told to adopt a more moderate tone, so as not to "create a feeling of dissatisfaction among colored people," and suggested that Studin act as a kind of censor of *Crisis* material, to prevent any "misconstruction" of its aims. The NAACP board, having little choice, accepted this arrangement, and the *Crisis* committee, which included Du Bois, agreed to restrict the magazine's content to constructive criticism.[112]

Three days after Studin's meeting with Barnes, Du Bois told Archibald H. Grimké, president of the NAACP's Washington branch, that he "would not dare" to publish the latter's ninety-two-line poem about the Houston executions, since he had "just been specially warned by the Department of Justice that some of our articles are considered disloyal." Du Bois was probably glad to have an excuse to return Grimké's rambling and repetitive poem about the ingratitude shown by the United States toward its black soldiers, the insults suffered by them in the South, and the readiness of the army to side with white civilians rather than its own men. Grimké's biographer, Dickson D. Bruce, has argued that the rejection worsened already strained relations between Du Bois and Grimké, whose Washington branch was a vital cog in the machinery of the NAACP. (The poem was eventually published in the *Messenger* in October 1919.)[113]

For all Studin's assurances that the *Crisis* would give no further cause for concern, A. H. Pike was determined that its publishers should be prosecuted for having, as he saw it, set out deliberately to undermine the morale and loyalty of African Americans, perhaps as part of a carefully conceived German plot. However, he had difficulty in convincing Alfred Bettman, the attorney general's special assistant, who shared responsibility with John Lord O'Brian for prosecutions under the Espionage Act. Since at this time the content and policy of the *Crisis* was nominally controlled by a committee of board members, a prosecution would have entailed action against the board of directors of the NAACP, which included a number of prominent and well-respected white Americans. Bettman could see that black protest could be a cause for concern if "non-participation in war activities or military service should be used as a hold-up weapon to force greater equality of treatment," but he was uneasy about "prosecution of men for membership in groups rather than for their individual actions." He wanted Pike to come up with some concrete evidence that the magazine was deliberately sabotaging the war effort.[114] Instead of this, Pike concentrated on collecting opinions which supported his own belief that publication of the *Crisis* was undesirable in wartime purely because its objectives—equal rights and the suppression of lynching—were controversial and its tone was offensive to many white people. Pike hoped that Bettman would be persuaded to prosecute by the sheer weight of adverse comment.[115]

In the summer of 1918, as further reports came into the BI from its agents about the *Crisis,* almost exclusively from the South, Pike saw to it that those that were critical were annotated by Bielaski and sent to Bettman, while those that suggested the *Crisis* was innocuous were laid aside.[116] The May 1918 issue of the *Crisis,* which was in print before the warning was issued to Charles Studin on May 1, came in for a good deal of criticism from white southerners. The leading editorial, "The Negro and the War Department," drew attention to the army's unwillingness to promote, or even properly train, black officers, and the news sections carried a detailed account of a lynching in Tennessee in February and William Pickens's report on racial discrimination by the YMCA.[117] Officials of both the Justice Department and the War Department regarded reports of this kind as, at best, unnecessarily demoralizing for black readers, and, at worst, a form of German propaganda.

An Atlanta BI agent obliged Pike by reporting that the May *Crisis* carried articles "which tend to excite the negro race in this section against the white people" and that this had nearly caused a riot between black and white soldiers at Camp Gordon, near Atlanta, and the BI's man in Waco, Tex., identified the *Crisis* as the kind of propaganda that had caused the Houston riot nine months earlier. Bettman began to show more sympathy with Pike's point of view upon receiving information from the U.S. attorney at Roanoke, Va., that black preachers in that area were giving out the *Crisis* free of charge and that this distribution was intended "to stir up the negroes and make them disloyal"; it was felt this might connect with reports that blacks in western Virginia were holding secret meetings at night. Bettman concluded that the May issue did not violate the Espionage Act and that its prosecution was not warranted

> without proof, outside of the periodical itself, of enemy or hostile origin, instigation, financing or purpose, [but] . . . the fact that the periodical is distributed free of charge is suspicious and warrants running down the source of the financial support of the periodical and of its distribution.[118]

Pike, armed with this opinion, and with his conviction strengthened by further warnings from the commanding officer of the 24th Infantry "that possibly enemy propoganda [*sic*] may be behind the publication," alerted the BI's agents in New York City and Virginia. He warned them that because

of reports of free distribution of the *Crisis* "it is thought that German propagandists may be using this magazine in their work," but only the Norfolk
office was told that the *Crisis* had not yet violated any federal law.[119] The
hard-pressed New York office passed the matter on to the APL for investigation.

Pike's initial surge of anti-*Crisis* activity was abruptly ended when on June
5, 1918, Bettman told Bielaski that "nothing should be done which would
lead to prosecution." He had talked to Maj. Joel Spingarn, the chairman
of the NAACP, who had recently been posted to military intelligence and
was in the early stages of an imaginative, but doomed, initiative within the
MIB designed to improve American race relations. Spingarn had assured
Bettman that the *Crisis* was "a genuinely negro publication . . . [having] no
connection whatsoever with an enemy source" and that he had spoken to
Du Bois, who had "promised to change the tone."[120] For the time being, the
BI's interest in the *Crisis* lapsed and Bettman's views prevailed. Nevertheless, the fact that for the first half of 1918 the *Crisis* had been the subject
of numerous reports suggesting an epidemic of pro-German agitation
among blacks caused the magazine to become firmly associated in the
minds of BI field agents and some Justice Department central officials with
the myth of enemy-inspired subversion of American race relations. As a
result, general reports concerning "German Propaganda among the Negroes in Harlem" or a lack of enthusiasm for the war shown by black house-
maids on Long Island—containing no mention of the *Crisis,* Du Bois, or
the NAACP—were filed in Washington with material on the journal, as if
the probability of a connection was taken for granted.[121]

The reports compiled by the New York City branch of the APL are
significant in that, when compared with others, they demonstrate how
much the APL differed regionally, in both its thoroughness and the racial
attitudes of its members. Whereas the typical southern APL member regarded Jim Crow laws and white supremacy as part of the Americanism
which he was sworn to protect from subversive influences, northern APL
agents, especially in New York, often took a more liberal view of black protest against lynching and other abuses. The reports also show that, at the
local level at least, the APL may have been less impressed by the urgency
of amassing evidence against non-German groups than were the BI and the
MIB. The first APL investigation of the *Crisis* was made in response to an
original report from the San Antonio BI office, which described the journal
as "seditious literature."[122] A New York APL agent, W. T. Carothers, visited

the *Crisis* offices in early June and "had a very satisfactory talk with A. G. Dill (colored), Business Manager, regarding their activities and sentiments." Dill was able to satisfy Carothers that the NAACP supported the war effort wholeheartedly. Carothers concluded that while the *Crisis* might sometimes "express ideas rather heated and critical of the treatment accorded their race," it was not being deliberately disloyal. He went to the trouble of asking A. Philip Randolph and Chandler Owen of the *Messenger* for their opinion of the NAACP and the *Crisis*. Randolph and Owen, by no means supporters of the NAACP, wrote to Carothers defending its motives and describing the contents of the *Crisis* as "very largely propaganda of a truthful and service-able nature" and judging Du Bois and Dill to be "able." They also insisted that there was

> no pro-German movement among Negroes—organized or unorganized. But there is great discontent with the lynching, disfranchisement, segre-gation, Jim Crowism and all kinds of discrimination practised against col-ored people, especially at a time when they are fighting and dying side by side with their white fellow citizens.[123]

The editors of the *Messenger* also let the Department of Justice know what they thought of its investigative methods hitherto:

> May we now, in closing, congratulate this new method the Department of Justice has adopted of going directly to intelligent, honorable and capable colored and white people, to ascertain information. It is the only proper way. . . . We trust your Department will continue this and dispense with ignorant white or colored detectives, sneaks and scheming politicians as sources of information.[124]

This gave Carothers "much satisfaction" and he concluded that they had expressed "concisely the prevalent feelings held by colored people."[125]

In his second report, following Pike's request that the New York BI office look into the possibility that German propaganda work included distribu-tion of the *Crisis,* Carothers provided detailed information about the maga-zine's income and circulation. Again, he was convinced that it was backed by a sincere organization, committed to much-needed reforms.[126] It is ironic that the most objective, accurate, and unsensational reports filed with the Department of Justice about the *Crisis* in this period should have come from an essentially amateur organization with a deserved reputa-tion for overzealous spy-hunting and exaggeration, while the professionals chased after and fueled rumors that Germany was manipulating the African-American population. Indeed, by the summer of 1918, even the most mundane NAACP activity, such as a visit by Mary White Ovington to Omaha, Neb., to help organize a local branch, was being monitored by the BI.[127]

The final burst of BI activity concerning the NAACP was concentrated in the South, allowing A. H. Pike once again to draw the attention of the Department of Justice to the inadvisability of allowing NAACP literature to circulate freely. The episode also revealed the firm conviction of the BI, if not the Department of Justice as a whole, that putting forward a doctrine of racial equality in a part of the country where it was wholly unacceptable to the white population was so subversive and disloyal in wartime that it might well be a form of German propaganda. In August 1918, the APL branch in Birmingham, Ala., reported on recent events connected with the NAACP. The Rev. J. G. Robinson, a local NAACP organizer, speaking to drafted blacks on their way to an army training camp, was alleged to have told them that he had just returned from seeing Woodrow Wilson in Washington and that the president had said, "with tears streaming down his face," that he knew southern blacks were being denied their rights and that, if the whites would not grant them, then "'some colored leader is going to spring up like a flame in the night and lead a revolution that cannot be stopped until you get your rights.'" (Robinson had indeed seen Wilson, as part of an AME Church delegation on March 14, 1918, but the account of the meeting that he was alleged to have given in his speech, with its intriguing reference to Wilson's tears—just as Jernagin's NRC delegation would report in October—was rather more dramatic than the account he published a year later. Then, he had Wilson expressing great admiration for the wartime efforts of African Americans and promising that "full citizenship rights" would be their reward.[128]) Robinson was further alleged to have urged his Alabama audience to fight well in France and then "take the rifles with which you have whipped the Germans and blow hell out of the prejudice of the South." How much of this was exaggeration on the part of the witness is impossible to tell, but it was sufficiently provocative to help convince certain BI officials that the NAACP should no longer be allowed to operate in the South.[129]

At about the same time, the Birmingham APL found a disturbing circular which originated in Montgomery. It was addressed to "Slackers and Traitors, Spreaders of German Propaganda, Fighters against World Wide Democracy" and purported to be from the Royal Demon of the Mysterious Order of Dragons, "organized to create a love of Country, Race and Fair Play"—apparently a secret black fraternal order. The circular contained a passionate declaration of the loyalty of African Americans to their country and a demand that white southerners repay this loyalty with "Fair Play, Justice in the Courts—A Place among Men." White residents of Montgomery were asked to give blacks the same chance as any other ethnic group, and instances of generous contributions by southern blacks to the Liberty Loans were cited. (The same figures had also appeared in the July *Crisis*.) Despite the overall patriotic tone of this leaflet, this kind of insistence on rights by blacks was guaranteed to arouse the white population, especially when voiced by an anonymous and possibly vengeful-sounding sect.[130] The Birmingham APL alerted its division chief in Atlanta, who passed on the report to the Atlanta BI office, which in turn informed Washington. On October 22, the BI in Birmingham sent a black undercover agent, W. L. Hawkins, to investigate the Montgomery leaflets. Hawkins spent over a week in Montgomery, interrupted by an outbreak of Spanish influenza, attempting to find out who had printed and distributed the leaflets. Posing as "a man who believed in doing all I could for the uplifting of my race," he acquainted himself with local NAACP officials and concluded that they were probably responsible for the leaflets.[131]

Meanwhile, the BI's Montgomery agent, J. S. Edson, was instructed by Washington to investigate the Rev. J. G. Robinson. Edson suspected a connection between the tone of Robinson's speech and the "Dragons" leaflet, which he reckoned had been printed by the local black paper, the *Emancipator*. Robinson had left the area, however, and the investigation was hampered by a complete lack of cooperation between the Montgomery APL and the Montgomery BI, and between the latter and the Birmingham BI. The "Dragons" leaflet had "created some alarm" in Montgomery and led to a conference of city officials, the local APL, and the state council of defense, after which the Montgomery APL chief refused to tell Edson anything, although the APL operated nationally under the auspices of the Department of Justice. Edson then met Hawkins, the black infiltrator from the Birmingham BI office, who refused to give any information because he "was under instructions to talk to no white man, except Mr. Fred Gormley of the Council of Defense." Edson traveled to Birmingham to see the BI's special-agent-in-charge, but got no further information from him. Further confused by a letter from military intelligence stating that it was "not expedient to deal formally with Robinson for flagrantly misquoting the President," Edson wrote to Bielaski asking "upon what theory, if any, the Government is interested." He received a reply after the Armistice, when the national directors of the APL in Washington forwarded their Atlanta file on Robinson and the NAACP to the Justice Department. Pike explained to Edson that the BI had "been making an investigation with a view to learning whether or not any enemy interests were behind this negro propaganda."[132]

Pike made one last effort in November 1918 to get Alfred Bettman to take action against the NAACP. Under Bielaski's signature, he forwarded to Bettman the material on Robinson and the NAACP in the South and added a report by the Atlanta APL on local NAACP recruitment in August 1918. On the advice of the local U.S. attorney, the APL was looking out for "anything that may be circulating among the negroes of a harmful nature," and submitted, as examples of its vigilance, two advertisements for the weekly Atlanta NAACP meetings. Pike ignored a much more specific report by an Atlanta BI agent, who had an NAACP meeting covered by a black undercover agent and concluded that there was no attempt to spread ill feeling between the races and that the NAACP was not engaged in any German propaganda.[133] Pike reminded Bettman that his decision not to prosecute the *Crisis* had been contingent upon the NAACP keeping its promise to the Justice Department "to eliminate all objectionable literature and endeavour to confine its activities to legitimate work among the negroes." As far as Pike was concerned, and his view probably reflected that of the majority of BI agents and other officials in the South: agitation in wartime to eradicate lynching and dismantle barriers to black advancement did not qualify as "legitimate work among the negroes." The NAACP recruitment leaflets, urging blacks to fight for their rights, and the "Mysterious Order of Dragons" leaflet were, Pike asserted, "of a very doubtful character for circulation at this time, especially in the South."[134] Bettman, perhaps hopeful that with the end of the war in Europe the matter would be forgotten, did not hurry to reply. When he did, in January 1919, he firmly quashed any suggestion that the NAACP should be prosecuted for anything said or done during the war. Regarding the material Pike had sent, he declared himself "very thoroughly of the opinion that there is nothing therein contained which warrants any further action by this Department." It related "exclusively to the domestic treatment of the negro" and, in its frequent urgings of loyalty to the U.S., it seemed to Bettman "to tend to encourage rather than discourage military service of negroes."[135]

The Surveillance of African-American Leadership

As a proportion of the black press in the United States, the range of journals which attracted the unfriendly attention of the government's investigative agencies during the war was limited, but it included some of the most forward-looking and widely read newspapers and magazines—publications which forcefully denounced all racial discrimination and which after the war were to herald the emergence of the "New Negro." Their editors put the concerns of their own race first, refused to behave subserviently toward whites, and advocated responding to racial violence with equal ferocity. The simmering anger which the investigation of the black press and organizations such as the NERL revealed evidently came as a surprise to most of the government officials involved and helped to convince them that the black population as a whole was becoming increasingly volatile and militant in thought and, imminently perhaps, in deed. This was a distorted view, for journals like the *Crisis* and the *Messenger* attempted to be leaders of black opinion, rather than mere reflections of it. Nevertheless, they undoubtedly represented an increasingly politically conscious black community.

Perusal of the black press tended to arouse in the white officials who undertook it, many of whom plainly regarded demands for equality with considerable personal distaste, a belief that such protest should be swiftly quelled—by open persuasion and subtle threats, if possible; otherwise, by federal prosecution. During the war, most government officials equated true patriotism—"100% Americanism"—with completely uncritical support for the administration. Justice and War Department officials reacted with irritation, tinged with considerable racial prejudice, to suggestions that the United States ought to put its own house in order before attempting to secure democracy abroad by force. Even more galling to federal officers was that, by coupling discussions of the contribution of blacks to the war effort to demands for equality and by advising readers that American entry into the war could turn out to be to their advantage, some journals seemed to be implying that black support for the war was conditional and should be withdrawn if these demands were not met. At best, this was regarded as impertinent and selfish; at worst, it was seen as tangible evidence that German efforts to undermine black loyalty had succeeded.

The more rational and less alarmist views of Alfred Bettman were shared by only a minority of officials, but they were decisive in preventing widespread prosecutions that would plainly have been based on political denunciation rather than evidence of actual offences against the law. Bettman and many others who had come to Washington in wartime returned to their previous occupations within a few months of the Armistice, leaving behind bureaucrats who were still convinced that the loyalty of African Americans could not be taken for granted and that they were especially susceptible to the approaches of subversive alien agitators. Just as black civil rights agitation during the war was frequently attributed to German intrigue, so the same analysis, which presumed that black people were gullible and that lynching, disfranchisement, and segregation were not appalling enough to explain the level of protest, led the government's investigators in 1919 to attribute renewed demands for equal rights to the malign influence of the new alien threat—Bolshevism.

Five

W. E. B. Du Bois, Joel Spingarn, and Military Intelligence

In the summer of 1918, NAACP chairman Joel Spingarn, now a major in the U.S. Army, seized the opportunity of an unexpected posting to the MIB to put forward a "constructive programme" to transform the work of military intelligence on racial issues. In so doing, he was attempting to exploit the peculiar circumstances of the national emergency and the expansion of federal powers during World War I. One of his central aims was the passage of a bill to make lynching in wartime a federal offense, while his other, more modest, initiatives were designed to lessen discrimination and raise black morale generally. The official reaction to the arguments he advanced in support of his ideas sheds light on the reluctance of Woodrow Wilson's Democratic administration to develop a policy on race relations. It also suggests some of the problems and hazards facing a would-be reformer working from within, since the two unintended outcomes of Spingarn's efforts were the consolidation of the MIB's view of African Americans as a potentially disloyal group and the precipitation of an ideological crisis within the equal rights movement in general and the NAACP in particular. During his eleven-week spell in the MIB, Spingarn displayed characteristic resourcefulness and imagination in promoting fundamental reforms within a conservative and hostile bureaucracy, but his efforts were ultimately counterproductive.

Although racial equality was not a primary concern of the Progressive movement, the leaders of the NAACP during World War I included many influential and energetic reformers of the kind Nancy Weiss has called "social justice progressives."[1] Joel Spingarn was, perhaps, the most committed and radical of these "New Abolitionists." The independently wealthy son of a Viennese Jewish immigrant, Spingarn had achieved scholarly recognition after 1899 as the brightest member of the department of comparative literature at Columbia University. In 1911, however, when he opposed infringements of academic freedom, he was fired by university president

Nicholas Murray Butler. Spingarn nevertheless continued to publish literary criticism, poetry, and botanical tracts. He became the first chairman of the New York branch of the NAACP in 1911 and was elected national chairman in 1914. Until his death in 1939, he served the association as chairman, treasurer, and, finally, president. In politics, he was a Rooseveltian Progressive and a known critic of the Wilson administration, particularly when it extended the segregation of black and white federal employees.[2]

Of all the NAACP's senior white officials, Spingarn was probably the most sympathetic to W. E. B. Du Bois's radical opposition to Tuskegee, and he shared Du Bois's determination to make the *Crisis* a magazine of national importance. Although Spingarn was the younger man, his relationship with Du Bois at times resembled that of an avuncular professor and a gifted, but wayward, junior colleague. In 1914 he told Du Bois, "You have an extraordinary unwillingness to acknowledge that you have made a mistake, and if accused of one, your mind will find or even invent reasons and quibbles of any kind to prove that you were never mistaken." This reproach was intended to be collegial, but Du Bois would not have taken it from any other NAACP director. In December 1916 and January 1917, Spingarn gave Du Bois generous financial help to pay for urgent kidney operations. Thus, although each man respected the other's intellect and opinions and their personal rapport transcended race, Spingarn's influence on Du Bois was probably considerable. In his first autobiography, soon after Spingarn's death, Du Bois wrote, "I do not think that any other white man ever touched me emotionally so closely as Joel Spingarn."[3]

During the first few months of 1918, when black radicalism continued to cause concern to domestic intelligence, particularly as equal rights protest in the black press grew louder, the army general staff showed every sign of sharing the view that black protest was disloyal. However, it also recognized that a rapid deterioration of race relations could harm civilian and military morale and that special measures to avoid deterioration might be needed. The "Counter-Espionage Situation Summary" for the week ending May 18, compiled by the MIB for the War Department, claimed that German agents were actively subverting black loyalty and warned that "every lynching, or other unlawful act against the negroes, tends to assist their labors."[4] Three days later, Spingarn was posted to MI-4, the counterespionage division of the MIB, and given responsibilities covering Bolshevism, the Industrial Workers of the World, and, in particular, "negative intelligence work in matters concerning negro subversion."[5] The General Staff were thus entrusting the task of counteracting the erosion of black loyalty to a well-connected white liberal, with views on race that appealed to African Americans but were anathema to the great majority of white Americans in both the North and South.

At first glance, Joel Spingarn's recruitment into the MIB looks like an aberration, but it was not untypical of Van Deman's methods of expanding his organization and enhancing its expertise. Under the competitive bureau system still operating in the War Department, Van Deman was free to poach newly commissioned army officers to serve as his specialists on key subjects whenever necessary, and after 1917 most intelligence officers were selected for their familiarity with a particular area of work, rather than for their general competence. In March 1918, when the new chief of staff, Gen. Peyton C. March, returned from the front, he began a thorough shake-up of the army's bureaucracy in which the MIB was expanded and reorganized, so that more specialized intelligence subsections could be created.[6] March endorsed Van Deman's policy of recruiting officers with a wide range of civilian experience into the MIB. He later wrote that

> before the war was over its roster resembled a Who's Who of writers. This brilliant collection of educated men and women thus did their bit in the war, in capacities where their brains could be used, instead of being square pegs in round holes, in camp or field, performing duties which could be done better by some husky son of the soil.[7]

When the decision was taken to strengthen the surveillance and counteraction of "Negro Subversion," Van Deman was alerted to Spingarn's availability, possibly by Emmett Scott, who had been asked by Du Bois to find the NAACP chairman a staff posting in Washington after severe ulcers prevented him from sailing with his regiment to France.[8] Spingarn seemed to fit the bill as an unusually well educated officer and a competent administrator, with a keen interest in a key subject, and one who had already given thoughtful advice on black wartime opinion to the MIB via Herbert Parsons in August 1917.

Spingarn accepted the MIB post, believing that he had been given a great opportunity to change government policy and influence black opinion. He had regarded the creation of the black officers' training camp in 1917 as a major victory, and it may have encouraged him to believe that with sufficient pressure the government might bend in other areas. He had already witnessed deliberate efforts by the government to overcome black alienation through the appointment of black professionals, such as Emmett Scott by the War Department and the economist George E. Haynes by the Department of Labor, and the taking of black leaders into the confidence of the government, as in the cases of Robert Russa Moton and, for a time, W. E. B. Du Bois. Spingarn's own presence in Washington, in an agency which enjoyed direct access to the secretary of war, seemed to offer further tantalizing possibilities. Although he saw bolstering black loyalty and dampening equal rights protest in wartime as his chief responsibilities, he also hoped that liberal analyses of racial problems would encourage the government to respond sympathetically to black aspirations.

On his arrival at the MIB, Spingarn initiated the drafting of a bill to make lynching in wartime a federal offense. He then read existing reports on the question of race, before submitting a wide-ranging plan to deal with "Negro Subversion" to the new director of the MIB, Col. Marlborough Churchill, a career artillery officer who succeeded Van Deman when the latter was posted to France after falling out with Peyton C. March. Some of Spingarn's suggestions clearly derived from the earlier analyses of Maj. Walter H. Loving, particularly the idea of a nationwide counterintelligence network within the black population. Citing the expressions of anxiety among African Americans recorded by Loving about the treatment of soldiers, Spingarn called on the War Department to give assurances that black men would be dealt with fairly in France and that more black officers would be trained. He suggested the formation of an "Advisory Committee to the Chief of Staff," composed solely of black representatives, to develop effective methods for countering enemy propaganda. He also called for greater efforts to discourage "vicious anti-negro utterances in [the] white press" and made plans for a conference of black newspaper editors in Washington to rekindle their patriotism. Above all, he stressed the need for President Wilson to declare "that during the war lynching will be regarded as disloyal, and aiding the enemy, since it causes disaffection among 12,000,000 people."[9] This dual approach of propaganda initiatives aimed at blacks and federal action to address their grievances had military relevance, Spingarn claimed, since it would guarantee black participation in the war. However, in linking a "war for democracy" fought in France to the extension of democracy at home, Spingarn was trying to further the aims of the NAACP as much as the war effort. He was one of the few pro-war progressives who referred specifically to the racial dimension when arguing that intervention in Europe would produce reform in American life. Blacks would earn fairer treatment, he believed, through selfless demonstrations of loyal citizenship in wartime. Spingarn was sincere, but his ideas and methods as a military intelligence officer were hastily improvised, unfocused, and overambitious, and his task was made harder by confidential reports, already sitting in the files of the MIB and other federal surveillance agencies, that questioned the loyalty of the NAACP.

In an attempt to counteract these reports and to protect himself, Spingarn made a show of demanding assurances from the NAACP that it recognized its patriotic duty. Over the signature of the MIB director, he warned the NAACP's legal adviser, Charles H. Studin, that the *Crisis* had laid itself open to criticism. Studin was told that the government would deal fairly with grievances, but could "not tolerate carping and bitter utterances likely to foment disaffection and destroy the morale of our people for the winning of the war." He was advised to "make a special effort to eliminate all matter that may render the paper liable to suppression in the future." Studin promised that "no pains" would be spared "to make all future issues of this magazine comply with the wishes of the Government both in letter and spirit." The staff of the *Crisis* and its management committee, he wrote, were "loyal to the last degree" and "their paramount purpose" was to support the war effort. Indeed, because of the national recognition achieved by the NAACP and the influence of its journal, Studin suggested, the association could "render certain services better than other agencies." This was not simply abject groveling; Spingarn was using Studin to sanitize the NAACP. Perhaps unwittingly, Studin also made Spingarn's plans in the MIB more plausible by hinting that NAACP personnel could act as intermediaries between black Americans and the administration.[10]

Spingarn was well aware that the kind of expression routinely identified by MIB officers as "Negro Subversion" was no more than outspoken agitation against discrimination that had nothing to do with disloyalty or pro-Germanism. Nevertheless, he was prepared to exploit the myth of a potential black uprising—a real possibility in the minds of most military intelligence officers and Justice Department agents and of some congressmen —in order to convey the urgency of measures that he claimed would gain the confidence of blacks and secure their support for the government.

Spingarn faced three main obstacles. The first was the reluctance of the Wilson administration to begin substantial intervention on behalf of the black population, which Secretary of War Newton D. Baker had made plain to Du Bois and Emmett Scott in the fall of 1917 in his reference to there being "no intention on the part of the War Department to undertake at this time to settle the so-called race question."[11] Second, as episodes such as the 1913–14 debates on the Smith-Lever agricultural extension bill had shown, conservative and southern opinion in Congress was hostile to measures specifically designed to assist blacks.[12] Clearly, any scheme requiring legislation was going to encounter opposition. Third, Spingarn had to overcome the skepticism of his fellow officers, few of whom shared his view of the war as an opportunity to reform backward aspects of American society, and least of all race relations. Moreover, some officers were plainly hostile to the NAACP; one described the *Crisis* as having "much literature in it which would inflame and stimulate race feeling; it might even be considered a form of German propaganda."[13] Thus Spingarn was never able to present his ideas as the considered and united opinion of military intelligence, and he was vulnerable when his plans began to falter. Spingarn's credentials in the MIB rested on his close connection with the NAACP, yet that connection was to cause his eventual failure. While the NAACP chairmanship gave him nationwide contacts and access to current research, it also allowed his fellow officers to point to the irregularity of a man holding senior positions in both military intelligence and a civilian protest organization.

Spingarn had suggested to Parsons in 1917 that the welfare of black troops be assigned to a special agency, staffed by black officers and a few whites "in whom colored people have implicit confidence."[14] He now resurrected this idea and broadened it so as to address the question of racial discrimination throughout American society. Early in June 1918, he secured approval for the formation of a subsection of MI-4 to do special work on "Negro subversion." He found himself a separate office in the business area of Washington and began identifying eligible black army officers to staff the projected Negro Subversion subsection. He was assisted by Lt. T. Montgomery Gregory, a Howard University instructor who gained a commission after playing a leading role in the fight to establish the training camp at Fort Des Moines. As Spingarn's "constructive programme" gathered pace, any aspect of racial discrimination and prejudice that could be construed as having a bearing on the war, however remote, began to feature in his reports and recommendations.[15]

The "Negro Subversion" subsection maintained direct contact with the secretary of war's office through Emmett Scott, who suggested several projects for Spingarn to undertake. Plans were made to hold an interracial conference at East St. Louis, to head off a predicted recurrence of rioting due to continuing northward migration of black labor. Spingarn and Scott also attempted to prevent the showing of D. W. Griffith's film *The Birth of a Nation* because, they argued, its portrayal of black men as thieves and rapists during Reconstruction was likely to provoke violence and impede the war effort. The Charleston, S.C., intelligence officer was ordered to determine why the distribution of various black newspapers, including the *Chicago Defender*, had been interfered with in Georgia, while the San Antonio, Tex., officer was sent to warn the editors of *K. Lamity's Harpoon* that their articles attacking the conscription of black troops laid them open to prosecution under the Espionage Act.[16]

In order to allay growing fears at home about the conditions experienced by black soldiers in France, Spingarn persuaded the General Staff to cable Pershing in mid-June to ask for a "clear, specific and emphatic" rebuttal of rumors, apparently circulated by German agents, alleging that black troops were being put on the front lines to minimize white casualties and left to die when wounded. In a detailed reply, Pershing showed that so far just twenty-five black soldiers had died, and only two others had serious wounds. Black regiments, he reported, were in high spirits and were "especially amused at the most dangerous positions and . . . desirous of having more active service." Spingarn turned this into a rousing press release, headed "Pershing Nails a Lie."[17]

The contradictions inherent in Spingarn's position—a bold civil rights activist in the most reactionary agency of an anti-radical administration—were reflected in his views on political expression by blacks. Spingarn knew how real their grievances were, but he had misgivings about their being aired during the war and believed an important objective of MIB work on race should be the molding of black opinion. Hence came the elaborate plan he conceived for convening black newspaper editors and other spokesmen, giving them a closed forum in which to impress on government officials the causes and extent of black dissatisfaction, and, in turn, allowing the administration to remind the African-American leadership of its duty to sustain morale and patriotism during the war.

The conference was modeled on the gathering of black leaders hosted by the NAACP in Washington in May 1917. Although credit for the latest conference was claimed by both George Creel of the Committee on Public Information and Newton D. Baker, the idea plainly originated with Spingarn. Through Emmett Scott, he recommended it to Creel as something the CPI could usefully sponsor, so that "Negro public opinion should be led along helpful lines rather than along lines that make for discontentment and unrest." Creel had recently been stung by the charge of the National Committee of Patriotic Societies that he was not doing enough to combat growing German influence among blacks in the South, so he welcomed Spingarn's proposal and offered to pay the traveling costs involved. Creel then tried to get Woodrow Wilson involved, telling the president how eager he was to bring black spokesmen and editors to the White House "for one of your informal talks." He reminded Wilson that the black population had been "torn by rumor and ugly whisperings ever since we entered the war." Their representatives at the conference would be "all loyal and enthusiastic," and meeting the president was, he thought, "just the inspiration they need." Wilson replied that it "probably would do no good. . . . I have received several delegations of negroes and am under the impression that they have gone away dissatisfied." He made his standard evasion concerning his silence on lynching—that he had "never had an opportunity to actually do what I promised them I would seek an opportunity to do"—and asked Creel to carry on without him.[18]

The man who more than anyone had given Wilson cause to be wary of black delegations was William Monroe Trotter. The editor of the *Boston Guardian* had been a persistent thorn in the side of Booker T. Washington and had engaged Wilson in a well-publicized squabble in the Oval Office in 1914.[19] Trotter's National Liberty Congress, jointly organized by the NERL and Hubert Harrison's Liberty League, was due to begin in Washington just a few days after the CPI gathering. Spingarn got the Boston MIB officer to ask the NERL to delay its congress "for four or five months [because] . . . agitation likely to cause trouble at this time must be discouraged." When the officer ill-advisedly showed him Spingarn's letter, Trotter insisted his aims were basically no different from Spingarn's and that it was too late to postpone the NERL gathering. He noted that "Major Spingarn is connected with a white organization for the benefit of the colored people," whereas the NERL was "distinctly a colored man's movement." The Boston field officer reckoned that Trotter wanted "to be a savior of his own race rather than be under obligation to white men," hence his "childish egotism and desire to get into the limelight." Trotter had indicated that he might attend the final day of the CPI conference, in which case, the officer suggested, "some man of very high position in the government" could take him aside and convince him of the need to delay his convention.[20] In the event, Trotter's knowledge that Spingarn of the NAACP was behind an attempt to silence him ensured that he would persevere with his original plans, and gave him ready ammunition and grounds for suspicion concerning later controversies.

The CPI editors' conference consisted of three four-hour sessions in the Department of the Interior building on June 19–21, 1918. Trotter did not show up, but out of the forty-seven men invited, only two others were missing. The great majority of the participants were newspaper and magazine editors, representing thirty-one publications from cities across the nation, with the exception of the west coast. The rest included churchmen, educators, and holders of public office.[21] Women and labor were absent and the South was underrepresented, but Spingarn and Scott had succeeded in convening most of the prominent figures of black America in a forum that cut across political and professional barriers. It was a rare ecumenical opportunity for key individuals normally divided on many issues. In the working sessions, a variety of perspectives were aired and open discrimination was more strongly attacked by some than by others, but the government-imposed agenda produced a general consensus in which black American support for the war was affirmed. Scott set the tone when he opened the proceedings with a reminder of why they had been brought together: "This is not the time to discuss race problems. Our first duty is to fight, and to continue to fight until the war is won. Then we can adjust the problems that remain in the life of the colored men. This is the doctrine we are teaching to the Negroes of the country."[22]

The black leaders were addressed by Newton D. Baker, George Creel, Franklin D. Roosevelt, and representatives of the Shipping Board and the Food Administration. Spingarn, who stayed in the background as much as possible, arranged for his younger brother, Arthur, a captain in the Medical Corps, to deliver a message from the surgeon general, asking the editors to alert soldiers and draft registrants to the dangers of venereal disease. Three senior French army officers described the contribution of African colonial troops to the French war effort. According to Joel Spingarn, they made "a deep impression on the conference, and perhaps no other incident created so much enthusiasm." Between official speeches, he allowed general debates to take place "so as to permit each man to 'let off steam' as much as he desired, and to guide the discussion in the right direction."[23]

The conference produced two documents, an "Address to the Committee on Public Information" and a "Bill of Particulars." The former, for Creel to give to the president, was signed by all who attended but was primarily the work of W. E. B. Du Bois and reflected his own views. It stated an "unalterable belief" that Germany's defeat was "of paramount importance to the welfare of the world in general" and of black people in particular. The signatories promised, "as students and guides of public opinion among our people," to do their utmost to keep blacks "at the highest pitch, not simply of passive loyalty, but of active, enthusiastic and self-sacrificing participation in the war." They were grateful for all indications that their citizenship was valued, such as the service of black officers in France, but there were signs at home that "justifiable grievances" were producing,

> not disloyalty, but an amount of unrest and bitterness which even the best efforts of [Negro] leaders may not be able to always guide unless they have the active and sympathetic cooperation of the National and State governments. German propaganda among us is powerless, but the apparent indifference of our own government may be dangerous.[24]

Prompt government action was sought in three areas to raise black morale. Foremost was racial violence. The fact that seventy-one lynchings had taken place since the United States declared war, without the conviction for murder of a single mob member, was "indescribably depressing." The situation required "a strong clear word on lynching from the President of the United States" and federal legislation to stamp it out. Second, the successive refusals of the Red Cross to accept black nurses, the civil service to hire black stenographers, and the navy to recruit black sailors were condemned. Finally, the conference raised the question of segregation on the railroads. Under the wartime Railroad Administration, Jim Crow seemed to have federal sanction, so that blacks felt "with special keenness the injustice of first-class fares and third-class accommodation and frequent other embarrassing discriminations." The spokesmen stressed that they were "not seeking to hold-up a striving country and a distracted world by pushing irrelevant personal grievances as a price for loyalty." The black American was "willing to do his full share in helping to win the war for democracy," but he expected "his full share of the fruits thereof." All he wanted was "that minimum of consideration which will enable him to be an efficient fighter for victory."[25] The "Bill of Particulars," echoing Woodrow Wilson's Fourteen Points, specified fourteen required reforms and was circulated among the heads of various government departments and bureaus.[26]

Joel Spingarn reported to the MIB that the conference "conformed throughout" to the organizers' intentions. "Heated argument was not infrequent," he admitted, "but on the whole the tone of the discussion was sober and statesmanlike." The editors "were pleased at having been taken into the confidence of the Government and asked for advice and cooperation." Nearly all of their grievances could be removed "without any fundamental social readjustments," he argued, and it was "the part of military statesmanship to remedy as many as possible of them at this time."[27] He drafted a more sober account for Churchill to submit to the General Staff, conceding that the proceedings seemed to "confirm the existence of widespread unrest among the colored people." German agents may have been responsible "in isolated cases, but the real causes [were] more fundamental." Since the United States had entered the war in Europe, Spingarn explained, "a reaction against Dr. Washington's more conciliatory attitude has set in and been diffused throughout the colored world. This would have taken place even if we had not declared war on Germany; it is due to consciousness of their inferior status on the part of large masses of negroes, for the first time in American history." Granting the black leaders' demands, he concluded, "would stimulate negro morale to an extraordinary degree," whereas refusal would leave them unable to deliver black support for the war. Both Peyton C. March and Newton D. Baker noted this report.[28]

George Creel's analysis of the conference was less thoughtful, but overall he was satisfied, assuring Wilson that "after the first day of ugly feeling" (when Creel had spoken), the event produced "all that we could have wished for in the way of support and understanding."[29] Soon afterward, he hired one of the participating journalists, Ralph W. Tyler of the *Cleveland Advocate,* the secretary-founder of the National Colored Soldiers Comfort Committee, to work for the CPI in France as the only official black war correspondent. Tyler's longstanding Tuskegee connections made him the natural choice.[30]

Spingarn's prediction that the conference would have a dramatic effect on black opinion proved overoptimistic, although its coverage in the black press was mostly favorable. The editors of the papers that had been represented obediently based their reports on Emmett Scott's press release. "Dignity and unity were the predominating features" of the "epoch-making" conference, according to the *Washington Bee,* while the *Baltimore Afro-American* applauded Scott's "admirably-tempered addresses." According to the MIB officer at St. Louis, the event "had a salutary effect" on *St. Louis Argus* editor John E. Mitchell, who had earlier been warned by military intelligence to tone down his crusading editorials. Mitchell declared that the black leaders called to Washington "to deliberate on the destiny of a race and the welfare of a nation" had "been signally honored by the nation of which they and their people were a part." The *Argus* stated that the black press now had a dual role to play in wartime, "keeping morale high, as well as fighting for justice."[31]

An entirely different perspective on the conference was given by William Monroe Trotter when his National Liberty Congress met a few days later. He told the delegates, "Quite a number of people tried to stop this congress from convening in Washington, but we could not be stopped by a Jew, nor by a Jim Crow Negro"—meaning Spingarn and Scott. Another speaker, also from Boston, said, "We do not want a Jew to represent our race, we have competent colored men for our leaders," and accused Scott ("this self-styled leader") of luring "a number of colored editors to come to Washington to be wined and dined at the Government's expense for the sole purpose of muzzling them."[32]

Despite such lingering suspicion and dissent among black radical activists, the editors' conference provided Spingarn with the foundation for his two most ambitious projects, the virtually single-handed attempt to secure the passage of a federal anti-lynching law and the recruitment of W. E. B. Du Bois to help run a special subsection of military intelligence devoted to racial matters.

Of all his ideas as an intelligence officer, the anti-lynching law was the one that owed most to the existing policy of the NAACP. It also had a certain amount of support already on Capitol Hill. Two bills for the extension of federal jurisdiction to cases of mob violence had been introduced in 1918, by Rep. Leonidas C. Dyer (R-Mo.) and Rep. Merrill Moores (R-Ind.). However, both bills, and especially Dyer's, several versions of which were reintroduced on subsequent occasions, had drawn conservative and southern objections that they threatened to infringe states' rights and were unconstitutional.[33] A further southern complaint, repeated throughout the interwar period whenever anti-lynching bills were debated, was that such legislation would remove the only effective deterrent against rape by black men, in spite of the reality that fewer than one-fifth of lynch-mob victims were accused of rape, let alone demonstrably guilty.[34] Some of the congressional reservations were shared by the administration. Even after the particularly barbaric lynching of Jim McIllheron, tortured and burned to death at Estill Springs, Tenn. (on Lincoln's birthday, and only two days after the lynching of another black man in the same town), the Justice Department's

W. E. B. Du Bois, Joel Spingarn, and Military Intelligence

response to the protests of the NAACP had been that Supreme Court decisions left the government with "absolutely no jurisdiction." Moreover, the attorney general argued, lynchings were not "connected with the war in such a way as to justify the action of the Federal Government under the war power." Equally discouraging, from Spingarn's point of view, was the War Department's decision in August 1917 that the lynching of William Page, a drafted black man, at Lilian, Va., was a crime against that state, and not against the federal government.[35] Spingarn nevertheless promoted his bill as an emergency wartime measure to eradicate behavior that was destroying black loyalty and playing into the hands of German propagandists.

The idea that the war made federal legislation to suppress lynching timely was not especially new, nor was it peculiar to Spingarn and the NAACP, having already been called for by religious organizations, congressmen, and the liberal press. In February 1918 the New England Baptist Missionary Convention's Committee on the State of the Country had resolved, "It is the merest folly to wait until the war is over to ask for a real place in a real democracy. If the President can give his influence on the side of woman suffrage as a war measure, it is but fair for us to ask the same for racial justice in the South as a war measure." Three weeks prior to Spingarn's transfer to the MIB, Leonidas Dyer had asked the House to consider the contrast between the U.S. government's eagerness to crush tyranny abroad and its refusal to act against lynch mobs at home.[36] And in the first week of June, the New York weekly, *Outlook*, had commented,

> Lynching is recognized by an increasing number of people as a danger to National safety and to success in the war. It is treason to the country to do anything which will take the heart out of [black troops] and make them feel that they have no country. Is there anything that would be more likely to do that than to allow Negroes at home to be murdered by mobs?[37]

The suggestion that the MIB had a law-making role was not new, either, since it had an active Legislative Branch. There, Spingarn found an ally in Capt. George Sanford Hornblower, a New York lawyer in civilian life. Within four days of Spingarn's arrival, Hornblower had drafted a bill to punish lynching, "in so far as such crimes tend to prevent the success of the United States in war." The draft provided that participants in a riot that resulted in the death of an employee of the United States, or a person liable to military service, or any prisoner of the United States, or "the dependent wife, brother, sister, father, mother, son, daughter, nephew or niece, whether whole or half blood, of any person in the military or naval forces of the United States, shall be deemed guilty of a capital offense against the United States."[38] The NAACP president, Moorfield Storey, one of the country's leading jurists—who had criticized the Dyer and Moores bills for their reliance on the Fourteenth Amendment, which the Supreme Court had decided only covered "encroachment by the states" upon the rights of citizens—thought that Hornblower's reliance on the war powers granted to the federal government in Article 1 of the Constitution and the new bill's War Department origins gave it a fair chance of enactment and efficacy. He also liked the absence of any mention of race and advised the NAACP not to arouse southern opposition by overt lobbying.[39]

Without the MIB's prior knowledge, Spingarn and Hornblower appeared on June 6 before the House Committee on the Judiciary, after Dyer invited them to a hearing on his bill. Spingarn testified that military intelligence was interested because it had gathered "evidence of a great deal of bitterness among the colored people as a result of lynching." He thought Dyer's bill was excellent, but argued that the situation demanded a law that was "distinctly a war measure intended to accelerate the prosecution of the war, and nothing else." The two officers presented their own bill to the committee. To justify such sweeping legislation, Spingarn went to some lengths to portray the black population as demoralized and an easy target for German propagandists. He claimed to know that spies were busy circulating false rumors about the treatment of black soldiers, while Hornblower added general remarks about "a great class . . . of ignorant persons easily reached by a lying propaganda of secret enemy agents."[40] Spingarn stated that this was not a sectional phenomenon—disaffection was to be found "virtually everywhere"—but any receptiveness among African Americans to enemy overtures was primarily caused by the unabated frequency of lynching. He claimed there had been 212 lynchings since the United States entered the war, more than double the known figure. Consequently, "as part of the military statesmanship of the General Staff," anti-lynching legislation was "thought necessary [as] some kind of counteroffensive." Black civilians and soldiers were not disloyal, but they *were* embittered, and yet the white population was largely oblivious to the conflicting emotions felt by many African Americans. They loved their country but were disgusted by what it habitually allowed, a tension that was communicated through word of mouth and the black press. Spingarn argued that if the federal government would undertake to protect members of a soldier's family from mobs—it protected them financially, after all, under the war-risk insurance scheme—then the prosecution of the war would be substantially assisted. If no such law was forthcoming, he warned, the morale of black troops and civilians would suffer and recruitment might be hampered.[41]

Despite some sharp argument between Hornblower and the committee as to the bill's constitutionality, the members appeared to readily accept that blacks were susceptible to enemy propaganda. They were clearly less certain about the motives and authority of the two officers before them. In response to an assertion by Robert Y. Thomas (D-Ky.) that "a man found guilty of rape should be lynched," Spingarn offered statistics on the alleged crimes of lynch-mob victims in the standard manner of the NAACP, prompting William L. Igoe (D-Mo.) to ask whether the bill was an independent venture of Spingarn's or the result of full discussion at the War Department. Spingarn countered with a refusal to talk about the secret internal affairs of military intelligence. When pressed, he said he had permission to appear before the committee, but he was evasive as to how far the War Department endorsed the bill.[42] The truth was that he was acting alone. The first indication that senior MIB officers had of his appearance was the published record of the committee hearing, about which he told his wife, "It looks terrifyingly public in print, but I am hoping that my superiors will survive the shock."[43]

At the request of the committee chairman, Hornblower prepared a brief on the bill, stressing that it represented his own view "as a lawyer, since questions of constitutional law are not in the purview of the Military Intelligence Branch." Referring to the congressional war powers, he argued that his draft was as much in keeping with the Constitution as existing wartime legislation, such as the Sedition Act, the Sabotage Act, and the War-Risk Act, and that it made as much military sense. "In a war recognized as ultimately turning upon comparative man power," he reasoned, "the lynching of men registered or registerable for the United States military service necessarily reduces the factor of national safety." He repeated his claim about "secret machinations by German agents and subtle propaganda among large groups of our population," although he made no mention of race.[44] Spingarn, meanwhile, began to seek support from prominent individuals and civilian organizations, recognizing that the bill would need more than its military origins to stand a chance of passing. He contacted William Mather Lewis, executive secretary of the National Committee of Patriotic Societies, and Bolton Smith, of the Tennessee Law and Order League, assuring them that any help they could give to hasten the end of lynching would "serve a highly patriotic purpose."[45]

The hardest part, however, was trying to persuade the War Department to approve the anti-lynching initiative. The General Staff took three weeks to give grudging permission to Hornblower on July 12 to submit his brief to the Judiciary Committee. On July 22, in an attempt to force the department's hand, Spingarn compiled a special file on the bill, containing Hornblower's brief, a four-thousand-word memorandum for Churchill to forward to Peyton C. March, and letters for the signature of the secretary of war calling on the Senate and House Judiciary Committees to approve the bill "at the earliest opportunity . . . for military reasons." He drew heavily on the words of black spokesmen, the black press, and existing "Negro Subversion" reports to construct a picture of a brutally wronged people, infuriated by the indifference of the government to their plight, and now ripe for disastrous incitement by enemy agents.[46] Spingarn wrote that over the past year the bitterness caused by a wave of unpunished murders had been deepened by the East St. Louis riot and the rapid execution of thirteen of the Houston mutineers. He cited black bishops who had told the MIB, "after the latest lynching, that they no longer cared who won the war." He quoted from the correspondence between Woodrow Wilson and Robert Russa Moton, in which the principal of Tuskegee had written, "There is more genuine restlessness and dissatisfaction on the part of the colored people than I have ever before known." Moton attributed this anger to incidents such as the recent killing of six people in Georgia, among them a pregnant woman, and asked Wilson to do something "pretty definitely to change the attitude of these millions of black people." This was a piece of selective quotation by Spingarn, since the presidential action that Moton sought was "a strong word" on lynching, not legislation.[47] Further evidence came from the Rev. D. D. Crawford, secretary of the General Missionary Baptist Convention of Georgia, who had warned Emmett Scott in May 1918, "The morale and enthusiasm of our people are broken, and they are discouraged as never before. . . . Germany is going to use these outrages, I fear, to demoralize our soldiers in France. . . . A disheartened people cannot give their best." Spingarn also cited examples of favorable southern white opinion on the question of anti-lynching legislation.[48]

Spingarn pointed out that the moral principle on which American belligerency rested had raised many questions in the minds of blacks; they were not passive, unthinking onlookers. Conscription, in particular, "made them alive to the larger issues of the world. They hear the phrases of the hour, that the war is a war for freedom, for the protection of smaller nations, a war 'to make the world safe for Democracy,' and apply these to their own situation." To illustrate, he offered the declaration of the *Amsterdam News* of May 29, 1918 (the issue that the Post Office declared non-mailable), that "Cracker Prussianism" in the South posed a more immediate menace to black Americans than the Kaiser's army. He repeated that black opinion could no longer be divided into conservative and radical schools. The whole race had "suddenly become conscious of its inferior status and resentful of discrimination against it." At the same time, its leaders had "adopted a bolder and more truculent tone." This threatened national security, because, while black people had made great strides since slavery,

> large masses still remain in comparative ignorance and poverty, to which is added a native bent toward emotionalism and religious devotion. Rumors spread with extraordinary rapidity in the colored world, and are exaggerated and distorted with repetition. This makes enemy propaganda easy to spread, while the absence of the "newspaper habit", especially in rural districts, makes such propaganda difficult to combat.[49]

Since his bill rested entirely on its relevance to the war effort, Spingarn speculated in alarmist tones about the law-and-order implications of black unrest and insisted that an anti-lynching law was a "military necessity." Putting the number of African Americans at between eleven and twelve million, he identified, for effect, twenty-seven countries with smaller total populations. "The cooperation of this large element of our population in all civilian and military activities is of vital importance," he warned the General Staff, so that

> the alienation, or worse, of eleven million people would be a serious menace to the successful prosecution of the war. Leaving aside the military problem involved in the repression of two and a half times the population of Ireland, the dislocation of Southern agriculture and of Northern and Southern industry would in itself be sufficiently severe.[50]

Citing alleged cases of German propaganda from MIB files, Spingarn concocted a thoroughly misleading impression of a carefully orchestrated plot to undermine black loyalty. He classified each case according to type: "Religious propaganda. . . . Propaganda based on German sympathy. . . .

Propaganda based on lynching and other discriminations at home. . . . Propaganda based on false rumors from abroad. . . . Propaganda based on fear." He warned that this subversion "was falling on fruitful soil," requiring "not only counter-propaganda, but elimination of obvious and legitimate grievances." Without government action to eradicate lynching, he stated, "it will be impossible to cope with the present unrest and dissatisfaction."[51] This was utter nonsense, and Spingarn knew it. In desperation, he had gone much further in his characterization of black alienation than in his assessment following the editors' conference. In effect, he gave the "Negro Subversion" scare further credibility, playing on prevalent images of the devious German agent and the insolent, yet gullible, black civilian, in the hope that the government would respond by confronting lynching.

There can be little doubt that he was trying to rush an anti-lynching law onto the federal statute books, so that the wartime measure could be retained in some form for peacetime (as was to happen with the long-standing objective of the temperance movement). However, as Michael Handel has shown for the modern period, the political context in which intelligence operations are conducted can determine the willingness of intelligence chiefs and governments to act on the recommendations of officers, however valid.[52] The same was true in World War I. The wartime anti-lynching bill was introduced into Congress, but it was never passed, not because Spingarn failed to get his message through to the administration, but because of insurmountable political and bureaucratic barriers.

Ultimately, Spingarn's analysis did help to produce some government action—Woodrow Wilson made a long-awaited public condemnation of lynching, which was an outcome Spingarn welcomed, as far as it went, but, ironically, Wilson's statement also accelerated Spingarn's downfall in the MIB. Since 1912, Woodrow Wilson had been pressed to issue a public denunciation of lynching by Booker T. Washington, Robert Russa Moton, the NAACP, and many other petitioners. Although he repeatedly said he was willing to do something once he had formed "a confident judgment as to what would be effective and influential," he hesitated until the summer of 1918.[53] When he did speak out, on July 26, it was in large part because Joel Spingarn's "constructive programme" had shown the relevance to the war of such a statement. In addition to the anti-lynching bill, Spingarn had provided a platform in Washington for African-American leaders in the editors' conference and had driven home a warning about the dangers of ignoring black opinion. The key resolution of the editors' conference was the call for federal efforts to eradicate lynching. Although the government's objective in holding the event was not to invite, still less to entertain, a number of controversial demands, the resolution did add to the pressure on Wilson to condemn mob violence and it is clear that the advice the president received as a result of the conference was important in spurring him to act.

Newton D. Baker was one of those who pressed the president from within the administration. After claiming the conference had been called at his own suggestion so that he could refute, "in a very authoritative way," rumors about the treatment of black soldiers, Baker warned Wilson that lynching was a cause of considerable animosity. He acknowledged that "of course, no Federal legislation is likely on the subject," but urged the president to break his silence. Baker had read the MIB reports on "Negro Subversion," including Spingarn's, and he now confessed to Wilson, "I have been much disturbed and my anxiety is growing at the situation in this country among the negroes." He endorsed Moton's suggestion that Wilson should write an open letter to the governor of a state where a lynching had recently occurred, calling for the prosecution of the offenders. He might even offer "the voluntary and sympathetic cooperation of the Department of Justice." This "would operate as a deterrent and would certainly allay some feeling among the leaders of the negro people."[54] Wilson rejected this politically dangerous form of broadcast, but within a month he had issued his denunciation, calling lynching, especially during war, "this disgraceful evil."[55] Although George Creel omitted any mention of the black editors' conference in his memoirs, claiming that Wilson's attack on vigilantism was prompted solely by the lynching of a German immigrant, Robert Praeger, in Illinois in April 1918, the president's statement actually referred to "many lynchings" in "widely separated parts of the country," and the text responded in several other ways to points made by black lobbyists.[56] This was the first clear condemnation of mob murders of African Americans by a senior political figure since Theodore Roosevelt's attack on the East St. Louis rioters a year before, and black leaders were delighted. However, it made no difference to the level of racial violence in America: sixty blacks were lynched in 1918 and seventy-six in 1919 (the highest number since 1908), and hundreds more were to die in race riots across the United States before Wilson left office.[57]

Spingarn's second ambitious project as an intelligence officer—the recruitment of W. E. B. Du Bois to the MIB—called for a further demonstration of audacity and cunning, for Du Bois, on the face of it, was an even less obvious choice as an intelligence officer than Spingarn himself.

It was a fateful initiative, with far-reaching consequences for Du Bois, Spingarn, and the equal rights movement as a whole. Du Bois had been clear all along about where the duties of black Americans lay; he supported the war effort wholeheartedly and he wanted the fullest African American involvement in it, but he did not intend simply to abandon protest against discrimination. In the year prior to June 1918, he delivered some of his most powerful denunciations of racism, such as his report on the East St. Louis riot of July 1917, which was an indictment of the United States itself, and a furious editorial denouncing the 24th Infantry executions in the January 1918 issue of the *Crisis:*

> We raise our clenched hands against the hundreds of thousands of white murderers, rapists, and scoundrels who have oppressed, killed, ruined, robbed and debased their black fellow men and fellow women, and yet, today, walk scot-free unwhipped of justice, uncondemned by millions of their white fellow citizens, and unrebuked by the president of the United States.[58]

In May 1918, he virtually accused the War Department of the deliberate ill-treatment of black troops and warned the government that "[i]ntentional injustice to colored soldiers is the poorest investment that the nation can make just now."[59] As Du Bois explained to Emmett Scott in April 1918, there were three strands to his position on the war. He believed the defeat of Germany was "absolutely necessary for the emancipation and uplift of the colored races," that blacks had already "gained more than at any time since emancipation" because of the war, and that through "strong organization and careful thought" they would continue to strengthen their hold on these gains and extend them.[60]

Soon after his arrival in Washington, Spingarn began to tempt Du Bois into applying for a commission. At a meeting between the two in Washington on June 4, 1918, Spingarn explained that his intelligence posting represented an opportunity to create a new agency generating enlightened government policy on racial matters, while also sustaining black enthusiasm for the war, but he did not attempt to recruit Du Bois on this occasion. Later that day he sent Du Bois a copy of the anti-lynching bill as an example of the kind of thing he was hoping to achieve in the MIB.[61] Knowing the unpopularity of the *Crisis* among federal officials, Spingarn then set out to make Du Bois more acceptable to the War Department, but the manner in which Du Bois was to comply with this exercise created a massive controversy.

First, however, an intervention by the Justice Department had to be deflected. On the day Spingarn met Du Bois in Washington, BI Chief Bruce Bielaski had instructed his agent-in-charge in New York City to get information on the financial support of the *Crisis*. Bielaski was worried by reports that because the magazine was available "free of charge in large numbers, . . . German propagandists might be securing copies for distribution." When a carbon copy of this letter reached Churchill at the MIB the next day, Spingarn visited Alfred Bettman, the attorney in the war division of the Justice Department who had alerted Bielaski to the alleged free distributions. Assured by Spingarn that the *Crisis* had no connection with enemy agents and that Du Bois had "promised to change the tone" of the magazine, Bettman had the investigation suspended. Du Bois's pledge to "change the tone" of the *Crisis* and make it "an organ of patriotic propaganda hereafter" must have been made at the June 4 meeting in Washington.[62] On Saturday, June 8, Du Bois was back in Washington and this time, as Spingarn afterward told his wife,

> I gave him the shock of his life by offering him a commission, but don't breathe a word of this to a human soul until it goes through. I think it will, for the bait of olive drab is strong even for such a man as he. If it does, it will mean a good deal, not only for him and his, but for the whole country. . . . I have given him (and my own chief too) a big vision of things to be accomplished and I like the way the vision stirs them.[63]

Spingarn was not exercising his authority over Du Bois as NAACP chairman, although he did so on other occasions; he was offering an enthusiastic invitation to collaborate. Spingarn's plans were still hazy, but they appealed to Du Bois because they coincided so well with the *Crisis* editor's own belief that full black participation in the war was vital and would prompt an official commitment to upholding civil rights. Here was a chance to show blacks that the domestic dimension of Wilson's ideal of international democracy genuinely applied to them. Other factors also attracted Du Bois to the idea of an army commission. Throughout his career, he was prepared at short notice to take up new posts, in new organizations and cities, whenever he felt his freedom and usefulness were being restricted. His move from Atlanta University to the NAACP in New York in 1910 can be explained partly in these terms, as can his return to Atlanta in 1934. In 1918, his relations with some of the directors of the NAACP were strained and his closest ally on the board, Joel Spingarn, was absent. Du Bois also felt hampered by the wartime limitations on freedom of expression. In these circumstances, he could regard a temporary move to Washington as worthwhile. Moreover, the cohort of over six hundred black officers commissioned at Fort Des Moines consisted largely of students and graduates of Howard and Fisk Universities and Hampton Institute. Du Bois had already volunteered intellectual and political guidance to the Talented Tenth, the black elite nurtured mainly by such institutions. Now, by joining a branch of the General Staff, he could confirm his leadership of the younger generation. After brief contemplation, influenced by his affection and respect for Spingarn and his own urge to do something tangible for the war effort, Du Bois agreed to seek a commission. He seized upon Spingarn's depiction of the Negro Subversion program as "constructive," and this became a recurrent theme in his subsequent defense.[64]

Spingarn repeated to Churchill in his progress report of June 10 that Du Bois had promised to "change the tone" of the *Crisis*. He also advised the MIB director that all the material for each issue was being submitted before publication to Studin, who would ensure that it was innocuous.[65] Military intelligence began to receive letters recommending Du Bois for a commission from prominent residents of the District of Columbia, including Rep. Frederick W. Dallinger (R-Mass.), Du Bois's contemporary at Harvard, and two friends of the NAACP, Wendell Phillips Stafford, a District of Columbia Supreme Court judge, and Sen. Wesley L. Jones (R-Wash.). As a result, when Du Bois returned to the capital a fortnight later for the editors' conference, Churchill arranged a physical examination for him at the Army Medical School. The doctors were told that Du Bois, who was fifty years old, was being considered only for a desk job. He nevertheless failed the medical tests, because of the series of operations he had undergone in January 1917, when he lost his left kidney and "looked death in the face."[66] At this point, the medical report did not seem significant. On June 18, Spingarn told his wife he was "certain that I can get this waived. (If not, all my plans will go to smash.)" He knew that he was dealing with a sensitive matter, and that War Department officials had to be handled carefully, and he obviously expected African Americans to be surprised, but in his excitement he seems to have had no idea of just how great a controversy was looming. He told his wife, "I think that everyone will be amazed at this news when it gets out, but you must not breathe a word about it now." Churchill made no mention of the medical report or any other difficulty when advising the general staff the following day that formation of the Negro Subversion subsection was proceeding steadily. On June 22, Spingarn assured Churchill that the *Crisis* editor was playing a vital role in voicing and shaping the political and racial consciousness of the black population. Not only were Du Bois's editorials the clearest expressions of the desire for equal rights; he was also one of the strongest black supporters of American involvement in the war. He could, therefore, monitor and analyze African-American opinion and be relied upon to head off anything that veered toward disloyalty. Spingarn sent the head of MI-4 details of Du Bois's career, and the latter formally applied on June 24 for a commission in military intelligence, listing his chief interest as "race problems."[67]

In the same week, the July issue of the *Crisis* appeared, containing an editorial by Du Bois titled "Close Ranks":

> This is the crisis of the world. For all the long years to come men will point to the year 1918 as the great Day of Decision, the day when the world decided whether it would submit to military despotism and an endless armed peace—if peace it could be called—or whether they would put down the menace of German militarism and inaugurate the United States of the World.
>
> We of the colored race have no ordinary interest in the outcome. That which the German power represents today spells death to the aspirations of Negroes and all darker races for equality, freedom and democracy. Let us not hesitate. Let us, while this war lasts, forget our special grievances and close our ranks shoulder to shoulder with our own white fellow citizens and the allied nations that are fighting for democracy. We make no ordinary sacrifice, but we make it gladly and willingly with our eyes lifted to the hills.[68]

The timing and tenor of the "Close Ranks" editorial were vital to the decision of the War Department to offer Du Bois a commission. On June 26, a week after the editors' conference and two days after the submission of Du Bois's application for a commission, but before the reaction of *Crisis* readers to "Close Ranks" had begun to register, Spingarn told his wife,

> The DB situation looks brighter than ever. I have won Scott over, and effected an almost epoch-making alliance of all the factions,—if the thing goes through. It means that twelve millions are unanimously mobilized

in support of the country, and the sleeping volcano may not become dangerous, after all.[69]

Spingarn was referring to the fact that a few hours earlier Newton D. Baker had granted an interview to Emmett Scott. Briefed in advance by Spingarn, Scott had commented to Baker on the success of the black editors' conference and the especially "fine attitude" displayed by Du Bois. He then showed Baker "the Crisis editorial" and placed before him a letter addressed to Marlborough Churchill which, "after a few moments of conversation etc., [Baker] signed without further parley." In the letter, Baker gave his approval to a particular "designation," making Scott "most happy" that Spingarn had allowed him "to put this thing through for the cause." In view of Scott's satisfaction, it may be assumed that the letter conveyed the secretary of war's approval that Du Bois be commissioned at the rank of captain for military intelligence work with the Negro Subversion section. A week later, after Spingarn showed Churchill a clipping from the Crisis as "evidence of the effect of MIB policy," the MIB director described the "Close Ranks" editorial as "very satisfactory."[70]

Du Bois had certainly supported Woodrow Wilson's decision to go to war in April 1917, but during the following year he had attacked racial injustice in the United States as caustically as ever. Thus, the conciliatory terms he used in the July 1918 issue of the Crisis seemed to contradict the mounting radicalism of black politics and all that Du Bois, in particular, stood for. To the growing number of African Americans who endorsed explicit campaigns for equal rights during the war, Du Bois's exhortation to "forget our special grievances and close our ranks shoulder to shoulder with our own white fellow citizens" was the language of abject submission. They complained that Du Bois was asking them to be silent about injustice and squander the political opportunities of war by declining to exploit the national emergency to negotiate appropriate rewards for their participation. William H. Wilson, a Washington physician, wrote Du Bois immediately that he was astonished by what he had just read in his copy of the Crisis: "In no issue since our entrance in the war am I able to find so supine a surrender— temporary though it may be—of the rights of man."[71] There was speculation that Du Bois had lost his nerve in the prevailing anti-radical atmosphere following the warning he had received in May 1918 from the assistant United States attorney in New York that the Crisis was being monitored for breaches of the Espionage Act of 1917 and the forthcoming Sedition Act.[72]

W. E. B. Du Bois, Joel Spingarn, and Military Intelligence

When the news that Du Bois was seeking a commission emerged in the first week of July, his critics believed they had found another, more disturbing, explanation for "Close Ranks." Mere disagreement with the editorial gave way to denunciation of the author. The conjunction of application and editorial brought down a deluge of abuse on Du Bois, damaging his reputation as an unbending opponent of racial discrimination, almost splitting the NAACP, and deepening the divisions between various factions in the increasingly vigorous black political vanguard. Du Bois stood accused of vanity and mercenary opportunism, and he risked losing the confidence of many would-be supporters, just when it seemed he might fill the gap left by Washington's death. He continued to be highly influential in the interwar period, but the ill-feeling caused by "Close Ranks" was slow to subside, and in the 1920s it contributed to his poor relations with other black radicals, notably socialists such as A. Philip Randolph and Pan-Africanists such as Marcus Garvey. Partly because of "Close Ranks," Du Bois was to recall World War I with a mixture of shame and bitterness for the next forty years.

Du Bois was more alert than Spingarn to anti-militarist sentiment among the directors of the NAACP. In the days following Baker's approval of his recruitment, he attempted to sound them out, advising them that if he joined the army he would be working with Spingarn "in a constructive attempt to guide Negro public opinion by removing pressing grievances of colored folk which hinder the prosecution of the war." If offered a commission, he would be obliged to accept it, but only on condition that the NAACP let him retain editorship of the *Crisis,* an arrangement he defended on the grounds that his work for military intelligence should be regarded as furthering the aims of the association. Finally, "in view of past services," he asked the board to supplement his captain's pay, so that he suffered no fall in income.[73]

By the date of the next NAACP board meeting, July 8, Du Bois had gathered a dozen favorable replies and was quite content to have the directors discuss the matter.[74] However, attendance was low and, in Du Bois's words, "strongly pacifist." The NAACP board included some of the most vocal opponents of American belligerency and they were represented at the meeting by Oswald Garrison Villard, a founder of the American Union against Militarism, the social reformer Florence Kelley, and the presidents of the Boston and Washington NAACP branches, Joseph Prince Loud and Archibald H. Grimké. The latter took the chair. Among the absentees were some directors who would have undoubtedly been able advocates of

Du Bois's acceptance of the commission, including Joel Spingarn and his brother Arthur, Col. Charles Young, right-wing socialist William English Walling, and Prof. George W. Cook of Howard University. As it was, Du Bois could count on the support of only three of those present.[75] Du Bois spelled out the terms on which he proposed to combine the roles of MIB officer and *Crisis* editor. The board promptly rejected them, resolving instead that the need for a full-time editor was "imperative." For Du Bois to be distracted by time-consuming work elsewhere would be a disservice to the 79,000 readers of the journal and the 39,000 members of the association. The wording of the resolution was left to Studin, Du Bois, and the NAACP secretary, John R. Shillady, but as a summary of the board's views, it told less than half the truth. The already skeptical meeting was swayed less by its concern for the quality of the *Crisis* than by the fear that Du Bois's recruitment by an intelligence agency of the southern-dominated Wilson administration would "spread suspicion and discouragement." Grimké, the only prominent black person at the meeting other than Du Bois, was especially clear on this point, expressing the "passionate belief" that such an overt switch of allegiances would split his Washington branch. It was rapidly growing and, because of its lobbying role, was the most important branch in the country.[76]

Du Bois afterward told Joel Spingarn that even a fully attended meeting could have accepted his proposals only after a "sharp and unsatisfactory division," which he wished to avoid. He thought the board's decision was the end of the matter and that he had been denied "a great opportunity for service."[77] Joel Spingarn was enraged; the majority at the meeting were "a damn lot of pacifists and theorists and fools," he told his wife. "They say that DB's coming here is bad, and refuse to sanction it; he cannot afford a captaincy unless they help out a little with their funds. I must resign from the whole thing immediately if they continue in this unpatriotic attitude." He made good this threat in a letter to Studin, adding that he intended to speak to Grimké.[78] Mary White Ovington, the acting chairwoman of the NAACP, traveling in the West, wrote Du Bois she was "most relieved" by the board's decision and suspected that he was, too, and that he must have realized that he could have been powerless in Washington: "I believe that the southern attitude is quite inimical to the advance of any Negro in the higher walk of life. I think they are like a stone wall on that matter." Du Bois's reply was full of equivocation and frustration: "I have decided not to go to Washington. I may change my mind but probably not. The Board was pretty evenly divided but it happened to be a 'pacifist' meeting. I am meaning these days everything that I say in THE CRISIS but I am not saying all that I would like to say."[79]

Two days later, the Washington NAACP branch made it clear that the issue was far from dead. In its "stormiest meeting ever," the membership justified Grimké's fears and virtually accused Du Bois of trying to buy himself a commission with the "Close Ranks" editorial. Some of those who attacked him most fiercely had attended the editors' conference a fortnight earlier and were now shocked to find that while drafting resolutions pledging black loyalty he was also actively seeking a post in military intelligence. Spingarn attended the branch meeting, thereby absenting himself from one of the regular interagency intelligence conferences, at which he had been expected to outline the plans for his new MIB subsection. Speaking as national NAACP chairman, he tried to defend Du Bois, but found the audience equally critical of his own role in the affair. Du Bois's determination to retain two sources of income was condemned almost as bitterly as his political retreat, even though he sought no increase in his total salary for doing two jobs.[80]

Not all black opinion in Washington was so hostile. The *Washington Bee* cautioned its readers not to pre-judge Du Bois, predicting that he would be able to do useful work in the MIB. The *Bee* was also confident that the appointment would not seduce him politically, but favorable comment of this kind was rare and short-lived. The *New York News,* a black weekly with little time for the NAACP, reported the branch meeting with some satisfaction:

> Many of the speeches were radically denunciatory of Editor Du Bois' alleged selfishness in desiring to draw salary from two positions and "traitor" and "Benedict Arnold" were some of the endearing terms applied to him because of his "Close Ranks" editorial in the last issue of the Crisis. . . . In short it has been made plain to him that he cannot serve two masters.[81]

If the reaction of the board in New York left Du Bois in a defeatist mood, the venom of the public attack on his integrity roused him to fight back. Thanking Spingarn for his support and sympathizing with him for the criticism he, too, was attracting, Du Bois attempted to explain why he had placed conditions on his acceptance of a commission. He had to consider three things: his family's income, his future employment prospects, and the effects on the NAACP and its journal if he were to leave. He realized that "we must all expect when we essay to lead a crowd that the crowd will at times be incredibly stupid," but he was surprised at the strength of black feeling. He was "all at sea and disposed to simply sit and wait" until he could see where his duty lay. As his confidence returned, he suggested to his close friend John Hope, president of Morehouse College in Atlanta, that since editors were "muzzled" during the war, it was questionable whether he would be any more restricted editing the *Crisis* as an army officer than he already was as a civilian. Less than a week after the board's decision, he decided that it could probably be overturned, although the extent of popular opposition still worried him. In reply, Hope asked if Du Bois was certain that his work in military intelligence would be "constructive"; might he not become "a secret serviceman pure and simple" and, if so, would that be an "efficiently patriotic" use of his talents?[82]

For several weeks, members of the NAACP and other equal rights activists gave Du Bois their advice freely, many rebuking him, others regretting the loss of his editorship of the *Crisis* should he join the army, and some giving him wholehearted support. From Atlanta, J. W. E. Bowen, vice-president of Gammon Theological Seminary, a long-standing friend and colleague of the late Booker T. Washington, took a predictable line: "Hold your ground; don't surrender; your principles are right; get on the inside and you will be able to continue the struggle for right." Washington's successor, Robert Russa Moton, also congratulated Du Bois on the commission and at the same time let him know that Tuskegee still had the inside track in Washington: "I of course knew that the matter was under consideration." In contrast, George C. Bradford, the white Bostonian who had sponsored Du Bois's research at Atlanta University, warned that in accepting the commission he would be "bound by official etiquette and red tape . . . your hands would be tied. Furthermore, you would lose your influence in the community. The row in Washington illustrates that." Possibly for party political reasons, the black Georgian Republican regular Henry Lincoln Johnson also advised Du Bois not to join up, and the Memphis branch of the NAACP appealed to him to stay where he was most needed, at the helm of the *Crisis*.[83] Byron Gunner, a Niagara Movement veteran and co-organizer of the NERL, who at first congratulated Du Bois on his commission, apparently before reading the July *Crisis*, was "amazed beyond expression" by the call to "close our ranks." He told Du Bois that blacks should be doing

W. E. B. Du Bois, Joel Spingarn, and Military Intelligence

"just the reverse," since a war in the name of democracy was "the most opportune time" for their complaints to be aired.[84]

Spingarn had hardly expected the NAACP board or the Washington branch to be obstacles. He had already begun circulating news of Du Bois's enlistment in government circles, and his own credibility was at stake. His mood changed daily. On the Sunday after the board meeting he fretted about the difficulty of getting suitable assistants and wished his brother, Arthur, could join him, but he remained optimistic: "The colored world is boiling hot about the Spingarn–Du Bois affair. Heaven knows what the result will be, but I am mighty cheerful and feel hopeful about everything." By the following Tuesday, after attending the African-American community's Bastille Day celebrations at the Howard Theater, he had become fully aware of his weakened and isolated position in Washington and the extent of the furor which "Close Ranks" and the commission had stirred up. He told his wife:

> The situation still remains doubtful here, especially in regard to DB, who I learned today has telegraphed a friend "I do not think I shall accept the commission." The poor fellow is frightened by the clamor of his enemies, and in fact all of his people,—the first want to hurt him, and the others are afraid that he will be muzzled. I don't want to do anything to hurt his leadership with his race, but I hate to let him miss the wonderful opportunity that awaits him here.[85]

He was reduced to pleading with Du Bois not to abandon him: "My whole constructive programme here is on trial, and in danger of toppling over if you do not join forces with me now." He insisted it would be "madness" to let an unrepeatable opportunity slip by and predicted that the outcry of "a few bitter men" would soon subside. He suggested that if the NAACP gave Du Bois a leave of absence and a firm promise of reappointment after the war, others could produce the journal in the interim. If the association would not help Du Bois financially, the shortfall in his income could be "taken care of in other ways," apparently by Spingarn himself.[86]

Du Bois clashed frequently with other white members of the board, especially Villard, but he always found it difficult to resist a direct appeal from the only comparable academic among the creators of the NAACP. Indeed, Spingarn was one of the few people who could persuade him that he might sometimes be mistaken. He relented, promising Spingarn that he would accept the commission on only one condition: a guarantee that he could return to the *Crisis* after the war. He still wanted to explain why he had been so difficult at first. The journal was his own "carefully built up machine," and he wished to preserve it. His request that the business manager, Augustus Dill, become acting editor had already been vetoed by Villard, who wanted to give the job to the NAACP field secretary, James Weldon Johnson. This, wrote Du Bois, "would be almost fatal," probably because he knew that Johnson's most recent editorial experience had been gained on a Tuskegee-backed newspaper, the *New York Age*. Du Bois again referred to his reluctance to inconvenience his family, meticulously demonstrating that a captain's pay of $2,400 fell far short of his annual outgoings, which were based on his current salary of $4,200.[87]

By mid-July 1918, criticism of Du Bois for apparently abandoning his principles in the "Close Ranks" editorial was reaching a peak. In the past, he had been critical of the standards and integrity of the black press; now the tables were turned. The *New York News*, still raging at Spingarn and Du Bois for advocating a separate officers' training camp, denounced them as "genuflecting gentlemen . . . playing both ends of the game against the middle." It was all very well for Du Bois to want to join the army, but not at the financial and political expense of the NAACP, and for him to aspire no higher than the rank of captain was an insult to his race. The *News* blamed Spingarn's "mad meddling"—he was "the evil genius . . . of Dr. Du Bois." Du Bois also made a sitting target for the pen of William Monroe Trotter. Harking back to their collaboration in the Niagara Movement, and claiming to be the man who persuaded Du Bois to lead "the fight for equality, human brotherhood and liberty," Trotter wrote in the *Boston Guardian* of his deep disappointment that Du Bois should have "finally weakened, compromised, deserted the fight, betrayed the cause of his race." He found the claim that Germany posed a grave threat to black hopes for democracy "a strange statement." In Trotter's eyes, the editor of the *Crisis* was "no longer a radical" but "a rank quitter in the fight for equal rights," betraying his race just when demands for equality and liberty should be most vigorously advanced. On the subject of the commission, Trotter remarked only that its coincidence with "Close Ranks" and the wrangle over the future editorship of the *Crisis* could "not help Dr. Du Bois."[88]

By the end of July 1918, few black newspapers took the charitable view expressed by the *Baltimore Afro-American*, that Du Bois deserved the benefit of the doubt and might well be able to embark "on a new line of attack" on prejudice from within the War Department. Instead, the bulk of the black press concurred with the verdict of Du Bois's onetime supporter, the *Washington Bee,* that any confidence in him had been destroyed.[89]

Spingarn's fellow MIB officers quickly exploited the damage done to his standing as an expert on racial matters. They had four main reasons for doing this. First, the prevailing atmosphere in the MIB was hostile to reform. Although, as Roy Talbert, Jr., has shown, the MIB allowed its specialists a degree of freedom in analyzing social problems, most officers doing "negative" intelligence work sought only to identify and counter enemy propaganda within the United States. Since it was not an intelligence officer's primary duty to expose, still less to solve, the failings of American democracy, Spingarn's ideas exceeded the normal boundaries. Second, for almost a year the dominant MIB view of the NAACP had been that it was causing unnecessary unrest among blacks by criticizing the government and drawing attention to racial inequality. Third, some officers, seeing their own positions as "Negro subversion" specialists threatened by the establishment of a new subsection with a distinct ethos of its own, were quick to express doubts about the fitness of the newcomers to senior officers. Finally, in a predominantly Anglo-Saxon enclave, racial prejudice and anti-Semitism played a part in the antipathy toward Du Bois and Spingarn. In quick succession, as Spingarn's plan to recruit Du Bois faltered, three MIB officers submitted memorandums attacking the *Crisis,* its editor, and the NAACP.[90]

Capt. James L. Bruff's "Memorandum re. Officers and Directors of the National Association for the Advancement of Colored People" typified the attitude of junior intelligence officers toward liberal organizations. Pacifism was the most pernicious of the radical tendencies he detected within the NAACP. He made no comment about Spingarn, his senior officer, but his assessment of Du Bois was tailored to contradict all the arguments for recruiting him. Du Bois, wrote Bruff, was "the leader of a faction of his race which believes, so it is understood, in its equality with the white race and insists upon recognition of this alleged right." Spread through the seditious medium of the *Crisis,* these views tended "to cause discontent among the colored population" and had provoked rioting. Bruff conceded that Du Bois was brilliant and well educated but noted that "many persons of discernment seriously question his capacity for leadership because of his radical beliefs and rather extreme views on the race problem."[91]

Capt. Harry A. Taylor followed this with an "Extremely Confidential" report on the *Crisis* for the director of the MIB's Negative Branch. Until Spingarn arrived, Taylor had usually monitored "Negro subversion," operating through unreliable African-American informants in the apparent belief that he was receiving ample intelligence on alleged black disloyalty. Spingarn and Du Bois represented a threat to his status as the MIB's specialist on racial matters. The *Crisis,* he wrote, was "extremely radical and antagonistic in tone" and was the real cause of any black unrest. Indeed, it was "apparently published for the sole purpose of creating antagonism and race prejudice with a view to inciting the colored race to acts of violence against the whites." On the cover of his report, Taylor printed prominently, "W. E. BURGHARDT DU BOIS, DIRECTOR OF PUBLICATIONS AND RESEARCH. DR. J. E. SPINGARN, CHAIRMAN OF THE BOARD." Churchill personally annotated Taylor's report.[92]

The third blow, and probably the most effective, was dealt by Walter H. Loving, now operating mainly from New York. Loving was the only black person in military intelligence when Spingarn joined the MIB. Tactful, capable, and objective—willing to condemn and quash intemperate black expression in wartime and yet openly committed to the ultimate objective of equal rights—he had gained the respect of his superiors, who were often prepared to forward his unamended reports to the secretary of war's office as the considered MIB position on questions of black troop morale and civilian race relations. He had hoped to be recommissioned into the army during the war, but by June 1918 nothing had come of his request. Yet it now seemed that Du Bois, five years older and with no military background, was about to walk into a commission on the strength of his connections. A Negro Subversion subsection, containing Captain Du Bois and several younger Talented Tenth black officers, would have eclipsed Loving's solo operation and would, he felt, perform no more effectively than he had on his own. His response was to emphasize his own value to the MIB by questioning that of Du Bois and, less directly, that of Spingarn, despite his own high regard for the NAACP and his undoubted approval of the content of "Close Ranks."[93]

Loving first sent Churchill an editorial from the *New York Voice,* written by Hubert Harrison. Harrison had ridiculed "Close Ranks," claiming that it amounted to a suggestion that blacks should "consent to be lynched 'during the war' and submit tamely and with commendable weakness to being Jim-crowed and disfranchised." Aware of the kind of barrage Harrison could deliver, Loving asked him for a further "summary" of the debate raging among blacks over Du Bois's commission. In response, Harrison explained that black leaders who owed their positions to whites were being "re-evaluated and, in most cases, rejected." They had "established unsavory reputations by advocating surrender of life, liberty and manhood, masking their cowardice behind the pillars of wartime sacrifice." Du Bois was "a most striking instance." His pursuit of a commission in military intelligence was not, in itself, the reason for "the stormy outburst of disapproval"; he had "first palpably sinned" by asking blacks to forget their grievances until after the war. That could have been excused as an error of judgment, but

> when it was learned that Du Bois was being preened for a berth in the War Department as a captain-assistant (adjutant) to Major Spingarn, the words used by him in the editorial acquired a darker and more sinister significance. The two things fitted too well together as motive and self-interest.[94]

Moreover, they were part of a steady slide into gradualist accommodation in the wake of the black editors' conference. Although he had not been present, Harrison rightly guessed that Du Bois was responsible for the conference resolutions, which seemed to him to extol "servile virtues of acquiescence and subservience." In sum, the conference, the commission, and "Close Ranks" seemed, even to NAACP supporters,

> to afford proof of that which was only a suspicion before, viz: that the racial resolution of the leaders had been tampered with and that Du Bois had been privy to something of the sort. The connection between the successive acts of the drama (May, June, July) was too clear to admit of any interpretation other than that of deliberate cold-blooded, purposive planning. And the connection with Spingarn seemed to suggest that personal friendships and public faith were not good team-mates.

By asking Harrison to spell out "radical" opinion on the "Close Ranks" affair for the MIB, Loving deftly demolished the argument that Du Bois ought to be recruited because he best understood the changing views of black Americans. Harrison's account seemed to show that Du Bois was so distrusted by those he purported to represent that he could be of only limited value to military intelligence. Shortly after the war, Harrison claimed that Loving had judged his analysis a major reason why the MIB eventually withdrew its offer of a commission to Du Bois.[95]

For good measure, on July 22 Loving followed up with his own analysis, in which he wrote that the editors' conference had backfired badly. It had been unwise to hold the sessions in secret and to allow the CPI to control publication of the proceedings, because it looked to outsiders like "a hand picked, star chamber affair, where certain Negro editors and others had met with officials of the War Department to compromise race issues." It also appeared to be an official attempt to undermine Trotter's and Harrison's subsequent National Liberty Congress, which was much better publicized, "establishing their conference as the one most representative of popular feeling." Secondly, Loving argued, the "Close Ranks" editorial should not make Du Bois a more attractive candidate for a commission. It had caused protests across the country and led to the widespread belief that Du Bois had sold out and was about to become the government's black newspaper censor: "A man cannot desert overnight the principles he has followed for twenty-five years without incurring the suspicion and mistrust of his people." If Du Bois were appointed to military intelligence, "it would give the radicals a continued theme for discussion and opportunity to implicate the government in this affair"; moreover, his "career as a race leader would be cut short," an outcome Loving wished sincerely to avoid. In sum, Du Bois should be left to edit the *Crisis,* "subject to the same laws that apply to all other publications." Finally, in language that suggested that he did not entirely trust the journalist in Du Bois, Loving recommended that to avoid the leaking of his reports no black officers at all be assigned to the MIB unless "absolutely necessary," in which case they should be "men who have long military experience and who realize the importance of protecting the interests of the government in matters of this character."[96] Given the faith that senior MIB officers had in Loving's integrity and acuity, this report was a deadly summary of Du Bois's unfitness for a commission and Spingarn's lack of judgment. The head of the New York military intelligence office, Maj. Nicholas Biddle, telephoned Churchill about Loving's report, supporting its conclusions regarding Du Bois's commission and adding some weasel words about Spingarn's capacity to do his duty—that Spingarn's past was as radical as Du Bois's and that it seemed to African Americans, therefore, that both "Du Bois and Spingarn are in the positions of men who have been bought by the government, and that the negroes have thereby lost their leaders. Major Spingarn, of course, as you know, is of Jewish race, and has often experienced the results of race prejudice."[97]

Spingarn, meanwhile, not knowing whether Du Bois would ignore his critics and rightly suspecting the pressure mounting on Churchill to scrap the idea of a Negro Subversion subsection, was becoming increasingly agitated. On July 20, he protested to the new head of the Negative Branch, Maj. Henry T. Hunt, that he was still waiting to be moved into his new office and that a month had passed since Du Bois had filed his application with a request that the physical disqualification be waived, and yet no decision had been made. Hunt did not reply.[98] On July 30, as Spingarn confessed to Charles Studin that he was in confusion, Churchill told Hunt that the special propaganda program for blacks was to be abandoned. Following the public condemnation of lynching by Woodrow Wilson at the end of the previous week, the anti-lynching bill was now "considered superfluous" and Baker's office wanted the work on it stopped.[99] Churchill told Spingarn that he was "firmly convinced" that the MIB should confine its future work on racial matters to the morale of black troops—a job for the Morale Section (part of MI-3), rather than the Negative Branch (MI-4). Du Bois's application for a commission was formally rejected, partly on medical grounds, but primarily, so Churchill claimed, because "any attempts on the part of the Military Intelligence Branch to solve the question of negro subversion among the civil population would necessarily lead it beyond the proper limits of military activity and would duplicate the efforts of agencies already charged with the solution of the same problem."[100] Hunt took the trouble to send Du Bois a remarkable letter, which, if sincere, demonstrated that the Negative Branch had once been fully committed to the creation of the Negro Subversion subsection and Du Bois's recruitment. In the days before Spingarn and "Close Ranks," Hunt had disapproved of the *Crisis* and ordered that it was to be kept "out of not only the Y.M.C.A. huts, but all other places" in army camps.[101] A former mayor of Cincinnati, who in the 1920s would act as lawyer for A. Philip Randolph and the Brotherhood of Sleeping Car Porters, Hunt told Du Bois that he personally regretted the abandonment of the subsection.

> I must bow to it as a decision of higher authority. For my own part, I am far from regretting the [whole] incident, for it has enabled me to add much to my former very slight knowledge of your character, abilities and program. I always had a strong sympathy with Americans of African descent and with efforts to bring about equality before the laws, as well as equal economic opportunities for them. Major Spingarn has referred to me several copies of the "Crisis", containing your editorials, which I read with the deepest interest. They seem to me extraordinarily eloquent and tragically poetic. I know that they have already been valuable toward the

object which we are all trying to achieve—towit [*sic*], crushing German autocracy.

I hope to have the opportunity some time in the future to state to you verbally my very strong feelings on this subject.

With best wishes, . . . [102]

Spingarn and Emmett Scott exchanged expressions of regret, but both appeared to think that the former would, nonetheless, remain in the MIB. In fact, within three days Spingarn was ordered to Hoboken, N.J., to board ship "for extended field service" in France.[103] A month later, he received a letter from Churchill in which the MIB director wrote of his personal regret that the subsection had not been formed and his hope that Spingarn understood "how difficult for me was the situation which made it necessary for me to withdraw my unqualified support."[104]

Before dispensing with Spingarn, the MIB had taken advice on alternative race relations experts from Thomas Jesse Jones, a conservative white authority on black education. The field of "Negro Subversion" was now entrusted to the Morale Section and all Spingarn's remaining projects, such as the suppression of *The Birth of a Nation,* were abandoned. Walter Loving was retained and transferred to the Morale Section.[105] A year later, when a U.S. senator from Arkansas sent Newton D. Baker a newspaper clipping about Joel Spingarn's speech at the Tenth Annual Conference of the NAACP and demanded an explanation of a reference therein to Spingarn's service in military intelligence, Churchill drafted "an appropriate reply" for the secretary of war's signature. The truth—that the MIB had almost fostered something imaginative and liberal in the field of race relations, before conforming to the conservative and repressive instincts of the administration as a whole—was too complicated and embarrassing to relate. Instead, Churchill provided what was required—a plausible lie—stressing that when Spingarn had been transferred to the MIB it was desperately short of staff, and that when "his service there did not prove satisfactory" he had been posted to France.[106]

W. E. B. Du Bois suspected he was robbed of his commission by intrigue, later accusing white southerners of obstructing him after "Negro sources" revealed his radical politics. Emmett Scott and Arthur Spingarn preferred a different but equally simple explanation: the subsection was blocked because of the fuss surrounding "Close Ranks" and its plainly divisive effects on black opinion. Joel Spingarn essentially agreed, but he held the NAACP board primarily responsible, since their refusal to accept Du Bois's conditions had produced the controversy. He confirmed his determination to resign the chair, being "wholly out of sympathy with the attitude of some of the directors on various problems."[107]

The controversy dragged on until the Armistice and thereafter remained a convenient stick with which to beat Du Bois. He insisted throughout that his conscience was clear and that the outcry left him in "unruffled serenity," but he went to some lengths in correspondence and in print to defend himself. In the August 1918 *Crisis,* he tried to clarify "Close Ranks," maintaining that since the United States was "the hope of mankind and of black mankind," the war was "for the survival of the Best against the threats of the Worst." Rather than "bargain" with their loyalty, he argued, blacks should contribute to a victory won by "manliness, and not by the threat of the footpad." He advised "patience, then, without compromise; silence without surrender." In the following issue, he dealt at length with both the commission and the July editorial but treated them as if they were unconnected. The commission, he wrote, was part of a planned "far-reaching constructive effort to satisfy the pressing grievances of colored Americans" and, as such, should not have been questioned. The "Close Ranks" editorial was consistent with the principles of the NAACP and the loyalty shown by blacks throughout the war. He then tried to show, by distorting history, that since 1776 blacks in the United States had gained civil rights "rapidly and effectively" by fighting in the country's wars and that new rights were being gained in 1918. Concerning the attacks on himself, he concluded, "No one who essays to teach the multitude can long escape crucifixion."[108]

Given the scale of governmental and civil animosity toward groups and individuals who opposed the American war effort in 1918, Du Bois's pro-war and pro–equal rights position was far more realistic than his critics' insistence that the war represented a great opportunity for blacks to bargain with the state. His enemies nevertheless brushed his protestations aside, preferring to concentrate on his abnormally meek language in "Close Ranks." To the emerging black nationalist organizer Marcus Garvey, writing in the fledgling *Negro World* in August 1918, Du Bois's defense was "a desperate effort to bolster up a bad case by far-fetched conclusions." Garvey dismissed the idea that blacks would ultimately benefit by putting their country before their rights during the war. By "dickering with an official position," he claimed, Du Bois had shown he was no longer the leader he had been in the Niagara Movement. Instead, he was "a follower of the masses."[109]

In his attempts to rebut the charge that the editorial and the commission were connected, Du Bois tinkered with the truth. A few days after Spingarn departed for France, Du Bois replied to a sympathetic request for information about "Close Ranks" and the commission from Lafayette Hershaw, a Niagara Movement stalwart who had defended him at the Washington branch meeting. Du Bois assured Hershaw that the invitation to apply for a commission had "absolutely nothing to do with the editorial utterances of The Crisis" and that the journal had already been in print for two weeks when he was "summoned to Washington." There, to his "great surprise," he was asked if he would accept a post in the MIB.[110] This version of events is scarcely credible; his surprise was genuine, but the timing he gave was misleading. Although he implied in the September *Crisis* that the first he heard about a commission was on June 15, he later stated that he was called to Washington on June 1. He certainly spoke to Spingarn in the capital on June 4 and again on June 8 when the commission was offered, which would have required the July *Crisis*, editorials and all, to have been in print by about May 20, if the sequence he described were true. It is clear from the content of other issues in 1918 that the journal was never in its final form four to five weeks in advance of appearing on the newsstands.[111] Du Bois further stated in his defense that the "Close Ranks" editorial had been "in exact accord" with the resolutions adopted at the editors' conference on June 21. In fact, the resolutions, written by Du Bois with the scrutiny and approval of his fellow editors, were far less conciliatory than the July editorial. The conference presented specific and urgent demands to the government; "Close Ranks" called for setting them aside.[112]

The "Close Ranks" controversy undoubtedly harmed the struggle for equal rights. The affair removed the veneer of unity applied in the years after Booker T. Washington's death by such gatherings as the Amenia Conference of 1916, when Joel Spingarn had convened black leaders at his home in upstate New York.[113] It also fueled personal and organizational quarrels, by pointing up the divergent paths taken by black leaders on questions of strategy and basic philosophy. The paths included intellectual elitism, radical equal rights protest, nationalism, socialism, and accommodation.[114]

Within the NAACP, the "Close Ranks" affair earned Du Bois a persistent opponent in Neval H. Thomas, who led the attack on the commission proposal in the Washington branch and continued to raise the matter for months afterward. In September 1918, he told Oswald Garrison Villard that he agreed with what he called Villard's "desire to rid the Association of its greatest liability, DuBois [*sic*]. . . . He has reversed his whole life, and is no more good to us." Thomas unfairly accused Du Bois of being more interested in making money than in furthering the aims of the NAACP: "His service has not been philanthropic, but commercial." In May 1919, Thomas told Villard that Du Bois would "never get back to the place he once occupied before people found him out. . . . You did us valiant service in not letting him make some extra money and make our magazine an organ of the war department."[115] Villard declined the invitation to reopen the debate, but a month later, Emmett Scott, stung by Du Bois's accusation that he had made insufficient efforts on behalf of black troops during the war, fanned the flames further. By now secretary-treasurer of Howard University, Scott released a letter from Neval Thomas in which the latter denounced Du Bois's apparent silence on the subject of "burning wrongs" in the summer of 1918 as "seeking honors at the price of complete surrender." When Thomas was later elected to the national board of the NAACP—"a calamity," according to Du Bois—a lengthy wrangle ensued. The animosity between them, one of several open feuds at the highest levels in the organization, lasted throughout the 1920s.[116]

Du Bois's critics outside the NAACP also maintained a steady chorus of indignation. In February 1919, the *Half-Century Magazine,* a middle-class black monthly published in Chicago, castigated him for having spoken "bunk" during the war. It declared that since leaders like Du Bois were "blown the way the white man wishes them to be blown, they constitute nothing less than carbuncles on the race." Two months later, at a meeting of Marcus Garvey's Universal Negro Improvement Association (UNIA), resolutions criticizing Du Bois were carried with the support of W. A. Domingo, a Jamaican-born socialist. Domingo admitted he had "favored, honored and respected [Du Bois] for many years," but he felt "compelled to dishonor and disfavor him" because of "Close Ranks." When Du Bois attended the UNIA's vast convention in August 1920, Garvey made a gratuitously cutting comment from the platform: "We believe Negroes are big, not by the size of their pocket book, not by the alien company they keep but by their being for their race. You cannot advocate 'close ranks' today and talk 'dark water' tomorrow; you must be a hundred percent Negro." There were echoes of this in Garvey's charge in 1923 that "Du Bois and those who think like him can see and regard honor conferred only by their white masters."[117] Cyril Briggs, who now combined his editorial work for the

Amsterdam News with the publication of a new left-nationalist monthly, *The Crusader*, described "Close Ranks" as Du Bois's "Surrender Editorial" and included the *Crisis* editor in an attack on "coward and traitor leaders . . . , surrendering and selling the Race they claim to lead."[118] Other young black radicals in New York in the 1920s derisively referred to Du Bois as "Der Kapitan." Among them were A. Philip Randolph and Chandler Owen, editors of the socialist *Messenger* magazine. They mainly scoffed at Du Bois's weak grasp of economics, but they were not above using "Close Ranks" as an additional line of attack. It would, they wrote, "rank in shame and reeking disgrace" with Booker T. Washington's Atlanta Compromise address of 1895. From the wings, conservative, accommodationist black leaders also enjoyed the spectacle of their erstwhile critic's embarrassment, and they may have covertly helped increase it. Robert Russa Moton confided to the editor of the *New York Age*, "Our methods seem to be prevailing. Our friend Du Bois seems to be persona non grata with his own people."[119]

Undoubtedly, then, Du Bois's flirtation with military intelligence and the ensuing controversy severely dented the reputation he had earned during two extraordinarily productive decades as a perceptive analyst of disadvantage and an uncompromising opponent of discrimination. Historians have used "Close Ranks" to support arguments about the impact of World War I on American society and, in particular, on blacks.[120] In their analyses of the dilemmas of black leadership and the pressures on W. E. B. Du Bois, they have consistently overlooked the deliberate purpose he had in mind when he wrote it. Du Bois was not as passive as he later claimed. The editorial was a conscious deviation in the trajectory of his wartime writings and was specifically included in the July 1918 issue of the *Crisis* to help get him into military intelligence. To explain it as simply the apogee of his pro-war thinking, or as a frightened response to pressure exerted on the NAACP by the New York United States attorney's office, is to miss the point. Although his enthusiasm for the war was genuine and he was certainly being careful not to offend the Justice Department, the meekness of the July editorial was an astonishing departure from the magazine's declared commitment to exposing and attacking all racial injustice. Above all, it did not square with the editor's known rejection of accommodationism. The only plausible explanation for the editorial is that Du Bois wrote it at Spingarn's request, knowing that its appearance in the July *Crisis* would coincide with his formal application for a commission. This ensured that the most current example of his advice to black Americans would be impeccably loyal, allowing Scott and Spingarn to use it to persuade their respective superiors—the secretary of war and the director of the MIB—that Du Bois could perform valuable service in uniform. The wreckers within military intelligence thus behaved logically, by their own lights at least, since the invective of Bruff, Taylor, and Loving was designed to undermine the appeal of "Close Ranks." Du Bois's black political critics, such as Harrison and Thomas, were equally astute (although they willfully misread his longer-term intentions and his concern over his income): their charges linking the editorial and the commission were well founded.

Viewed in these terms, the editorial ceases to be an adequate summary of Du Bois's response to the war, still less of the views of black Americans (the use to which many historians have put it). It becomes, instead, an address to the War Department, in which its author distorted his real beliefs and for which he paid a heavy price.

The wider significance of the controversy over "Close Ranks" and the proposed commission lies in what it reveals about the mood of the African-American population at the height of the nation's engagement in World War I and the potential for schism among black leaders and organizations at a pivotal moment in the development of civil rights thought. Faced with bitter frustrations and nationwide racial violence, blacks embraced various political ideologies and methods during and immediately after World War I, most of which entailed uncompromising opposition to discrimination. Far from serving as a handy précis for sorely tried black patriotism during the war, "Close Ranks" commands attention for two quite different reasons: firstly, because of the hubristic propaganda exercise from which it emerged, and, secondly, because of the immediacy and vigor with which equal rights activists dissented from the burden of its key sentence: "Let us, while this war lasts, forget our special grievances and close our ranks shoulder to shoulder with our own white fellow citizens and the allied nations that are fighting for democracy." In rejecting this injunction, the more principled of Du Bois's African-American critics were making three clear and fundamental points: first, that unflagging and loud protest against all discrimination was the only honorable option; second, that there should be no obligation on black people to align themselves with whites so long as reciprocation was highly unlikely; and third, that African Americans had no particular reason to identify with the allied cause or to believe that the democracy for which Wilson declared war was ever meant to be shared by them. Moreover, "Close Ranks" and the response it provoked emphatically demonstrated the lack of solidarity and the primacy of the individual that existed within the movement for equal rights.

Finally, Spingarn's entire "constructive programme" suggests that, in the area of race relations at least, black and white Progressive reformers who imagined in 1917 that the mobilization of American society for war represented an opportunity to harness the powers of the federal government to their particular cause were wildly overoptimistic. Spingarn's work in the MIB helped to produce a long-overdue presidential statement, but none of his original objectives was achieved, save that of temporarily influencing the editorial comment of the black press. His intelligence activities may even have been a disservice to black Americans. This was hardly intentional, but he knew the risks. The manner in which he compiled his evidence and conclusions provided Washington intelligence agencies, executive chiefs, and influential legislators with apparent confirmation of a supposition that most of them were inclined to accept: that German propagandists had selected blacks as an American Achilles' heel, and that they had done so for good reason. Spingarn by no means invented this scare, but he certainly exploited it and thereby strengthened the view that the activities, speeches, writings, and alliances of black campaigners for equal rights should continue to be monitored. When he was removed, his twin legacies to the MIB were a series of highly colored assertions that blacks were succumbing to the blandishments of a German spy network and a furious ongoing protest among African Americans over an editorial which to all white officials seemed impeccably loyal. His reports endorsed current beliefs about the innate impressionability of black people and bolstered the suspicion that the outspokenness of their leaders was becoming dangerous. Thus, far from challenging prejudice and transforming government policy, Joel Spingarn's attempts to shock his fellow officers, the administration, and Congress into complying with his agenda, particularly in the case of the anti-lynching bill, merely lent extra weight to the argument that blacks were a potentially subversive element of American society.

Six

Diplomacy and Demobilization, 1918–1919

In the final months of the war, military intelligence in Washington was reorganized, largely on the initiative of Gen. Peyton C. March, who had begun a thorough shake-up of the General Staff on his return to the United States from France in March 1918.[1] His later assertion that when he arrived the Military Intelligence Branch was no more than "a minor appendage of the War Plans Division" was inaccurate, but his changes did enable intelligence officers to initiate new projects and communicate more effectively with the rest of the War Department and other federal agencies. He replaced Ralph Van Deman as director of military intelligence with Col. Marlborough Churchill, a Harvard-educated regular officer who had been part of the U.S. mission to France when Congress declared war and afterward a member of March's staff at the American artillery training center at Valdahon. March then rearranged the General Staff into four full-fledged divisions: Operations; Military Intelligence; Purchase, Storage and Traffic; and War Plans.[2] Thus, on August 26, 1918, the MIB became the Military Intelligence Division (MID) and Churchill was promoted to the rank of brigadier general.[3] From late November 1918 to April 1919, Col. John M. Dunn, normally chief of the Positive Branch of the MID, served as the acting director of military intelligence during Churchill's absence in France, where he joined Ralph Van Deman on attachment to the U.S. Commission to Negotiate Peace.[4]

After the reorganization, matters relating to "Negro Subversion" and "Negro Soldier Problems" were turned over to Capt. James E. Cutler and the Military Morale Section of the MID until October 1918, when a separate Morale Branch of the General Staff was established under the command of a Medical Corps officer, Brig. Gen. Edward L. Munson.[5] Thereafter, information on blacks was gathered by both the MID and the Morale Branch, with the latter concentrating on troops, so that in December 1918 Cutler described himself as working officially within the Morale Branch, but "acting more or less in the capacity of Liaison Officer with MID."[6] Morale Branch reports on black radical activity were referred to the MID, which maintained the files on that subject. Regional intelligence officers across the U.S. continued to send information on race to the MID, whence it might be forwarded to the Morale Branch.

Within a fortnight of the announcement of the Armistice, MID officers were instructed to undertake no new investigations into disloyalty or enemy alien agitation among the civilian population. Information on such matters was to be turned over to the Department of Justice.[7] Military intelligence operations in the United States were accordingly run down in December 1918, and existing investigations were concluded. The General Staff decided to reduce the number of officers assigned to the MID from almost 300 to just 103, some of whom would be officers returning from Europe. On January 24, 1919, the MID was ordered to end its investigation of civilians, although it was allowed to receive information from individuals who were not connected with military intelligence. As a result, former members of the American Protective League, which was disbanded between January 1 and February 1, 1919, found there was still a demand for amateur sleuthing and regrouped themselves into independent vigilance organizations.[8]

This order appeared to rule out further military investigation of "Negro Subversion" and many other areas of interest to the MID, but it was evaded in a number of ways. In New York City, the MID office was able to draw on the intelligence work enthusiastically conducted by the British assistant provost marshal, Col. Norman Thwaites, and the better publicized, but equally unreliable, efforts of men like the prominent New York lawyer and red-baiter Archibald E. Stevenson. (Both Thwaites and Stevenson covered the subject of racial agitation.)[9] Postal Censorship continued to be another regular source of information for the MID, since the military representatives were retained on the postal censorship committees. They continued to send transcripts of suspicious correspondence found in the international mails to the MID and the Office of Naval Intelligence. In this way, for instance, Marcus Garvey's growing reputation in the Caribbean was monitored.[10] Walter Loving, still the MID's most useful and perceptive authority on the strength of black feeling, was retained until September 1, 1919, but his status became less clear-cut. Although he reported on black civilian and military matters continually until August, mostly from New York, intelligence officers kept this fact to themselves when discussing "Negro Subversion" with other agencies. For instance, when the MID referred in March

1919 to Loving's wartime dealings with Robert Abbott and the *Chicago Defender,* it described him to the BI as "formerly attached to the War Department," although he was clearly still part of MID personnel.[11]

Despite the efforts of MID officers to circumvent restrictions placed on civilian investigations, Churchill resumed control of a smaller, weaker organization when he returned to Washington in April 1919. Under Churchill and his assistant, Col. A. B. Coxe, who had accompanied him to France and who in June took over the Negative Branch from the more cautious Col. K. C. Masteller, the rules were habitually stretched and civilian investigations carried on beyond 1920. Churchill's main task was to preserve military intelligence as a separate entity. In 1919, those government agencies created during the war which believed they had a peacetime role to play were attempting to justify their continued existence in the face of Congressional cost-cutting. The 1918 appropriation for military intelligence had been $2.5 million.[12] In June 1919, Churchill asked for $500,000 and received $400,000. He based his appeal for funds on the need for positive intelligence gathering abroad, but considerable energy was subsequently expended on investigation of radical movements at home.[13] This was curtailed in February 1920, after complaints both in the press and by the Department of Justice.[14] Churchill made a weak attempt to rebut criticism of his division for exceeding its authority. He claimed that, since the war, the MID had made

> a very sincere effort . . . to comply with the spirit and the letter of our laws as fully as is possible during the period of great industrial unrest which must necessarily be a source of concern to all law-abiding men. . . . Due to the unrest naturally produced by the reconstruction period there are elements in the existing situation in this country which, as law-abiding citizens and officers of the Army, we can but regard with concern. The Regular Army is the one sure bulwark against possible disorder. No other force can be made ready so quickly. None other is so good.[15]

It was, he asserted, the duty of military intelligence officers to provide information to the army's department commanders, especially since troops had had to be used to quell civil disturbances. Ideally, he agreed, the BI and the Treasury Department's Secret Service ought to "find out everything there is to know," but he felt that those agencies were working under unspecified but "almost insuperable difficulties which tend to complicate the situation and make almost impossible the normal relation between civil and military authority." Therefore, the MID's Foreign Influence Section, as MI-4 was now known, was charged with the task of preparing a "Weekly Situation Survey of Radical and Racial Movements."[16]

Churchill succeeded in preserving the MID's separate identity—it was made one of the five peacetime divisions of the General Staff in the Army Reorganization Act of 1920, and renamed G-2. However, it became the poor relation of the General Staff, suffering severe cuts in appropriations and being reduced to only twenty-seven officers and fifty civilian employees by 1927. As late as 1923, the Adjutant General's office had to remind G-2 to stop investigating individuals, either directly or through volunteers, in peacetime.[17]

Throughout 1917 and 1918, African-American equal rights activists recognized that although lasting reforms were unlikely to be enacted during the war itself, the pressure for change had to be maintained, so that, as soon as the war ended, equal rights campaigning could be stepped up. An important element of this outlook was an increasing internationalism. In January 1918, Woodrow Wilson had announced his Fourteen Points for European and world peace, the fifth of which called for "absolutely impartial adjustment of all colonial claims," in which "the interests of the populations concerned must have equal weight with the equitable claims of the government whose title is to be determined." Thereafter, forward-looking African Americans urged that the future of Africa should be linked to the worldwide problem of racial discrimination and placed high on the agenda for discussion during the post-war settlement.[18] A. Philip Randolph and Chandler Owen of the *Messenger* were among the first to contemplate the peace conference in any detail: "The Negro ought to be there to insist upon international equity as regards the treasures of Africa and its inexhaustible labor supply. He needs further to call upon America to make good her claims of fighting 'to make the world safe for democracy.'"[19] The editors implied that they themselves could perform this duty at the peace conference as well as anybody.

In the month following the Armistice, a number of black organizations confidently elected delegates to travel to Paris to submit resolutions to the peace conference. The delegates were instructed to draw world attention to the plight of African Americans by lobbying the conference through a variety of sketchily conceived peripheral congresses, which were expected to gather in the early months of 1919. Hubert Harrison, ever the loner, thought they were wasting their time; he could not foresee the quality of

American democracy being an issue for discussion at the peace conference, nor could he picture black organizations being allowed to present their case.[20] Harrison was essentially right; Woodrow Wilson was spared any embarrassment as he assumed the role of world statesman by the State Department's refusal to grant passports to black delegates to the peace conference. Following the passage of the Passport Control Act of May 1918, U.S. residents could not leave the country without a passport or permit issued by the State Department and, although this was a wartime security measure, it remained in force during the Armistice.[21] The handful of black people who did secure passports to travel to France before the end of 1918 were only able to do so at the request, or with the assistance, of members of the federal government. Robert Russa Moton, the only black man in whose judgment Woodrow Wilson seemed to place any trust, was informed by Emmett Scott that both the president and the secretary of war were keen that he should go to France to examine, and advise upon, the conditions under which black soldiers were serving. It was also hoped that the conservative educator would have a soothing effect on the troops. Moton was accompanied by two like-minded men—his secretary, Nathan Hunt, and Lester A. Walton of the *New York Age,* a newspaper with strong Tuskegee connections. They were joined by the white educationalist Thomas Jesse Jones, who opponents of Moton claimed had been selected to keep an eye on their behavior. Passage was arranged for them on George Creel's press boat, the *Orizaba,* which departed from New York four days before the president sailed aboard the *George Washington* on December 4, 1918.[22]

A late decision by the board of the NAACP to fund the collection of material for a history of black involvement in the war led to W. E. B. Du Bois's joining this party at the last moment. (He and Moton shared a cabin and appear to have enjoyed each other's company.) Du Bois revealed in the May 1919 *Crisis* and in his report to the NAACP board that he had approached Emmett Scott and others in November 1918 with the suggestion that they collaborate on a history of blacks in the world war, but that Scott had rejected this offer because he had already made arrangements to write such a study alone.[23] Walter Loving's investigations led him to believe that relations between Scott and Du Bois at this point were not so clear-cut. He informed the MID that, although the two men had had their differences in the past, a deal had been struck between "the foxy Dr. Du Bois" and Scott, with the blessing of the latter's publisher, by which Scott would help Du Bois secure a passport in return for his cooperation on a joint book.

This volume would combine Scott's recollections and access to War Department data with the results of Du Bois's research in France and his literary skills. The beauty of it was that the NAACP would be paying Du Bois's expenses throughout. Loving alleged that Scott, in particular, was hoping by this arrangement "to clean up financially. . . . [H]e cares not what embarrassment might befall the War Department so long as he can profit by the deal." This extraordinary swipe at Scott, the only other black man with any direct influence over War Department policy on racial matters, reflected a general disenchantment among African Americans with the assistant to the secretary of war's efforts in the war. It also showed a certain ingratitude on Loving's part, since Scott had lobbied Secretary of War William Howard Taft on his behalf in 1906–07.[24] According to Loving, Du Bois had repudiated the agreement with Scott on arriving in France, but his report was almost entirely wrong. Du Bois had tried to interest Scott in a joint project in November 1918, but Scott declined, having begun negotiations with a publisher ten months earlier.[25]

Whatever the status of their discussions about a history of the war, it is certain that Emmett Scott had given Du Bois crucial assistance in the matter of getting to France by securing at short notice the necessary documents from the State Department's Division of Passport Control. Indeed, without Scott's help, Du Bois would never have got on the *Orizaba,* which must have made Du Bois's searing criticisms of Scott in the spring of 1919 all the more galling. The Division of Passport Control was swamped with applications from American citizens wishing to travel to Europe and those submitted by African Americans were being treated with particular suspicion, but Scott was able to have Du Bois's forms processed on the day they were submitted —Saturday, November 30, just twenty-four hours before the *Orizaba* sailed. In the absence of Du Bois's birth certificate, Scott agreed to fill out an affidavit as a reputable person, "having actual knowledge of the applicant's birth" in the United States. Scott also secured for Du Bois a letter of introduction to the passport officials from Harvey O'Higgins, the Canadian-born acting chairman of the Committee on Public Information, who declared that he had no objection to Du Bois covering the peace conference for the *Crisis.* Du Bois wrote on his application form that he intended to be a "newspaper correspondent" while in Europe and a few hours later was handed his passport.[26] Before being allowed to board the *Orizaba,* however, he still had to badger George Creel on the quayside for press credentials,

Diplomacy and Demobilization, 1918–1919

since Scott had neglected to tell the CPI chairman that Du Bois would be coming along.[27]

Du Bois had already informed the administration of his interest in the outcome of the post-war settlement for African people, but only to the extent of seeking American action; he made no mention of a non-white convention in Paris. Four days before sailing from New York, he submitted his "Memoranda on the Future of Africa" to the White House and asked Woodrow Wilson to discuss the African colonies with "a small delegation of representative colored men," which would have included himself and Moton. Du Bois hoped to have his ideas placed "before the Peace Conference and before the world." In the mildly worded document, drawn up after consultation with George Foster Peabody, the millionaire banker and treasurer of the Southern Education Board, Du Bois suggested that the great powers should listen to educated black people in various countries: "It would be a wise step to ascertain by a series of conferences the desires, aspirations and grievances of these people and to incorporate [these] to some extent in the plans for the reconstruction of the world." Du Bois speculated that this might eventually lead to international agreement on decolonization in Africa, "under the guidance of organized civilization."[28] Wilson's secretary, Joseph Tumulty, had replied that the President would be shown the document, but that his impending departure for France left him no time to see the delegation, in view of which, Du Bois later reported to the NAACP Board, "[a] Pan-African Congress in Paris seemed the next step."[29] Du Bois wisely made no mention on his passport application of his plan to call a Pan-African Congress. Had he done so, as he readily admitted afterward, his passport would have been delayed and probably refused outright. This element of Du Bois's trip was only made public by the NAACP after he had arrived in France.[30]

While Du Bois and Moton were making their way to Paris, other, less well connected African-American delegates attempted to finalize their own plans to join them. William Monroe Trotter's National Equal Rights League had announced at its September 1918 meeting in Chicago that it would call a National Race Congress in January 1919 in Washington, D.C., "to elect race petitioners to be sent to intercede for full democracy for Colored Americans." This had been reported to the BI by informant Arthur U. Craig.[31] When the war ended earlier than Trotter had expected, the National Race Congress was brought forward, and early in December Craig alerted Washington BI agent J. G. C. Corcoran to the imminent arrival in the capital of the *Boston Guardian* editor and his followers. Corcoran advised Justice Department attorneys A. H. Pike and Alfred Bettman of Trotter's plan to send delegates to the peace conference, and suggested that efforts should be made to discover their financial backers.[32] He also recommended that the State Department be notified and that "these so-called delegates' passports to France be . . . held up at least until the Peace Conference is over." On the subject of Du Bois, who was halfway to France, Corcoran warned, "this is a 'Rock-the-Boat' type. . . . His associations have been along German lines. He is further alleged to be a rank Socialist and all of his associations are the same. He may attempt to introduce socialistic tendencies at the Peace Conference."[33] This, he concluded, was part of Du Bois's master plan "to establish himself as a leader in this country among the colored people, which in turn will prove all the negroes here to be socialists [if] following this leader."[34] The meeting of Trotter's National Race Congress, held from December 16 to 19 at one of the largest churches in the district, was covered for the BI by another black civil servant, John E. Bowles, an employee of the Bureau of Mines, who had gathered information on Hubert Harrison's friends in Washington three months earlier. Corcoran may have felt that Craig, after covering the June and September NERL meetings, was in danger of being unmasked. Bowles attended the daily sessions of the National Race Congress and remarked to Corcoran afterward, "I have no regrets in going as it was quite amusing."[35]

Thirty-nine states were represented among the 250 attendees at the National Race Congress. Ten delegates to the peace conference were elected, including Ida B. Wells-Barnett, who, Bowles reported, abused white people generally throughout, and William Monroe Trotter, whose name was only added to the list after some discussion as to whether his inclusion would jeopardize the whole enterprise, given Woodrow Wilson's well-known aversion to him. A collection of several hundred dollars was taken up immediately, and a target set of $25,000. Ida B Wells-Barnett presided, but, according to Bowles, the outstanding single influence at the gathering was Elder R. D. Jonas, a white man with "a great flow of fine language."[36] Rupert Jonas was a squat, bearded, Welsh-born itinerant preacher, based in Chicago. He took delight in meddling in the affairs of black political organizations, while at the same time reporting what he knew of their activities to the BI and to the British military representatives in New York City, who in turn passed his often inaccurate information to the MID. On this occasion, he distributed leaflets in which he announced that he, too, was planning to travel to France, to help the black delegates obtain a hearing at Versailles, and that he was forming a "League of Colored Races" for this purpose. Bowles, who was plainly disenchanted with the proceedings of the National Race Congress, and especially with Jonas's posturing, commented, "It is very strange to me just at this time to have so many queer looking people raise so much Hell over us poor downtrodden people as he says we are."[37]

The BI was thus able to give the State Department immediate details about the National Race Congress's intention to send delegates to Versailles, thereby killing any chance that they would be permitted to travel. Walter Loving also recommended to the MID, immediately after the National Race Congress dispersed, that a careful check be made on the records of Trotter and his fellow delegates before any of them were issued passports, especially Ida B. Wells-Barnett—"a known race agitator." Loving put the total number of delegates elected to travel to Paris by various black organizations at over a hundred and warned, "If this plan is successfully carried out, I fear that the result may be a little embarrassing for this government."[38] He stressed the case of Wells-Barnett because by the time the National Race Congress convened she had already been nominated as a delegate by another radical organization—Marcus Garvey's Universal Negro Improvement Association (UNIA).[39] On Sunday, November 10, 1918, the eve of the Armistice, Garvey had held one of his first large Harlem meetings at the Palace Casino, attended, according to the New York press, by five thousand people. (A BI agent who attended in the guise of a newspaper reporter reckoned the audience was nearer two thousand.) The meeting had been advertised in the *Negro World* as a vital opportunity for black New Yorkers to link up with other non-white people of the world: "The Irish, the Jews, the East Indians and all other oppressed peoples are getting together to demand from their oppressors liberty, justice, equality, and we now call upon the 400 millions of Negro people of the world to do likewise."[40] After referring to the future status of black people in the New World, Garvey presented the meeting with resolutions on Africa which the UNIA would be commending to the powers gathered around the peace table. He placed great emphasis on the principle of self-determination and declared that the only way to avoid future warfare was through recognition of the rights of non-Europeans. He insisted on the dismantling of economic barriers, freedom of travel, equal educational opportunity, no European interference in African tribal custom, no segregation, and the repeal of the South African land acts. He called for all former German colonies to be entrusted to the administration of black people educated in Europe and America and for non-white nations to be accorded proportional representation in the event of a world government.[41]

Announcing another mass meeting to be held on Sunday, December 1, to elect three delegates to the peace conference, Garvey repeated his warning that Africans were in danger of being overlooked in the post-war settlement:

> Every oppressed group of people will be represented in some way or other at the Peace Conference.
>
> Remember, men, the time is now. There must be liberty, justice and equality, and that can only be when the Negro takes proper steps to make his power felt.
>
> Let there be no compromise. Let us unite to get all that is ours. At the Peace Conference great issues are to be decided, and the Negro must prepare to take his stand without faltering.
>
> It is your duty to be at the Palace on Sunday.[42]

Again, the *New York Times* reported, around five thousand people attended. As well as Wells-Barnett, they elected A. Philip Randolph and a Haitian follower of Garvey, Eliezer Cadet, who would also act as their interpreter in Paris, where they were to put forward the resolutions adopted by the UNIA on November 10. A collection of $3,000 was taken up for their mission, which they hoped to begin within ten days, if passports could be secured from the State Department within that time.[43] If the travel and living expenses of W. E. B. Du Bois are any indication, the $3,000 collected on December 1 would easily have covered round-trip passage and a three-month stay in Paris for all three UNIA delegates.[44] Garvey continued, nevertheless, to publicize the mission and to collect additional funds in its name.

Garvey's meetings were being regularly monitored by this time and the various investigative agencies of the federal government kept each other well informed about his new plans. Two agents compiled shorthand reports on the December 1 UNIA meeting for the BI, which copied one report to the MID. In addition, Postal Censorship in New York City intercepted letters from Eliezer Cadet to friends in Haiti, in which he wrote enthusiastically about his forthcoming voyage and his ambition to secure an administrative post in a former German colony. Copies of this correspondence were passed to the Justice Department, the State Department, naval and military intelligence, and the British and French liaison officers in New York.[45]

On December 17, in the midst of Trotter's National Race Congress, Walter Loving was summoned to the MID offices to arrange for a black shorthand reporter to cover a UNIA meeting in Baltimore on the following day, at which Garvey and Wells-Barnett were due to speak. Loving secured the services of Woolsey W. Hall, an employee of the Treasury Department, who was to become a frequent reporter of radical meetings in and around the capital over the coming year. Hall made a lengthy transcript of the Baltimore meeting, in spite of an announcement by one of the organizers that a government "spy" was rumored to be present and a request that the audience identify him, to prevent evidence being gathered on which Wells-Barnett could be denied a passport.[46] Loving produced an edited version of Hall's report, but could find "nothing of interest" in her speech, which covered twenty-three pages. He concluded that she had decided to tone down her material rather than endanger her trip to France, but urged that nevertheless "special attention be given to her record before a passport is granted her."[47] On receiving Loving's reports on the Garvey meeting in Baltimore and Trotter's congress in Washington, the acting MID director made it clear to Emmett Scott that, with or without hard evidence of seditious intent, Ida B. Wells-Barnett's presence in Paris during the peace conference would not be welcomed by the government.[48] The MID's request was unnecessary, for an apparatchik like Emmett Scott would never have supported Wells-Barnett's passport application, or that of A. Philip Randolph. Eliezer Cadet was able to travel to France unhindered, apparently on papers provided by the Haitian consulate (which he gave as his New York address), but neither Randolph nor Wells-Barnett was granted a passport to travel on behalf of the UNIA.

The efforts of yet another black equal rights organization which hoped to be represented at Versailles were undoubtedly hampered by Trotter's scheme. Trotter had dubbed his December 16–19 assembly a "National Race Congress" and, not for the first time, government agents confused his activities with those of another group—the Rev. William H. Jernagin's National Race Congress of the United States (NRC), a much less confrontational body than the NERL or the UNIA. To add to the confusion, Jernagin applied for his passport on December 21, 1918, just two days after Trotter's National Race Congress ended, and most of the documentation which he submitted in support of his application was dated in the preceding week.[49]

These were letters to certify that Jernagin's NRC had nominated him to be "a delegate to the Conference of Darker Races and also a delegate to the League of Small Nations and Weak Peoples to be held in France during the session of the Peace Council in AD 1919," and that, in addition, the Federal Council of Churches had appointed both Jernagin and a fellow member of the NRC, John R. Hawkins, to its own fourteen-member Special Commission to the Peace Conference.[50] The latter document did not assist Jernagin, because Hawkins had attended some of the sessions of Trotter's National Race Congress. On top of this, just prior to Trotter's National Race Congress, Postal Censorship intercepted a letter sent by J. Milton Waldron of the NRC to a prominent Indian nationalist in Stockholm, who had previously been based in Berlin. Waldron wrote that he and his associates were looking forward to meeting the Indian nationalists at the Conference of Darker Races in Paris, to which the NRC had already elected delegates. American officials had already expressed concern about the activities of Indian nationalists in the United States during the war, and this letter was taken to be "evidence of rapprochement between the negro and Hindu agitators."[51]

Jernagin asked for his passport to be issued in time for him to sail from New York on January 4, 1919, but three weeks after that date he was still waiting for it. Meanwhile, he had secured further written assurances from the Federal Council of Churches that it wished to include him among its delegates to Paris. He also had a statement from the management of the *Pittsburgh American* that he would be the journal's sole reporter on the peace conference.[52] On January 27, Jernagin submitted to the State Department an undertaking that, if granted a passport, he would confine his activities to those of a newspaper correspondent and a member of the Federal Council of Churches commission, with responsibility for the religious future of Africa: in other words, that he would in no way represent the NRC or raise the issue of racial discrimination in America while in France. On the strength of this undertaking, and perhaps after separate representations from the Federal Council of Churches, Third Assistant Secretary of State William A. Phillips intervened on Jernagin's behalf. The references on his original application to his plans to attend the Conference of Darker Races and the meeting of the League of Small Nations and Weak Peoples were deleted and, with "Religious work" substituted, the passport was issued on January 29.[53]

When it became clear that the State Department was being less than helpful with passports for African Americans, Hubert Harrison predicted that none of "the seventy-odd Negro 'delegates' to the Peace Conference who have got themselves 'elected' at mass meetings and concerts" would be allowed to travel to France and that the decision had already been taken. As usual, Harrison had captured the essence of what was going on:

> Of course, the government isn't telling them so in plain English. That wouldn't be like our government. It merely makes them wait while their money melts away. Day after day and week after week, they wearily wend their way to the official Circumlocution Office where they receive a reply considered sufficient for their child-minds: "Not yet." . . . The government will not let them go to France, because the government's conscience is not clear. And the government ordered that ludicrous lackey, Mr. R. R. Moton to go—for the same reason. In fact, the creation of sinecures for Mr. Scott and the other barnacles is due largely to an uneasy conscience.[54]

When it finally came, the calculated response of the State Department to groups of blacks who wished to travel to France was to act as if the question was not one for the United States government to decide. Du Bois's plan to call a Pan-African Congress had been publicized after his arrival in France and, on the basis of this, the State Department assumed that the various black delegations were all intending to participate in this congress. On February 1, 1919, the government stated:

> The State Department has been approached by various colored delegations with a view to sending representatives to Paris to participate in a Pan-African congress composed of colored people from different parts of the world. The department has been in touch with the French Government on the subject and is now in a position to state that the French Government has not been approached, but does not consider this a favorable time to hold such a conference. In the circumstances the department will be unable to grant passports to persons desiring to proceed to Paris for the purpose of attending such a congress.[55]

During the next few days, this statement was incorporated into letters from Second Assistant Secretary of State Alvey A. Adee to the peace conference delegates elected by black organizations as an explanation of why they would not be issued passports.[56] Unfortunately for the State Department, NAACP Secretary John R. Shillady had already released a cablegram from Du Bois which read, "Clemenceau permits Pan-African Congress February 12, 13, 14. North, South America, West Indies, Africa represented.

Two of our delegates, Haiti, Liberia, sit in Peace Conference." In releasing this, Shillady tactfully omitted Du Bois's final sentence: "Carefully selected delegates welcome." It was obvious, as the *New York Call,* a socialist daily, observed, that the French government had not been consulted by the United States before the State Department issued its statement.[57]

In taking repressive action regarding passports, the State Department had sought to avoid embarrassing protests in Paris over racial discrimination in the United States, but it may also have been influenced by the concerns of Allied diplomats about the sensitivity of Japan on the question of race, and particularly American attitudes on this subject. In December 1918, the Japanese government had announced that its leading negotiator at the peace table, Baron Makino, had been instructed to obtain guarantees from the other participants against racial discrimination in international relations.[58] Since the ending of the war, American investigative agencies had picked up clear indications that black radicals hoped to be able to capitalize on Japanese dissatisfaction with American attitudes. Most notably, both the BI and the MID collected information on the activities of the International League of Darker Peoples (ILDP), which surfaced in New York in January 1919. This was the title eventually adopted by the body for which R. D. Jonas had been trying to attract support at Trotter's National Race Congress in December 1918 under the name of a "League of Colored Races." It was not connected with either the Conference of the Darker Races or the League of Small Nations and Weak Peoples, to which the Rev. W. H. Jernagin was hoping to travel. The ILDP was born at the New York country estate of the famous African-American cosmetics tycoon, Madame C. J. Walker, who had been chosen as a delegate by the Washington gathering. Attended by around thirty blacks and two whites (Jonas and his wife), the inaugural meeting elected the Rev. Adam Clayton Powell, Sr., as president of the ILDP, Madame Walker as treasurer, and A. Philip Randolph as secretary. Among the other noteworthy participants were Marcus Garvey and the Rev. George Frazier Miller. The immediate program of the league was that it should act as a coordinating body for the various organizations that had elected delegates to travel to Paris—arranging tours of European cities for them and securing accommodation, providing press facilities, lobbying the participants in the peace conference, and organizing "an international conference of the darker peoples" in Paris. The longer-term ambition of the ILDP was to be the benevolent world representative of all

"darker peoples" and a disseminator of educational and political information.[59]

On January 7, 1919, a committee of seven ILDP members, including
Walker, Jonas, and Randolph, held a meeting at the Waldorf-Astoria Hotel
with Shuroku Kuroiwa, a leading Tokyo newspaper proprietor, who was on
his way to Paris to join the Japanese mission to the peace conference. The
BI in New York described Kuroiwa as "the Japanese William Randolph
Hearst." According to the ILDP's account, published by Randolph in the
organization's short-lived journal, *World Forum,* Kuroiwa expressed "his unqualified and genuine approval of the darker peoples making common
cause against the common enemy—race prejudice based upon color." Randolph entrusted the ILDP's "Memorandum of Peace Proposals" to Kuroiwa,
who promised that the question of race would be raised at Versailles. The
memorandum called for an international agreement on the "abolition and
prohibition of all economic, political, and social discriminations in all countries, based upon color." It also demanded freedom of movement, revision
of African treaties "entered into through force or duress, threat or intimidation," the removal of restrictive barriers to trade, and self-determination.
The ILDP argued that the German colonies should be entrusted to a
"supernational commission," and that an "International Commission of
Darker Peoples," made up of educated blacks and Asians, should give tech-
nological advice to developing countries and monitor interference in their
affairs by industrial nations. Labor conditions should be improved, universal suffrage introduced, and revenue raised from import duties. Finally,
the ILDP asked the nations participating in the peace conference to recognize that

> [t]he egalitarian theory of mankind is the only sound one upon which
> the new world society must be founded.
>
> All races and nations must be accorded free access to the instrumen-
> talities of civilization. Races and nations are different because of differ-
> ences in opportunity and not on account of differences in capacity.[60]

R. D. Jonas included an account of the Waldorf-Astoria meeting in his secret
report to the BI and also, apparently, in his report to British military intelligence, since it was later mentioned by the New York City MID office, along
with the names of Japanese radicals with whom Jonas claimed black leaders
were working.[61] (The ILDP dissolved early in 1919, weakened by its failure

Race, War, and Surveillance

to make an impression on the Peace Conference, the divergent interests of its members, and the death of C. J. Walker.)

In Paris, American negotiators were ultimately forced to acknowledge that Japan was serious in pursuing formal recognition of the equality of races and the right of aliens to equal treatment, but Wilson and his advisors would certainly not have welcomed additional lobbying on this issue in France by groups of African Americans. After its introduction into the League of Nations discussions early in February 1919, the Japanese proposal was never favored by Wilson for domestic political and, possibly, personal reasons, although the most active opposition came from Australia and Great Britain.[62] Thus, the State Department's refusal to grant passports to black delegations in the early months of 1919 was based partly on a determination to avoid international comment on American racial discrimination, and partly on a general desire to discourage equal rights agitation at home.

By no means all African Americans regretted the government's refusal to grant passports to the delegations, revealing the factionalism and personal rivalries at the heart of black politics. Several newspapers questioned the usefulness and even the sincerity of certain would-be travelers. The *New York Age* declared that it saw "no sense or reason in this multiplying of so-called Peace delegates that will never get as far down the harbor as the Statue of Liberty."[63] The *Baltimore Daily Herald* referred to what it called "that class of professional Negroes . . . , always and eternally ready to hand around the hat to lift a donation for themselves for their great services to the race," and added,

> We did not expect that class of men to secure passports and it is fortunate for the race in this country that they will not be permitted to lower the dignity of the race and destroy the splendid impression of the race given the peoples of Europe by the manly, sensible, and brave bearing and exploits of the Black American soldiers, by their wild rantings and most foolish attempt to intrude the domestic ills from which we suffer into the presence of men gathered together upon matters of international import, and concerning which they could neither give aid nor give counsel.[64]

The *Chicago Defender* suggested that the withholding of passports might be "a great help to protect the pocket books of the poor people who have recently fallen victim to graft schemes instigated by people seeking to have a good time in Paris."[65]

Most black people, however, were angered at the government's concoction of an excuse to refuse passports to virtually all blacks, even those who would have traveled independently and at their own expense. A. Philip Randolph was particularly incensed, ridiculing the government's favoritism toward "'good niggers', safe and sound leaders who will take orders."[66] Cyril Briggs, who devoted most of the early issues of the *Crusader* to internationalist ideals such as self-determination, but whose own small organization, the Hamitic League of the World, made no attempt to send delegates to France, compared the radicalism and vigor of the UNIA's envoys with the moderation of those blacks who had been allowed to travel in December 1918. He speculated that Du Bois might be on an intelligence mission for the government, and could think of only one useful purpose for Moton's trip:

The South has been greatly troubled of late with its guilty conscience and fear of what those Black Soldiers, who have chased the white Huns, will do to murderous crackers when they get back home.

It may be possible that the South intends sending white men's "niggers" across to placate the Black warriors of Democracy before they get back home, to the end that they will have been prepared by "nigger" leaders to go back South in the old spirit of servile submissiveness to wrongs and insults that no self-respecting race or man can further tolerate?

We merely ask the question. In the meantime we prefer to pin our faith in the Randolphs, the Geo. Frazier Millers, the Monroe Trotters, the Harrisons and the Garveys of the race.[67]

In Paris, meanwhile, Du Bois had pressed ahead with the arrangements for the Pan-African Congress. It began a week later than the date agreed to by the French government, running from February 19 to 21. Fifty-seven people attended, from fifteen countries, but there were only twelve African participants. Blaise Diagne, a Senegalese member of the French Chamber of Deputies, who had been instrumental in securing Clemenceau's permission to hold the gathering in Paris, was elected president of the congress, while Du Bois served as its secretary. The United States was the most heavily represented country, with sixteen individuals, including YMCA worker Addie W. Hunton, William Jernagin (whose own race gatherings never took place), a number of black army officers, and three white members of the NAACP board. Robert Moton had said he would attend the congress, according to Du Bois, but he left France before it began.[68] Thirteen members of the congress were from the French West Indies, seven from France, and seven from Haiti, including the UNIA delegate, Eliezer Cadet, who distributed copies of the *Negro World*. France, Belgium, and Portugal sent official observers.[69] The report of the French official, colonial administrator Maurice Delafosse, made it clear that his government did not regard the Pan-African Congress as a radical threat. Indeed, Diagne began the opening session with a salute to French colonialism, and, as a historian of Africa has noted, "the anti-American edge of the movement was actually much sharper than the anti-colonial one." Delafosse acknowledged that

> The nations which until now have been marginalized, the races which are victims of prejudice, are naturally the most anxious of all those nations and races which are awaiting, with justifiable impatience, decisions upon which the fate of humanity will depend.[70]

He also had no doubts about the representativeness of the congress: "I am therefore convinced that, despite its restricted membership, the Pan-African Congress had sufficient authority to speak for all black people."[71] The Pan-African Congress adopted a number of resolutions, including one calling on the League of Nations, when formed, to monitor the welfare of native peoples. In particular, the congress asked for the recognition of native ownership of land, prevention of the exhaustion of natural wealth, the abolition of slavery, the provision of technical education, improvement of hygiene and medical care, native participation in government at a local level, eventual self-government, and resistance to the imposition of foreign culture and religion. The most important resolution, so far as black Americans were concerned, was that

> Where ever persons of African descent are civilized and able to meet the tests of surrounding culture, they shall be accorded the same rights as their fellow-citizens; they shall not be denied on account of race or color a voice in their own government, justice before the courts and economic and social equality according to ability and desert.[72]

While in Paris, Du Bois met Woodrow Wilson's adviser, Col. Edward M. House, and the American colonial expert George Beer, but he later admitted that if the Pan-African Congress had any slight influence, it was limited to encouraging acceptance of the mandate system for dealing with the problem of the former German colonies.[73]

At the end of February, one week after the Pan-African Congress dispersed, the State Department announced that it was looking into the four-week-old news that the French government had, after all, given permission for the congress to go ahead. If that was the case, the State Department conceded, with feigned generosity, then it would ask for a delay in the holding of the congress, so as to allow "a limited number of delegates of the colored race from the United States to reach Paris in order to participate."[74] Early in March, State Department officials must have felt that their original position had been the right one, after receiving a report from Harry F. Worley, the white Virginia-born financial adviser to the Republic of Liberia. Although he did not attend "the so-called Pan-African Congress," Worley claimed to have heard from those who had that "the speeches of the American Negroes were highly inflammatory and condemnatory of the social conditions in the United States and inveighing against the Government of the United States for permitting such conditions to exist." This, wrote Worley, was especially true of Du Bois. In fact, Du Bois's Pan-African Congress did not cause any great political or diplomatic difficulty to the Wilson administration, but one consequence of his visit to France almost certainly caused government officials, including those who had helped to get him a passport, to regret that he had been allowed to travel. During his time in France, Du Bois had spectacular success in unearthing documentary evidence of hostile and prejudiced attitudes on the part of white army officers toward black troops. [75]

William Monroe Trotter claimed that he never even bothered to apply for a passport, so sure was he that it would be refused. This did not prevent him from reaching France, but he arrived alone and long after the Pan-African Congress had closed. Du Bois was already back in the United States before Trotter left on April 18, 1919. Nevertheless, Trotter enhanced his reputation for selflessness and determination in the fight for equal rights. He had left Boston in mid-February, as the Pan-African Congress was preparing to meet, but it took him two months to secure a job as a cook on a small freighter sailing out of New York. Trotter jumped ship at Le Havre in the first week of May and made his way to Paris, where he turned out a number of well-received articles for the French press on the conditions facing black Americans and sent copies of the resolutions of the National Race Congress to all the negotiators. Throughout June, he pestered the American commission to the peace conference for an interview, or for some indication that the petition which he had sent would be discussed, but he was ignored. In early July, after the treaty had been signed, he returned to a hero's welcome in Harlem.[76] The only one of the delegates elected at Trotter's National Race Congress to secure a passport was Bishop Lynnwood W. Kyles, of the African Methodist Episcopal Zion (AMEZ) Church, and this came only after government officials had been carefully obstructive. Kyles, from St. Louis, submitted his first application to the State Department in person on December 20, 1918, the day after the National Race Congress closed, stating that he intended to sail from New York a month later, but omitting to mention that he had just been elected to Trotter's delegation. He ostensibly applied for the passport as part of an AMEZ Church delegation to Methodist conferences in West Africa, and commented that he wanted to visit France only "en route." This reference to France was enough to ensure that no action was taken on his application. Finally, a few days after the State Department's February 1, 1919, announcement about alleged French unwillingness to allow black delegates to congregate in Paris, and almost three weeks after his intended date of departure, Kyles was informed that his passport application was being denied. His one-dollar application fee was returned. In May, almost three months after the Pan-African Congress, Kyles appealed to Assistant Secretary of State Adee to reconsider his application, in view of the recent granting of passports to other members of the AMEZ Church mission to West Africa. He now hoped to leave New York in June. After a further two weeks, Kyles was issued a passport on May 26, 1919, on the basis of his December application, except that his request to be allowed to visit France en route was specifically denied.[77]

The State Department had relaxed slightly once the Pan-African Congress was over. Discreet and conservative black leaders who had the backing of white groups or politicians rather than of black organizations could now secure passports, so long as they made it clear that they would not be engaging in political activity in Paris. Even so, the process was dominated by an air of skepticism and reluctance on the part of the bureaucrats. In April 1919, Mary Church Terrell, the wife of District of Columbia municipal court judge Robert H. Terrell (one of the few black Republican appointees to retain office during the Wilson years), was granted a passport to travel as a delegate from the American Section of the International Committee of Women for Permanent Peace (ICWPP) to the forthcoming International Congress of Women at Berne. She was able to support her application with a letter of invitation from the ICWPP, signed by its chairwoman, Jane

Addams, and the secretary for the American delegates, Alice Thacher Post, the wife of Assistant Secretary of Labor Louis F. Post.[78] Richard R. Wright, president of the Georgia State Industrial College at Savannah, applied for a passport on June 20, 1919, in order to travel on July 3 to England, France, and Belgium, "to study school conditions." His application fee was promptly returned with a request that he provide evidence that this was the real object of the trip. Wright forwarded to the State Department a letter from Emmett Scott supporting Wright's plans and stating that Robert Moton had asked Scott to give Wright assistance. In addition, Governor Hugh M. Dorsey of Georgia telegraphed the State Department in support of Wright's proposed tour. These endorsements persuaded Assistant Secretary of State Phillips to allow a passport to be sent on July 3 to Wright in Philadelphia, where his son was a teacher and editor. From there, Wright traveled to New York, where his passport was visaed by the representatives of the French, Belgian, and British governments, before he sailed on July 11. The British military representative was uneasy about Wright's departure, however, informing the BI a few days later that Wright had seemed suspiciously hurried when asking for his visa, and that he had admitted knowing and agreeing with various black radicals, including William Monroe Trotter. The British remained convinced that Wright was planning to join forces with Trotter in Paris, although Wright had denied this. (In fact, Trotter had left France by the time Wright sailed from New York and the two probably passed each other in mid-Atlantic.) The State Department took the view that it was too late to do anything about it.[79]

The demobilization of the American army in 1919, in the context of inflation, the growing red scare, and labor unrest, was widely recognized as a potential emergency, and the racial dimension was frequently noted. In March 1919, soon after the return from France of the African-American combat divisions (92nd and 93rd), the black director of a large, segregated YMCA branch in Chicago warned a group of the city's leading businessmen that

> [m]any of the colored boys who have been in the army are coming back with new ideas about what life ought to be. America, which fought to make the world safe for democracy, has an acid test for democracy here at home. The negro soldier is coming back with a consciousness of power hitherto unrealized, a sense of manhood, and a belief in his ability to carry responsibility. He believes that his strength is the same as that of other men.[80]

Such frankness might have been appreciated in northern industrial cities, but elsewhere black leaders were trying to get across a subtly different message to white audiences, while acknowledging that the war would have had an impact on African Americans. On a visit to the South, Emmett Scott sought to allay white apprehension about assertive returning black soldiers. At the Twenty-Eighth Annual Tuskegee Conference, he stated that black men would have benefited physically and mentally from military training and would return with "a broader vision and appreciation of American citizenship, as well as with new ideas of what Liberty and Freedom (not license) mean." The black American veteran, said Scott, would avoid anything which might "jeopardize or impair the honor and fame his race has won in this war by any thoughtless or unmanly word or deed."[81]

For American military intelligence officers, who had been uneasily contemplating the probable mood of returning black soldiers since November 1918, the immediate concern had been with discipline after the Armistice and the way in which contact with French civilians might influence the soldiers' future attitudes toward American society. White officers in France had expressed the contradictory views that blacks would indulge in general rape and looting in France and that the friendly reception accorded to them by French civilians would lead to demands for "social equality" at home. During the war, senior AEF officers had made it plain to the French army that they disapproved of the local population's "treating the Negro with familiarity and indulgence." French officers were advised that the "vices of the Negro" represented "a constant menace to the American who has to repress them sternly." Strict orders were issued after the Armistice to limit contacts between members of black regiments and French civilians, especially women.[82] Even before the war ended, Newton D. Baker had begun to receive advice that he should repatriate black soldiers as soon as possible. On November 7, a War Department official attached to the Services of Supply wrote Baker,

> If I may recommend one thing from observation as to what is going on here, get the colored troops out of France as soon as you can. The French treat them like they do their Algerians and our men misunderstand this and it has resulted in quite a bit of crime.[83]

Less than a fortnight later, a cable from a State Department investigator was passed to military intelligence. He reported that on a visit to the front he had been told by white American officers of the "excesses indulged in by our negro troops at Chateau-Thierry." The alleged collapse of discipline was attributed to the fact that French civilians had shown the black soldier "more courtesy and social attention than he was accustomed to at home." It was claimed that villagers had been terrorized by drunken soldiers and that cases of murder and attempted rape had followed. Northern blacks were said to have behaved worse than those from the South. The State Department agent concluded that, "with no reflection on their service in the war, I believe every effort possible should be made to have all negro troops immediately returned to America." Otherwise, he envisaged a situation in which black soldiers, through excessive drinking "and with passions aroused, would be a menace not only to the localities in which they are quartered but would necessarily discredit the United States."[84] Such views were actively promoted by racist senior officers who were determined to denigrate African-American soldiers and officers at the end of the war. The commanding general of the 92nd division, Gen. C. C. Ballou, was said to have referred to it as his "rapist" division, while in December 1918, Ballou's chief of staff, Col. Allen J. Greer, the author of Bulletin No. 35, wrote Sen. Kenneth D. McKellar of Tennessee a lengthy letter accusing black officers and men of cowardice, dishonesty, and inefficiency, adding that they had been "dangerous to no one but themselves and women." Another general claimed that by mid-December there had been twenty-six cases of rape in the 92nd division—an outright lie, which Robert Russa Moton exposed when he examined the division's records soon afterward and found that seven of the twelve thousand men in the division had been charged with rape, of whom two had been convicted. One of the convictions had been set aside at General Headquarters and the one certainly guilty man had been executed.[85]

Shortly afterward, Newton D. Baker was shown a lengthy memorandum prepared by Walter Loving, in which the black agent listed, as he saw them, "some of the impending dangers which will undoubtedly confront the military authorities should negro troops be kept in France for any great length of time."[86] Loving at no time traveled to France to view conditions for himself, and so his opinions were necessarily colored by his own experiences of active service in the Philippines, some twenty years earlier, and by the misleading and biased reports of white field officers which reached Washington in 1918. He felt there had been an undercurrent of racial friction within the AEF ever since it had arrived in France, and now that the war was over he expected this tension to surface in places of entertainment, where whites would insist on segregation. Black soldiers would naturally seek diversions, wrote Loving,

> and with them diversion and women are synonymous. No American white man, whether he comes from the north or the south, wants to see colored men mingling with white women in sporting houses and other questionable places, no more so than a colored man would want to see a white man enter the house of a respectable colored family and claim one of the race's best to serve him as his mistress—a practice which is in vogue in this late day in the south.[87]

He predicted that if black and white American soldiers were allowed to compete for the attentions of French women, it would result in "an American race war in France." Such a "catastrophe would be disastrous and disgraceful before the whole civilized world," especially if, as Loving thought possible, French troops took the side of the black men: "Just imagine a mix-up of this kind." Loving was aware of a further complication: a number of black men were contemplating marriage to French women. This, he stated, would not be looked on with favor by either race at home; for one thing, many black women were "looking forward to such opportunities themselves." Loving's advice to the War Department, given, he wrote, "for the good of the service and to the best interest of the colored race in general," was that no discharges be granted in France, that all black soldiers "be shipped home with the least possible delay," and that "strict measures" be adopted to prevent soldiers of different races encountering each other in brothels.[88]

Marlborough Churchill endorsed these suggestions, advising the chief of staff that "Major Loving's recommendations to this division with respect to questions concerning his own race have always been valuable and are believed to be entirely without race prejudice." The chief of staff clearly concurred and Newton D. Baker wrote on Loving's memorandum that it was "very thoughtful and judicious."[89] The secretary of war was concerned about the management and demeanor of the African-American regiments for a variety of reasons: to preserve good order within the army, to enhance the reputation of the black soldier, to avoid criticism of the administration, and to promote peaceful race relations in the United States. Baker had been appalled by two earlier instances of gang rape of white women by black soldiers in the United States, particularly an assault at Rockford, Ill., by nineteen black soldiers from Camp Grant, and was alert to what he called "popular feeling aroused in these cases," which led to "very widespread and bitter resentment."[90] He may thus have been predisposed to accept as true some of the uglier characterizations of black troops as they prepared to return from France, but he was also well aware that if whites in the South came to regard these veterans as lawless and corrupted, many African Americans could suffer terribly.

In early December 1918, Baker was supplied with the southern white supremacist view of the returning black soldier by one of the MID's volunteer officers, the Missouri-born Capt. Frederick Sullens. In civilian life, as the editor of a leading Mississippi newspaper, the *Jackson Daily News*, Sullens had written sympathetically about the efforts of black farmers to undertake agricultural improvements, and opposed the successful bid of the virulently racist former governor James K. Vardaman to gain election to the U.S. Senate in 1912 and the election of Theodore G. Bilbo to the governorship in 1915.[91] In the interwar period, Sullens would nonetheless be a firm opponent of extending civil rights to black Mississippians and retained from his army service the MID's view of black leaders. His description of W. E. B. Du Bois in the 1920s contained loud echoes of Capt. James A. Bruff's slanted portrait of Du Bois and other NAACP board members at the time of the commission controversy. Sullens called Du Bois "a Northern Negro who hates the South and everything Southern. He is brilliantly educated but has a warped mind. He is perhaps the most vicious, vindictive, volatile, and uncompromising hater of the Southern white man who ever lived."[92] According to Sullens, southerners with whom he corresponded and spoke were expecting racial trouble to follow the war, unless black veterans were carefully handled. In the first place, they thought it imperative that the men should be prevented from returning to their homes in uniform. Anyone familiar with the South, he declared, knew that "the negro soldier strutting about in uniform three months after his discharge will always be a potential danger." (Only a danger to himself, Sullens might have added if he were being truthful.) He predicted that the black veteran would be a changed man—one who had gained "new ideas and social aspirations . . . , particularly from his association with the French demi-monde." If veterans tried to carry these ideas back to the South, and Sullens was sure that some would, he foresaw "an era of bloodshed . . . as compared with which the history of reconstruction will be mild reading, indeed." He recommended that the federal government cooperate with the state authorities to help turn black soldiers back into submissive civilians. (This problem had already been given considerable attention in Alabama, for instance, in meetings between the governor and various bodies, including the American Protective League, leading the Alabama Council of Defense to ask Baker to delay the return of black soldiers until the threat of German subversion had passed.[93]) Sullens suggested that the Morale Branch should contact state governors as soon as possible to discuss the return of black troops, and that the War Department should engage in propaganda through black churches and the southern press, to dampen the veterans' political and social ambitions and calm white fears. He claimed that his main concern was for the welfare of the soldiers: "If many of them have had false ideas instilled in their minds during the period of service, that is more a misfortune than their fault."[94]

Capt. James E. Cutler of the Morale Branch subsequently discussed the probable mood of returning black soldiers with Newton D. Baker and George Foster Peabody, from whom Baker often sought advice on racial matters. Cutler found them in favor of allowing conservative black speakers to address the troops prior to their discharge, but unwilling to go along with Sullens's other proposals, which they felt would have exceeded the War Department's authority.[95] Of all Wilson's cabinet officers, Baker was probably the least likely to be attracted to the idea of collaborating with semi-official organizations like the APL to assist southern whites to reassert their dominance over the black population. Peabody's reservations stemmed from other sensitivities; a native of Georgia, he opposed any action that might later be construed as outside interference in an essentially southern racial problem.[96]

The War Department heeded the advice to recall black troops without unnecessary delay. Although the combat regiments were involved in the occupation of Germany in December 1918, they were withdrawn to France to await transport home in January 1919. Black labor battalions of the Services of Supply (SOS) were deployed away from centers of population and given the task of clearing the battlefields and reburying the dead. At the Argonne National Cemetery near Romagne, six thousand African Americans prepared and filled twenty-three thousand graves. No black soldiers were taken to Paris to take part in the Victory Parade.[97] Instead, they were treated to homilies in their camps by men like Robert Russa Moton, who had carefully discussed what to say to them with the Morale Branch before leaving for France. Cutler reported to his superiors soon after Moton sailed that he was going "to add his influence in favor of common sense and right conduct on the part of the returning colored soldiers."[98] Moton gave the men a set speech on the need to behave "in a straightforward, manly, and modest way" on their return to the United States, to get a job or a piece of land and a wife and to avoid doing "anything in peace to spoil the magnificent record you have made in war." Both Woodrow Wilson and Newton D. Baker expressed satisfaction at the way in which Moton accomplished his task, but black radicals were less impressed by this impersonation of Booker T. Washington at his most submissive.[99] Cyril Briggs, delighted to have been proved right about the object of Moton's voyage, weighed in against its "shameless treachery and disgusting servility." Moton, he wrote, was "living in the wrong era":

> [T]imes and the Negro's spirit have undergone a radical change since the servile days of fool advice to own pigs and land and give no thought to the political rights that alone could protect the owner of land and pigs in his property rights. The Negro has learned from sad experience that begging and crawling and following "handpicked" leaders will win nothing that is worthwhile. He has seen Suffrage and Labor triumphant through a policy of *demanding* and *agitating*. And neither the Negro men who fought for Democracy on the shell torn fields of France, nor the Negro women and men who stood by the country and backed up all its soldiers, are going to adopt the "modest and unassuming" attitudes that Robby recommends. . . . No man can serve two masters and we commend Robby to his white 'massas.' The Negro Race is forever done with the spineless Judas Iscariot type of leader.[100]

In France, meanwhile, intelligence officers with the AEF were becoming anxious about the mood of the African-American regiments. Before the Armistice, there had been no suggestion that black soldiers were disloyal, even though the enemy attempted to lure them away from the Allied lines. German planes had dropped leaflets in which African Americans were asked what harm had ever been done to them by Germany and whether they had benefited at all from the "Democracy" for which they now fought:

> You have been made a tool of the egotistic and rapacious rich in America, and there is nothing in the whole game for you but broken bones, hor-

rible wounds, spoiled health, or death. No satisfaction whatever will you get out of this unjust war. You have never seen Germany, so you are fools if you allow people to make you hate us. Come over and see for yourself. Let those do the fighting who make the profit out of this war. Don't allow them to use you as cannon fodder.

To carry a gun in this service is not an honor but a shame. Throw it away and come over to the German lines. You will find friends who will help you.[101]

Such overtures had no effect, but white officers in the AEF had nevertheless been made uneasy by unsubstantiated rumors during the war that black soldiers had covertly formed an organization to fight post-war discrimination in the South.[102] These suspicions grew after the Armistice, and in January 1919, as the black combat regiments waited to return home, the AEF's intelligence arm, the original G-2, began to receive fresh reports that black officers of the 370th Infantry (originally the 8th Illinois National Guard, from Chicago) had formed a new secret society for "the promotion of social equality between colored and white after demobilization." The movement seemed to have spread to two other 93rd Division regiments, the 369th, formerly the 15th New York National Guard, and the 371st, made up of southern draftees. All three regiments were encamped at Brest and it was believed that the organization had made contact with African-American leaders and with French politicians. As far as G-2 could determine, its object was to resist the continued imposition of "white ascendancy," especially in the South, and to "maintain and strengthen the social equality between the races as established in France." The difficulty which intelligence officers encountered in securing any further information about the organization— even its name—led G-2 to conclude that it was "probable that there were motives other than the above in the minds of the promoters."[103]

Brig. Gen. Dennis E. Nolan, the New York–born chief of G-2, advised his officers to be on the lookout for signs of such a society wherever black troops were stationed, adding, "In the circumstances it is essential that the utmost discretion be exercised in making observations." In mid-February, when the 93rd Division had returned to the United States and the 92nd was at sea, Nolan warned the MID that the mysterious organization probably existed, but that G-2 had been unable to prove it before the combat divisions departed. He hoped the on-board investigation being conducted by the 92nd Division's G-2 officer, Maj. F. P. Schoonmaker, a Pennsylvania lawyer in civilian life, would yield more information, but the latter, in his final communication from Camp Meade on February 25, could only report that there had been some sort of meeting at the Le Mans Forwarding Camp on the "[p]olitical, economical, educational betterment and co-ordination of the negro in the United States on the principles of Democracy as won on the Battlefields of Europe."[104]

The black SOS regiments, returning to the United States some weeks after the combat divisions, provoked a spate of new concerns. In April 1919, Col. John M. Dunn, chief of the Positive Branch of the MID, claimed that practically every black soldier in the labor battalions was bringing back an army revolver. He suggested to Churchill that extra efforts be made in France to prevent this and that the military authorities in the United States should search black regiments for weapons on arrival. The seriousness of the matter could not be exaggerated, he warned,

> since it is a well-known fact that there is a great deal of social and labor unrest among the negro population of the United States, who are demanding social equality as well as other changes in their post-war status. Negro publications openly advocate race war and violence, and if there be any truth in this report about the revolvers, this would seem to indicate one of the sources from which they are obtaining, or could obtain, firearms for illegal purposes.[105]

Dunn's warning was backed up by the statement of a white officer stationed in a supply area in Belgium from January to March 1919. After hearing frequent bouts of shooting coming from the direction of the salvage ammunition and small arms dumps, he had discovered that all the black pioneer soldiers detailed to sort the weapons were armed with revolvers and automatic pistols.[106] Churchill approved Dunn's request that extra care be taken to ensure that black soldiers did not bring home private arsenals, but he stipulated that "*all troops* and not only the black ones should be inspected on arrival." However, in alerting the intelligence community to the problem, the MID placed clear emphasis on the particular need to crack down on black troops. The U.S. military attaché in Paris was advised of the reports that African Americans were preparing to return home illegally armed and was asked to recommend appropriate action "which will not raise a race discrimination issue in case of publicity." This request was forwarded to G-2, and at the same time intelligence officers at U.S. military ports of entry were warned that black soldiers might be bringing in guns, "which certain classes may attempt to use in the future in race or radical movements." G-2 replied that thorough kit inspections already made sure that only officers and senior NCOs were able to leave France with their guns, as they were entitled to do, and that the original information about black troops was probably unreliable. At Hoboken, Maj. Lawrence Dunham also testified to the effectiveness of the inspections and added that if any German revolvers were to be smuggled in, they would prove useless since ammunition of the necessary caliber was unavailable in the United States.[107] At Newport News, the port intelligence officer reacted to the MID's call for extra vigilance by imposing an especially detailed kit inspection at the surrounding dispersal camps for a trial month, but this revealed no great problem with soldiers landing in possession of unauthorized weapons.[108] Like so much else in the chronic fear of externally inspired African-American disloyalty which gripped parts of the American government, the press, and the white civilian population during and after World War I, the episode revealed far more about a need to seek and find conspiracy and a deep-seated anxiety about the vengefulness of black men than it did about the undoubted determination shared by the majority of African-American veterans and their civilian peers to urgently advance the cause of equal rights.

Meanwhile, G-2 reported that it had picked up new information that an organization and journal for black officers was about to be set up in the United States along the lines of a Masonic lodge. The man behind the scheme was "a Methodist or Baptist minister of Galveston, Texas, radical and probably militant in his views." An investigation revealed nothing, but on March 1, 1919, Walter Loving recounted what little he had been able to discover about yet another group, the Soldiers' Association for the Fight for a True Democracy, said to have been formed by the men of the 371st Infantry at Camp Jackson, S.C., prior to their discharge. Loving reported that although it was led by a "very conservative and very intellectual" regimental sergeant major from Pittsburgh, the men had joined this association on the basis that, "having fought and won the cause overseas, they must enjoy it in America, [even] if it costs another battle." The intelligence officer of the 371st Infantry suggested that the best way to tackle the organizers of this group might be to get them involved in some kind of swindle and then expose them through leaks to selected newspapers, "and thus 'get them in bad' with the colored people." This proposal was quickly ruled out by Col. K. C. Masteller, chief of the Negative Branch of the MID, who felt that military intelligence should obey the restrictions imposed in January 1919 on its work outside the army. The MID consoled itself with the thought that the Soldiers' Association, which it compared in its basic aims to the NAACP, had had little time to organize before demobilization and that "perhaps it is safe to assume that after the men become scattered their organization will very soon fall to pieces and nothing much will come of it."[109] This assessment proved to be largely correct. Most black veterans' groups were weak and disunited and their proliferation was less an expression of political determination than a response to the American Legion's refusal to admit non-white servicemen on an equal basis. State branches of the Legion were permitted to either exclude blacks or establish separate posts for them, and would not permit them to hold office above post level.[110]

During March and April, G-2 closely examined the mail of African-American officers, chaplains, and YMCA secretaries. The latter remained under suspicion because of the establishment of the "Honey Bee" club by a YMCA secretary for "protecting negro interests, improving negro morals, and creating social equality between the colored and whites in the United States after demobilization." The letters contained accounts of French hospitality and "a certain amount of dissatisfaction and grumbling" on racial problems, but no references were found to nascent veterans' groups.[111] This seemed to confirm an earlier MID suspicion that sensitive correspondence on such subjects was being carried home by black naval personnel or sent via the civilian postal services by newly acquired French wives of black servicemen.[112] In mid-April, Loving became aware of a further black veterans' organization, the Grand Army of Americans, run from Washington, D.C., by Samuel F. Sewall, a former member of the 10th Cavalry. Sewall had emerged from the Des Moines officers' training camp with the rank of captain, but had been invalided out soon afterward. In June 1918, he had supplied military intelligence with a list of the delegates to the National Liberty Congress organized by Trotter and Harrison. He was not thought to be especially radical and his organization was not considered subversive; nor was it particularly successful.[113]

Walter Loving was much impressed by the determination of black soldiers to ensure that their wartime contribution should prove to have been worthwhile. After a reception in March 1919 for the 1st Separate Battalion of the District of Columbia National Guard, recently mustered out of the 372nd Infantry at Camp Meade, he commented,

> The thought of fighting for democracy abroad and expecting democracy at home seems to be the key note and when the soldiers themselves are

not using the expression, they can always find someone to express their sentiments on these public occasions.[114]

In other words, W. E. B. Du Bois's famous, if hackneyed, editorial in the May *Crisis,* "Returning Soldiers," in which he slashed away at America's injustice to its darker-skinned people, was not merely a new rallying cry to African Americans, but also a faithful reflection of what the veterans, in particular, felt after the Great War:

> . . . [W]e are cowards and jackasses if now that that war is over, we do not marshal every ounce of our brain and brawn to fight a sterner, longer, more unbending battle against the forces of hell in our own land.
> We *return.*
> We *return from fighting.*
> We *return fighting.*
> Make way for Democracy! We saved it in France, and by Great Jehovah, we will save it in the United States of America, or know the reason why.[115]

This sentiment was given its fullest organizational expression on April 7, 1919, with the formation in Harlem of the League for Democracy (LFD), the most radical and successful of the black veterans' associations. The driving force behind the LFD was its secretary, Lt. Osceola E. McKaine, "an energetic young man of excellent education and ability," according to Loving. Born in South Carolina, he had studied in Washington and Boston before becoming a freelance journalist, supporting Booker T. Washington's gradualist approach to black advancement. He joined the army in 1914, serving in the Philippines and afterward with the 24th Infantry at Columbus, N.M., and under Pershing during the latter's pursuit of Pancho Villa. Soon after the United States declared war in Germany, and prior to the ill-fated transfer of the 24th to Houston, McKaine was selected for officer training at Des Moines, and was assigned to the 367th Infantry. While stationed at Camp Upton, N.Y., in the spring of 1918, McKaine had written an optimistic article for the *Outlook* on the high morale of black soldiers and their eagerness to fight for democracy.[116] In stark contrast with this was a piece published by the *Independent* in January 1919, which McKaine had written in France immediately after the Armistice. In it, he dwelt upon the affection which black soldiers had quickly formed for the French people because of their apparent lack of racial prejudice: "France was a terrestrial heaven where they could forget that they were sinners simply because they were black. . . . France had no man made laws governing social equality; . . .

America suffered by comparison." The black soldier was in no mood to accept the pre-war American status quo:

> For the duration of the war he has put aside his grievances; but he is determined that the new physical liberation of Belgium, Rumania and Serbia will also mean complete economic, political and educational liberation for himself and his race. . . . He feels that any inhabitant of a country who willingly, nay eagerly, offers himself for the supreme sacrifice in defending that country's honor, liberty and peace has an inalienable right to share equally in that honor, liberty and the prosperities of peace.[117]

The LFD, which may have had its origins in the Le Mans meeting described by Schoonmaker, was organized by black officers, but membership was open to all black veterans, YMCA staff, essential war workers, and the relatives of those killed in the war. It was pledged to press for improved promotion prospects for blacks in the armed services, electoral emancipation, the eradication of lynching and Jim Crow laws, equal economic and educational opportunity, and justice in the courts. The initial membership fee was one dollar, with subscriptions at twenty-five cents per month, and badges were sold for two dollars to former members of the black regiments. Each branch, or "camp," was to be sold a charter for five dollars. The New York City camp, with three hundred members, attempted to find jobs and accommodation for veterans and ensured that they received their two months' bonus on discharge from the army. Within two weeks of its foundation, the LFD had branches in Atlanta, Boston, Brooklyn, Chicago, the District of Columbia, Newark, Patterson, N.J., Philadelphia, Providence, R.I., St. Louis, and Tallahassee, Fla.[118] The LFD made its mark with a campaign to defend the record of black troops during the war. The men had fought well, especially those under French command, despite being often ill equipped and having their morale undermined by the frequent replacement of allegedly incompetent black officers by unsympathetic whites. The black combat regiments played an important part in Allied advances which hastened the end of the war, suffering heavy losses, while the "laborers in uniform" of the SOS worked long and hard for scant recognition.[119] Initially, the contribution of blacks to the AEF was acknowledged by other Americans in the press and on public platforms, often on the basis of information supplied by Emmett Scott.[120] Such gratitude was short-lived, however, in the face of a whispering campaign intended to deny the courage of the soldiers and the efficiency of their black officers. More by word of mouth and private communication than by public statement, those whites who found it difficult to give blacks due credit for their war record had their prejudices confirmed.[121] Thus, a year after the Armistice, Sen. John Sharp Williams of Mississippi felt qualified to declare that African-American soldiers had

> "flickered." . . . I think the boys who came home can be trusted to tell the truth about the negro's service in France without my raising the subject in the Senate. I never expected them to do any great service, and I rather pitied than blamed them when I found out they had not. The whole thing after all was a "white man's fight" in which the negro was not interested. If I had had my way, I would not have had a negro soldier in the entire army except behind the lines in transport and communication service, etc.[122]

Ray Stannard Baker, the progressive journalist and biographer of Wilson, sailed back from France on the same vessel as the president and witnessed the readiness of men at the highest levels of American government to assume that blacks had been rotten soldiers. Among the anecdotes current among Wilson's party, which Baker jotted down, was one about "the Negro company that ran away."[123] This hearsay originated with white army officers, many of whom, especially the regulars and southerners, had opposed the awarding of commissions to blacks. In the field, they had removed black officers by referring them to efficiency boards which could usually be relied upon to find them unfit for command. The white southern sociologist Thomas J. Woofter, who sailed to France with black troops and was in the AEF HQ during the latter months of the war, saw several negative reports about the 92nd Division which he knew to be false.[124] In the months after the war, white officers made a special effort to discredit those blacks who had retained their commissions, in order to reduce the likelihood of their becoming a widespread feature of the post-war army. W. E. B. Du Bois published some of the most flagrant examples of this campaign in the May *Crisis*. On his visits to the camps in France, prior to the Pan-African Congress in Paris, Du Bois had collected a number of revealing documents, with the aid of black clerical staff of the 92nd Division, despite Maj. F. P. Schoonmaker's order to intelligence officers that a "prompt report will be made to G-2 of all Du Bois's moves and actions while at station of any unit." These documents were taken back to the United States for Du Bois by Frederic C. Howe, a former muckraking journalist and reformer, who served as commissioner of immigration at the port of New York from 1914 to 1919.[125]

One of the items which appeared in the May *Crisis* was Colonel Greer's letter to Senator McKellar, in which he drew attention to the question of black officers, in view of the invitation to all army officers to apply for regular commissions. Greer described black troops as having been a complete failure under fire, for which he held black officers responsible:

> The undoubted truth is that the Colored officers neither control nor care to control the men. They themselves have been engaged very largely in the pursuit of French women, it being their first opportunity to meet white women who did not treat them as servants. . . . Accuracy and ability to describe the facts is lacking in all and most of them are just plain liars in addition.[126]

The other documents which Du Bois reproduced were further testimony to the hostility and lack of consideration shown to black soldiers by white officers.

A week or so after the May *Crisis* appeared, the extent of white opposition to black officers in the post-war army was further revealed by publication of the proceedings of the board which vetted applicants for permanent commissions at Camp Meade in February 1919. Thirty applications from the 368th Infantry were turned down, including that of Capt. Thomas M. Dent, whose marks for physical ability, intelligence, leadership, and personality were deliberately adjusted, so that the total fell below that which would have resulted in an automatic recommendation for a commission. Recommending no further examination of Dent, the board's verdict damned all who aspired to follow in the footsteps of Charles Young:

> Unqualified by reason of qualities inherent in the Negro race. An opinion of the Board based on the testimony of five white officers serving with the 368th Infantry, Negroes are deficient in moral fiber and force of character rendering them unfit as officers and leaders of men.[127]

Walter Loving was stunned by such blatant discrimination. Although he was troubled by Du Bois's unapologetic disclosure of confidential army documents in the *Crisis*, he was also disgusted by the prejudice displayed by the white officers: "these articles are degrading and humiliating to the War Department and should be thoroughly investigated. And if true the officers responsible for such orders should be called upon to account for the same." Loving reported to Churchill on May 6 that men like Colonel Greer should never have been assigned to the 92nd Division. He stated that black soldiers were known to be good fighting men, but their morale had been destroyed by white officers; Greer ought to be court-martialed for his letter to McKellar, while General Ballou, the commanding officer of the 92nd Division, plainly lacked "the tact and judgment usually expected in an officer of such high rank." To command black soldiers, he explained, white officers had to be "broad minded men, fully in sympathy with the principle that 'a man is a man' and should never allow the idea of race to enter into the administration of military affairs." Above all, black officers had to be given a fair chance to prove themselves and earn promotion. Otherwise, the War Department would be laying itself open to "a just charge of ingratitude." As it was, Loving expected the League for Democracy to make an issue out of Greer's letter. He advised that if the War Department accepted black officers in the peacetime army it would "blot out some very unpleasant memories connected with the war in France" for soldiers and civilians alike.[128]

In the Morale Branch, Captain Cutler had become increasingly worried about the effects of black alienation during the period of demobilization and advised Churchill that Loving was right. Citing Greer's letter and the Dent case, he warned that blacks now regarded the army and, by extension, the government as openly hostile toward them. Repeating Loving's observation that Filipinos were being admitted to West Point and assigned to white regiments, Cutler urged that the War Department produce a clear policy on black officer training in peacetime, beginning with an announcement that discrimination would be eradicated and that all commissions in black regiments were open to competent officers, with no limits placed on their promotion prospects. Churchill sent Loving's and Cutler's views to Gen. Peyton C. March with a strong personal endorsement. These memorandums, wrote Churchill,

> one prepared by a colored man who is believed to be as impartial and tolerant as a man of his race can be in the treatment of this subject, and the other by a very well-informed and entirely tolerant and impartial student of the race question, indicate the seriousness of the negro question in relation to the Army, and the fact that all officers do not carry out the spirit of the War Department policy with respect to a square deal for the negro.[129]

March took prompt action, but not the sweeping measures which Loving and Cutler had hoped for. He announced that the placing of an insurmountable obstacle in the way of would-be army officers—rejection on the grounds of supposedly inherent racial qualities—would cease.[130] Nonetheless, the discharging of officers continued, to Cutler's obvious dismay: "The failure of the General Staff and of the War Department to get into a position which is openly and publicly defensible, as regards the handling of colored troops, leaves the way entirely open for radical propaganda among these ex-service men."[131]

The most obvious manifestation of this radicalism was the continued growth of the League for Democracy, which began an energetic campaign to have Greer disciplined for attempting to bring about southern political interference in army deliberations. Loving traveled to New York to attend the next meeting of the LFD in Harlem and arranged for a stenographer to record Osceola McKaine's speech, which was an unrestrained attack on Greer and his kind. McKaine called on African Americans to "rise as one man in their righteous anger and deluge the War Department with petitions to have the scoundrel and liar court-martialed." On the more general issue of the struggle for equal rights in America, McKaine told the veterans, "You have shown your willingness to die for the white man. Now show your willingness to die, if need be, that your descendants may not look upon your grave with scorn."[132] Loving openly approached the protesting officers of the 92nd Division, with whom he sympathized, and was given copies of five hitherto unpublished orders by white officers relating to black troops. Loving thought one of the orders, generally commending blacks but warning them that any failings would be magnified by unfriendly superiors, was fair; the others showed "incompetence and inefficiency" on the part of the white officers who drafted them. One order, issued in the final days of the war, invited any black officer who was waiting to undergo an efficiency board "to demonstrate his fitness by being assigned to front line duty with the special mission of taking prisoners. Undertaking this duty will demonstrate courage—succeeding in it will demonstrate efficiency and courage." And failure, no doubt, would relieve the army of an inefficient hero.[133]

As the black press began to take up the LFD's cry of "Greer Must Go," McKaine told Newton D. Baker that blacks now wanted to know what he was going to do about this "vile, vicious premeditated insult to the race. . . . The War Department is on trial in this matter; we have scores of just grievances against its policies." Cutler advised Baker's private secretary that a response was best left to Emmett Scott, who could state that the protest was "receiving the Secretary's attention and will be given very careful consideration." Unappeased, the LFD staged a mass meeting at the Howard Theater in Washington on June 8, at which calls for action against Greer were reiterated amid declarations that blacks owed "no special allegiance to a government that discriminates, segregates and permits lynching and burning at the stake."[134] Two days later, Baker agreed to see a delegation of seven discharged officers of the 92nd Division, including McKaine and Dent, local officials of the LFD, two black journalists, and a black YMCA official who had worked in France. The group argued that Greer ought to be court-martialed "for conduct to the prejudice of good order and military discipline, for attempting to influence legislation, and for aiding the enemy." On the following day, the Adjutant General's Office asked McKaine to furnish proof, firstly, that Greer actually wrote the letter complained of, and, secondly, that Greer had made it public. Loving pointed out to Cutler that this was blatant obstructionism by the army, since Baker had told the LFD delegation during their interview that McKellar had denied having published the letter which he received from Greer, the implication being that the letter was undoubtedly genuine. And, in any case, the question of who had made the letter public was irrelevant, since it was well known that Du Bois was responsible for this. The LFD, for its part, could only protest that Greer had not denied writing to McKellar and that it did not know how Du Bois had acquired his copy of the letter. As far as the Adjutant General's Office was concerned, however, no action could be taken against Greer in the absence of further evidence.[135]

At a meeting of the three-hundred-strong LFD branch in Washington on June 15, 1919, McKaine had hinted that he was expecting this outcome: "We are not after Greer, but we are after what Greer represents."[136] In that sense, at least, the efforts of the LFD were not entirely wasted. In addition to the Greer matter, Baker was also faced at this time with the problem of the fate of four black officers found guilty of cowardly misconduct during a disorderly retreat by the 368th Infantry in a battle on the Argonne front in September 1918. They had originally been sentenced to death by firing squad, but this had been commuted to terms of between five and ten years in prison.[137] By the time the LFD delegation called on him, Baker had already seen some evidence to suggest that African-American soldiers rarely received fair treatment from white officers. McKaine and his associates helped to convince him that this was so. Soon afterward, he arranged to interview the four convicted officers—a meeting which left him "strongly inclined" to "recommend to the President clemency" in their cases and also determined "to try to find out just what had gone on in the 368th at the time in question." The "conservative and moderate tone spoken by these young men . . . made a most favorable impression."[138]

For Baker to take such a close interest in the welfare of individuals affected by his decisions was not unusual. In September 1917, he had traveled to Camp Meade, Md., to meet a group of young conscientious objectors and had written sympathetically about them to Wilson.[139] Although Baker was in charge of an army that was riddled with racism (from which he was not always immune), it is plain that if certain other members of Wilson's cabinet had held the post of secretary of war—Albert Burleson, for example, or Josephus Daniels—the ill-treatment dished out to black officers and drafted men during and after the war might have been greater, and any willingness to correct injustices afterward would almost certainly have been less evident.

At Baker's request, Cutler put together a file of material relating to the treatment of blacks in the army. This included uncomplimentary reports by white officers, black officers' complaints about their lot, Loving's memorandums on the behavior of Greer and other white officers, the May *Crisis* containing the original disclosures, and the June *Crisis*, which carried Du Bois's lengthy essay on the black man's part in the war. Cutler added a copy of an article by the one black journalist accredited by the CPI for front-line reporting in France, Ralph Tyler of the *Cleveland Advocate*, in which the courts-martial of the four officers were fiercely denounced.[140] On Emmett Scott's advice, Tyler, who had three sons serving in the AEF, had made his articles written in France uncritical of the army and the welfare facilities provided for black troops, but on his return he had felt free to tell the truth. He claimed that racial prejudice had destroyed the morale of the 368th Infantry even before it reached the front, that it was ill equipped, and that during the battle the white major commanding the battalion that retreated had disappeared without explanation and later suffered a nervous collapse. The subsequent courts-martial were, according to Tyler, "necessarily star-chamber affairs—the findings usually anticipated" and were "characterized more by expeditiousness than by justice."[141] Baker instructed the inspector general to embark on a lengthy review of the court proceedings and the allegations about both the treatment of black troops and their performance. On the basis of the inspector general's report, Baker issued a detailed statement in November 1919, conceding that there were cases of discrimination, that the 368th had been insufficiently trained and equipped for the terrain and the intensity of the fighting, and that the advance of the disgraced battalion had been given inadequate artillery support. Baker exonerated white officers, but added that there was "no basis at all for any of the general assumptions with regard to the action of colored troops in this battle or elsewhere in France." The four convicted officers were freed.[142]

The official rebuttal of slurs on the abilities and fortitude of African-American soldiers made little difference to how they were perceived by white people in the South. To Sen. James K. Vardaman of Mississippi, they would remain "Frenchwomen-ruined niggers."[143] It was southern determination to dash quickly any heightened black hopes of political and social advancement as a result of the war that partly caused the steady growth of the new Ku Klux Klan, which had progressed slowly after its revival in 1915. On a program of "uniting native-born white Christians for concerted action in the preservation of American institutions and the supremacy of the white race," the Klan's membership rose to over a hundred thousand within a year of the end of the war. Frank S. Dickason from Tennessee, a wagoner in the 50th Artillery, was one of many southern soldiers looking forward to joining the Klan on their return from Europe. In a letter to a relative in Alabama, intercepted by G-2, he wrote that he was "itching to get in the new Ku-Klux, it would be Heaven itself to become one of the instructors in the school of differentiation of the two colors. I would like to shoot down just a few [blacks] to see them kick, they are getting too egotistical and important to suit me."[144]

Exemplary violence of the kind that Dickason fantasized about had been increasing since the United States entered the war. In 1917, thirty-eight blacks were lynched and an equal number had died in the riot at East St. Louis. In 1918, fifty-eight blacks died at the hands of lynch mobs, and in 1919 this figure would rise to over seventy, not including the dozens more who died in the race riots of that year. Black soldiers who were reckoned by whites to have worn their uniforms for too long after being discharged were frequent targets. Many were beaten and at least ten died in a rash of lynchings in Mississippi (three), Georgia (three, two of them at Blakely), Arkansas (two), Florida and Alabama (one each).[145] If oppression of this kind did not square with the idealism which had fueled American mobilization for war, it sat no more easily with the post-war solicitude for the downtrodden and unrepresented to be found in Wilson's advocacy of the League of Nations Covenant. Such apparent hypocrisy persuaded many African Americans that the United States was unfit for the international role that Wilson envisaged. In the *Baltimore Afro-American,* the author of a poem about the mob-murder of a black veteran, titled "A Burnt Offering to Democracy," asked,

> How can a nation dare dictate to men
> Of foreign climes what their conduct should be,
> In dealing with their weaker subjects, when
> Their own are lynched with all impunity;
> Restricted and deprived of every right,
> Because they were born black, instead of white?[146]

In the northern states, where racial violence was an everyday occurrence but black people were less likely to be lynched, the economic strides they had made during the war began to falter in the post-war months—a problem that was compounded by the rapid demobilization of the army. Moving from the South in order to fill the demand for labor caused by rising war-related production and declining immigration, blacks had for the first time become an important part of the northern industrial workforce. Although the number of black skilled artisans in the United States was falling, the number of unskilled blacks employed in iron- and steel-making, mining, shipbuilding, and meatpacking had almost doubled since 1910. When demand for the products of those industries fell after the war, thousands of black migrants were among those fired. In one week, for instance, the American Steel Company at East St. Louis reduced its payroll from 1,282 workers to 25, and almost 700 of those who lost their jobs were black.[147] The returning veterans added to the number of unemployed urban blacks, since many from the South chose to settle in northern cities, even though they were generally discharged in their home states. For example, fewer than 40 percent of soldiers from Louisiana continued to live in that state after leaving the army; most sought work in the North.[148] As a result, one month after most of the men had been discharged, the Department of Labor's Division of Negro Economics (DNE) estimated that 99 percent of the black veterans in Chicago were unemployed and had little prospect of getting work in a city where jobs had been scarce since the beginning of the year.[149] This problem was discussed by a number of federal agencies, including the DNE, the MID, the Morale Branch, and the Bureau of Returning Soldiers and Sailors (BRSS). The national superintendent of the BRSS remarked to the Morale Branch that black soldiers were showing "a tendency to flock to the northern states and a disinclination to go back to the South; although there is in the South an actual shortage of colored help." He blamed the black press for this and wondered whether the men could be persuaded to return to the South from the more congested cities, like Philadelphia. Emmett Scott advised the Morale Branch that he was working on the question of how best to encourage blacks to go to "occupations and sections of the country that would be of most benefit to themselves and most helpful in the reconstruction period." He avoided, however, any suggestion that this necessarily meant the South.[150]

The General Staff recognized quickly that nothing could be done by the government to prevent the migration. For the Morale Branch, Cutler argued that since the war blacks had been "inclined to put what they understand to be their rights as American citizens above all other considerations" and that where migration was concerned, economic prospects were "a secondary matter." African Americans were increasingly preferring to live where they had some rights. Cutler thought that only a policy of "tolerance and conservatism" on the part of leading southerners would halt the flow.[151] When the intelligence officer at Camp Wheeler, Ga., reported in March that the enthusiasm shown by men of a recently discharged labor battalion for the idea of moving to the North might have been the work of "propagandists," he was informed by the MID that this enthusiasm was "general rather than local." In any case, it seemed to Col. K. Masteller of the Negative Branch "inadvisable to attempt to identify civilian propagandists of this sentiment. It must be remembered that we are very likely to exceed our authority if we take action in a matter of this nature."[152]

In January 1919, the DNE had established Negro Workers' Advisory Committees in a number of states to tackle employer and union resistance to black workers, but the level of unemployment in Chicago rendered this scheme nearly useless. The Chicago branch of the BRSS ran an unemployment office for veterans, with separate lists of vacancies for black and white workers, and toward the end of April it attempted to ease the situation by agreeing "to fill orders for shipment of a number of discharged negro servicemen to the South."[153] In May, with the promise of cooperation by the BRSS, the Chicago Association of Commerce wired southern chambers of commerce to ask if they could make use of Chicago's excess black labor, much of it made up of ex-servicemen. This plan made no headway, however, partly because of southern unease about the kind of person who might be sent—too fond, perhaps, of northern freedom—but mostly because very few veterans came forward to seek a job in the South; to leave the North would be to admit defeat and lend support to white claims that the South was the proper home of African Americans. Hence the comment of the radical middle-class black Chicago monthly, *Half-Century Magazine:* "Any Negro who boards a train for Dixie should be derailed into the Mississippi River."[154]

African-American political and racial awareness, which had been increasing steadily in the pre-war years, grew apace during the war. Membership of organizations with political, as much as social or economic, objectives rose sharply after 1918, as did the readership of radical journals. Their strident demands for equal rights, coming at a time of labor unrest and nationwide fear of an alien plot to bring about revolution in the United States, caused African Americans to be identified by government officials and the white press as one of the groups in society most affected by Bolshevik propaganda. As an unprecedented wave of race riots broke out across the United States in what James Weldon Johnson called the "Red Summer" of 1919, the rhetoric indulged in by the leaders of black veterans undoubtedly helped to foster this misunderstanding.[155] Employing a tone as belligerent as that to be found in Du Bois's "Returning Soldiers" editorial, the League for Democracy began publication on June 25, 1919, of a short-lived newspaper, the *Commoner,* which was to be

> the written expression of the returned veteran and war worker. As such it knows that determined, radical action will give us a fuller participation in domestic democracy.
>
> Therefore the Commoner will be radical. We denounce the spirit of compromise and apology.
>
> We denounce watchful waiting and hoping.
>
> Demand every right because you have merited it.
>
> Organize and fight. Be aggressive. Fight for the ballot where you are denied its use. Resist to the utmost of your physical strength impositions of force and physical violence which tends to intimidate, humiliate or harm. Fight. Be proud. Be aggressive. Fight.[156]

On the same day, the *Veteran,* published by a New York group calling itself the National Colored Soldiers and Citizens Council, quoted a black soldier:

We offered our lives to save this country and we are willing to give our lives for our rights. We hope this will not be necessary. We do not want war. But they are beating Colored women and children every day and if something isn't done about it we shall be forced to fight.[157]

Pursuing this theme further, the *Veteran* advised its readership,

The slightest acquaintance with the psychology of the gang ought to be sufficient to convince us that the cringing pleading attitude is not going to get the black man any favorable consideration at the hand of the mob. Mobs are not moved that way. They are too brutally inhuman to respond to any argument except the argument of cold steel and fire. The race man who determines that if he must at all die at the hand of a mob he will die game, makes an incalculable contribution to the majesty of the law.[158]

In its exhortation to blacks not to turn the other cheek, the *Veteran* anticipated the literary symbol of black resistance to the violence unleashed in the race riots, Claude McKay's poem "If We Must Die," first published in Max Eastman's *Liberator* magazine in July 1919:

If we must die, let it not be like hogs
Hunted and penned in an inglorious spot
While round us bark the mad and hungry dogs,
Making their mock at our accursed lot.
If we must die, O let us nobly die,
So that our precious blood may not be shed
In vain; then even the monsters we defy
Shall be constrained to honor us though dead!
O kinsmen! we must meet the common foe!
Though far outnumbered let us show us brave,
And for their thousand blows deal one death blow!
What though before us lies the open grave?
Like men we'll face the murderous cowardly pack,
Pressed to the wall, dying, but fighting back![159]

Although the conflict in Europe was over and the United States was the decisive victor, to most African Americans Woodrow Wilson's war for democracy and its bloody aftermath reeked of triumphant white supremacy; any hopes that the war would rapidly advance the cause of black freedom at home and abroad were extinguished. There was ample justification for such disappointment, but after the experience of World War I the trenchancy and fire with which black publicists condemned racism, and the resolve with which ordinary African Americans stood up to white rioters, heralded the emergence of a New Negro and laid the foundations of the civil rights movement of the middle of the twentieth century.

Seven

Conclusion

The federal government's intelligence files record fascinating bureaucratic excursions into what to white officials was the "other" world of black America, as attempts were made to account for the increasing exasperation of African Americans with the effects of racial prejudice. The wartime intelligence agencies conceived of legitimate black political activity only in terms of Tuskegee-ite gradualism and habitual Republicanism. Many government officials were therefore easily persuaded, or simply assumed, that militant demands by African Americans for fair treatment during the war and the immediate post-war years had not simply resulted from growing black dissatisfaction and better organization, but might be the product of some sinister foreign incitement that could be counteracted. In 1917–18, this was believed to be German propagandists, seeking to burden the United States with racial strife on the home front.

Despite the significant scale of the racial component of the government's massive domestic surveillance activities during World War I and the subsequent red scare, none of the hundreds of BI and MIB investigations into alleged German subversion of black loyalty in 1917 and 1918, and Bolshevik subversion thereafter, resulted in the discovery of a genuine plot against the United States developed by foreign agents actively working to subvert the loyalty of the African-American population as a whole or even the loyalty of individual African Americans. In Senate hearings into German propaganda after the war, the BI did not attempt to attribute reported instances of black disloyalty to any official German subversion. Although Military Intelligence did claim that black anti-war sentiment was a product of general German propaganda, this was heavily influenced by hindsight and not substantiated by wartime investigation.[1]

The files are therefore compelling testimony to three things. First, they convey, with varying degrees of distortion, the profound sense of alienation which very many African Americans felt from most aspects of American society, at a time when they might have been expected to alter their opin-

Conclusion

ions, or at least moderate their complaints, for the sake of the war effort. Second, the language and assumptions of white federal officials are redolent of the animosity and contempt which they felt toward the diverse efforts of black people to improve their situation by securing their constitutional rights. Third, in the readiness of white citizens and officials to see treason in such efforts, the files are evidence of the power of rumor and exaggeration when existing racial hatreds and fears are propelled by the emotional pressures of war.

That said, there is little purpose in arguing that federal surveillance of African Americans during World War I represented especially oppressive behavior by the government. Certainly, the super-patriotic atmosphere conjured up by the government and civilian pro-war enthusiasts made life difficult for radical black publicists. W. E. B. Du Bois later recalled the World War I spy scare as "a national psychosis of fear that German intrigue would accomplish among Negroes . . . disloyalty and [an] urge toward sabotage and revenge."[2] But by comparison with other groups in American society, such as German Americans (and especially Hutterites and Mennonites), non-naturalized aliens, members of the Industrial Workers of the World (of which only one leading member, Ben Fletcher, was black), and other radicals, African Americans were subjected to relatively little specifically war-induced persecution. Although many black publications were monitored, only a few single issues were held up in the mails and no journals were suppressed; few black critics of the war were arrested for political crimes and fewer still jailed. This amounted to virtual immunity, compared to the kinds of official and unofficial harassment to which others were subjected.[3] Moreover, the intelligence agencies' efforts regarding African Americans involved relatively little subterfuge; their dealings with black leaders through Loving, Spingarn, and agents of the BI and the APL were largely open and direct. In other words, even though the civil liberties of some black people were undoubtedly infringed during the war and its aftermath, and some deeply racist officials gave free rein to their prejudices on paper, and the power of equal rights campaigning was reduced by being labeled subversive, federal surveillance can not be said to have worsened the already greatly disadvantaged circumstances of the African-American minority.

The importance of the files from the viewpoint of public history is what they reveal about American racial attitudes, particularly of those in government. One of the most striking features of the day-to-day reports on racial matters by domestic intelligence agents across the United States and the conclusions drawn afterward in central digests is the general lack of insight achieved or even sought by senior officials. Indeed, the government's real doubts about the loyalty of the black population unquestionably reflected and, to some extent, stemmed from just how little whites typically knew, or could be bothered to know, about their black fellow citizens. It was common for white people, particularly in the South, to claim that they already knew black people well enough and understood their nature and outlook—this was a familiarity that could encompass occasional affection and sometimes even a degree of sympathy, but was normally expressed in a standard set of negative images and phrases, rather than factual information. Government officials under the Wilson administration consistently exhibited this capacity for confident generalization about the capabilities and inclinations of black people, and they often deferred to the views and preferences of the white South. This tendency was reflected in analyses of racial matters at all levels within the federal bureaucracy, ranging from field reports to executive summaries. There were some exceptions, naturally. A few northern federal officials, mostly in the War Department under Newton D. Baker, were troubled by a difficulty that the war only intensified: on the one hand, the government had no wish to promote and protect equal rights for racial minorities, but officials also found it impossible to deny the fundamental reasonableness of what African Americans insisted they were entitled to, as they fought and labored in the war for democracy: voting rights, representation, economic justice, due process, and protection from gross acts of violence. While constitutional and political considerations meant that nothing of any significance would be done in any of these areas, it is clear that a number of officials felt obliged to treat black soldiers and civilian petitioners with basic respect, at the very least.

As Paul A. C. Koistinen has shown, the mobilization of American society for World War I was extraordinarily complex and further complicating factors, such as collapsing race relations, would have been unwelcome.[4] At first the Wilson administration tried to play down or deny the importance in 1917 of the East St. Louis riot, the Houston mutiny and the executions that followed it, the persistence of lynching, and the black spy scare. These events related to only a tenth of the population, after all, and one that had little formal political power. However, two considerations made the government take hesitant, inadequate steps to acknowledge the race problem. Firstly, black protesters had friends in the press such as Oswald Garrison

Conclusion

Villard and Lyman Abbott, who were in frequent contact with members of the administration and could expect that, as they were members of the same caste, their questions would be answered. Secondly, the African-American population was a large enough minority, and was possibly cohesive enough, to have had a disruptive effect on the economy, the armed forces, and national morale if its demands for equal rights were ever to escalate into civil disobedience. Jane Lang Scheiber and Harry N. Scheiber have argued persuasively in a brief study that, while the government was in no sense sympathetic to black aspirations, it was prepared to make a number of concessions in wartime to preserve order and retain black cooperation. Thus when black protest and lobbying reached a sufficient pitch, or black unrest was alleged to be reaching a worrying level, the administration attempted to prevent widespread disaffection, while avoiding any commitment to long-term reform.[5]

The Wilson administration relied on the support of southern senators and congressmen, who had shown themselves quick to react to any suggestion of federal interference in southern racial matters. The demands of black spokesmen for federal anti-lynching legislation, fair promotion of black army officers, and the ending of Jim Crow regulations on the now federally controlled railroads were not entertained by the Wilson administration because of the vehement objections they would have produced from the South. Hence the cultivation of friendly relations with conservative black leaders, such as Robert Moton of Tuskegee Institute, in the hope that they might prevent black political protest from getting out of hand. Hence, also, the sharp warnings handed out to black spokesmen and editors by both the Justice Department and the War Department. The paradox was that while government officials were expressing fears that radical black leaders would refuse to support the government's war policy until their race's treatment improved, most of the same leaders were pointing to the fine contributions blacks were making to the war effort as proof of their entitlement to the full rights of citizenship.

Organizationally and ideologically, black politics became more diverse during the war years, and new options presented themselves in all parts of the country, but the schismatic nature of the equal rights campaign was also fully revealed—a problem that would bedevil the formation of a broad national campaign for years to come. World War I touched all aspects of the lives of African Americans, but did not transform them. The war saw the geographic center of the black population shift northward, and as the

Great Migration accelerated, it offered black people work in industries that had previously been closed to them, it put them in uniform and trained them, it sold them Liberty Bonds, and it reminded them of the substandard citizenship that they endured, particularly in the South, and gave them a new certainty that they were entitled to demand something better. Out of the war also came a greater willingness on the part of some white southerners to take a stand against lynching, prompted by both the campaigns of black activists and a desire to reduce migration.[6] Neil R. McMillen, writing specifically about Mississippi, has suggested that World War I was "a racial watershed [which] . . . signaled the beginning of a journey toward freedom, the early departure point for the freedom struggles of our time."[7] That conclusion can be extended across the South.

At no time, however, in the interwar period did the federal government formulate a clear policy on race relations—the creation of advisory commissions under men like Moton and the insertion of bland planks in party platforms were as far as administrations would go, for fear of provoking revolts in Congress. Instead of reform, continued black protest in peacetime attracted further surveillance, as federal intelligence agencies switched abruptly from investigating alleged "Pro-Germanism among the Negroes" to hunting for "Bolshevik Influence," a concern that would endure until the 1970s.[8]

Notes

Abbreviations

APL	American Protective League
BI	Bureau of Investigation
CO	commanding officer
DJ	Department of Justice
DMI	director of military intelligence
HL	Houghton Library, Harvard University
IO	intelligence officer
JWJC	James Weldon Johnson Collection, Beinecke Rare Book and Manuscript Library, Yale University
LC	Library of Congress
MIB	Military Intelligence Branch
MID	Military Intelligence Division (formerly the MIB)
M-SRC	Moorland-Spingarn Research Center, Howard University
NA	National Archives, Washington, D.C.
NRC	National Records Center, Suitland, Md.
NYPL	New York Public Library
ONI	Office of Naval Intelligence
RG	Record Group
ROC	Records of the Office of the Counselor
UML	University of Massachusetts Library, Amherst
WRHS	Western Reserve Historical Society, Cleveland

Introduction

1. Bruce Kellner, ed., *The Harlem Renaissance: A Historical Dictionary for the Era* (London: Methuen, 1987), xvi.

2. Howard W. Odum, *Race and Rumors of Race: Challenge to American Crisis* (Chapel Hill: University of North Carolina Press, 1943), 180–81. See also George Brown Tindall, *The Emergence of the New South, 1913–1945* (Baton Rouge: Louisiana State University Press, 1967), 143–83, 565.

3. Richard B. Sherman, *The Republican Party and Black America from McKinley to Hoover, 1896–1933* (Charlottesville: University Press of Virginia, 1973), passim.

4. William A. Link, *The Paradox of Southern Progressivism, 1880–1930* (Chapel Hill: University of North Carolina Press, 1992), 69. See also ibid., 63–78, 248–67; Ralph E. Luker, *The Social Gospel in Black and White: American Racial Reform, 1885–1912* (Chapel Hill: University of North Carolina Press, 1991), passim; Nancy J. Weiss, *The National Urban League, 1910–1940* (New York: Oxford University Press,

1974), passim; Morton Sosna, *In Search of the Silent South: Southern Liberals and the Race Issue* (New York: Columbia University Press, 1977), passim; Ronald C. White, Jr., *Liberty and Justice for All* (San Francisco: Harper & Row, 1990), passim.

5. See, for example, W. E. B. Du Bois, *The Souls of Black Folk: Essays and Sketches* (Chicago: McClung, 1903); Du Bois, "Credo," *Independent* 57 (Oct. 6, 1904), 787; Kelly Miller, *Race Adjustment: Essays on the Negro in America* (New York: Neale Publishing, 1908); Ray Stannard Baker, *Following the Color Line: An Account of Negro Citizenship in the American Democracy* (New York: Doubleday, Page, 1908); Mary White Ovington, *Half a Man: The Status of the Negro in New York* (New York: Longmans, Green, 1911); Edgar Gardner Murphy, *Problems of the Present South: A Discussion of the Educational, Industrial, and Political Issues of the Southern States* (New York: Macmillan, 1904); Harlan Paul Douglass, *Christian Reconstruction in the South* (Boston: Pilgrim Press, 1909); W. D. Weatherford, *Negro Life in the South: Present Conditions and Needs* (New York: Young Men's Christian Association Press, 1910); Weatherford, *Present Forces in Negro Progress* (New York: Association Press, 1912).

6. See Thomas Dixon, *The Leopard's Spots: A Romance of the White Man's Burden, 1865–1900* (New York: Doubleday, Page, 1902); Dixon, *The Clansman: An Historical Romance of the Ku Klux Klan* (New York: Doubleday, Page, 1905). See also Luker, *Social Gospel in Black and White*, 293, 295–300. Steven Biel has noted that, with a few exceptions, white American intellectuals and critics made no effort to engage with their African-American counterparts in this period. Biel, *Independent Intellectuals in the United States, 1910–1945* (New York: New York University Press, 1992), 8–9.

7. Robert R. Moton, "The South and the Lynching Evil," *South Atlantic Quarterly* 18 (July 1919), 191–96; *Historical Statistics of the United States, Colonial Times to 1957* (Washington, D.C.: U.S. Bureau of the Census, 1960), 218; Herbert Shapiro, *White Violence and Black Response: From Reconstruction to Montgomery* (Amherst: University of Massachusetts Press, 1988), 93–157; George C. Wright, *Racial Violence in Kentucky, 1865–1940: Lynchings, Mob Rule, and "Legal Lynchings"* (Baton Rouge: Louisiana State University Press, 1990), 185–213; Edward L. Ayers, *The Promise of the New South: Life after Reconstruction* (New York: Oxford University Press, 1992), 155–58; Leon F. Litwack, *Trouble in Mind: Black Southerners in the Age of Jim Crow* (New York: Alfred A. Knopf, 1998), 280–319. See also Stewart E. Tolnay and E. M. Beck, *A Festival of Violence: An Analysis of Southern Lynchings, 1882–1930* (Urbana: University of Illinois Press, 1995). On the mechanics, scope, costs, defense, impact, and evolving economy of segregation, see the essays in *The Age of Segregation: Race Relations in the South, 1890–1945*, ed. Robert Haws (Jackson: University Press of Mississippi, 1978).

8. Charles Flint Kellogg, *NAACP: A History of the National Association for the Advancement of Colored People, Volume 1: 1909–1920* (Baltimore: Johns Hopkins University Press, 1967), 9–30, 209–46; Robert L. Zangrando, *The NAACP Crusade against Lynching, 1909–1950* (Philadelphia: Temple University Press, 1980), 350. See, for example, NAACP resolution on lynching, O. G. Villard and M. W. Ovington to G. W. Wickersham, Dec. 16, 1911, DJ File 158260-7, section 1, 1911–19, RG 60, NA; Claudine L. Ferrell, *Nightmare and Dream: Antilynching in Congress, 1917–1922* (New York: Garland, 1986), 77–91.

9. Kellogg, *NAACP,* 149–54.

10. W. E. B. Du Bois, *The Autobiography of W. E. B. Du Bois: A Soliloquy on Viewing My Life from the Last Decade of Its First Century* (New York: International Publishers, 1968), 248; Booker T. Washington, *My Larger Education: Being Chapters from My Experience* (Garden City: Doubleday, Page, 1911), 118; David Levering Lewis, *W. E. B. Du Bois: Biography of a Race, 1868–1919* (New York: Henry Holt, 1993), 297–342, 402–404.

11. Louis R. Harlan, *Booker T. Washington: The Wizard of Tuskegee, 1901–1915* (New York: Oxford University Press, 1983), 427. On John Hope and the Washington–Du Bois divide, see Leroy Davis, *A Clashing of the Soul: John Hope and the Dilemma of African American Leadership and Black Higher Education in the Early Twentieth Century* (Athens: University of Georgia Press, 1998), 145, 181, 188–215.

12. Joel Williamson, *The Crucible of Race: Black-White Relations in the American South since Emancipation* (New York: Oxford University Press, 1984), 368.

13. Woodrow Wilson to Howard Allen Bridgman, Sept. 8, 1913, in *Papers of Woodrow Wilson,* vol. 28, ed. Arthur S. Link (Princeton: Princeton University Press, 1978), 265–66.

14. Nancy J. Weiss, "The Negro and the New Freedom: Fighting Wilsonian Segregation," *Political Science Quarterly* 84 (March 1969), 61–79; Sherman, *Republican Party and Black America,* 116–17; Williamson, *Crucible of Race,* 364–94.

15. Ayers, *Promise of the New South,* 426–30; Litwack, *Trouble in Mind,* 206–16.

16. Thomas J. Woofter, *Southern Race Progress: The Wavering Color Line* (Washington, D.C.: Public Affairs Press, 1957), 100.

17. See RG 65 (Bureau of Investigation), RG 165 (Military Intelligence Division), RG 38 (Office of Naval Intelligence), RG 59 (Department of State), RG 28 (Post Office), RG 174 (Department of Labor), NA and NRC. Records from these files have been edited for microfilm by Theodore Kornweibel, Jr., as *Federal Surveillance of Afro-Americans (1917–1925): The First World War, the Red Scare, and the Garvey Movement* (Frederick, Md.: University Publications of America, 1986), 25 reels. On wartime anti-radicalism and dissent, see William Preston, Jr., *Aliens and Dissenters: Federal Suppression of Radicals, 1903–1933* (New York: Harper & Row, 1966), 88–180; H. C. Petersen and Gilbert C. Fite, *Opponents of War, 1917–1918* (Seattle: University of Washington Press, 1968), passim; Christopher N. May, *In the Name of War: Judicial Review and the War Powers since 1918* (Cambridge: Harvard University Press, 1989), 133–44, 164–72; Christopher C. Gibb, *The Great Silent Majority: Missouri's Resistance to World War I* (Columbia, Mo.: University of Missouri Press, 1988).

18. Homer S. Cummings and Carl McFarland, *Federal Justice: Chapters in the History of Justice and the Federal Executive* (New York: Macmillan, 1937), 376–82; Sanford J. Ungar, *F. B. I.* (Boston: Little, Brown, 1976), 39–40; Harry and Bonaro Overstreet, *The FBI in Our Open Society* (New York: W. W. Norton, 1969), 12–27. In 1935, the Bureau of Investigation was renamed the Federal Bureau of Investigation.

19. Cummings and McFarland, *Federal Justice,* 381.

20. Joan Jensen, *The Price of Vigilance* (Chicago: Rand McNally, 1968), 13; "Bielaski of the Secret Service," *Delineator* 92 (May 1918), 13; "German Plotters Fear

Him," *Literary Digest* 55 (Sept. 29, 1917), 60–64. An outstanding athlete at college, he was recruited by the Department of Justice in 1907 from the Bureau of Printing and Engraving, allegedly to strengthen the Justice baseball team.

21. Jensen, *Price of Vigilance,* 22; Cummings and McFarland, *Federal Justice,* 414–15, 420; *New York Times,* May 13, 1917.

22. Jensen, *Price of Vigilance,* 17–25. Jensen's remains the most detailed study of the APL. For a contemporary account, see Emerson Hough, *The Web* (Chicago: Reilly and Lee, 1919). By June 1917, there were almost six hundred branches of the APL, with a membership of over 100,000, rising to 250,000 in 1918. See Cummings and McFarland, *Federal Justice,* 421.

23. Jensen, *Price of Vigilance,* 29; Cummings and McFarland, *Federal Justice,* 416–18. In 1916–17, the BI compiled an index of aliens suspected of violation of the neutrality laws. On March 31, 1917, Bielaski provided Gregory with a summary, showing that, of the 1,770 individuals named, only 367 had been cleared of specific offenses, while 574 were strongly suspected and there were doubts about another 589. It was recommended that a group of 98 be arrested immediately war was declared and a further 140 required to post bonds. In April 1917, 63 enemy aliens were detained, rising to 125 by early May, to 295 by the end of June, and to 895 by the end of October. In all, 6,300 people were arrested in wartime under presidential warrant, of whom 2,300 were interned by the military; most of the rest were paroled. See Cummings and McFarland, *Federal Justice,* 418, 427.

24. Marc B. Powe, *The Emergence of the War Department Intelligence Agency: 1885–1918* (Manhattan: Kansas State University Press, 1975), passim; Marc B. Powe and Ed E. Wilson, *The Evolution of American Military Intelligence* (Fort Huachuca, Ariz.: U.S. Army Intelligence Center & School, 1973), 10–11; Frederick P. Keppel, "The General Staff," *Atlantic Monthly* 75 (April 1920), 541. See also Walter C. Sweeney, *Military Intelligence: A New Weapon in War* (New York: Frederick A. Stokes, 1924). On military intelligence in the U.S. Army before 1903, see Elizabeth Bethel, "The Military Information Division: Origin of the Intelligence Division," *Military Affairs* 11 (Spring 1947), 17–24; Roy Talbert, Jr., *Negative Intelligence: The Army and the American Left, 1917–1941* (Jackson: University Press of Mississippi, 1991), 3–6; Elihu Root, *Military and Colonial Policy of the USA* (Cambridge: Harvard University Press, 1916), 109, 391–94, 426–31, 436. In 1915, the General Staff were wary of appearing to exceed their authority by overenthusiastic war planning. In 1913, Wilson and his cabinet rejected the joint army and navy board's contingency plan for a war with Japan, and when the board persisted in pressing Secretary of the Navy Josephus Daniels for an endorsement, Wilson threatened to abolish the board. See Arthur S. Link, *Wilson: The New Freedom* (Princeton: Princeton University Press, 1956), 297–99. See also Mary T. Reynolds, "The General Staff as a Propaganda Agency, 1908–1914," *Public Opinion Quarterly* 3 (July 1939), 391–408; James Hewes, "The United States Army General Staff, 1900–1917," *Military Affairs* 38 (April 1974), 67–71.

25. Powe, *Emergence,* 79–82; Talbert, *Negative Intelligence,* 5–6; "The General Staff (1903–16)," *The Military Historian and Economist* 1 (Oct. 1916), 385–93.

26. Powe and Wilson, *Evolution,* 12–13, 18; Powe, *Emergence,* 37, 48, 71–73, 82–87; Root, *Military and Colonial Policy,* 85–89; Talbert, *Negative Intelligence,* 6–9; Marl-

borough Churchill, "The Military Intelligence Division, General Staff," *Journal of the United States Artillery* 52 (April 1920), 293–315. See also the chart of the "Military Intelligence Division—General Staff," in MID File 10560-135/8, RG 165, NA. (The Military Intelligence Branch was reformed as the Military Intelligence Division in 1918, and its records are archived under that name.) Until the responsibility of military intelligence was widened to include non-military investigations, information sent by members of the public to the secretary of war about German agents was returned to senders by the adjutant-general's office, with the suggestion that it be readdressed to the BI. Information which Van Deman came across directly was passed on to BI Chief Bielaski. See, for example, J. E. Boze to secretary of war, March 29, 1917; adjutant general to J. E. Boze, April 3, 1917; Bielaski to Billups Harris, Baltimore, March 28, 1917, BI File OG 3057, RG 65, NA.

27. Talbert, *Negative Intelligence*, 11–18; Powe and Wilson, *Evolution*, 19; Powe, *Emergence*, 90.

28. See all MID files with prefix 10218-, RG 165, NA, and, for a BI example, report of Rose B. Mix, Newport, R.I., Oct. 17, 1918, BI File OG 311586, RG 65, NA.

1. African Americans and the War for Democracy, 1917

1. Cited in William Toll, *The Resurgence of Race: Black Social Theory from Reconstruction to the Pan-African Conferences* (Philadelphia: Temple University Press, 1979), 194.

2. "World War and the Color Line," *Crisis* 9 (Nov. 1914), 28–30; "The Perpetual Dilemma," ibid. 13 (April 1917), 270–71; "We Should Worry," ibid. 14 (June 1917), 60–61; "The Present," ibid. 14 (Aug. 1917), 165; W. E. B. Du Bois, "The African Roots of War," *Atlantic Monthly* 115 (May 1915), 707–14. See also Du Bois, *Darkwater: Voices from within the Veil* (New York: Harcourt, Brace and Howe, 1920), 59; Du Bois, *Dusk of Dawn: An Essay toward an Autobiography of a Race Concept* (New York: Harcourt, Brace, 1940), 238–41; David W. Noble, *The Paradox of Progressive Thought* (Minneapolis: University of Minnesota Press, 1958), 47–49. Other black writers made connections between the war, colonialism, and African-American fortunes, including Benjamin Brawley in *A Social History of the American Negro* (New York: Macmillan, 1921), 365–71. Du Bois's view of different styles of colonial government was influenced by his experiences in 1900 at the Paris Exposition Universelle and the London Pan-African Congress and by the opinions of the late Pan-Africanist pioneer Alexander Crummell. See David Levering Lewis, *W. E. B. Du Bois: Biography of a Race, 1868–1919* (New York: Henry Holt, 1993), 247–51; Wilson Jeremiah Moses, *Alexander Crummell: A Study of Civilization and Discontent* (New York: Oxford University Press, 1989), 252. For discussion of a southern black intellectual response to the war, see Leroy Davis, *A Clashing of the Soul: John Hope and the Dilemma of African American Leadership and Black Higher Education in the Early Twentieth Century* (Athens: University of Georgia Press, 1998), 216–18, 224, 229–33.

3. June Sochen, *The Unbridgeable Gap: Blacks and Their Quest for the American Dream, 1900–1930* (Chicago: Rand McNally, 1972), 7–8, 119.

4. B. Joyce Ross, *J. E. Spingarn and the Rise of the NAACP, 1911–1939* (New York:

Atheneum, 1972), vii, 3–9; Marshall Van Deusen, *J. E. Spingarn* (New York: Twayne, 1971), 62–63.

5. Ross, *J. E. Spingarn*, 84, 96–97; Van Deusen, *Spingarn*, 62–63; Lewis, *W. E. B. Du Bois*, 528–29; Hal S. Chase, "Struggle for Equality: Fort Des Moines Training Camp for Colored Officers, 1917," *Phylon* 39 (Dec. 1978), 297–310; *Norfolk Journal and Guide*, March 3, May 5, 1917; *Crisis* 13 (April 1917), 270–71.

6. *Cleveland Gazette*, March 10, 1917; *New York News*, Feb. 22, 1917 (and reprinted in ibid., July 18, 1918).

7. *Norfolk Journal and Guide*, March 17, 1917; ibid., April 14, 1917.

8. Ibid., May 5, May 19, 1917; Chase, "Struggle for Equality," 297, 301–302, 306. Chase gives less credit than some other historians to Spingarn for the creation of the training camp, emphasizing instead the efforts of black students, particularly in Washington. See also Ross, *J. E. Spingarn*, 84–97; Charles Flint Kellogg, *NAACP: A History of the National Association for the Advancement of Colored People, Volume 1: 1909–1920* (Baltimore: Johns Hopkins University Press, 1967), 250–57; Hasia R. Diner, *In the Almost Promised Land: American Jews and Blacks, 1915–1935* (Westport, Conn.: Greenwood Press, 1977), 133–34; George S. Schuyler, *Black and Conservative* (New Rochelle, N.Y.: Arlington House, 1966), 87–91; Arthur E. Barbeau and Florette Henri, *The Unknown Soldiers: Black American Troops in World War I* (Philadelphia: Temple University Press, 1974), 56–62; Gerald W. Patton, *War and Race: The Black Officer in the American Military, 1915–1941* (Westport, Conn.: Greenwood Press, 1981), 54–68; Bernard C. Nalty and Morris J. McGregor, eds., *Blacks in the Military: Essential Documents* (Wilmington, Del.: Scholarly Resources, 1981), 75–76; Bernard C. Nalty, *Strength for the Fight: A History of Black Americans in the Military* (New York: Free Press, 1986), 109–21; Lucy France Pierce, "Training Colored Officers," *Review of Reviews* 56 (Dec. 1917), 640; "Training Negroes for Officers," *Literary Digest* 55 (July 21, 1917), 50–51. Fort Des Moines was an established location for the stationing of black troops. See Douglas Kachel, "Fort Des Moines and Its African American Troops in 1903/04," *Palimpsest* 74 (Spring 1993), 42–48. See also Davis, *A Clashing of the Soul*, 224–27.

9. R. K. McWoodson to *New York Sun*, reprinted in *New York Age*, Feb. 15, 1917, and in *McDowell* (W.Va.) *Times*, clipping, n.d. (1917), cited in U.S. attorney, West Virginia, to A. B. Bielaski, April 25, 1917, BI File OG 3057, RG 65, NA.

10. *Savannah Morning News*, March 12, 1917.

11. *New York Age*, Feb. 15, 1917. On Booker T. Washington's relationship with the *New York Age*, see Samuel R. Spencer, Jr., *Booker T. Washington and the Negro's Place in American Life* (Boston: Little, Brown, 1955), 164–167, 174; Louis R. Harlan, *Booker T. Washington: The Wizard of Tuskegee, 1901–1915* (New York: Oxford University Press, 1983), 321, 324, 393.

12. *New York Age*, March 29, 1917. The opinion of leading papers such as the *Age* was often reprinted elsewhere, as in this case. See *Norfolk Journal and Guide*, March 30, 1917.

13. See, for example, "Declaration of Loyalty" by black residents of McDonagh County, Ga., in *Henry County Weekly*, March 30, 1917; "Open Address to Wilson and Baker," in *Topeka Plaindealer*, March ?, 1917.

14. *New York Tribune,* April 4, 1917.

15. Ibid., April 5, 1917; *New York Globe,* April 6, 1917.

16. *New York Tribune,* April 5, 1917.

17. *New York Times,* April 7, 1917.

18. *Florence (S.C.) Daily Times,* April 5, 1917.

19. On the Zimmerman telegram, see Arthur S. Link, *Wilson: Campaigns for Progressivism and Peace, 1916–1917* (Princeton: Princeton University Press, 1965), 342–59.

20. James A. Sandos, *Rebellion in the Borderlands: Anarchism and the Plan of San Diego, 1904–1923* (Norman: University of Oklahoma Press, 1992), passim; Senate Foreign Relations Committee, *Investigations of Mexican Affairs, Report and Hearings,* 2 vols., 66 Cong., 2 sess., Sen. Doc. 285, 1201–1207, 1232, 1295, 1303, 3241. The hearings in which the Plan of San Diego was outlined were convened by a subcommittee chaired by Senator Albert B. Fall in San Antonio in January 1920. See Barbara Tuchman, *The Zimmerman Telegram* (London: Constable, 1958), 96–97; William H. Hager, "The Plan of San Diego: Unrest on the Texas Border in 1915," *Arizona and the West* 5, no. 4 (1963), 327–36; Alan Gerlach, "Conditions along the Border: The Plan of San Diego," *New Mexico Historical Review* 43 (July 1968), 195–212; Charles Harris III and Louis Sadler, "The Plan of San Diego and the Mexican War Crisis of 1916: A Re-Examination," *Hispanic American Historical Review* 57 (Aug. 1978), 381–408. The Plan of San Diego gained a mythical status. See *Baltimore Afro-American,* Dec. 5, 1919, and Hilton Howell Railey, "The Bootleggers," *Saturday Evening Post,* Aug. 28, 1920, 177, which links the plan to an unlikely story about twenty-five Prohibition agents rounding up 150 out of 500 blacks who were plotting an armed uprising in western Arkansas. See also John B. McClung, "Texas Rangers along the Rio Grande, 1910–1919" (Ph.D. diss., Texas Christian University, 1981).

21. *New York Tribune,* April 5, 1917; *New York Globe,* April 6, 1917. See also Patricia A. Turner, *I Heard It through the Grapevine: Rumor in African-American Culture* (Berkeley: University of California Press, 1993), 42–45.

22. Reinhard R. Doerries, *Imperial Challenge: Ambassador Count Bernstorff and German-American Relations, 1908–1917* (Chapel Hill: University of North Carolina Press, 1989), 39–76; Mark Ellis, "German-Americans in World War I," in *Enemy Images in American History* (Providence: Berghan, 1997), ed. Ragnhild Fiebig–von Hase and Ursula Lehmkuhl, 188–194.

23. "President Wilson's Flag Day Address, 14 June 1917," in John Price Jones and Merrick Hollister, *The German Secret Service in America* (Boston: Small, Maynard, 1918), frontis.

24. *Congressional Record,* May 31, 1918, 65 Cong., 2 sess., 7237.

25. *Montgomery (Ala.) Advertiser,* cited in *Literary Digest* 54 (April 21, 1917), 1153.

26. *Macon (Ga.) Telegraph,* cited in *Literary Digest* 54 (April 21, 1917), 1153.

27. Ray Stannard Baker, *Following the Color Line: An Account of the Negro Citizenship in the American Democracy* (New York: Doubleday, Page, 1908), 81.

28. Forrest G. Wood, *Black Scare: The Racist Response to Emancipation and Reconstruction* (Berkeley: University of California Press, 1968), esp. 130–155.

29. I. A. Newby, *Jim Crow's Defense: Anti-Negro Thought in America, 1900–1930* (Ba-

ton Rouge: Louisiana State University Press, 1965), 113–40; Lewis, *W. E. B. Du Bois,* 425–26, 477–78, 680 n. 20. Anti-integrationist blacks, including Marcus Garvey, expressed doubts as to the merits of "social equality" as an objective. See Marcus Garvey, "Aims and Objects of Movement for Solution of Negro Problem," in *Philosophy and Opinions of Marcus Garvey, or Africa for the Africans,* ed. Amy Jacques Garvey (London: Frank Cass, 1977), 2nd ed., part 2, 40–41; Marcus Garvey, "Appeal to the Soul of White America" (Oct. 1923), reprinted in Amy Jacques Garvey, *Garvey and Garveyism* (London: Collier, 1970), 16–26.

30. Joel Williamson, *The Crucible of Race: Black-White Relations in the American South since Emancipation* (New York: Oxford University Press, 1984), 464–68, 473 n. 17.

31. *New York Age,* April 12, 1917; *Crisis* 14 (May 1917), 23–24; George Coleman Osborn, *John Sharp Williams: Planter-Statesman of the Deep South* (Gloucester, Mass.: Peter Smith, 1964), 295; *Vicksburg Herald,* cited in Neil R. McMillen, *Dark Journey: Black Mississippians in the Age of Jim Crow* (Urbana: University of Illinois Press, 1990), 304.

32. *New York Evening Post,* April 4, 1917.

33. *New York Age,* April 12, 1917.

34. Christopher F. Drewer to Thomas Watt Gregory, April 9, 1917, BI File OG 3057, RG 65, NA. The philanthropic work among African Americans of the Synodical Conference of the Lutheran Church, which donated $60,000 annually to black education projects, was described in the May 1917 issue of the *Crisis* (14), p. 38.

35. *Washington Bee,* n.d., cited in *Crisis* 14 (May 1917), 23; *Norfolk Journal and Guide,* April 14, 1917.

36. *Norfolk Journal and Guide,* May 5, 1917; see also ibid., April 7, 14, 21, 28, 1917; *Amsterdam News,* April 11, 1917; *Columbia (S.C.) State,* April 16, 1917. See also I. A. Newby, *Black Carolinians: A History of Blacks in South Carolina from 1895 to 1968* (Columbia: University of South Carolina Press, 1973), 186–87.

37. *Boston Herald,* April 9, 1917. During April 1917, Johnson addressed several other NAACP branch meetings in a similar vein. See *Norfolk Journal and Guide,* April 28, 1917.

38. "To the Editors of the Colored Newspapers in the United States," NAACP press release, n.d., Papers of the NAACP, Manuscript Division, LC.

39. *Crisis* 14 (May 1917), 8.

40. *New York Age,* April 12, 1917.

41. *New York Tribune,* April 11, 1917; *Crisis* 14 (May 1917), 37.

42. *New York Times,* April 6, 13, 1917; *Norfolk Journal and Guide,* May 5, 1917.

43. R. R. Moton to *Richmond Planet,* cited in *Crisis* 14 (June 1917), 76.

44. *Cleveland Gazette,* April 14, 1917.

45. *Richmond Planet* editorial, cited in *Boston Guardian,* November 3, 1917. After the Armistice, other editors expressed regret that the war had not lasted longer and that American casualties had not been greater. If they had been, it was argued, the black contribution to the Allied victory might have been more vital and better

appreciated. See Andrew Buni, *Robert L. Vann of the Pittsburgh Courier: Politics and Black Journalism* (Pittsburgh: University of Pittsburgh Press, 1974), 102.

46. *Amsterdam News,* April 11, 1917. At other times, Briggs picked out the southwest as the best location for a black republic within U.S. borders.

47. *New York Age,* April 5, 1917; *Boston Advertiser,* April 9, 1917; *New York Tribune,* April 11, 1917.

48. *Crisis* 14 (June 1917), 59.

49. Theodore Kornweibel, Jr., *"No Crystal Stair": Black Life and the Messenger, 1917–1928* (Westport, Conn.: Greenwood Press, 1975), 3–34; Kornweibel, "Apathy and Dissent: Black America's Negative Responses to World War I," *South Atlantic Quarterly* 80 (Summer 1981), 322–38; Gerald R. Gill, "Afro-American Opposition to the United States' Wars of the Twentieth Century," (Ph.D. diss., Howard University, 1985), 38–41, 135–40, 185–86, 189–93, 234–52, 349–69; Steven A. Reich, "Soldiers of Democracy: Black Texans and the Fight for Citizenship, 1917–1921," *Journal of American History* 82 (March 1996), 1478–1504.

50. George S. Schuyler, "Our White Folks," *American Mercury* 12 (Dec. 1927), 386.

51. Robin D. G. Kelley, "'We Are Not What We Seem': Rethinking Black Working-Class Opposition in the Jim Crow South," *Journal of American History* 80 (June 1993), 75–112, and reprinted in *The New African American Urban History,* ed. Kenneth W. Goings and Raymond A. Mohl (Thousand Oaks, Calif.: Sage, 1996), 187–239. See also Kelley, *Hammer and Hoe: Alabama Communists during the Great Depression* (Chapel Hill: University of North Carolina Press), 1990; Al-Tony Gilmore, "The Black Southerner's Response to the Southern System of Race Relations: 1900 to Post–World War II," in *The Age of Segregation: Race Relations in the South, 1890–1945,* ed. Robert Haws (Jackson: University Press of Mississippi, 1978), 67–88.

52. Cited in Henry Justin Ferry, "Patriotism and Prejudice: Francis James Grimke on World War I," *Journal of Religious Thought* 32 (Spring–Summer 1975), 90–91.

53. Major R. W. Pullman to Bielaski, April 6, 1917, BI File OG 3057, RG 65, NA; Bielaski to Billups Harris, Baltimore, March 28, 1917, ibid.; Bielaski to C. S. Wheatley, Cincinnati, March 29, 1917, ibid.; Bielaski to A. J. Devlin, Roanoke, Va., April 2, 1917, ibid. Pullman, the Washington police commissioner and a former high school classmate of Bielaski, wrote, "My Dear Bruce, . . . the negro agitation that we spoke about some time ago. . . . " See Louis Brownlow, *Passion for Anonymity* (Chicago: University of Chicago Press, 1958), 45.

54. A. B. Bielaski to McLeod, March 26, 1917, BI File OG 3057, RG 65, NA; report of F. C. Pendleton, Jr., New Orleans, May 1, 1917, ibid.; U.S. Attorney R. E. Byrd, Roanoake, Va., to attorney general, April 7, 1917, ibid.

55. Charles A. Webb to attorney general, April 9, 1917, BI File OG 3057, RG 65, NA; A. D. Pitts to attorney general, April 13, 1917, ibid.; Bielaski to J. R. Murray, Birmingham, Ala., April 25, 1917, ibid. See 60 Cong., 1 sess. (1909), U.S. Criminal Code, Section 37, Statute 35, Ch. 321, p. 1096.

56. John Dittmer, *Black Georgia in the Progressive, Era, 1900–1920* (Urbana: Uni-

versity of Illinois Press, 1977), 186; *Columbia (S.C.) State*, cited in George Washington Ellis, "Psychic Factors in the New American Race Situation," *Journal of Race Development* 7 (April 1917), 474. On lynching, see Stewart E. Tolnay and E. M. Beck, *A Festival of Violence: An Analysis of Southern Lynchings, 1882–1930* (Urbana: University of Illinois Press, 1995); Herbert Shapiro, *White Violence and Black Response: From Reconstruction to Montgomery* (Amherst: University of Massachusetts Press, 1988), 31–63, 93–118. On the lynching tradition, see Christopher Waldrep, *Roots of Disorder: Race and Criminal Justice in the American South, 1817–80* (Urbana: University of Illinois Press, 1998).

57. James R. Grossman, *Land of Hope: Chicago, Black Southerners, and the Great Migration* (Chicago: University of Chicago Press, 1989), 23–37, 98–99, 109–11; Emmett J. Scott, *Negro Migration during the Great War* (New York: Oxford University Press, 1920), 3, 29, 50, 62–68; Scott, "Letters of Negro Migrants of 1916–1918," *Journal of Negro History* 4 (July 1919), 290–340; Scott, "Additional Letters of Negro Migrants of 1916–1918," ibid. (Oct. 1919), 412–65; Henderson H. Donald, "The Negro Migration of 1916–1918," ibid. 6 (Oct. 1921), 383–498; Hannibal Gerald Duncan, *The Changing Race Relationships in the Border and Northern States* (Lancaster, Pa.: Intelligence Printing, 1922), 14; Darlene Clark Hine, "Black Migration to the Urban Midwest: The Gender Dimension, 1915–1945," in Goings and Mohl, eds., *New African American Urban History*, 240–65; Jacqueline Jones, "From Farm to City: Southern Black Women Move North, 1900–1930," in *Major Problems in the History of American Workers*, ed. Eileen Boris and Nelson Lichtenstein (Lexington: D. C. Heath, 1991), 200–14; McMillen, *Dark Journey*, 262–72; Lester C. Lamon, *Black Tennesseans, 1900–1930* (Knoxville: University of Tennessee Press, 1977), 119, 126; Jerrell H. Shofner, "Florida and the Black Migration," *Florida Historical Quarterly* 57 (Jan. 1979), 267–71; Preston William Slosson, *The Great Crusade and After, 1914–1928* (New York: Macmillan, 1935), 254; Allan H. Spear, *Black Chicago: The Making of a Negro Ghetto, 1890–1920* (Chicago: University of Chicago Press, 1967), 131–40; Thomas J. Woofter, *Southern Race Progress: The Wavering Color Line* (Washington, D.C.: Public Affairs Press, 1957), 61–69; Carole Marks, *Farewell—We're Good and Gone: The Great Black Migration* (Bloomington: Indiana University Press, 1989). See also W. E. B. Du Bois, "The Migration of Negroes," *Crisis* 14 (June 1917), 63–66; Arna Bontemps and Jack Conroy, *Any Place but Here* (New York: Hill & Wang, 1966); St. Clair Drake and Horace R. Cayton, *Black Metropolis: A Study of Negro Life in a Northern City*, 2 vols. (New York: Harper & Row, 1962). On movement within the South, see Edward L. Ayers, *The Promise of the New South: Life after Reconstruction* (New York: Oxford University Press, 1992), 22–25, 196–98, 457. See also Leon F. Litwack, *Trouble in Mind: Black Southerners in the Age of Jim Crow* (New York: Alfred A. Knopf, 1998), 483–96. One of the most dramatic increases in the black population of a southern city occurred in Miami, but much of this was due to immigration from the Bahamas. See Charles Garofolo, "Black-White Occupational Distribution in Miami During World War I," *Prologue* 5 (Summer 1973), 98–101.

58. White newspapers that regretted the migration included the *Memphis Commercial Appeal*, the *Columbia (S.C.) State*, the *Atlanta Constitution*, and the *Chattanooga*

Times; among those content to see blacks go were the *New Orleans Times-Picayune,* the *Nashville Banner,* and the *Vicksburg Herald.* Scott, *Negro Migration,* 152–69. For detailed analysis of the cotton belt economies in relation to migration, see Thomas J. Woofter, Jr., *Negro Migration: Changes in Rural Organization and Population of the Cotton Belt* (New York: AMS Press, 1971, first published 1920). See also James R. Grossman, "Black Labor is the Best Labor: Southern White Reactions to the Great Migration," in *Black Exodus: The Great Migration from the American South,* ed. Alferdteen Harrison (Jackson: University Press of Mississippi, 1991), 51–71; Neil R. McMillen, *Dark Journey,* 272–74.

59. See, for example, *Norfolk Journal and Guide,* Oct. 21, 1916, Jan. 13, 1917, Feb. 3, 10, 24, 1917, March 10, 17, 24, 30, 1917, April 7, 14, 21, 28, 1917, May 5, 12, 1917, Aug. 4, 1917.

60. Bielaski to Divisional Superintendent Lewis J. Bailey, Atlanta, March 21, 1917, BI File OG 3057, RG 65, NA; Newby, *Black Carolinians,* 189; James C. Cobb, *The Most Southern Place on Earth: The Mississippi Delta and the Roots of Regional Identity* (New York: Oxford University Press, 1992), 115–19.

61. Scott, *Negro Migration,* 38, 55, 72–73, 76; Florette Henri, *Black Migration: Movement North, 1900–1920* (Garden City: Anchor-Doubleday, 1975), 61; Grossman, *Land of Hope,* 45–47. On the role of the Pennsylvania Railroad in transporting the migrants from Florida, see G. Z. Phillips to L. F. Englesby, Jacksonville, Fla., Oct. 30, 1916, BI File MISC 10015, RG 65, NA. For probable examples of labor agents being mistaken for German spies, see report of J. R. Murray, Birmingham, Ala., April 27, 1917, BI File OG 3057, RG 65, NA.

62. BI File MISC 10015, RG 65, NA, passim.

63. Report of M. Hanna, Birmingham, June 17, 1917, BI File OG 3057, RG 65, NA; report of J. S. Menefee, Cincinnati, April 25, 1917, ibid.; report of H. L. Scott, Cincinnati, May 10, 1917, ibid.; reports of R. L. Barnes, San Antonio, May 17, July 26, 1917, ibid.

64. Report from Birmingham, n.d., BI File OG 4978, RG 65, NA; report of Leverett Englesby, West Palm Beach, Fla., April 20, 1917, BI File OG 3057, RG 65, NA.

65. E. M. Harris, York, Ala., to Post Office Dept., Washington, March 31, 1917, ibid.; Bielaski to postmaster, Blockton, Ala., April 2, 1917, ibid.; Bielaski to Lewis, April 3, 1917, ibid. See also *New York Times,* April 7, 1917.

66. J. B. Moakley, Jackson, to Bielaski, April 11, 1917, BI File OG 3057, RG 65, NA. See also report of J. L. Webb, Galveston, April 5, 1917, ibid.; Arthur Smith, Clarksdale, Miss., to Post Office inspector-in-charge, Chattanooga, Tenn., April 5, 1917, ibid.; report of L. Y. McLeod, Mobile, Ala., April 10, 1917, ibid.; report of B.C. Baldwin, San Antonio, April 17, 1917, ibid.

67. Reports of F. M. Spencer, Dallas, April 9, 1917, BI File OG 3057, RG 65, NA; R. L. Barnes to U.S. Marshal J. H. Rogers, Austin, April 14, 1917, ibid.; report of R. L. Barnes, San Antonio, May 3, 1917, ibid.; report of B.C. Baldwin, San Antonio, May 6, 1917, ibid.; reports of McElveen, Memphis, April 10, 16, 1917, ibid. BI Divisional Superintendent R. L. Barnes had been a BI agent on the Mexican border

in 1912 before taking over the San Antonio office in 1913 with responsibility for Texas, Arizona, and New Mexico. In October 1917, he became the intelligence officer for the army's Southern Department with the rank of major. He organized intelligence work regarding the "German System in Mexico." Senate Committee, *Investigations of Mexican Affairs,* 1232.

68. Spear, *Black Chicago,* 81–82, 114–15, 134–37, 184–85; Scott, *Negro Migration,* 17–18, 30, 40, 45; Henri, *Black Migration,* 64; Grossman, *Land of Hope,* 67–97, report of P. R. Hilliard, Chicago, April 17, 1917. See also Carolyn A. Stroman, "The Chicago 'Defender' and the Mass Migration of Blacks, 1916–1918," *Journal of Popular Culture* 15 (Fall 1981), 62–67; "Urging Blacks to Move North (W. Allison Sweeney in *Chicago Defender,* June 23, 1917)," in *Voices of a Black Nation: Political Journalism in the Harlem Renaissance,* ed. Theodore G. Vincent (San Francisco: Ramparts Press, 1973), 47–48.

69. Report of F. C. Pendleton, New Orleans, April 9, 1917, BI File OG 5911, RG 65, NA; Bielaski to Division Superintendent Hinton G. Clabaugh, Chicago, April 9, 1917, ibid.

70. Clabaugh to Bielaski, April 16, 1917, BI File OG 5911, RG 65, NA; report of John E. Hawkins, April 16, 1917, ibid.; report of P. R. Hilliard, April 17, 1917, ibid.; report of Mercantile Agency, R. G. Dun & Co., April 11, 1917, ibid.; reports of Hawkins, April 12, 13, 16, 17, 1917, BI File OG 3057, RG 65, NA. Abbott was to become one of the first black millionaires in the United States. Stroman, "The Chicago 'Defender,'" 65–66. See also Frederick Detweiler, *The Negro Press in the United States* (Chicago: University of Chicago Press, 1922), 62, 64–67; Roi Ottley, *The Lonely Warrior: The Life and Times of Robert S. Abbott* (Chicago: Regnery, 1955).

71. Report of E. S. Chastain, Jacksonville, Fla., April 24, 1917, BI File OG 3057, RG 65, NA; report of B. A. Davis, Pensacola, Fla., April 16, 1917, ibid.

72. Durand Whipple to A. M. Briggs, July 3, 1917, ibid.; Furbershaw to Bielaski, July 10, 1917, BI File OG 5911, RG 65, NA.

73. H. B. Cocker to Woodrow Wilson, March 29, 1917, BI File 3057, RG 65, NA; report of G. W. Dillard, Washington, March 15, 1917, ibid.; H. W. Kinney, Lynchburg, Va., to DJ, March 31, 1917, ibid.; J. A. Malone, Grayson, Ky., to DJ, March 13, 1917, ibid. Regarding servants, see also Tera W. Hunter, "Domination and Resistance: The Politics of Wage Household Labor in the New South," in Goings and Mohl, eds., *New African American Urban History,* 167–86; Litwack, *Trouble in Mind,* 167–74.

74. Collier H. Minge to Joseph Tumulty, April 6, 1917, BI File 3057, RG 65, NA.

75. Report from New Orleans, June 18, 1917, BI File OG 26527, RG 65, NA; report of R. N. Daughton, Norfolk, Va., May 1, 1917, BI File OG 3057, RG 65, NA; report from Chicago, June ?, 1917, BI File OG 25436, RG 65, NA; report of C. P. Tighe, Indianapolis, July 24, 1917, BI File OG 39951, RG 65, NA.

76. Report of W. J. Patrick, Birmingham, April 18, 1917, BI File OG 3057, RG 65, NA; unidentified clippings and letter, Asheville, Ala., September ?, 1918, BI File OG 196145, RG 65, NA; report from New Orleans, May 28, 1917, BI File OG 19755, RG 65, NA.

77. Report of B.C. Bocock, Charleston, May 10, 11, 1917, BI File OG 3057, RG 65, NA.

78. Report of McElveen, Memphis, April 30, 1917, ibid.

79. Anon. letter to U.S. Government, n.d., ibid. (punctuation added). The possibility that this letter was written by a white scaremonger cannot be completely discounted.

80. R. L. Barnes to B.C. Baldwin, Sept. 12, 1917, ibid.; report of B.C. Baldwin, Waco, Tex., Sept. 13, 1917, ibid. See Alwyn Barr, "The Texas 'Black Uprising' Scare of 1883," *Phylon* 41 (June 1980), 179–86.

81. Report of Stephen Pinckney to Division Superintendent Baley, Atlanta, Aug. 17, 1917, BI File OG 3057, RG 65, NA; clipping from *Cincinnati Post*, April 22?, 1917, ibid.; report of J. B. Wilson, Wheeling, W.Va., April 24, 1917, ibid.; report of M. Hanna, Birmingham, May 29, 1917, ibid.

82. Report of T. F. Weiss, Oklahoma City, April 11, 1917, ibid.; report of E. S. Chastain, Jacksonville, May 13, 1917, ibid. For examples of patriotic letters from African Americans, see in the same file J. Silas Harris (Negro Protective League of Missouri) to Woodrow Wilson, April 23, 1917; Dr. L. J. Johnson, Helena, Ark., to DJ, June 19, 1917. L. J. Johnson, a chiropractor, was almost certainly one of the four medically employed Johnson brothers killed by a white posse near Helena at the height of the Elaine race riot in October 1919.

83. Tolnay and Beck, *Festival of Violence*, 32–34; Woofter, *Southern Race Progress*, 26–33; McMillen, *Dark Journey*, 395. For examples of near-lynchings of blacks accused of plotting in World War I, see ibid., 243. Between 1900 and 1919, an average of sixty-nine blacks were murdered by mobs each year and in 1918 the figure would rise again to sixty.

84. Reports of B. Bocock, Charleston, S.C., May 10, 11, 23, 1917, BI File OG 3057, RG 65, NA.

85. Woofter, *Southern Race Progress*, 32.

86. Report from Oklahoma, December 6, 1917, BI File OG 106027, RG 65, NA; report from Waco, Tex., May 29, 1917, BI File OG 1889, RG 65, NA; Durand Whipple to Bielaski, May 25, 1917, BI File OG 3057, RG 65, NA.

87. Cocker to Wilson, March 29, 1917, BI File OG 3057, RG 65, NA; report of R. S. Phifer, Jr., Jackson, Miss., April 30, 1917, ibid.; Hermon Carlton to W. S. Goodwin, April 9, 1917, ibid.; Goodwin to attorney general, April 12, 1917, ibid.; Bielaski to C. M. Walser, Little Rock, April 16, 1917, ibid.; report of Walser, April 23, 1917, ibid.; McMillen, *Dark Journey*, 230–32, 394–95; Jacqueline Jones, *The Dispossessed: America's Underclass from the Civil War to the Present* (New York: Basic Books, 1992), 86–87. See also Tolnay and Beck, *Festival of Violence*, 40–41; Cobb, *Most Southern Place on Earth*, 113–15.

88. Winfield H. Collins, *The Truth about Lynching and the Negro in the South: In Which the Author Pleads That the South Be Made Safe for the White Race* (New York: Neale Publishing, 1918), 63.

89. Ralph E. Luker, *The Social Gospel in Black and White: American Racial Reform, 1885–1912* (Chapel Hill: University of North Carolina Press, 1991), 85, 233–34. For

a lurid account of the Statesboro case, see also Baker, *Following the Color Line,* 177–90. On secret societies, see David M. Tucker, *Black Pastors and Leaders: Memphis, 1819–1972* (Memphis: Memphis State University Press, 1975), 25–41.

90. Report of J. M. Bauserman, Jr., Richmond, Va., June 13, 1917, BI File OG 3057, RG 65, NA; report of Leverett Englesby, Cocoa, Fla., May 14, 1917, ibid.

91. McMillen, *Dark Journey,* 30–31, 304–305.

92. Elliott M. Rudwick, *Race Riot at East St. Louis, July 2, 1917* (New York: Atheneum, 1972), 16–33, 36–37. On the chaos and corruption of the city government in East St. Louis, see Roger Baldwin, "East St. Louis—Why?" *Survey* 38 (Aug. 18, 1917), 447–48.

93. Rudwick, *Race Riot,* 10–11; *New York Times,* Nov. 4, 1916.

94. Rudwick, *Race Riot,* 12–13; *New York Times,* Nov. 6, 1916; *Chicago Herald,* Nov. 4, 1916; *Chicago Tribune,* Nov. 6, 1916.

95. Rudwick, *Race Riot,* 13; multiple reports and correspondence in BI Files MISC 9744 and MISC 10015, RG 65, NA.

96. Report of J. J. McLaughlin, St. Louis, July 5, 1917, BI File OG 28469, RG 65, NA; Rudwick, *Race Riot,* 15.

97. Rudwick, *Race Riot,* 38–56; *St. Louis Post-Dispatch,* July 3, 1917; *Chicago Defender,* July 7, 1917; *Crisis* 15 (April, 1918), 269; Robert Asher, ed., "Documents of the Race Riot at East St. Louis," *Journal of the Illinois State Historical Society* 65 (Autumn 1972), 327–36. The *Crisis* put the number of deaths at 125 and Du Bois continued to use this figure. See W. E. B. Du Bois, *The Autobiography of W. E. B. Du Bois: A Soliloquy on Viewing My Life from the Last Decade of its First Century* (New York: International Publishers, 1968), 269. See also Alfreda Duster, ed., *Crusade for Justice: The Autobiography of Ida B. Wells* (Chicago: University of Chicago Press, 1970), 383–95; Turner, *I Heard It through the Grapevine,* 46–50.

98. Bielaski to E. J. Brennan, July 3, 1917, BI File OG 28469, RG 65, NA; *New York Sun,* July 8, 1917.

99. Reports of J. J. McLaughlin and K. C. Coes, July 5, 1917, BI File OG 28469, RG 65, NA; report of E. J. Brennan, July 6, 1917, ibid.

100. Rudwick, *Race Riot,* 136. On the accusations made by the employers and by the unions, see "Negro Labor and the Unions," *American Industry in Wartime,* August 10, 1917, 6–7; Samuel Gompers, "East St. Louis Race Riots—Their Causes," *American Federationist* 24 (Aug. 1917), 621–26.

101. Herron to Fitts, July 20, 1917, cited by Rudwick, *Race Riot,* 262; "Authority of USA to Protect Negroes in the States in Enjoyment of Civil Rights," DJ memo, March ?, 1910, BI File OG 3057, RG 65, NA.

102. Bielaski to Brennan, July 21, 1917, BI File OG 28469, RG 65, NA.

103. Report of E. J. Brennan, July 24, 1917, ibid.; Karch to Gregory, July 23, 1917, cited by Rudwick, *Race Riot,* 137; Wilson to Gregory, July 23, 1917, case file 152, series 4, Papers of Woodrow Wilson, LC.

104. H. G. Clabaugh to Bielaski, July 21, 1917, BI File OG 28469, RG 65, NA; *Chicago Defender,* July 28, 1917. McGlynn was a leading figure in the East St. Louis Chamber of Commerce's "committee of 100," formed to see that rioters were prose-

cuted and the police department reformed (Rudwick, *Race Riot,* 98–99). He was later condemned by the congressional committee which visited East St. Louis in October 1917 for defending policemen charged with rioting.

105. William T. Hutchinson, *Lowden of Illinois: The Life of Frank Lowden* (Chicago: University of Chicago Press, 1957), 338; Rudwick, *Race Riot,* 18–19, 29, 32, 35, 82.

106. Clabaugh to Bielaski, July 21, 1917, BI File OG 28469, RG 65, NA.

107. Reports of E. J. Brennan, July 23, 25, 1917, ibid.; report of W. Brashear, July 24, 1917, ibid.

108. Gregory to Wilson, July 27, 1917, case file 152, series 4, Papers of Woodrow Wilson, LC; Wilson to Leonidas C. Dyer, July 28, 1917, ibid.; Gregory to Karch, July 27, 1917, cited by Rudwick, *Race Riot,* 262.

109. Reports of W. Brashear, July 24, 25, 26, 27, 28, 1917, BI File OG 28469, RG 65, NA.

110. "The Massacre of East St. Louis," *Crisis* 14 (Sept. 1917), 219–38. See also Martha Gruening, "Democratic Massacres in East St. Louis," *Pearson's Magazine* 38 (Sept. 1917), 106–18.

111. Unidentified clipping, BI File OG 37586, RG 65, NA. See also *Chicago Defender,* July 7, 1917, and Linda O. McMurry, *To Keep the Waters Troubled: The Life of Ida B. Wells* (New York: Oxford University Press, 1998), 314–16.

112. Clabaugh to Bielaski, July 5, 1917, BI File OG 37586, RG 65, NA; Bielaski to Clabaugh, July 24, 1917, ibid.; report of S. Krautzburg, Chicago, Sept. 14, 1917, ibid.; Clabaugh to H. F. Schuettler, July 13, 1917, BI File OG 3057, RG 65, NA.

113. *Norfolk Journal and Guide,* July 7, 1917; *Baltimore Afro-American,* July 7, 1917; *The Voice,* July 4, 1917, reprinted in Hubert H. Harrison, *When Africa Awakes: The 'Inside Story' of the Stirrings and Strivings of the New Negro in the Western World* (New York: Porro Press, 1920), 14; *Chicago Defender,* July 7, 1917.

114. *Norfolk Journal and Guide,* July 14, 1917; "What Some Americans Think of East St. Louis," *Outlook* 116 (July 18, 1917), 435–36; "The Illinois Race War and Its Brutal Aftermath," *Current Opinion* 63 (Aug. 1917), 75–77; "The East St. Louis Riot", *Outlook* 116 (July 11, 1917), 392; Oscar Leonard, "The East St. Louis Pogrom," *Survey* 38 (July 14, 1917), 331–33. See also "East St. Louis Riots," *Literary Digest* 55 (July 14, 1917), 10–11.

115. Reprinted in the *Norfolk Journal and Guide,* July 14, 1917.

116. Desha Breckinridge to Oswald Garrison Villard, May 31, 1918; "Lynchers Are Allies of the Hun," clipping from *Lexington Herald,* May 25, 1918, folder 347.6, correspondence files, Papers of Oswald Garrison Villard, HL.

117. *Baltimore Afro-American,* July 14, 1917; J. Milton Waldron to Wilson, July 10, 1917; Joseph P. Tumulty to Wilson, July 10, 1917, case file 152, series 4, Woodrow Wilson Papers, LC. See also John M. Blum, *Joe Tumulty and the Wilson Era* (New York: Archon Books, 1969, first published 1951), 137.

118. *Baltimore Afro-American,* July 14, 1917.

119. *Baltimore Afro-American,* Aug. 4, 1917; *Norfolk Journal and Guide,* Aug. 11, 1917.

120. "The Riots in East St. Louis," *Pan-American Magazine* 25 (Aug. 1917), 173–

74; "The Illinois Race War and Its Brutal Aftermath," *Current Opinion* 75 (Aug. 1917), 75–77.

121. *Baltimore Afro-American*, July 14, 1917; *Norfolk Journal and Guide*, July 14, 1917; Lewis, *W. E. B. Du Bois*, 538.

122. James Weldon Johnson, *Along This Way: The Autobiography of James Weldon Johnson* (New York: Penguin, 1990, first published 1933), 319–20.

123. Anthony Platt, ed., *The Politics of Riot Commissions, 1917–1970: A Collection of Official Reports and Critical Essays* (New York: Macmillan, 1971), 58–82.

124. *Baltimore Afro-American*, Aug. 4, 1917; Robert H. Ferrell, *Woodrow Wilson and World War I, 1917–1921* (New York, Harper & Row, 1985), 217; Johnson, *Along This Way*, 321; Ralph Ginzburg, *100 Years of Lynching* (New York: Lancer, 1962), 104–106; David M. Kennedy, *Over Here: The First World War and American Society* (New York: Oxford University Press, 1980), 30. Silent protest marches were later held in other cities, including Newark, N.J.. See *Baltimore Afro-American*, Sept. 29, 1917; Audrey O. Faulkner, et al., eds., *When I Was Coming Up: An Oral History of Aged Blacks* (Hamden, Conn.: Archon, 1982), 215.

125. Harrison, *When Africa Awakes*, 14–15.

126. Report of L. Loabl, St. Louis, Sept. 20, 1917, BI File OG 28469, RG 65, NA.

127. "GET OFF THE EARTH," leaflet in Central File 158260-43, Records of the Department of Justice, RG 60, NA; also BI File OG 3057, RG 65, NA; also MID File 10218-132, RG 165, NA. *Baltimore Afro-American*, Sept. 29, 1917.

128. Desha Breckinridge to postmaster, Lexington, Aug. 17, 1917; Postmaster, Lexington, to chief inspector, Post Office Dept., Aug. 20, 1917, Central File 158260-43, RG 60, NA. Although theirs was a wealthy southern family, the Breckinridges were unusually liberal. Desha's sister, Sophonisba, worked with Jane Addams and was an early supporter of the NAACP, and his wife was invited to be a member of a national race commission which Oswald Garrison Villard unsuccessfully proposed to Woodrow Wilson in 1912–13. Kellogg, *NAACP*, 124, 160 n20.

129. Report of J. L. Webb, Galveston, Tex., Aug. 23, 1917, BI File OG 3057, RG 65, NA; Charles Burke to Bielaski, Sept. 3, 1917, ibid.; report of A. L. Barkley, Buffalo, N.Y., Sept. 12, 1917, ibid.; U.S. Attorney, Southern District, Texas, to Attorney General, Aug. 31, 1917, Central File 158260-42, RG 60, NA.

130. T. W. Quinlan to Bielaski, Aug. 27, 1917, BI File OG 3057, RG 65, NA; Bielaski to Quinlan, Sept. 1, 1917, ibid.; Quinlan to Bielaski, Sept. 10, 1917, BI File OG 55468, RG 65, NA; *Baltimore Afro-American*, Sept. 29, 1917.

131. *Illinois State Journal*, Sept. 20, 1917; *Illinois State Register*, Sept. 20, 1917; Zechariah Chafee, Jr., *Freedom of Speech* (London: George Allen & Unwin, 1920), 45. In October 1917, military intelligence made an inconclusive investigation of the "GET OFF THE EARTH" leaflet, after being informed by a black Washington clergyman that it might be the work of a local printer. F. W. Scheick to Capt. H. A. Taylor, Oct. 9, 1917, MID File 10218-32, RG 165, NA; report of Mark A. Keefe to Taylor, Oct. 9, 1917, ibid.

132. *Norfolk Journal and Guide*, July 21, 1917.

133. *Baltimore Afro-American*, Aug. 11, 1917; *Norfolk Journal and Guide*, Aug. 11, 18, 1917; *Washington Bee*, Aug. 11, 1917.

134. D. J. Jordan to Woodrow Wilson, July 4, 1917, BI File 0G 28649, RG 65, NA; Herbert Parsons memo, Sept. 29, 1917, MID File 10218-24, RG 165, NA.

135. Robert V. Haynes, *A Night of Violence: The Houston Riot of 1917* (Baton Rouge: Louisiana State University Press, 1976); Nalty, *Strength for the Fight*, 101–106. Six more members of the Twenty-fourth Infantry were executed in September 1918. Ibid., 105.

136. Report of V. F. Kilborn, Mobile, Ala., Aug. 31, 1917, MID File 10218-12, RG 165, NA. For similar sentiments, see report of L. O. Thompson, Lexington, Ky., April 26, 1918, MID File 10218-132, RG 165, NA.

2. The Wilson Administration and Black Opinion, 1917–1918

1. Leland Harrison to R. H. Van Deman, Aug. 2, 1917, MID File 10218-113, RG 165, NA; report of P. T. Rellihan, July 28, 1917, ibid. For more on Kuhn, Loeb and Co., see John Price Jones and Merrick Hollister, *The German Secret Service in America* (Boston: Small, Maynard, 1918), 238. On Philip Payton, see Gilbert Osofsky, *Harlem: The Making of a Ghetto, Negro New York, 1890–1930* (New York: Harper & Row, 1971), 93–104; Jervis Anderson, "Harlem: I, The Journey Uptown," *New Yorker*, June 29, 1981, 68.

2. Van Deman had previously submitted his own reports on racial matters to the BI. See A. B. Bielaski to Billups Harris, March 28, 1917, BI File OG 3057, RG 65, NA.

3. *Who Was Who in America*, vol. 1 (Chicago: Marquis–Who's Who, 1943), 939. Parsons's Republican party work had brought him into contact with James Weldon Johnson in 1916. Eugene D. Levy, *James Weldon Johnson: Black Leader, Black Voice* (Chicago: University of Chicago Press, 1973), 166–70; James Weldon Johnson to Herbert E. Parsons, Aug. 11, 1916, folder 365, box 15, James Weldon Johnson Papers, JWJC; Parsons to Johnson, Nov. 13, 1916, ibid.; Johnson to Charles W. Anderson, Oct. 31, 1916, folder 22, box 2, ibid.; E. J. Scott to W. E. B. Du Bois, May 15, 1918, Papers of Joel Spingarn, NYPL; Scott to Spingarn, June 26, 1918, Joel E. Spingarn Papers, M-SRC. Parsons later served in France with the 5th Division as an assistant chief of staff in military intelligence and then as assistant military attaché at Berne. He became chairman of the New York State Republican Party in 1920 and died in a motorcycle accident in 1925. Levy, *James Weldon Johnson*, 208; Oswald Garrison Villard, *Fighting Years: Memoirs of a Liberal Editor* (New York: Harcourt, Brace and World, 1939), 407–408. See also Robert F. Wesser, *A Response to Progressivism: The Democratic Party and New York Politics, 1902–1918* (New York: New York University Press, 1986), 11, 125, 168–69; J. W. Jenks to H. Parsons, Aug. 13, 1917, MID File 10218-1, RG 165, NA. Jeremiah Jenks worked for the Aircraft Production Board of the Advisory Commission of the Council for National Defense. Hallie Queen accepted a teaching post at Tuskegee Institute in 1909, but, finding it too academically parochial, resigned soon afterward and spent four years as a government employee in Puerto Rico. See William Toll, *The Resurgence of Race: Black Social Theory from Reconstruction to the Pan-African Conferences* (Philadelphia: Temple University Press, 1979), 110; *The Correspondence of W. E. B. Du Bois*, vol. 1, *Selections,*

1877–1934, ed. Herbert Aptheker (Amherst: University of Massachusetts Press, 1973), 125–26; Willard B. Gatewood, *Aristocrats of Color: The Black Elite, 1880–1920* (Bloomington: Indiana University Press, 1990), 404 n10.

4. *Chicago Defender,* July 28, 1917; *Baltimore Afro-American,* July 28, 1917; Hallie E. Queen, "East St. Louis As I Saw It," in "Documents of the Race Riot at East St. Louis," ed. Robert Asher, *Journal of the Illinois State Historical Society* 65 (Autumn 1972), 330–336. This account of the riot was sent by Queen to U.S. Senator William Y. Sherman of Illinois on Aug. 20, 1917. Parsons memo, Aug. 23, 1917, MID File 10218-1, RG 165, NA.

5. Parsons to Spingarn, Aug. 15, 1917, MID File 10218-1, RG 165, NA.

6. Parsons memo, Aug. 19, 1917, MID File 10218-3, RG 165, NA; Spingarn to Parsons, Aug. 25, 1917, MID File 10218-7, RG 165, NA.

7. Spingarn to Parsons, and enclosure, Aug. 25, 1917, MID File 10218-7, RG 165, NA.

8. Parsons to Spingarn, Aug. 27, 1917, ibid. Parsons still used Du Bois for odd pieces of information. See, for example, Parsons to Du Bois, Sept. 20, 1917, MID File 10218-22, RG 165, NA; Du Bois to Parsons, Sept. 25, 1917, ibid.

9. Van Deman to chief of staff, Sept. 1, 1917, MID File 10218-7, RG 165, NA.

10. Hal S. Chase, "Struggle for Equality: Fort Des Moines Training Camp for Colored Officers, 1917," *Phylon* 39 (Dec. 1978), 297–310; "Training Camp for Negro Officers," *Literary Digest* 55 (July 21, 1917), 50–51; B. Joyce Ross, *J. E. Spingarn and the Rise of the NAACP, 1911–1939* (New York: Atheneum, 1972), 84–97.

11. On the treatment of black officers in World War I, see Proceedings of a Board of Officers, Feb. 26, 1919, NAACP Papers, Admin. File, LC; J. E. Cutler to DMI, 20 June 1919, MID File 10218-279, RG 165, NA; *Crisis* 18 (May 1919), 1621; ibid. 19 (Dec. 1919), 45–46; *New York Age,* May 10, 1919; *Cleveland Advocate,* June 14, 1919; *New York Times,* Nov. 8, 1919; "Newton D. Baker, Official Statement about Negro Troops," *Southern Workman* 48 (Dec. 1919), 636–39. See also Addie W. Hunton and Kathryn M. Johnson, *Two Colored Women with the U.S. Expeditionary Forces* (New York: Brooklyn Eagle Press, 1920), 57–61; Gerald W. Patton, *War and Race: The Black Officer in the American Military, 1915–1941* (Westport, Conn.: Greenwood Press, 1981), 54–68, 81–122; George S. Schuyler, *Black and Conservative* (New Rochelle, N.Y.: Arlington House, 1966), 86–93; Emmett J. Scott, *The American Negro in the World War* (Chicago: Homewood Press, 1919), passim, especially chapters 7–9, 30; Bernard C. Nalty, *Strength for the Fight: A History of Black Americans in the Military* (New York: Free Press, 1986), 107–24.

12. Robert Ewell Greene, *Black Defenders of America, 1775–1973* (Chicago: Johnson Publishing, 1974), 158–63; Florette Henri, *Black Migration: Movement North, 1900–1920* (Garden City: Anchor-Doubleday, 1975), 278–84, 381–83; J. E. Spingarn memo, n.d., MID File 10218-154, RG 165, NA; Charles Young to W. E. B. Du Bois, June 20, 1917, Papers of W. E. B. Du Bois, reel 5, UML.

13. John Sharp Williams to Woodrow Wilson, June 22, 1917, Papers of Woodrow Wilson, series 2, reel 88, LC; Williams to Wilson, June 27, 30, 1917, special correspondence, 1917–19, box 2, Papers of John Sharp Williams, LC; Wilson to Newton D. Baker, June 25, July 3, 9, 1917, Papers of Newton D. Baker, reel 3, LC.

14. Baker to Wilson, June 25, July 7, 1917, Papers of Newton D. Baker, reel 3, LC; Baker to Tasker H. Bliss, n.d., ibid.; Wilson to Williams, June 29, 1917, ibid.; Arthur E. Barbeau and Florette Henri, *The Unknown Soldiers: Black American Troops in World War I* (Philadelphia: Temple University Press, 1974), 67–68. See also William W. Giffin, "Mobilization of Black Militiamen in World War I: Ohio's Ninth Battalion," *Historian* 11 (Aug. 1978), 686–703.

15. David Levering Lewis, *W. E. B. Du Bois: Biography of a Race, 1868–1919* (New York: Henry Holt, 1993), 532–34; Greene, *Black Defenders of America,* 163. See also Rayford W. Logan and Michael R. Winston, eds., *Dictionary of American Negro Biography* (New York: W. W. Norton, 1982), s.v. "Young, Charles."

16. Robert Russa Moton to Wilson, July 7, 1917, Papers of Woodrow Wilson, series 4, reel 362, LC; Wilson to Moton, July 9, 1917, series 3, letterbook 42, ibid. Moton's letter enclosed clippings about Young from the *New York Age,* June 28, 1917; the *Nashville Globe,* June 29, 1917; the *St. Louis Argus,* June 29, 1917; the *Chicago Defender,* June 30, 1917; and the *Indianapolis Freeman,* June 30, 1917. See also *Crisis* 14 (Oct. 1917), 286; ibid. 15 (Feb. 1918), 165; *Baltimore Afro-American,* July 5, 1918; J. E. Spingarn to M. Churchill, June 15, 1918, MID File 10218-154, RG 165, NA. On the NAACP campaign to restore Young to active service, see Newton D. Baker to Gen. McCain, Feb. 2, 1918, Papers of Newton D. Baker, LC; McCain to Baker, Feb. 6, 1918, ibid.; Oswald Garrison Villard to John R. Shillady, Feb. 9, 1918, Papers of W. E. B. Du Bois, reel 7, UML; Villard to Frederick P. Keppel, Feb. 9, 1918, ibid.; Richetta Randolph to Young, Feb. 13, 1918, ibid.; John R. Shillady to Young, March 19, 1918, ibid.; Young to Du Bois, March 21, 1918, ibid.; Young to Shillady, March 21, 1918, ibid.; Young to Baker, April 26, 1918, ibid. The journalist George Schuyler later claimed that, while traveling to begin officer training at Fort Des Moines, he met Charles Young in Oakland at the time of the latter's medical examinations in June 1917 and that Young attributed the obstruction of his promotion to a dispute with fellow officers in 1916, during their pursuit of Pancho Villa with Gen. John J. Pershing's Punitive Expedition to Mexico. Schuyler, *Black and Conservative,* 86–87. Nancy Gordon Heinl, "Colonel Charles Young," *Army Magazine,* March 1977, 30–33.

17. Van Deman to Bielaski, Sept. 11, 1917, MID File 10218-9, RG 165, NA; Van Deman to Bielaski, Sept. 22, 1917, MID File 10218-6, RG 165, NA, and BI File OG 60095, RG 65, NA; Van Deman to IO, Central Department (Chicago), Oct. 2, 1917, MID File 10218-24, RG 165, NA.

18. Van Deman to Biddle, Sept. 11, 1917, MID File 10218-10, RG 165, NA; Biddle to Van Deman, Sept. 25, 1917, ibid. On the rioting in New York, see *New York Times,* May 27, 28, 31, July 4, 1917; *Baltimore Afro-American,* July 14, 1917. On Biddle and the New York Bomb Squad, see Richard Polenberg, *Fighting Faiths: The Abrams Case, the Supreme Court, and Free Speech* (New York: Viking, 1987), 56–61.

19. R. R. Moton to Van Deman, Sept. 12, 1917, MID File 10218-15, RG 165, NA; Van Deman to Moton, Sept. 18, 1917, ibid.; Van Deman to Felix Frankfurter, Sept. 26, 1917, ibid.

20. "The Problem of the Negro Soldier," *Outlook* 117 (Oct. 24, 1917), 279–80. See also Scott, *American Negro in the World War,* chapter 3.

21. Logan and Winston, eds., *Dictionary of American Negro Biography,* s.v. "Scott,

Emmet Jay"; Louis R. Harlan, *Booker T. Washington: The Wizard of Tuskegee, 1901–1915* (New York: Oxford University Press, 1983), passim.

22. NAACP, Board Minutes, Sept. 17, 1917, Papers of W. E. B. Du Bois, reel 5, UML; W. E. B. Du Bois to Newton D. Baker, Sept. 18, 1917, ibid.; F. P. Keppel to Du Bois, Sept. 19, 1917, ibid.

23. NAACP, Board Minutes, Oct. 8, 1917, and Du Bois report, Oct. 6, 1917, ibid.

24. W. E. B. Du Bois, *Dusk of Dawn: An Essay toward an Autobiography of a Race Concept* (New York: Harcourt, Brace, 1940), 251.

25. Baker to Scott, Sept. 30, 1917, cited in David M. Kennedy, *Over Here: The First World War and American Society* (New York: Oxford University Press, 1980), 159. On Baker's various statements about black troops in 1917, see *Norfolk Journal and Guide*, Aug. 25, Sept. 15, Oct. 6, 1917; *Baltimore Afro-American*, Sept. 15, 22, Dec. 8, 1917. Paul A. C. Koistinen, *Mobilizing for Modern War: The Political Economy of American Warfare, 1865–1919* (Lawrence, Kans.: University Press of Kansas, 1997), 291.

26. Du Bois to E. J. Scott, Oct. 6, 1917, Papers of W. E. B. Du Bois, reel 5, UML; Scott to Du Bois, Oct. 11, 1919, ibid.

27. E. J. Scott to N. D. Baker, Oct. 8, 1917, "Memos for S/W" folder, box 2, Papers of Emmett J. Scott, Records of the Secretary of War, Entry 96, RG 107, NA. (Scott's main collection of papers, at Morgan State University, is closed to researchers.)

28. W. H. Davis to Scott, Oct. 13, Nov. 3, 8, 9, 10, 1917, folder D, box 2, Papers of Emmett J. Scott, Records of the Secretary of War, Entry 96, RG 107, NA; J. W. Johnson to A. H. Grimké, Nov. 13, 1917, folder G, ibid.; R. Hayes to Scott, Nov. 14, 1917, folder G, ibid.; R. Tyler to Scott, Oct. 26, 1917, folder T, ibid.

29. Scott to Baker, Nov. 9, 1917, "Memos for S/W" folder, ibid.; Baker to Scott (draft), Nov. ?, 1917, folder D, ibid.; Baker to Scott, Nov. 30, 1917, "Speeches, etc." folder, ibid.; Scott to Du Bois, Dec. 1, 1917, Papers of W. E. B. Du Bois, reel 5, UML.

30. Du Bois to Scott, Dec. 6, 31, 1917, ibid.; Scott to Du Bois, Dec. 13, 1917, ibid.; Du Bois to Baker, Dec. 6, 1917, ibid.; Baker to Du Bois, Dec. 13, 1917, ibid.

31. Scott to Du Bois, Jan. 26, Feb. 2, March 2, May 15, 31, 1918, Papers of W. E. B. Du Bois, reel 7, UML.; Du Bois to Scott, Feb. 21, March 4, March 11, April 2, 24, 1918, ibid.

32. Spingarn to Parsons, Aug. 25, 1917, MID File 10218-7, RG 165, NA.

33. Report of Queen, Sept. ?, 1917, MID File 10218-10, RG 165, NA; Parsons memo, Sept. 26, 1917, MID File 10218-24, RG 165, NA; Parsons memo, Oct. 5, 1917, MID File 10218-33, RG 165, NA; H. A. Taylor to Parsons, Oct. 27, 30, 1917, MID File 10218-46, RG 165, NA. The actual circulation of the *Crisis* in 1917 was probably half the figure Queen gave. See Charles Flint Kellogg, *NAACP: A History of the National Association for the Advancement of Colored People, Volume 1: 1909–1920* (Baltimore: Johns Hopkins University Press, 1967), 153.

34. C. C. Walcott to W. H. Loving, Sept. 6, 1917, folder 2, box 113-1, Papers of Walter Howard Loving, M-SRC; Van Deman to Loving, Sept. 19, 1917, folder 9, ibid.; Loving to Royal F. Nash, May 26, 1917, box B-1, Annual Conference file, NAACP Papers, LC; J. F. Bell to H. P. McCain, March 27, 1919, folder 4, box 113-1,

Papers of Walter Howard Loving, M-SRC. On Loving's career, see *The Marcus Garvey and Universal Negro Improvement Association Papers*, vol. 1, ed. Robert A. Hill (Berkeley: University of California Press, 1983), 327; Eileen Southern, ed., *Biographical Dictionary of Afro-American and African Musicians* (Westport, Conn.: Greenwood, 1982), s.v. "Loving, Walter"; Claiborne T. Richardson, "The Filipino-American Phenomenon: The Loving Touch," *Black Perspectives in Music* (Spring 1982), 3–27; "Walter Howard Loving, Military Band Conductor," *Negro History Bulletin* 33 (May 1970), 127; Greene, *Black Defenders of America*, 143; "Walter Howard Loving," obituary, *Journal of Negro History* 30 (1945), 244–45. On Loving's relatives in Los Angeles, see Charlotta Bass, *Forty Years* (Los Angeles: n.p., ca. 1960), 13–14, 197. Loving himself appears in the Los Angeles City Directory for 1917. On the work of the Philippine Constabulary between 1901 and 1907, see Heath Twitchell, Jr., *Allen: The Biography of an Army Officer, 1859–1930* (New Brunswick, N.J.: Rutgers University Press, 1974), 117–46. Loving resumed his career as a military musician in the Philippine army in October 1919. He was imprisoned by the Japanese in 1941 and killed by them during their retreat from Manila in February 1945.

35. M. Churchill to chief of staff, Aug. 20, 1919, MID File 10218-361, RG 165, NA; Loving to Nash, May 26, 1917, box B-1, Annual Conference file, NAACP Papers, LC; Loving to Van Deman, Nov. 7, 1917, MID File 10218-47, RG 165, NA; Loving to Van Deman, Dec. 30, 1917 MID File 10218-73, RG 165, NA.

36. Loving to Van Deman, Nov. 23, 1917, MID File 10218-50, RG 165, NA; Van Deman to Loving, Oct. 24, 1917, MID File 10218-39, RG 165, NA; Van Deman to Loving, Oct. 26, 1917, MID File 10218-41, RG 165, NA; Van Deman to Loving, Oct. 20, 1917, MID File 10218-37, RG 165, NA; Loving to Van Deman, Oct. 26, 1917, ibid.; Loving to Van Deman, Nov. 4, 1917, MID File 10218-48, RG 165, NA. See also APL reports from Chicago, BI File OG 80683, RG 65, NA.

37. Loving to Van Deman, Oct. 18, 1917, MID File 10218-36, RG 165, NA. See *Outlook* 117 (Oct. 1917), 279–80. On Trotter's differences with Washington, see Samuel R. Spencer, Jr., *Booker T. Washington and the Negro's Place in American Life* (Boston: Little, Brown, 1955), 140–44; Harlan, *Booker T. Washington*, 36, 44–47, 70–74. Loving had collaborated with Emmett J. Scott when the latter had lobbied the War Department with some success for the promotion of army bandmasters in 1907. See ibid., 313–17.

38. Loving to Van Deman, Oct. 16, 1917, MID File 10218-33, RG 165, NA.

39. Jenks to Parsons, Nov. 15, 1917, MID File 10218-49, RG 165, NA; Parsons to Jenks, Nov. 17, 1917, ibid.

40. Loving to Van Deman, Nov. 23, 28, 1917, MID File 10218-50, RG 165, NA. Robert Church's father, who had been born a slave, died in 1912, leaving him large property and banking interests. See Richard Bardolph, *The Negro Vanguard* (New York: Rinehart, 1959), 150; Andrew Buni, *Robert L. Vann of the Pittsburgh Courier: Politics and Black Journalism* (Pittsburgh: University of Pittsburgh Press, 1974), 114; Richard B. Sherman, *The Republican Party and Black America from McKinley to Hoover, 1896–1933* (Charlottesville: University of Virginia Press, 1973), 135, 138, 152. The Atlanta link in the "information chain" was still operating fitfully six months later. See report of John Brown, Atlanta, May 16, 1918, MID File 10218-149, RG 165, NA.

41. *Crisis* 14 (July 1917), supplement; *Chicago Defender,* Sept. 8, 1917; *Washington Post,* Dec. 3, 1917; *Baltimore Afro-American,* Dec. 8, 1917; James Weldon Johnson, *Along This Way: The Autobiography of James Weldon Johnson* (New York: Penguin, 1990, first published 1933), 317–18. See also Kenneth W. Goings and Gerald L. Smith, "'Unhidden' Transcripts: Memphis and African American Agency, 1862–1920," in, *The New African American Urban History,* ed. Kenneth W. Goings and Raymond A. Mohl (Thousand Oaks, Calif.: Sage, 1996), 142–166.

42. Loving to Van Deman, Dec. 3, 1917, MID File 10218-63, RG 165, NA.

43. *Washington Bee,* Aug. 11, 1917; reports of G. Lillard, Washington, Aug. 30–Oct. 5, Sept. 7, 15, 1917, MID File 10218-11, RG 165, NA; Loving memo, Nov. 7, 1917, ibid.; F. W. Scheick to H. A. Taylor, n.d., ibid.; Taylor to Parsons, Dec. 17, 1917, ibid.

44. Bardolph, *Negro Vanguard,* 150.

45. Loving to Van Deman, Dec. 12, 1917, MID File 10218-61, RG 165, NA; Haynes, *Night of Violence,* 7.

46. Van Deman to Keppel, Dec. 14, 1917, MID File 10218-61, RG 165, NA; Taylor to Parsons, Dec. 17, 1917, MID File 10218-11, RG 165, NA; Loving to Van Deman, Dec. 25, 1917, MID File 10218-73, RG 165, NA.

47. Loving to Van Deman, Feb. 20, 1918, MID File 10218-83, RG 165, NA.

48. Loving memo, "The Story of the Killing of Will Butler," n.d., MID File 10218-78, RG 165, NA; Loving to Van Deman, Jan. 10, 1918, ibid. The Memphis streetcar murder attracted nationwide black comment. See *New York Age,* Jan. 5, 1918; *Chicago Defender,* Dec. 8, 1917. Loving to Van Deman, Dec. 25, 1917, MID File 10218-73, RG 165, NA. Simmons had spoken regularly at Church's auditorium in Memphis during 1917. See *Chicago Defender,* July 7, Oct. 13, 1917.

49. Loving to Van Deman, Jan. 13, 1918, MID File 10218-78, RG 165, NA; Loving to Van Deman, Feb. 20, 1918, MID File 10218-83, RG 165, NA; Loving to Van Deman, Feb. 21, 1918, MID File 10218-95, RG 165, NA. Church refused to allow black citizens to hire his auditorium to hold a protest meeting over the streetcar murder, so as not to overshadow the Loving-Simmons performance. See Loving to Van Deman, Jan. 10, 1918, MID File 10218-78, RG 165, NA. The fact that Church owned a 135-acre subdivision of the Memphis streetcar lines may also have influenced his decision to refuse to help further publicize either the incident itself or the Jim Crow seating arrangements on the cars which led to it. See Buni, *Robert L. Vann,* 114. As Loving predicted, Church regarded a letter of thanks from Van Deman as adequate reward for his efforts on behalf of military intelligence. Loving to Van Deman, Feb. 21, 1918, MID File 10218-95, RG 165, NA; Van Deman to Church, Feb. 25, 1918, ibid.; Church to Van Deman, March 16, 1918, ibid.

50. Loving to Van Deman, Jan. 15, Jan. 19, Feb. 1, 1918, MID File 10218-83, RG 165, NA; *New Orleans Times-Picayune,* Jan. 16, 1918. On the Knights of Pythias Temple in New Orleans, see Charles H. Williams, *Sidelights on Negro Soldiers* (Boston: B. J. Brimmer, 1923), 126.

51. Loving to Van Deman, Feb. 20, 1918, MID File 10218-83, RG 165, NA.

52. Van Deman to Keppel, Jan. 21, 1918, ibid.; Keppel to Van Deman, Jan. 23, 1918, ibid.

53. Loving to Van Deman, Jan. 19, 1918, ibid. Loving was probably worried that the 2nd Battalion of the 24th Infantry might experience difficulties similar to those which led part of the 1st Battalion to riot in Houston in August 1917.

54. Loving to Van Deman, Feb. 1, Feb. 3, 1918, ibid. Issues of the *Los Angeles Times* (Jan. 28, 29, 31, 1918) and the *San Francisco Chronicle* (Feb. 5, 1918) in which the speeches could have been reported contain no such coverage.

55. Loving to Van Deman, Feb. 20, 1918, MID File 10218-83, RG 165, NA.

56. Ibid.; Loving to Van Deman, Feb. 21, 1918, MID File 10218-95, RG 165, NA.

57. *Amsterdam News,* March 6, 1918. The Negro American Alliance, an independent equal rights group, was in the midst of an unsuccessful recruitment drive for one million members. Its president was an Atlantic City attorney, James A. Lightfoot. See *Norfolk Journal and Guide,* Oct. 13, 1917.

58. State Negro Civic League of Louisiana, pamphlet, quoted in APL report, March 3, 1918, BI File OG 83071, RG 65, NA.

59. Report of J. Corwin, Austin, Tex., April 2, 1918, MID File 10218-142, RG 165, NA; report of A. W. Davis, Pensacola, Fla., Jan. 8, 1918, BI File OG 14296, RG 65, NA; report of S. D. Bradley, Washington, March 19, 1918, BI File OG 369936, RG 65, NA; report from Mineral, Va., June 1918, BI File 159218, RG 65, NA; report of E. Portley, Kansas City, Mo., July 10, 1918, BI File OG 161973, RG 65, NA; report from Campbello, S.C., Sept. 1918, BI File 42006, RG 65, NA.

60. Report from Lexington, Ky., May 1918, BI File OG 193446, RG 65, NA; report of IO, HQ, Southeastern Dept., April 22, 1918, MID File 10218-126, RG 165, NA; "History of Intelligence Service, Southeastern Department," March 19, 1919, p. 11, MID File 10560-152(87), Entry 65, RG 165, NA.

61. W. P. Smith to secretary of state, May 8, 1918, BI File OG 22310, RG 65, NA; report of "E. T. W.," Sept. 1917, MID File 10218-16, RG 165, NA. The Roman Catholic Church in the South did not make a more consistent habit of advocating better treatment for blacks than did the Protestant churches. See I. A. Newby, *Jim Crow's Defense: Anti-Negro Thought in America, 1900–1930* (Baton Rouge: Louisiana State University Press, 1965), 105–108.

62. Report of F. Skadden, Baltimore, May 2, 1918, BI File OG 186646, RG 65, NA.

63. Report of H. D. Williams to H. A. Taylor, Feb. 23, 1918, MID File 10218-99, RG 165, NA; report from Lexington, Miss., Sept. 1917, BI File OG 144128, RG 65, NA; *Vicksburg Post,* April 1, 1918; *New York Sun,* April 1, 1918; *New York Globe,* April 2, 1918; *Baltimore Afro-American,* April 5, 1918; Elmer T. Clark, *The Small Sects in America* (Nashville: Abingdon Press, 1949), 119; David M. Tucker, *Black Pastors and Leaders: Memphis, 1819–1972* (Memphis: Memphis State University Press, 1975), 87–100. On the Holiness phenomenon, including C. H. Mason, see Edward L. Ayers, *The Promise of the New South: Life after Reconstruction* (New York: Oxford University Press, 1992), 399–408.

64. "History of the Philadelphia Branch: Typical Cases," n.d., MID File 10560-152, RG 165, Entry 65, NA; Clark, *Small Sects,* 151–53. The Church of God and Saints of Christ was also known as "The Black Jews," but does not seem to have been connected with Harlem's Black Jews, led by Rabbi Arnold J. Ford, who allied

themselves to Marcus Garvey's Universal Negro Improvement Association. See Tony Martin, *Race First: The Ideological and Organizational Struggles of Marcus Garvey and the Universal Negro Improvement Association* (Westport, Conn.: Greenwood Press, 1976), 75, 77, 138.

65. Report of C. B. Ross to Dept. Int. Office, New York, April 10, 1918, MID File 10218-124, RG 165, NA; report from Gainesville, Fla., April 1918, BI File OG 22310, RG 65, NA; *Christian Science Monitor,* Feb. 16, May ?, 1918; *Detroit Free Press,* April 13, 1918. On the Gainesville lynchings of August 1916, see Kellogg, *NAACP,* 218–19; Ralph Ginzburg, *100 Years of Lynching* (New York: Lancer, 1962), 106.

66. R. F. Britton, St. Louis, to chief of MIB, July 9, 1918, MID File 10218-60, RG 165, NA; D. S. Groh, enc. report of Keaney, to MIB, Aug. 26, 1918, ibid.; F. P. Wells to Adj. Gen., Illinois, Sept. 9, 1918, ibid.; G. C. Van Dusen to A. H. Pike, July 23, 1918, BI File OG 28469, RG 65, NA; J. E. Spingarn, "Daily Summary" for July 23, 1918, ibid.

67. Report from West Virginia, March 1918, BI File OG 164306, ibid.; "History of Intelligence Service," MID File 10560-152, RG 165, NA; reports from South Carolina, May 1918, BI File OG 171747, RG 65, NA; *New York Telegram,* April 9, 1918.

68. Report of R. H. Daughton, Norfolk, Va., Nov. 28, 1917, MID File 10218-54, RG 165, NA; A. P. Wagner to MI-4, Aug. 30, 1918, MID File 10218-259, RG 165, NA; report of Louis De Nette, San Antonio, Tex., May 11, 1918, BI File OG 105390, RG 65, NA; "Memorandum re. Colored Situation," Oct. 19, 1917, MID File 10218-263, RG 165, NA; Howard Odum, *Race and Rumors of Race: Challenge to American Crisis* (Chapel Hill: University of North Carolina Press, 1943), 53–66.

69. See reports, Aug. 30, 1918–Sept. 30, 1920, in BI File OG 369936, RG 65, NA; Gatewood, *Aristocrats of Color,* 326.

70. Report of G. W. Lillard, Nov. 14, 1917, BI File 0G 369936, RG 65, NA; report of W. W. Grimes, March 19, 1918, ibid.; H. D. Williams to H. A. Taylor, April 19, 1918, MID File 10218-269, RG 165, NA; Van Deman to Bielaski, April 22, 1918, ibid.; M. Churchill to G. Creel, Sept. 17, 1918, MID File 10218-259, RG 165, NA.

71. C. Henry to H. A. Taylor, June 22, 1918, MID File 10218-90, ibid.; Queen to Taylor, July 18, 1918, ibid.; Henry to H. G. Pratt, Nov. 5, 1918, ibid.; Henry to Taylor, June 22, 1918, MID File 10218-291, RG 165, NA; Queen to Taylor, July 16, 1918, ibid.; Henry to Pratt, Nov. 5, 1918, ibid.; reports of Queen from New York, Feb. 1918, MID File 10218-100, RG 165, NA. The BI preferred informants to work for nothing, but paid small amounts if necessary. In May 1917, the BI agent-in-charge at Norfolk, Va., was told by Bielaski that a black informant's pay "should be kept as low as possible, and promptly discontinued unless something of importance is discovered." Bielaski to R. H. Daughton, May 21, 1917, BI File OG 3057, RG 65, NA.

72. Loving to Van Deman, Dec. 25, 1917, MID File 10218-73, RG 165, NA; Loving to Van Deman, Dec. 30, 1917, ibid.; report of G. W. Lillard, Jan. 2, 1918, ibid.; Garnet C. Wilkinson to Parsons, Jan. 5, 1918, ibid.; Parsons to Wilkinson, Jan. 8, 1918, ibid.; *Baltimore Afro-American,* Jan. 12, 1918. German language teaching was banned in at least fourteen states during the war, and many schools voluntarily suspended it from the curriculum. *New York Times,* July 22, 1918; *Chicago Defender,* May 4, 1918; *Messenger* 1 (Nov. 1917), 7; Senate Subcommittee on the Judiciary,

Brewing and Liquor Interests, and German Propaganda, 66 Cong., 1 sess., Sen. Doc. 62, 1787.

73. Queen to chief of staff, Feb. 13, 1918, MID File 10218-93, RG 165, NA; Van Deman to Queen, Feb. 26, 1918, ibid.

74. Loving to chief, MIB, March 5, 1918, MID File 10218-102, RG 165, NA. See also Eastern Dept. Weekly Summary, March 4–11, 1918, regarding "Negro Subversion," unnumbered, filed with MID File 10218, RG 165, NA. On Larmon Brown's part in the riot of August 23, 1917, see Robert V. Haynes, *A Night of Violence: The Houston Riot of 1917* (Baton Rouge: Louisiana State University Press, 1976), 128–129, 165, 167.

75. Van Deman to N. Biddle, March 18, 1918, MID File 10218-114, RG 165, NA.

76. Loving to chief, MIB, Dec. 3, 1917, MID File 10218-63, RG 165, NA.

77. "Counter Espionage Situation Summary," May 18, 1918, MID File 10641-196(51), RG 165, NA.

78. Stephen Vaughn, *Holding Fast the Inner Lines: Democracy, Nationalism, and the Committee on Public Information* (Chapel Hill: University of North Carolina Press, 1980), 207, 209; P. J. Bryant et al. to David F. Houston, March 5, 1918, MID File 10218-117, RG 165, NA; G. Creel to Van Deman, March 27, 1918, ibid. The Atlanta protest is also in case file 543, series 4 (Executive Office File, 1913–1921), Papers of Woodrow Wilson, LC. See also Leroy Davis, *A Clashing of the Soul: John Hope and the Dilemma of African American Leadership and Black Higher Education in the Early Twentieth Century* (Athens: University of Georgia Press, 1998), 235.

79. *Chicago Tribune,* April 15, 1918. The *Tribune* report was headlined "Creel Lulls U.S. As Foe within Helps Germany."

80. *New York Independent,* n.d., reprinted in *Crisis* 16 (May 1918), 24; *Christian Science Monitor,* May 31, 1918.

81. Vaughn, *Holding Fast the Inner Lines,* 124. When a speaker tried to deliver Bulletin No. 33 at a Dayton, Ohio, soldiers' home on July 4, 1918, he was refused permission to do so, because he was black. *Dayton Forum,* July 12, 1918. The speech was said to have been well received by an audience at Pasadena, Cal. *California Eagle,* July 13, 1918.

3. Black Doughboys

1. On the African-American contribution to the U.S. army's efforts in World War I, see Arthur E. Barbeau and Florette Henri, *The Unknown Soldiers: Black American Troops in World War I* (Philadelphia: Temple University Press, 1974); Gerald W. Patton, *War and Race: The Black Officer in the American Military, 1915–1941* (Westport, Conn.: Greenwood Press, 1981), 32–122; *Blacks in the Military: Essential Documents,* ed. Bernard C. Nalty and Morris J. McGregor (Wilmington, Del.: Scholarly Resources, 1981), 73–91; Bernard C. Nalty, *Strength for the Fight: A History of Black Americans in the Military* (New York: Free Press, 1986), 101–24; Charles H. Williams, *Sidelights on Negro Soldiers* (Boston: B. J. Brimmer, 1923); Chester D. Heywood, *Negro Combat Troops in the World War: The Story of the 371st Infantry* (Worcester, Mass.: Commonwealth Press, 1929); Emmett J. Scott, *The American Negro in the World War* (Chi-

cago: Homewood Press, 1919); W. Allison Sweeney, *History of the American Negro in the Great World War* (Chicago: G. G. Sapp, 1919); Keith Krawczynski, "World War I," in *A Historic Context for the African American Military Experience,* ed. Steven D. Smith and James A. Zeidler (Champaign, Ill.: U.S. Army Corps of Engineers, Construction Engineering Research Laboratories, 1998) (http://www.denix.osd.mil/denix/Public/ES-Programs/Conservation/Legacy/AAME/aame1.html); Nancy K. Bristow, *Making Men Moral* (New York: New York University Press, 1996), 137–78. African Americans in the U.S. navy were restricted to menial tasks.

2. Barbeau and Henri, *Unknown Soldiers,* 42–43; *Blacks in the Military: Essential Documents,* 78.

3. *Norfolk Journal and Guide,* Aug. 25, Sept. 15, Oct. 6, 1917; *Baltimore Afro-American,* Sept. 15, 22, Dec. 8, 1917; Bristow, *Making Men Moral,* 143–46.

4. Barbeau and Henri, *Unknown Soldiers,* 44; *Blacks in the Military: Essential Documents,* 79; Gary Mead, *The Doughboys* (London: Penguin, 2000), 78–79.

5. David M. Kennedy, *Over Here: The First World War and American Society* (New York: Oxford University Press, 1980), 17–18.

6. Patton, *War and Race,* 7–8, 47. See also Rep. J. W. Ragsdale (D-SC) to Newton D. Baker, Nov. 15, 1917, folder R, box 2, Papers of Emmett Scott, Entry 96, RG 107, NA.

7. *Baltimore Afro-American,* Aug. 2, 1917.

8. *Literary Digest* 55 (Sept. 29, 1917), 14–15.

9. "Negro Conscription," *New Republic* 12 (Oct. 20, 1917), 317–18. See also "The Problem of the Negro Soldier," *Outlook* 117 (Oct. 24, 1917), 279–80.

10. *K. Lamity's Harpoon* 16 (April 1918), 11–12, clipping in MID File 10218-164, RG 165, NA.

11. Jane Lang Scheiber and Harry N. Scheiber, "The Wilson Administration and the Wartime Mobilization of Black Americans, 1917–18," *Labor History* 10 (Summer 1969), 441; *Literary Digest* 55 (Sept. 29, 1917), 14–15. For a further example of southern support for a black draft, see Bolton Smith, "The Negro in War-Time," *Public* 21 (Aug. 31, 1918), 1110–13.

12. Assistant director, ONI, to Bielaski, Aug. 21, 1917, BI File OG 3057, RG 65, NA.

13. Sweeney, *American Negro in the Great World War,* 108–10; Barbeau and Henri, *Unknown Soldiers,* 36; Williams, *Sidelights on Negro Soldiers,* 22; Herbert J. Seligmann, Jr., *The Negro Faces America* (New York: Harper and Bros., 1920), 136–37.

14. Sweeney, *American Negro in the Great World War,* 111–12; Barbeau and Henri, *Unknown Soldiers,* 36.

15. Report from St. Paul, Va., June 1917, BI File OG 21663, RG 65, NA; John Dittmer, *Black Georgia in the Progressive Era, 1900–1920* (Urbana: University of Illinois Press, 1977), 197–98. See also Gerald E. Shenk, "Race, Manhood, and Manpower: Mobilizing Rural Georgia for World War I," *Georgia Historical Quarterly* 81 (Fall 1997), 622–62; K. Walter Hickel, " 'Justice and the Highest Kind of Equality Require Discrimination': Citizenship, Dependency, and Conscription in the South, 1917–1919," *Journal of Southern History* 66 (November 2000), 749–80.

16. Report of D. Trazivuk, Beaumont, Tex., April 1917, BI File OG 23364, RG 65, NA; report from Houston, Tex., June 1917, BI File OG 22371, RG 65, NA; report from Pittsburgh, June, 1917, BI File OG 27900, RG 65, NA; reports from San Antonio, Tex., June–August, 1917, BI File OG 29699, RG 65, NA; report from Tillman, S.C., Jan., 1918, BI File OG 42006, RG 65, NA; report from Galveston, Tex., June 1917, BI File OG 22977, RG 65, NA. In the latter case, one white and four blacks were arrested at the same time; the white man was referred to as "American" and the blacks as "African," although they were clearly American-born U.S. citizens. Report from Alvin, N.C., June 1917, BI File OG 20961, RG 65, NA. For other BI reports on black draft delinquency, see reports from St. Louis, June 1917, BI Files OG 22870, 27037, 27150, 28789, 28790, 28984, RG 65, NA; report from Atlanta, June 1917, BI File OG 23962, RG 65, NA; report from Dolen, Ala., June 1917, BI File OG 83967, RG 65, NA; reports from Norfolk, Va., June 1917, BI Files OG 22784, 29554, RG 65, NA; report from Dallas, June, 1917, BI File OG 26683, RG 65, NA; report from Wichita Falls, Tex., June 1917, BI File OG 28337, RG 65, NA; report from Oakley, S.C., June 1917, BI File OG 26826, RG 65, NA; reports from Philadelphia, June 1917, BI File OG 26739, 28794, RG 65, NA; report from Houston, June 1917, BI File OG 28758, RG 65, NA; reports from Pittsburgh, June 1917, BI Files OG 22807, 27174, RG 65, NA; report from Columbus, Ohio, June 1917, BI File OG 25808, RG 65, NA; report from Oklahoma City, June 1917, BI File OG 21864, RG 65, NA; report from Hannibal, Mo., Aug. 1917, BI File OG 42784, RG 65, NA; report from Dallas, Aug. 1917, BI File OG 24732, RG 65, NA; report from Moncks Corner, S.C., Aug. 1917, BI File OG 42006, RG 65, NA; report from Cincinnati, Dec. 1917, BI File OG 25808, RG 65, NA; report from Texarkana, Tex., Jan. 1918, BI File OG 105390, RG 65, NA; report from Portsmouth, Va., May 1918, BI File OG 159218, RG 65, NA; report from Galveston, Tex., June, 1918, BI File OG 105390, RG 65, NA; report from Indianapolis, June 1918, BI File OG 3065, RG 65, NA; report from North Dakota, Aug. 1918, BI File OG 258074, RG 65, NA; report from Tennessee, BI File OG 258049, RG 65, NA; report from Shreveport, La., Aug. 1918, BI File OG 253165, RG 65, NA; report from Memphis, Sept. 1918, BI File OG 266600, RG 65, NA.

17. Report from Cincinnati, June 1917, BI File OG 21869, RG 65, NA.; report from Corsicana, Tex., Aug. 1917, BI File OG 57042, RG 65, NA. See also report of J. H. Harper, Corsicana, Tex., Aug. 29, 1917, BI File OG 60093, RG 65, NA; report of Willard Uttley, San Antonio, Tex., Dec. 3, 1917, BI File OG 105390, RG 65, NA; report of D. S. Winn, Sherman, Tex., Oct. 1918, BI File OG 316726, RG 65, NA; National Civil Liberties Bureau, "War-Time Prosecutions and Mob Violence" (New York: NCLB, 1918), 5. In October 1918, the military intelligence office in New York picked up a rumor that Hindu agitators were "actively engaged in spreading propaganda among the negroes of the East and South, urging them to oppose the draft and the military service, and advising them to flee to Mexico." Churchill to Bielaski, Oct. 4, 1918, BI File OG 3057, RG 65, NA.

18. USFDA field representative to Van Deman, April 2, 1918, enc. *Vicksburg Post,* clipping, April 1, 1918, MID File 10218-299, RG 165, NA. On the Vicksburg draft board's corrupt behavior toward blacks, see Charles Flint Kellogg, *NAACP: A His-*

tory of the National Association for the Advancement of Colored People, Volume 1: 1909–1920 (Baltimore: Johns Hopkins University Press, 1967), 265–66.

19. Ammon Hennacy, "Atlanta—1917," in Staughton Lynd, ed., *Nonviolence in America: A Documentary History* (Indianapolis: Bobbs-Merrill, 1966), 196.

20. Osceola E. McKaine, "The Buffaloes: A First Class Colored Fighting Regiment," *Outlook* 119 (May 22, 1918), 144–47; Jervis Anderson, "Harlem: Shaping a Black Metropolis," *New Yorker,* July 6, 1981, 68. One group of black men who expressed "considerable dissatisfaction" at being drafted were British West Indian subjects in New York, who were inducted into the 367th Infantry. The intelligence officer at Camp Upton, N.Y., suspected "that this class may have been selected as a new group for propagandists to exercise." Report of J. S. S. Richardson, Dec. 20, 1917, MID File 10218-72, RG 165, NA. See also a letter from a Cuban living in Harlem to his mother in Havana, asking for proof of his nationality so that he could avoid the draft. He did not wish to fight for a country in which black people were despised. Postal Censorship Report, Jan. 22, 1918, MID File 10218-90, RG 165, NA. On Puerto Rican objections to being conscripted, see H. C. Peterson and Gilbert C. Fite, *Opponents of War, 1917–1918* (Seattle: University of Washington Press, 1968), 85–86.

21. Barbeau and Henri, *Unknown Soldiers,* 86; Bulletin No. 35, HQ, 92nd Division, Camp Funston, Kans., March 28, 1918, MID File 10218-120, RG 165, NA.

22. *Norfolk Journal and Guide,* July 28, Sept 8, 1917; Walter Loving to chief, MIB, April 16, 1918, MID File 10218-120, RG 165, NA. When two black officer cadets were arrested after refusing to sit in the Jim Crow part of a theater at Des Moines in 1917, Ballou issued an order demanding greater "co-operation" from the cadets under his command. This order had not produced anything like the reaction to Bulletin No. 35. See *Baltimore Afro-American,* July 14, 1917, April 12, 1918; *New York World,* April 19, 1918; *New York Age,* April 20, 1918; *New York News,* April 17, 1918; *Chicago Defender,* May 4, 1918, clippings in MID File 10218-120, RG 165, NA. See also *Baltimore Afro-American,* April 12, 19, 26, May 10, 1918; *Crisis* 16 (May 1918), 7. On Ferdinand Q. Morton, see Gilbert Osofsky, *Harlem: The Making of a Ghetto, Negro New York, 1890–1930* (New York: Harper & Row, 1971), 169, 173–74.

23. H. F. K. Cabell, Camp Sherman, to chief, MIB, April 11, 1918, MID File 10218-120, RG 165, NA. See also G. N. Northrop, Camp Dodge, to chief, MIB, May 11, 1918, enclosing letter from "A Negro Soldier" to the editor of the *Camp Dodger,* ibid; Bristow, *Making Men Moral,* 164–69.

24. C. C. Ballou to Emmett Scott, April 22, 1918, in *Baltimore Afro-American,* May 24, 1918. See also *Crisis* 16 (June 1918), 62. Scott sent out copies of Ballou's statement to all black newspapers except the *Boston Guardian,* or so it seemed to that paper's editor, William Monroe Trotter, who was preparing for the National Liberty Congress in Washington. *Boston Guardian,* clipping, n.d., MID File 10218-153, RG 165, NA.

25. Florette Henri and Richard Stillman, *Bitter Victory: A History of Black Soldiers in World War I* (Garden City, N.Y.: Doubleday, 1970), 84.

26. Report of Special Employee Darden, Shreveport, La., Sept. 26, 1917, MID File 10218-34, RG 165, NA; report of R. E. Corder, San Antonio, Tex., April 16,

1918, MID File 10218-122, RG 165, NA; report of L. H. C. Flinn, Cincinnati, Ohio, March 26, 1918, BI File OG 166802, RG 65, NA; report of Louis De Nette, San Antonio, Tex., June 11, 1918, BI File OG 105390, RG 65, NA; report of J. A. Baker, N.Y., June 24, 1918, BI File OG 17011, RG 65, NA; A. P. Wagner to MI-4, Aug. 30, 1918, MID File 10218-159, RG 165, NA. In the latter report, a black preacher at Braddock Heights, Md., was alleged to have told hotel waiters that black troops would be put in the front lines and would be given no medical attention if wounded, unless the Germans took care of them.

27. Report from Norfolk, Va., Jan. 1918, BI File OG 159218, RG 65, NA; report of S. D. Bradley, Washington, D.C., Feb. 21, 1918, MID File 10218-104, RG 165, NA; H. D. Williams to H. A. Taylor, Feb. 23, 1918, MID File 10218-99, RG 165, NA.

28. R. B. Fosdick to F. P. Keppel, March 23, 1918, MID File 10218-116, RG 165, NA; Barbeau and Henri, *Unknown Soldiers*, 111–16. On the 15th New York, see Anderson, "Harlem: Shaping a Black Metropolis," 67–68, 70–72, 76.

29. *New York American*, April 12, 1918; *New York Journal*, April 12, 13, 1918; unidentified clipping, datelined Washington, April 11, 1918, MID File 10218-116, RG 165, NA; Keppel to Van Deman, March 25, 1918, MID File 10218-116, RG 165, NA; Van Deman to Bielaski, April 4, 1918, BI File OG 3057, RG 65, NA; Van Deman to N. Biddle, April 10, 1918; Van Deman to Walter Loving, April 9, 1918, MID File 10218-116, RG 165, NA.

30. *Amsterdam News*, April 17, 1918. Loving was referred to in the *Amsterdam News* report as "a representative of the War Department." Van Deman thanked Loving for his "prompt and efficient measures . . . to suppress the dangerous propaganda among the colored people of Harlem." Van Deman to Loving, April 22, 1918, MID File 10218-116, RG 165, NA.

31. Report of C. E. Campbell, APL, New York, June 3, 1918, BI File OG 17011, RG 65, NA. For a vivid description of the activities of Harlem street speakers and the ways in which they directly influenced wider black discourse and writing, see Irma Watkins-Owens, *Blood Relations: Caribbean Immigrants and the Harlem Community, 1900–1930* (Bloomington: Indiana University Press, 1996), 92–111.

32. Hallie E. Queen to H. A. Taylor, May 23, 1918, MID File 10218-443, RG 165, NA; *Baltimore Afro-American*, June 21, 1918; Barbeau and Henri, *Unknown Soldiers*, 79, 129; *New York Age*, April 20, 1918. On James E. Walker's career, see *Dictionary of American Negro Biography*, ed. Rayford W. Logan and Michael R. Winston (New York: W. W. Norton, 1982), s.v. "Walker, James Edward." Rayford Logan was a member of the 1st Separate Battalion and served with the 372nd Regiment in France.

33. Queen to H. A. Taylor, July 16, 1918, MID File 10218-291, RG 165, NA; C. Henry to Taylor, June 22, 1918, ibid.; Loving to chief, MIB, June 31, 1918, MID File 10218-415, RG 165, NA.

34. *Chicago Herald-Examiner,* July 25, 1918; unidentified press clipping, datelined Amsterdam, July 24, 1918, MID File 10218-443, RG 165, NA; Paul J. Krausnick, Camp Grant, Ill., to chief, MIB, July 27, 1918, MID File 10218-192, RG 165, NA; F. T. Saussy to adjutant general, Atlanta, Ga., Aug. 3, 1918, MID File 10218-214, RG 165, NA.

35. H. E. James to H. A. Taylor, Sept. 5, 1918, MID File 10218-263, RG 165, NA;

"Quander E. Hall" (H. E. Queen) to H. A. Taylor, Sept. 28, 1918, MID File 10218-286, RG 165, NA.

36. Reports of V. W. Killick, Los Angeles, Aug. 21, 22, 1918, BI File OG 132476, RG 65, NA. After the war, Emmett Scott devoted a whole chapter (chapter 24) of *The American Negro in the World War* to "German Propaganda among Negroes," without providing any convincing evidence that such propaganda had ever been disseminated.

37. *Blacks in the Military: Essential Documents*, 71.

38. C. J. Harris, 18th Cavalry, to chief of staff, Sept. 5, 1917, "Negroes" folder, A. J. Glasser File, Records of the Department of Justice, RG 60, NA. In July 1917, a sergeant of the 1st Separate Battalion of the D. C. National Guard was beaten up by a gang of white railroad workers while on duty in the District of Columbia; he was afterward fined fifty dollars. *Baltimore Afro-American*, July 28, 1917. Another member of the 1st Separate Battalion, while on guard duty, shot and killed a white man who was illegally trying to enter a compound. The guard was sentenced to three years' imprisonment. *Baltimore Afro-American*, Dec. 29, 1917.

39. "Quander E. Hall" to H. A. Taylor, Aug. 22, 23, 1918, MID File 10218-215, RG 165, NA.

40. H. A. Taylor to chief, MIB, Oct. ?, 1917, MID File 10218-27, RG 165, NA.

41. Lee Kennett, "The Camp Wadsworth Affair," *South Atlantic Quarterly* 74 (Spring 1975), 197–211. In September 1917, it was reported in the white press that during the construction of Camp Wadsworth black workers were warned by German "emissaries" that when white troops arrived there would be an attempt to wipe out local blacks, in retaliation for the Houston riot. Any survivors were "to be rounded up and be used as targets for rifle practice." It was also alleged that black workers were offered financial inducements to leave for the Midwest and that there had been "a deliberate attempt to revive 'voodooism' [by] playing on the dense ignorance and credulity of the negroes." *New York Times*, Sept. 17, 1917.

42. William W. Giffin, "Mobilization of Black Militiamen in World War I: Ohio's Ninth Battalion," *Historian* 11 (Aug. 1978), 699–700.

43. Van Deman to chief of staff, Dec. ?, 1917, MID File 10218-53, RG 165, NA.

44. Report of "AEK" to Pratt, Newport News, Va., Sept. 24, 1918, and three unidentified newspaper clippings, MID File 10218-228, RG 165, NA; Harry Haywood, *Black Bolshevik: An Autobiography of an Afro-American Communist* (Chicago: Liberator Press, 1978), 52.

45. *New York Times*, Oct. 28, 1917; Mark Sullivan, *Our Times: The United States, 1900–1925*, vol. 5, *"Over Here"* (New York: Charles Scribner's Sons, 1933), 634; L. B. Dunham, Hoboken, N.J., to chief, MIB, Aug. 21, 1918, MID File 10218-209, RG 165, NA.

46. Reports of Harold Nathan, Newport News, March 3, 4, 6, 1918, BI File OG 57444, RG 65, NA. BI interest in army camps was generally slight, except when bootlegging was suspected.

47. G. B. Perkins to IO, Camp Meade, Aug. 9, 1918, MID File 10218-199, RG 165, NA; Harold F. Butler, Camp Meade, to chief, Military Morale Section, Aug. 13, 1918, ibid.

48. Anonymous letter to Emmett Scott, Aug. 18, 1918, MID File 10218-209, RG 165, NA. Initial reports in the black press were that all four of the wounded men had died. See *Negro World,* Aug. 29, 1918. L. B. Dunham to chief, MIB, Aug. 21, 1918, MID File 10218-209, RG 165, NA; E. J. Scott to G. B. Perkins, Sept. 3, 1918, ibid.; Dunham to chief, MIB, Aug. 21, 1918, ibid.; Dunham to Perkins, Aug. 30, 1918, ibid.; Perkins to IO, Hoboken, N.J., Sept. 7, 1918, ibid.; Dunham to Nicholas Biddle, June 25, 1918, MID File 10218-116, RG 165, NA.

49. Dunham to acting director, MIB, Jan. 15, 1919, MID File 10218-209, RG 165, NA.

50. "Quander E. Hall" to H. A. Taylor, Oct. 11, 1918, MID File 10218-287, RG 165, NA. See also C. A. Hedekin, Camp Lee, to adjutant general, U.S. Army, Oct. 5, 1918, Glasser File, RG 60, NA.

51. Barbeau and Henri, *Unknown Soldiers,* 49–51, 95–100; Dittmer, *Black Georgia,* 194–96; Heywood, *Negro Combat Troops,* 2; Scott, *American Negro in the World War,* chapters 6, 8, 9.

52. Williams, *Sidelights on Negro Soldiers,* 31–32; *Pontotoc (Miss.) Sentinel,* May 16, 1918, clipping in MID File 10218-151, RG 165, NA.

53. Barbeau and Henri, *Unknown Soldiers,* 101; C. W. B. Long, Camp Jackson, to commanding general, Camp Jackson, Oct. 30, 1918, MID File 10218-249, RG 165, NA.

54. W. H. Loving to Van Deman, Nov. 9, 1918, MID File 10218-47, RG 165, NA.

55. Report of Robert S. Judge, Pittsburgh, Dec. 7, 1917, BI File OG 98505, RG 65, NA; Loving to Van Deman, Dec. 12, 1917, MID File 10218-61, RG 165, NA. See also the report of S. D. Bradley, Washington, D.C., Feb. 21, 1918 (MID File 10218-104, RG 165, NA), in which a black soldier from Camp Lee was reported to have complained that he and his comrades had only been trained to use a pick and shovel.

56. Charles C. Lynde, "Mobilizing Rastus," *Outlook* 118 (March 13, 1918), 412–17; "Bush Germans Better Watch That 'Chocolate Front,' " *Literary Digest* 57 (June 1918), 43–47; Edwin R. Embree, "With the Negro Troops," *Survey* 40 (Aug. 1918), 537–38; "American Negro as a Fighting Man," *American Review of Reviews* 58 (Aug. 1918), 210–11; "Us Angry Saxyums," *Atlantic Monthly* 122 (Sept. 1918), 425–27. See also *Outlook* 118 (April 3, 1918), 562, and 119 (Aug. 14, 1918), 606.

57. E. L. Bryan, Camp Upton, to chief, MIB, June 3, 1918; Churchill to IO, Camp Upton, June 22, 1918; Bryan to chief, MIB, June 23, 1918; G. B. Perkins to Lincoln Schuster, War Risk Bureau, June 31, 1918, MID File 10218-168, RG 165, NA.

58. Anon. to R. M. Gates, n.d., MID File 10218-94, RG 165, NA (punctuation added and capitalization adjusted). There were frequent epidemics in the training camps, necessitating the quarantining of large numbers of soldiers. See *Blacks in the Military: Essential Documents,* 81; Barbeau and Henri, *Unknown Soldiers,* 49.

59. Van Deman to IO, Camp Dix, Feb. 26, 1918, MID File 10218-94, RG 165, NA; Fred T. Austin to IO, 78th Div., March 4, 1918, ibid.

60. "Capt. G. H. Hill" to H. B. Everett, April 27, 1918, MID File 10218-145, RG

165, NA (punctuation added). Perhaps convinced by Wilson's letter that black disloyalty was widespread, Everett began informing the army about other men about whom he had doubts. See, for example, H. B. Everett to adjutant general, Fort Dodge, Iowa, June 20, 1918, MID File 10218-187, RG 165, NA.

61. Bielaski to Van Deman, May 8, 1918, MID File 10218-145, RG 165, NA; Van Deman to IO, Camp Meade, May 23, 1918, ibid.; Churchill to IO, Camp Meade, Aug. 5, 1918, ibid.; Harold F. Butler to chief, MID, Aug. 7, 1918, ibid.; General Court Martial Order No. 136, HQ, 79th Div., Camp Meade, Md., July 2, 1918, ibid. Wilson died in Memphis in 1943. *Memphis and Shelby County Death Certificates (1940–1945)* (http://www.memphislibrary.lib.tn.us/ShelbyDR40/html/dr34.htm).

62. For complaints from the camps, see MID File 10218-206 (Camp Upton, N.Y., Aug. 1918); -220 (Camp Wheeler, Ga., Aug.–Sept. 1918); -229 (Camp Dix, N.J., Aug.–Oct. 1918); -227 (Camp Grant, Ill., Aug.–Nov. 1918); -216 (Camp Travis, Tex., Sept. 1918); -226 (Camp Sherman, Ohio, Sept. 1918); -234, -287 (Camp Lee, Va., Sept.–Oct. 1918); -233 (Camp Dodge, Iowa, Oct. 1918); -235 (Camp Upton, N.Y., Sept.–Oct. 1918); -238 (Camp Eustis, Va., Oct. 1918); -239 (Camp Devens, Mass., Oct. 1918); -243 (Camp Pike, Ark., Oct. 1918); -245 (Camp McClellan, Ala., Oct. 1918); -248 (Camp Knox, Ky., Oct. 1918); -293 (Camp Gordon, Ga., Oct. 1918); -260 (Camp Greene, N.C., Oct.–Nov. 1918); -271 (Camp Sevier, S.C., Nov.–Dec. 1918); -267 (Camp MacArthur, Tex., Dec. 1918); -268, -275 (Camp Alexander, Va., Dec. 1918).

63. Loving visited Camps Pike, Taylor, Humphreys, Wheeler, Gordon, Sheridan, Mills, Greene, Sevier, Jackson, and Lee. See MID File 10218-280, RG 165, NA. Williams sent copies of his reports on twenty camps between September 1918 and January 1919 to Cutler, as well as to the Committee on the Welfare of Negro Troops, possibly at the suggestion of Thomas Jesse Jones, who sat on the committee. See MID File 10218-279, RG 165, NA, and unnumbered contents of envelope marked "10218" with other material under that file number, RG 165, NA. On Williams's work, see also Williams, *Sidelights on Negro Soldiers,* 135–37; *Crisis* 16 (May 1918), 34–35.

64. Herbert Aptheker, *Afro-American History: The Modern Era* (New York: Citadel Press, 1971), 167; Bristow, *Making Men Moral,* 146–54.

65. MI-3 Bulletin for Intelligence Officers No. 31, "Special Bulletin: The Negro Problem in the Army," Oct. 21, 1918, MID File 10218-279, RG 165, NA. See also James Elbert Cutler, *Lynch-Law: An Investigation into the History of Lynching in the United States* (New York: Longmans Green, 1905).

66. J. E. Cutler, questionnaire on the welfare of black troops, Oct. 1918, MID File 10218-279, RG 165, NA. See also Bristow, *Making Men Moral,* 157–64.

67. Jesse E. Moorland, "The YMCA with Colored Troops," *Southern Workman* 48 (April 1919), 171.

68. John Hope Franklin, *From Slavery to Freedom: A History of Negro Americans,* 5th ed. (New York: Alfred A. Knopf, 1980), 329.

69. Williams, *Sidelights on Negro Soldiers,* 97. Another source gives the number of black YMCA workers in France as 150 in August 1918, but Williams is probably more accurate. See "American Negro as a Fighting Man," *American Review of Reviews*

58 (Aug. 1918), 210–11. The absence of a detailed YMCA policy regarding black troops meant that the standard of facilities offered to them varied from camp to camp and often depended to a large extent on the resourcefulness of the secretaries themselves. Basic educational, religious, and physical activities were usually provided, as well as entertainment and assistance with correspondence.

70. William Gilman Low to Van Deman, April 22, 1918, MID File 10218-130, RG 165, NA.

71. Reports of Agent Bernard, May 14 and 31, 1918, ibid.

72. Low to Van Deman, April 27, 1918, MID File 10218-138, RG 165, NA; Smiley to Low, May 11, 1918, ibid.

73. Low to Van Deman, May 9, 1918, MID File PF 11245, NRC. De Frantz had also worked as a YMCA secretary at the Fort Des Moines black officers' training camp in 1917, without provoking complaints. *Washington Bee*, Aug. 14, 1917.

74. Smiley to Low, May 27, 1918, MID File PF 11245, NRC; Smiley to IO, Camp Devens, May 27, 1918, ibid.; N. Harrower, Camp Devens, to Smiley, June 1, 1918, ibid.; Low to Masteller, May 17, 1918, MID File 10218-138, RG 165, NA; Smiley to Low, May 31, 1918, ibid.

75. *Crisis* 16 (May 1918), 23; Low to Van Deman, May 2, 1918, MID File 10218-139, RG 165, NA.

76. H. T. Hunt (per Malone) to Low, May 6, 1918, ibid.; E. G. Moyer, Camp Greene, to chief, MIB, May 8, 1918, ibid.; R. J. Malone to Hunt, May 25, 1918, ibid.; Hunt (per Malone) to Walter Loving, May 16, 1918, ibid.; Loving to Hunt, May 23, 1918, ibid.; Loving to chief, MIB, May 30, 1918, ibid. An Atlanta BI agent, who was passed a copy of the *Crisis* by the Camp Gordon intelligence officer, reported that the magazine, which was felt to have been responsible for a near-riot between black and white draftees, had been made available in the black YMCA huts, until banned by the camp's YMCA chief. Report of Howell E. Jackson, Atlanta, BI File OG 17011, RG 65, NA. On YMCA facilities at Camp Gordon, see Joseph H. Odell, "The New Spirit of the New Army: Making Democracy Safe for the Soldier," *Outlook* 117 (Nov. 28, 1917), 496–97.

77. Low to Van Deman, June 4, 1918, MID File PF 11245, NRC; Smiley to Low, June 8, 1918, ibid.; Low to Churchill, June 19, 1918, ibid.

78. Low to Churchill, June 13, ibid.; T. DeC. Ruth to Low, June 22, 1918, ibid.

79. Lt. Philip S. Weadock, Fort Huachuca, to Southern Dept. IO, Fort Sam Houston, July 25, 1918, MID File 10218-91, RG 165, NA.

80. Churchill to Low, Aug. 8, 1918, ibid.; Low to Churchill, Aug. 13, 1918, ibid.; R. L. Barnes to chief, MIB, Aug. 21, 1918, ibid.; Low to Churchill, Aug. 26, 1918, ibid.

81. Low to Churchill, Aug. 14, 1918, MID File PF 11245, NRC; Churchill to IOs, Camp Greene, Aug. 21, 1918, ibid.; Camp Lee, Aug. 21, 1918, ibid.; Camp Dix, Aug. 22, 1918, ibid.; Camp Devens, Aug. 22, 1918, ibid.; Ernest J. Hall, Camp Devens, to chief, MIB, Aug. 27, 1918, ibid.; W. W. Vaughn to Churchill, Aug. 29, 1918, ibid.; J. Termini to Churchill, Sept. 21, 1918, ibid.; J. E. Spingarn to Loving, July 6, 1918, MID File 10218-154, RG 165, NA.

82. Moorland, "YMCA with Colored Troops," 173. On the tireless work of More-

house College president John Hope for the YMCA in France, see Leroy Davis, *A Clashing of the Soul: John Hope and the Dilemma of African American Leadership and Black Higher Education in the Early Twentieth Century* (Athens: University of Georgia Press, 1998), 234–51.

83. Joseph Robie memo, Oct. 2, 1918, MID File 10575-596, RG 165, NA. According to two black employees who worked in France, there were objections by white army officers to the conduct of black secretaries in 1917 and at least one may have been repatriated then, but they are not clear on this. See Addie W. Hunton and Kathryn M. Johnson, *Two Colored Women with the U.S. Expeditionary Forces* (New York: Brooklyn Eagle Press, 1920), 23, 31, 138.

84. Hunton and Johnson, *Two Colored Women*, 135–36, 153; Robie memo, Oct. 2, 1918, MID File 10575-596, RG 165, NA; Curtis record card, n.d., ibid.; *Baltimore Afro-American*, Nov. 1, 1917. On James L. Curtis, see ibid.; *Washington Bee*, July 21, 1917; *Chicago Defender*, July 28, 1917; Willard B. Gatewood, "Booker T. Washington and the Ulrich Affair," *Journal of Negro History* 55 (Jan. 1970), 36–37; Richard B. Sherman, *The Republican Party and Black America from McKinley to Hoover, 1896–1933* (Charlottesville: University Press of Virginia, 1973), 116.

85. On William A. Hunton, see *Crisis* 13 (Jan. 1917), 119.

86. Williams, *Sidelights on Negro Soldiers*, 103, 106; Robert Russa Moton, *Finding A Way Out: An Autobiography* (London: T. Fisher Unwin, 1920), 262.

87. Robie memo, Oct. 2, 1918, MID File 10575-596, RG 165, NA.

88. C. L. Powell memo, Oct. 7, 1918, MID File 10575-596, RG 165, NA; Low to Churchill, Oct. 8, 1918, ibid.; Low to Churchill, Oct. 15, 1918, ibid.; Churchill to assistant chief of staff, G-2, Service of Supply, AEF, Paris, Oct. 10, 1918, ibid.; Low to Churchill, Oct. 29, 1918, ibid.; Churchill to assistant chief of staff, G-2, Service of Supply, AEF, Paris, Nov. 6, 1918, ibid.; assistant chief of staff, G-2, Service of Supply, AEF, Paris, to Churchill, Dec. 10, 1918, ibid. On May 6, 1921, Helen Curtis and Kathryn Johnson were arrested in their YMCA uniforms, picketing a New York City filmhouse showing *The Birth of a Nation*. Special Weekly Report of J. G. Tucker, May 7, 1921, BI File BS 202600-1628-20, RG 65, NA. Addie W. Hunton played a leading role in the 1927 meeting of the Pan-African Congress, in New York City. Aptheker, *Afro-American History*, 275.

89. "Quander E. Hall" to Henry G. Pratt, Nov. 9, 1918, MID File 10218-285, RG 165, NA; Hall to Harry A. Taylor, n.d., ibid.; K. A. Wagner to Henry G. Pratt, Nov. 25, 1918, ibid. One of the barred group was Helen Curtis's niece.

90. James E. Cutler memo, Oct. 21, 1918, MID File PF 11245, NRC; C. L. Powell memo, Oct. 11, 1918, ibid.; Cutler to Harry Taylor, Oct. 21, 1918, ibid.; "Quander E. Hall" to Harry Taylor, n.d., MID File 10218-285, RG 165, NA; "Quander E. Hall" to Henry G. Pratt, Nov. 9, 1918, ibid.; Cutler to chief, Morale Branch, Dec. 9, 1919, MID File 10218-289, RG 165, NA. When extra black YMCA staff were eventually allowed to travel to France, they did not always perform as the military authorities hoped. A YMCA secretary who arrived in January 1919 was reported to Washington four months later for having organized an "equality" group. Nolan to director, MID, April 22, 1919, MID File 10218-311, RG 165, NA.

91. Low to Dunn, Dec. 16, 1918, Jan. 4, 1919, MID File 10218-247, RG 165, NA;

A. Harrison to Henry G. Pratt (twice), Dec. 31, 1918, MID File PF 11245, NRC; W. K. Cooper to Pratt, Jan. 21, 1919, ibid.

92. Dunn to third assistant secretary of war, Jan. 15, 1919, MID File PF 11245, NRC; summary by C. L. Powell, Jan. 18, 1919, ibid.

93. Ibid.

94. Cutler memo, Feb. 4, 1919, ibid. De Frantz, at least, continued to work for the YMCA after the war, managing the black YMCA at Indianapolis. See *Crisis* 24 (Sept. 1922), 204. At least two other black military welfare organizations were inconclusively investigated by the government. In January 1918, the black journalist Ralph Tyler set up the National Colored Soldiers Comfort Committee with a fund-raising target of $2,000,000. The BI was concerned that its leaflets stressed the plight of the dependants of the thirteen executed members of the 24th Infantry, and seemed, to the BI, to be disloyally implying that the men had been the victims of injustice. See reports of J. E. Elliott, Washington, D.C., Jan. 18, 21, 22, 1918, BI File OG 369936, RG 65, NA; assistant U.S. attorney, Western District of Arkansas (Fort Smith), to Bielaski, Jan. 19, 1918, ibid.; report of McElveen, Memphis, Feb. 8, 1918, BI File OG 3057, RG 65, NA. The other distrusted organization was the Crispus Attucks Circle for War Relief (CACWR), which was investigated after the intelligence officer at Camp Meade, Md., voiced concern over Mexican approaches to black troops, which appeared to him to have originated in Philadelphia. The only organization connected with black soldiers that the BI could find in the city was the CACWR. It turned out to be an amateurish fund-raising group for the future welfare of black veterans, with one radical connection in the form of the Rev. George Frazier Miller of New York. Spencer Roberts, Camp Meade, to chief, MIB, May 10, 1918, MID File 10218-147, RG 165, NA; Van Deman to IO, Camp Meade, May 17, 1918, ibid.; Roberts to Van Deman, May 22, 1918, ibid.; Van Deman to Bielaski, May 27, 1918, BI File OG 98505, RG 65, NA; Bielaski to F. L. Garbarino (BI), Philadelphia, May 28, 1918, ibid.; reports of W. S. Carman, Philadelphia, June 11 (twice), 12, 1918, ibid.; report of F. B. Pond, Philadelphia, June 12, 1918, ibid.; reports of Elza W. Pond, Philadelphia, Aug. 30 (twice), Sept. 7, 1918, ibid.; report of "SA 16," Philadelphia, Aug. 1, 1918, ibid.; report of APL agent, New York, Aug. 23, 1918, ibid.

4. The Surveillance of African-American Leadership

1. Zechariah Chafee, Jr., *Freedom of Speech* (London: George Allen & Unwin, 1920), 43.

2. Ibid., 107; David M. Kennedy, *Over Here: The First World War and American Society* (New York: Oxford University Press, 1980), 16; Donald Johnson, *The Challenge to American Freedoms: World War I and the Rise of the American Civil Liberties Union* (Lexington: University of Kentucky Press, 1963), 58, 61, 82; William Preston, Jr., *Aliens and Dissenters: Federal Suppression of Radicals, 1903–1933* (New York: Harper & Row, 1966), 145. The Trading with the Enemy Act outlawed transportation around the country of material which had been declared non-mailable under the Espionage Act. See Preston, *Aliens and Dissenters,* 148.

3. James Weinstein, *The Decline of Socialism in America, 1912–1925* (New York: Monthly Review Press, 1967), 90–91, 144; Johnson, *Challenge to American Freedoms,* 57. For an account of the Post Office Department's harassment of the Industrial Workers of the World, see Preston, *Aliens and Dissenters,* 144–49.

4. Kevin Tierney, *Darrow: A Biography* (New York: Thomas Y. Crowell, 1979), 293; Burleson, speech to the National Hardware Association, Atlantic City, N.J., Oct. 15, 1919, General Correspondence, June 2–Oct. 15, 1919, Papers of Albert Sidney Burleson, LC.

5. Oswald Garrison Villard, *Fighting Years: Memoirs of a Liberal Editor* (New York: Harcourt, Brace and World, 1939), 357; Johnson, *Challenge to American Freedoms,* 56.

6. William H. Lamar, "The Government's Attitude toward the Press," *Forum* 59 (Feb. 1918), 129–40.

7. Kennedy, *Over Here,* 77.

8. Johnson, *Challenge to American Freedoms,* 63.

9. Lamar, "The Government's Attitude toward the Press," 132, 139.

10. *Documents of American History,* Henry Steele Commager, ed., 5th edition (New York: Appleton-Century-Crofts, 1949), 325–26.

11. Preston, *Aliens and Dissenters,* 145; Johnson, *Challenge to American Freedoms,* 69.

12. Villard, *Fighting Years,* 357; Johnson, *Challenge to American Freedoms,* 62. See also Ronald Schaffer, *America in the Great War: The Rise of the War Welfare State* (New York: Oxford University Press, 1991), 14–15, 28–30.

13. James R. Mock, *Censorship 1917* (Princeton: Princeton University Press, 1941), 62–65.

14. Frederick Detweiler, *The Negro Press in the United States* (Chicago: University of Chicago Press, 1922), 4. For a detailed list of black publications, see Warren Brown, *A Check List of Negro Newspapers in the United States (1827–1946)* (Jefferson City: Lincoln University School of Journalism, 1946). Herbert Aptheker, *Afro-American History: The Modern Era* (New York: Citadel Press, 1971), 127–58.

15. See *Norfolk Journal and Guide,* Oct. 21, 1916; Jan. 13, Feb. 3, March, 10, 17, 24, 30, April 7, 21, 28, May 5, 1917.

16. See David Levering Lewis, *W. E. B. Du Bois: Biography of a Race, 1868–1919* (New York: Henry Holt, 1993); Henry Lewis Suggs, *P. B. Young, Newspaperman: Race, Politics, and Journalism in the New South, 1910–1962* (Charlottesville: University Press of Virginia, 1988); Stephen R. Fox, *The Guardian of Boston: William Monroe Trotter* (New York: Atheneum, 1970); Theodore Kornweibel, Jr., *No Crystal Stair: Black Life and the Messenger, 1917–1928* (Westport, Conn.: Greenwood Press, 1975); Paula F. Pfeffer, *A. Philip Randolph: Pioneer of the Civil Rights Movement* (Baton Rouge: Louisiana State University Press, 1990), all passim.

17. Ray Stannard Baker, "Clouds along the Color Line," *World's Work* (June 1916), cited in *Crisis* 12 (Aug. 1916), 168. See also draft in Speeches and Writings File, 1881–1944, Papers of Ray Stannard Baker, LC.

18. Weinstein, *Decline of Socialism,* 144.

19. Gilbert Osofsky, *Harlem: The Making of a Ghetto, Negro New York, 1890–1930* (New York: Harper & Row, 1971), 133.

20. Harry Haywood, *Black Bolshevik: An Autobiography of an Afro-American Communist* (Chicago: Liberator Press, 1978), 122–31. See Briggs's letter to the *New York Globe,* April 10, 1918. See also *The Marcus Garvey and Universal Negro Improvement Association Papers,* vol. 1, ed. Robert A. Hill (Berkeley: University of California Press, 1983), 521–27; Robert A. Hill, "Introduction. Racial and Radical: Cyril V. Briggs, THE CRUSADER Magazine, and the African Blood Brotherhood, 1918–1922," in *The Crusader,* ed. Robert A. Hill, vol. 1 (New York: Garland, 1987), v–lxvi, esp. xiii–xvii. The idea of a separate state for blacks to depart to, or be deported to, had also been put forward by white southern segregationists. See William P. Calhoun, *The Caucasian and the Negro in the United States* (Columbia, S.C.: R. L. Bryan, 1902); Winfield H. Collins, *The Truth about Lynching and the Negro in the South: In Which the Author Pleads That the South Be Made Safe for the White Race* (New York: Neale Publishing, 1918). Collins, while recognizing it would never happen, suggested, "If about 100,000 square miles of territory on the Gulf of Mexico . . . were set apart as a State or States to which all the Negroes in other parts of the country might be encouraged or obliged to migrate, it might result in great good to both races." Ibid., 141–42.

21. Report of APL Operative Constant, New York, for Oct. 23, 1918, BI File OG 38201, RG 65, NA.

22. *Amsterdam News,* May 29, 1918, ibid.

23. Ibid.

24. H. C. Craig to chief, MIB, June 3, 1918, MID File 10218-163, RG 165, NA.

25. Report of Examiner 1731, U.S. Postal Censorship, Key West, June 4, 1918, BI File OG 38201, RG 65, NA.

26. Bielaski to Charles De Woody, July 12, 1918, BI File OG 38201, RG 65, NA.

27. Report of Constant, for Oct. 23, 1918, ibid.; Haywood, *Black Bolshevik,* 123; Hill, "Introduction," xxii–xxiii.

28. Report of Willard Utley, San Antonio, Nov. 27, 1917, MID File 10218-62, RG 165, NA.

29. Report of T. White, San Antonio, Jan. 14, 1919, MID File 10218-66, RG 165, NA; report of Louis Nette, San Antonio, Dec. 15, 1919, ibid.; *Atlanta Constitution,* Dec. 12, 1919.

30. Jervis Anderson, *A. Philip Randolph: A Biographical Portrait* (New York: Harcourt, Brace, Jovanovich, 1973), 54, 73–82; Kornweibel, *No Crystal Stair,* 25–32; Pfeffer, *A. Philip Randolph,* 6–10. See also Manning Marable, "A. Philip Randolph and the Foundations of Black American Socialism," *Radical America* 14 (March–April 1980), 6–29.

31. Weinstein, *Decline of Socialism,* 149–54. Chandler Owen's article "Peace," in the January 1918 *Messenger* (vol. 2, 17, 20), explains the journal's endorsement of the Socialist party's opposition to the war.

32. *Messenger* 1 (Nov. 1917), 6, 7; 2 (Jan. 1918), 31; 2 (July 1918), 11, 24–25.

33. *Messenger* 1 (Nov. 1917), 6, 10, 30, 36.

34. *Messenger* 2 (Jan. 1918), 7.

35. *Messenger* 2 (July 1918), 13. The circulation of the *Messenger* at this time was

estimated by Socialist party officials to be 45,000. Weinstein, *Decline of Socialism,* 71. However, in 1921, the editors themselves stated that 26,000 was the highest circulation they had achieved. Detweiler, *The Negro Press,* 171.

36. Report of Sawken, Cleveland, Aug. 10, 1918, BI File OG 234939, RG 65, NA.

37. Anderson, *A. Philip Randolph,* 106.

38. Report of Sawken, Aug. 10, 1918, BI File OG 234939, RG 65, NA; reports of A. W. Willett, Sept. 14, 30, 1918, BI File OG 259364, RG 65, NA.

39. Report of Sawken, Aug. 10, 1918, BI File OG 234939, RG 65, NA; indictment of Chandler Owen, Walter Bronstrup, A. Philip Randolph, and John Fromholz, n.d., in A. P. Randolph file, WRHS. Justice Department officials in Cleveland interpreted the Espionage Act and its amendment, the Sedition Act, particularly fiercely. On June 30, 1918, Socialist Party leader Eugene Debs was arrested at Cleveland and charged with ten different counts of having violated the Sedition Act during a speech at Canton, Ohio, two weeks earlier. In September, he was found guilty in federal district court and was confined in the Atlanta Penitentiary until Christmas Day, 1921. Ray Ginger, *Eugene V. Debs: A Biography* (New York: Collier Books, 1962), 377, 381–90.

40. Anderson, *A. Philip Randolph,* 107; Chandler Owen to Mary White Ovington, April 11, 1919, Admin File, NAACP Papers, LC. Seymour Stedman later defended Eugene Debs, and Assistant U.S. Attorney Kavanagh opened the prosecution. Ginger, *Eugene V. Debs,* 381, 384. That Stedman was a good friend of the *Messenger* can be seen from the message he sent to the journal when he was the Socialist Party's vice-presidential candidate in 1920. *Messenger* 2 (Nov. 1920), 156.

41. Owen to Ovington, April 11, 1919, Admin File, NAACP Papers, LC; index sheet from Owen, Bronstrup, Randolph, and Fromholz indictment, Randolph file, WRHS; report of Sawken, Aug. 10, 1918, BI File OG 234939, RG 65, NA.

42. Anderson, *A. Philip Randolph,* 108.

43. Kornweibel, *No Crystal Stair,* 52–53; Anderson, *A. Philip Randolph,* 108.

44. See postmaster, New York, to solicitor, Post Office Dept., July 1, 1919, unnumbered file on *Messenger,* Entry 40, RG 28, NA; Victor R. Daly (*Messenger* business manager) to postmaster general, July 3, 1919, ibid.; Lamar to postmaster, New York, July 8, 1919, ibid. If second-class mailing privileges were withdrawn between August 1918 and February 1919, the most likely cause is that the *Messenger*'s irregular publication had invalidated its registration as a journal with the Post Office.

45. Anderson, *A. Philip Randolph,* 108–109; Detweiler, *The Negro Press,* 171; Owen to Ovington, April 11, 1919, Admin File, NAACP Papers, LC; Ovington to Owen, April 14, 1919, ibid.; *Crisis* 17 (April 1919), 267.

46. Simmons and Abbott were on good terms. For excerpts from Simmons's speeches, see *Chicago Defender,* July 7, Aug. 11, Sept. 29, Oct. 6, 13, Nov. 10, 17, 24, Dec. 1, 8, 22, 1917.

47. H. B. Mock, Tucson, to H. G. Clabaugh, Dec. 20, 1917, BI File OG 5911, RG 65, NA; report of H. B. Mock, Dec. 28, 1917, ibid.; *Chicago Defender,* Dec. 8, 1917.

48. Report of B. D. Adsit, Chicago, Dec. 22, 1917, BI File OG 5911, RG 65, NA.

49. Report of E. J. Kerwin, Pine Bluff, May 7, 1918, ibid.

50. Report of B. D. Adsit, May 24, 1918, ibid.

51. Report of APL operative No. 38, Mobile, Sept. 24, 1918, ibid. The APL's belief in the need to control the black press was not confined to the South. In July 1918, the chief of the APL in Cincinnati told the MIB, "Disaffection among the Negroes, where found, can be traced to a very definite cause or grievance. If press utterances are guarded and they are made to feel that they are going to be dealt with fairly, such feeling will cease to exist." Joan Jensen, *The Price of Vigilance* (Chicago: Rand McNally, 1968), 186–87.

52. Report of Leon Spitz, MIB Chicago, April 25, 1918, MID File 10218-133, RG 165, NA.

53. A Citizen's Committee of Patriotic Negro Citizens to United States Intelligence Bureau [*sic*], n.d., ibid.; Carl Reichmann to chief, MIB, April 29, 1918, ibid.

54. W. H. Loving to chief, MIB, May 10, 1918, ibid.; R. S. Abbott to Loving, May 11, 1918, ibid.; Loving to chief, MIB, May 20, 1918, ibid.; *Chicago Defender,* May 18, 1918.

55. Lamar to postmaster, Chicago, Aug. 13, 1917, File 47522, Entry 40, RG 28, NA; letters from postmaster, Chicago, to Lamar, enclosing two copies of *Chicago Defender* for Oct. 13, 20, 1917, Jan. 12, Feb. 2, March 9, 16, 23, 30, June 8, 22, 29, July 6, 1918, ibid.

56. H. C. Piner, postmaster, Denison, Tex., to solicitor, Post Office Dept., June 8, 1918, ibid.

57. C. E. Boles to solicitor, June 13, 1918, ibid.

58. Ibid.

59. M. E. Nash, postmaster, Belcher, La., to solicitor, June 22, 1918, ibid.

60. John Sharp Williams to A. S. Burleson, June 22, 1918, ibid.; Madison Cy. Resolution, n.d., ibid.

61. "ZLD" to Horton, June 28, 1918, ibid.; "WS," memo on *Defender,* July 6, 1918, ibid.; Burleson to Williams, July 11, 1918, ibid.

62. "LH", Translation Bureau, to assistant U.S. attorney, New York, July 26, Aug. 16, 1918, ibid.

63. R. A. Bowen to assistant U.S. attorney, New York, July 26, 1918, ibid.

64. Roy F. Britton, IO, St. Louis, to chief, MIB, May 6, 1918, MID File 10218-144, RG 165, NA; *St. Louis Argus,* May 3, 1918.

65. *St. Louis Argus,* May 3, 1918.

66. Britton to chief, MIB, May 6, 1918, MID File 10218-144, RG 165, NA; Van Deman to Loving, May 13, 1918, ibid.

67. J. E. Mitchell to Loving, May 25, 1918, ibid.; Loving to Mitchell, May 28, 1918, ibid. (Loving's letter to Mitchell of May 21 is not in the file.)

68. Britton to chief, MIB, May 22, 27, 1918, ibid. (referring to the May 17 and May 24 issues of the *Argus*); Britton to chief, MIB, July 9, Aug 5, 1918, ibid. (referring to the July 5 and Aug. 2 issues of the *Argus*).

69. Radical black press clippings are in BI File OG 311587, RG 65, NA; *Washington Eagle* clippings are from the issues of June 14, July 6, and July 13, 1918.

70. Bielaski to W. Offley, New York, May 8, 1917, BI File OG 3057, RG 65, NA.

71. Don Whitehead, *The FBI Story* (London: F. Muller, 1957), 41–42.

72. Bielaski to Offley, May 8, 1917, BI File OG 3057, RG 65, NA. The Office of

Naval Intelligence recorded a suspicion that the *Washington Bee* was "Supposed to be Pro-German." Index to Suspect Cases (1917–1918), Series 78 and 84, Entry 77, RG 38, NA. Wilson probably knew that his chief rival, Calvin Chase of the *Washington Bee,* had kept afloat by covertly accepting Tuskegee money since 1905. See Louis R. Harlan, *Booker T. Washington: The Wizard of Tuskegee, 1901–1915* (New York: Oxford University Press, 1983), 90–91.

73. Harlan, *Booker T. Washington,* 36, 44–47, 103–104. See also Willard B. Gatewood, *Aristocrats of Color: The Black Elite, 1890–1920* (Bloomington: Indiana University Press, 1990), 306–309.

74. Hubert H. Harrison, *When Africa Awakes: The 'Inside Story' of the Stirrings and Strivings of the New Negro in the Western World* (New York: Porro Press, 1920), 10. In October 1916, the NERL had met in Washington in joint session with the National Colored Citizenship Rights Congress. *Norfolk Journal and Guide,* Sept. 30, 1916.

75. *The Voice,* July 4, 1917, reprinted in Harrison, *When Africa Awakes,* 10; Tony Martin, *Race First: The Ideological and Organizational Struggles of Marcus Garvey and the Universal Negro Improvement Association* (Westport, Conn.: Greenwood Press, 1976), 9–10, 92.

76. *Chicago Defender,* Aug. 4, 1917.

77. Fox, *Guardian of Boston,* 217; Bielaski to Clabaugh, Aug. 17, 1917, DJ Central File 158260-41, RG 60, NA; report of C. S. Weakley, Cincinnati, Sept. 17, 1917, BI File OG 57445, RG 65, NA; report of J. C. Dreutzburg, Chicago, Sept. 14, 1917, BI File OG 5911, RG 65, NA.

78. Fox, *Guardian of Boston,* 217; *Norfolk Journal and Guide,* Sept. 8, 29, 1917; Address to the Country by the National Equal Rights League, Tenth Annual Meeting, Sept. 30, 1917, case file 152, Series 4, Papers of Woodrow Wilson, LC.

79. *Norfolk Journal and Guide,* Sept. 29, 1917; Harrison, *When Africa Awakes,* 10. See also *New York Times,* July 5, 1917; *San Antonio Inquirer,* April 13, 1918, clipping in MID File 10218-66, RG 165, NA; *Hannibal Record,* May 30, 1918. The latter paper was held up by the U.S. postal censors at New Orleans, because of the references to the National Liberty Congress. It was being sent to Panama. See MID File 10218-170, RG 165, NA. *Southern Standard,* a Macon, Ga., paper, sent by IO, Southeastern Dept. (Charleston, S.C.), to chief, MIB, May 27, 1918, MID File 10218-153, RG 165, NA.

80. IO, Northeastern Dept. (Boston), to chief, MIB, June 5, 19, 1918, MID File 10218-153, RG 165, NA; Churchill to IO, Northeastern Dept., June 13, 1918, ibid.

81. *Hannibal Record,* July 18, 1918; list of delegates and accounts of speeches delivered to National Liberty Congress, June, 1918, unnumbered items with MID File 10218, RG 165, NA. In 1916, the Bureau of Education published a controversial two-volume study by Jones on black education in the United States. Charles Flint Kellogg, *NAACP: A History of the National Association for the Advancement of Colored People, Volume 1: 1909–1920* (Baltimore: Johns Hopkins University Press, 1967), 86, 310; Harlan, *Booker T. Washington,* 200–201; Lewis, *W. E. B. Du Bois,* 547–51; Thomas Jesse Jones, *Negro Education: A Study of the Private and Higher Schools for Colored People in the United States* (New York: Arno, 1969; first published 1917), 2 vols. See Eric Anderson and Alfred A. Moss, Jr., *Dangerous Donations: Northern Philan-*

thropy and Southern Black Education (Columbia: University of Missouri Press, 1999), passim.

82. Extracts from speeches transcribed in MID File 10218-153, RG 165, NA.

83. Report of J. G. C. Corcoran, July 1, 1918, BI File OG 369936, RG 65, NA.

84. *Hannibal Record,* July 18, 1918; Fox, *Guardian of Boston,* 221. On Martin Madden's reliance on black votes, see Harold F. Gosnell, *Negro Politicians: The Rise of Negro Politics in Chicago* (Chicago: University of Chicago Press, 1935, reprinted 1967), 53n, 66–67, 78–80.

85. Reports of J. G. C. Corcoran, June 29, Aug. 30, 1918, BI File OG 369936, RG 65, NA; Bielaski to Charles De Woody, Sept. 4, 1918, BI File OG 272751, RG 65, NA. On Arthur U. Craig and other informants used during this period, see Theodore Kornweibel, Jr., "Black on Black: The FBI's First Negro Informants and Agents and the Investigation of Black Radicalism during the Red Scare," *Criminal Justice History* 8 (1987), 121–136.

86. Reports of J. G. C. Corcoran, Sept. 11, 14, 20, 28, 1918, BI File OG 369936, RG 65, NA.

87. Report of J. G. C. Corcoran, Oct. 1, 1918, ibid. Craig's figure for the number of delegates was one-third of the number which the NERL itself claimed. See *Chicago Defender,* Sept. 28, 1918; Alfreda Duster, ed., *Crusade for Justice: The Autobiography of Ida B. Wells* (Chicago: University of Chicago Press, 1970), 379.

88. Report of J. G. C. Corcoran, Oct. 8, 1918, BI File OG 369936, RG 65, NA; Kellogg, *NAACP,* 278; Richard Bardolph, *The Negro Vanguard* (New York: Rinehart, 1959), 108. See also *Norfolk Journal and Guide,* Sept. 22, 1917.

89. National Race Congress leaflet, Oct. 1918, MID File 10218-292, RG 165, NA.

90. Kelly Miller to Woodrow Wilson, Aug. 4, 1917, case file 152, series 4, Papers of Woodrow Wilson, LC. Miller was born in South Carolina. He served Howard University for forty-four years. On his place in black intellectual circles, see Bernard Eisenberg, "Kelly Miller: The Negro Leader as a Marginal Man," *Journal of Negro History* 45 (July 1960), 182–97.

91. Report of Warren W. Grimes, Feb. 20, 1918, BI File 369936, RG 65, NA.

92. Bielaski to Van Deman, Feb. 21, 1918, MID File 10218-91, RG 165, NA; Van Deman to Loving, Feb. 28, 1918, ibid.; Loving to chief, MIB, March 14, 1918, ibid.; Miller to Loving, March 8, 1918, ibid.; Philip S. Weadock, 10th Cavalry, to dept. IO, Fort Sam Houston, July 25, 1918, ibid.; Churchill to dept. IO, Fort Sam Houston, Aug. 8, 1918, ibid.; Churchill to William Gilman Low, Aug. 8, 21, 30, 1918, ibid.; Low to Churchill, Aug 13, 26, 1918, ibid.; R. L. Barnes, IO, Southern Dept., to chief, MIB, Aug. 21, 1918, ibid.

93. Report of Horace A. Lewis, Boston, Aug. 19 (for Aug. 12), 1918, BI File OG 329980, RG 65, NA.

94. Report of Horace A. Lewis, Boston, Aug. 19 (for Aug. 15), 1918, ibid.

95. Reports of Horace A. Lewis, Boston, Sept. 20, Oct 24, 1918, ibid. An attempt was also made to provoke a breach of the Espionage Act by Miller's publishers, Austin Jenks, a black company based in Washington. In November 1918, a black informant inquired under a false name about the possibility of becoming a distributor of Miller's forthcoming book on the war and later visited Austin Jenks's office

to arrange for their material to be mailed to her, but no subsequent action was taken. K. A. Wagner to Henry G. Pratt, Nov. 22, 23, 1918, MID File 10218-91, RG 165, NA; Austin Jenks Co. to Miss Keichline, Nov. 6, 1918, ibid. The BI's most regular black informant in the capital, Arthur U. Craig, also tried this ruse on the Negro American Alliance. Craig got the NAA to send him some of their literature in February 1918, and offered to organize a Washington branch, but the offer was declined by the NAA secretary, Floyd Delos Francis. Floyd Delos Francis to Arthur U. Craig, Feb. 1, 1918, BI File OG 311587, RG 65, NA.

96. J. O. Carr, U.S. attorney, Wilmington, N.C., to Bielaski, Feb. 18, 1918, BI File OG 151080, RG 65, NA.

97. Bielaski to Carr, March 4, 1918, ibid. (This letter was drafted by an unidentified official, "S. D. B.")

98. See, for example, Bolton Smith, *Notes on the Negro Problem* (n.p., 1918), in BI File OG 374214, RG 65, NA; *A Philosophy of Race Relations* (Memphis: n.p., 1919), ibid.; "The Memphis Lynching," *New Republic* 12 (Aug. 11, 1917), 51. See also "A Southern Philanthropist on the Race Question," *Outlook* 122 (May 14, 1919), 59–60; Bolton Smith, "The Negro in War-Time," *Public* 21 (Aug. 31, 1918), 1110–13; Laurence C. Jones, *Piney Woods and Its Story* (New York: Fleming H. Revell, 1922), 98. On southern interracialism, see William A. Link, *The Paradox of Southern Progressivism, 1880–1930* (Chapel Hill: University of North Carolina Press, 1992), 248–61.

99. Bolton Smith to John Shillady, Nov. 19, 1918, Jan. 14, May 29, Aug. 1, l919, Admin File, Papers of the NAACP, LC; Ovington to Smith, Aug. 7, 15, 1919; Smith to Ovington, Aug. 13, 23, 1919, ibid.; Smith to John Sharp Williams, Oct. 6, 1919, box 48, Papers of John Sharp Williams, LC; Williams to Smith, Oct. 14, 1919, ibid. See also Bolton Smith to A. Mitchell Palmer, Aug. 1, 1919, DJ Central File 158260-102, RG 60, NA.

100. Report of McElveen, Memphis, April 30, 1917, BI File OG 17011, RG 65, NA.

101. Report of Paul Hofherz, New York, May 22, 1917, ibid.; *Crisis* 14 (July 1917), 112; Lewis, *W. E. B. Du Bois,* 552.

102. Lamar to postmaster, N.Y., Sept. 24, 1917, File 47732, Entry 40, RG 28, NA.

103. Leaflet for "Negro Silent Protest Parade," Oct. 14, 1917, BI File OG 67118, RG 65, NA; Bielaski to Tom Howick, Oct. 18, 1917, ibid.; Howick to Bielaski, Oct. 27, 1917, ibid.; *Baltimore Afro-American,* Oct. 27, 1917.

104. L. L. Burkhead to A. S. Burleson, Nov. 25, 1917, DJ Central File 189621, RG 60, NA; A. S. Burleson to Newton D. Baker, Dec. 10, 1917, ibid. Another event in 1917 which may have made the citizens of Columbus nervous was the internment there of 1,200 members of the Industrial Workers of the World, deported from Bisbee, Ariz., in cattle trucks in July by mining company gunmen. See *Outlook* 116 (July 25, 1917), 466; William D. Haywood, *Big Bill's Book* (New York: International Publishers, 1929, reprinted 1969), 300. The NAACP leaflet found at Columbus is no longer in the relevant Department of Justice file and may never have reached it.

105. Wilson Chase to commanding general, El Paso District, Dec. 22, 1917, DJ Central File 189621, RG 60, NA; John W. Ruckman to adjutant general of the Army,

Dec. 31, 1917, ibid. The *Crisis* was popular reading in the 24th Infantry, according to the regimental chaplain. *Crisis* 14 (Oct. 1917), 307–309.

106. "Thirteen," *Crisis* 15 (Jan. 1918), 114.

107. Secretary of war to attorney general, Jan. 10, 1918, DJ Central File 189621, RG 60, NA; John Lord O'Brian to Summers Burkhart, Jan. 15, 1918, ibid.; Burkhart to O'Brian, Jan. 29, 1918, ibid.

108. Post office inspector, Cincinnati Division, to Lamar, Jan. 29, 1918, File 47732, Entry 40, RG 28, NA; copies of letters from "LH/MR" to U.S. assistant district attorney, N.Y., during 1918, ibid.; Lamar to postmaster, N.Y., unused drafts March 19, May 17, 1918, ibid.; Boles to Lamar, May 17, 1918, ibid.; *Crisis* 15 (April 1918), 271–75. When the director of military intelligence asked whether any action was being taken against the *Crisis* by the Post Office Department in November 1918, Lamar replied that none was anticipated. Marlborough Churchill to Lamar, Nov. 8, 1918, File 47732, Entry 40, RG 28, NA; Lamar to Churchill, Nov. 16, 1918, ibid.

109. Report of G. C. Brautzburg, Chicago, Dec. 16, 1917, BI File OG 17011, RG 65, NA.

110. Report of Leverett F. Englesby, Palatka, Fla., April 5, 1918, ibid.

111. Report of Manuel Sorola, San Antonio, Tex., May 2, 1918, ibid.; J. R. Tolar to Bielaski, April 15, 1918, ibid.; Bielaski to Tolar, April 22, 1918, ibid.; C. D. Holt to Sen. O. M. James, April 21, 1918, ibid.; James to Bielaski, April 27, 1918, ibid.; Bielaski to James, May 10, 1918, ibid.; C. L. Butler to BI, April 21, 1918, ibid.; Bielaski to Butler, May 10, 1918, ibid. (Bielaski's replies were drafted by A. H. Pike.)

112. Charles Studin to W. E. B. Du Bois, May 1, 1918, Papers of W. E. B. Du Bois, reel 5, UML; minutes of the NAACP Board of Directors, May 13, 1918, ibid.

113. W. E. B. Du Bois to A. H. Grimké, May 4, 1918, Box 39-8, Papers of A. H. Grimké, M-SRC; "The Thirteen Black Soldiers," a poem by A. H. Grimké, ibid.; Dickson D. Bruce, Jr., *Archibald Grimké: Portrait of a Black Independent* (Baton Rouge: Louisiana State University Press, 1993), 220–29; *Messenger* 2 (Oct. 1919), 25–26.

114. Bettman to Bielaski, May 16, 1918, BI File OG 17011, RG 65, NA; Bettman to A. R. Gere, May 31, 1918, ibid.

115. Bielaski to Bettman, May 10, 1918, BI File OG 17011, RG 65, NA; Stanley Coben, *A. Mitchell Palmer: Politician* (New York: Da Capo Press, 1963), 201. Alfred Bettman had been a Cincinnati municipal and railroad lawyer prior to joining the Justice Department's War Division in 1917. *Who Was Who in America*, vol. 2 (Chicago: Marquis–Who's Who, 1950), 60. Bettman and Pike frequently clashed over what constituted a breach of the Espionage Act. Bettman and O'Brian also disapproved of Pike's willingness to let the Post Office, rather than the Justice Department, pronounce on the mailability of publications. They held that the interpretation of the Espionage Act was the sole prerogative of the Justice Department. See Bettman to Bielaski, May 16, 31, 1918; Bielaski to Bettman, May 17, 1918, BI File OG 185087, RG 65, NA. Bettman was also less willing than other Justice Department officials to condemn out of hand speeches containing criticism of government policy, especially when he felt he was only being shown selected passages. He had no qualms about declaring that a Justice Department stenographer's seventy-eight-

page transcript of an Irish Progressive League meeting was useless. See Bettman to Bielaski, May 10, July 11, Oct. 25, Nov. 12, 1918, BI File OG 181696, RG 65, NA; M. D. Allen to Van Dusen, Nov. 1, 1918, ibid.

116. Bielaski to Bettman, May 10, 1918, BI File OG 181696, RG 65, NA.

117. *Crisis* 16 (May 1918), 7, 16–20, 23.

118. Report of Howell E. Jackson, Atlanta, May 10, 1918, BI File OG 17011, RG 65, NA; Albert N—— to Bielaski, May 10, 1918, ibid.; Bettman to Bielaski, June 1, 1918, ibid.; R. E. Byrd to Bielaski, May 15, 1918, DJ Central File 189621-7, RG 60, NA.

119. Wilson Chase to U.S. district attorney, Albuquerque, N. M., May 22, 1918, DJ Central File 189621-8, RG 60, NA; Bielaski to R. H. Daughton, June 4, 1918, BI File OG 17011, RG 65, NA; Bielaski to Charles De Woody, June 4, 1918, MID File 10218-139(18), RG 165, NA.

120. Bettman to Bielaski, June 5, July 9, 1918, BI File OG 17011, RG 65, NA.

121. Report of C. E. Campbell, APL, June 3, 1918, ibid.; report of J. A. Baker, June 24, 1918, ibid.; report of D. Davidson, Dec. 5, 1918, ibid.

122. Report of Manuel Sorola, May 2, 1918, ibid.

123. Report of W. T. Carothers, APL, June 13, 1918, enc. letter from A. Philip Randolph and Chandler Owen to APL, New York, June 3, 1918, in New York APL report of June 13, 1918, ibid.

124. Ibid.

125. Ibid.

126. New York APL report of July 24, 1918, ibid. The response of the New York APL chief to the APL national directors' inquiries about "Propaganda among the Negroes," immediately after the war, was distinctly casual. See E. H. Rushmore to national directors, Dec. 13, 1918, MID File 10218-200, RG 165, NA.

127. *Omaha Monitor,* July 20, 1918, clipping, BI File OG 311587, RG 65, NA.

128. Part of address by Rev. J. G. Robinson to Negro selectmen, n.d., BI File OG 306451, RG 65, NA; *Literary Digest,* Aug. 9, 1919. Robinson received a number of death threats in 1919 after he reminded the president about his alleged promises to the AME delegation. See *Baltimore Afro-American,* April 22, 1919.

129. Robinson address, BI File OG 306451, RG 65, NA. Robinson had earlier drawn attention to himself by a bitter attack on President Theodore Roosevelt after the dishonorable discharge of three companies of the 25th Infantry, as a result of their involvement in a riot at Brownsville, Tex., in August 1906. See *Indianapolis Freeman,* Dec. 22, 1906.

130. *Slackers and Traitors. . . . ,* n.d., BI File OG 306451, RG 65, NA; *Crisis* 16 (June 1918), 83.

131. Report of J. S. Edson, Nov. 4, 1918, BI File OG 306451, RG 65, NA; A. M. Schoen to S. S. Doty, Nov. 14, 1918, ibid.; report of W. L. Hawkins, Oct. 29, 1918, BI File OG 17011, RG 65, NA; four reports by W. L. Hawkins, Oct. 31, 1918, ibid.; report by W. L. Hawkins, Oct. 30, 1918, BI File OG 327757, RG 65, NA.

132. Report of J. S. Edson, Nov. 4, 1918, BI File OG 306451, RG 65, NA; Churchill to Bielaski, Oct. 30, 1918, ibid.; Bielaski to Edson, Nov. 1, 22, 1918; Edson to Bielaski, Nov. 4, 1918, ibid.; A. M. Briggs to Bielaski, Nov. 21, 1918, ibid.

133. Report of Copeland, APL No. 61, Atlanta, Sept. 30, 1918, ibid.; report of C. P. Reynolds, Atlanta, Sept. 2, 1918, BI File OG 137812, RG 65, NA.

134. Bielaski to Bettman, Nov. 22, 1918, BI File OG 306451, RG 65, NA.

135. Bettman to Bielaski, Jan. 9, 1919, ibid.

5. W. E. B. Du Bois, Joel Spingarn, and Military Intelligence

Parts of this chapter appeared previously in Mark Ellis, " 'Closing Ranks' and 'Seeking Honors': W. E. B. Du Bois in World War I," *Journal of American History* 79 (June 1992), 96–124, and Mark Ellis, "Joel Spingarn's 'Constructive Programme' and the Wartime Antilynching Bill of 1918," *Journal of Policy History* 4, no. 2 (1992), 134–161.

1. For discussions of progressivism and World War I, see Warren I. Cohen, *The American Revisionists: The Lessons of Intervention in World War I* (Chicago: University of Chicago Press, 1967), 3–25; John F. McClymer, *War and Welfare: Social Engineering in America, 1890–1925* (Westport, Conn.: Greenwood, 1980), 153–84; Neil A. Wynn, *From Progressivism to Prosperity: World War I and American Society* (New York: Holmes and Meier, 1986), 35–38; John A. Thompson, *Reformers and War: American Progressive Publicists and the First World War* (Cambridge: Cambridge University Press, 1987), passim; Paul A. C. Koistinen, *Mobilizing for Modern War: The Political Economy of American Warfare, 1865–1919* (Lawrence, Kan.: University Press of Kansas, 1997), 10–14; 292–98. Nancy Weiss has argued that the NAACP "was an authentic product of the Progressive Era in which it was founded. . . . Racial reformers belong in the ranks of social justice progressives, and the organizations they founded are among the most important institutional legacies of the era of reform." See Nancy J. Weiss, *The National Urban League, 1910–1940* (New York: Oxford University Press, 1974), 47–48; also Robert L. Zangrando, *The NAACP Crusade against Lynching, 1909–1950* (Philadelphia: Temple University Press, 1980), 16–17; Leslie H. Fishel, Jr., and Benjamin Quarles, ed., *The Negro American: A Documentary History* (Glenview, Ill: Scott, Foresman, 1967), 359–62. Progressive sponsors and early organizers of the NAACP included Spingarn, Jane Addams, Ray Stannard Baker, Sophonisba Breckinridge, John Dewey, John Haynes Holmes, Florence Kelley, Mary White Ovington, Louis F. Post, Charles Edward Russell, Lincoln Steffens, Oswald Garrison Villard, Lillian Wald, and Stephen Wise. Charles Flint Kellogg, *NAACP: A History of the National Association for the Advancement of Colored People, Volume 1: 1909–1920* (Baltimore: Johns Hopkins University Press, 1967), 298–308. See, for progressive opinion, Ray Stannard Baker, "The Negro in a Democracy," *Independent* 67 (Sept. 2, 1909), 584–88. Thompson points out that progressivism was nevertheless broad enough to harbor a good deal of race prejudice (*Reformers and War,* 72–73).

2. B. Joyce Ross, *J. E. Spingarn and the Rise of the NAACP, 1911–1939* (New York: Atheneum, 1972), 3–12, 35–37, 62–80; Kellogg, *NAACP,* 61–62; Hasia R. Diner, *In the Almost Promised Land: American Jews and Blacks, 1915–1935* (Westport, Conn.: Greenwood, 1977), 120–22, 137–38. See also Nancy J. Weiss, "Long Distance Runners of the Civil Rights Movement: The Contribution of Jews to the NAACP and the National Urban League in the Early Twentieth Century," in *Struggles in the Prom-*

ised Land: Toward a History of Black-Jewish Relations in the United States, ed. Jack Salzman and Cornel West (New York: Oxford University Press, 1997), 123–154. For examples of Spingarn's academic work, see Joel Elias Spingarn, *A History of Literary Criticism in the Renaissance* (New York: Columbia University Press, 1899); J. E. Spingarn, ed., *Critical Essays of the Seventeenth Century,* 3 vols. (Oxford: Clarendon Press, 1908–1909). On his dismissal from Columbia University, see Joel E. Spingarn, *A Question of Academic Freedom* (New York: n.p., 1911), 6–7. Spingarn accused Nicholas Murray Butler of incompetence and dishonesty, and denounced the trustees of Columbia as pliant sycophants. Ibid., 9–10. See also Wilbur S. Scott, *Five Approaches to Literary Criticism* (New York: Macmillan, 1962), 18, 29–39; Marshall Van Deusen, *J. E. Spingarn* (New York: Twayne, 1971).

3. Joel E. Spingarn to W. E. B. Du Bois, Oct. 24, 1914, Joel E. Spingarn Papers, JWJC; Du Bois to Spingarn, Dec. 11, 1916, folder 141, box 95-2, Joel E. Spingarn Papers, M-SRC; Du Bois to Spingarn, Dec. 29, 1916, Jan. 2, 20, 1917, ibid.; Du Bois, *Dusk of Dawn: An Essay toward an Autobiography of a Race Concept* (New York: Harcourt, Brace, 1940), 255. On the literary relationship between Du Bois and Spingarn, see also George Hutchinson, *The Harlem Renaissance in Black and White* (Cambridge: Harvard University Press, 1997), 45–49.

4. Counter-Espionage Situation Summary, May 18, 1918, MID File 10641-196(51), RG 165, NA.

5. War Dept. Special Order No. 119, May 21, 1918, Papers of Joel E. Spingarn, NYPL; M. Churchill to Chief of Staff, July ?, 1918, MID File 10996-36, RG 165, NA; *Crisis* 15 (Jan. 1918), 112; Ross, *J. E. Spingarn,* 97–98.

6. Peyton C. March, *A Nation At War* (Garden City, N.Y.: Doubleday, Doran, 1932), 40–41. See also Edward M. Coffman, *The Hilt of the Sword: The Career of Peyton C. March* (Madison: University of Wisconsin Press, 1966), 53. On the bureau system, see Robert H. Ferrell, *Woodrow Wilson and World War I, 1917–1921* (New York: Harper & Row, 1985), 25–30; Koistinen, *Mobilizing for Modern War,* 90–93, 151–55, 184–87, 295–96.

7. March, *Nation at War,* 226–27.

8. Herbert Parsons to J. Spingarn, Aug. 15, 1917, MID File 10218-1, RG 165, NA; Parsons memo, Aug. 19, 1917, ibid.; Spingarn to Parsons, Aug. 25, 1917, MID File 10218-3, RG 165, NA; Van Deman to Chief of Staff, Sept. 1, 1917, MID File 10218-7, RG 165, NA; Du Bois to Scott, March 4, 11, 1918, Papers of W. E. B. Du Bois, reel 7, UML; Scott to Du Bois, May 15, 1918, ibid.

9. Spingarn to Churchill, June 10, 1918, MID File 10218-154, RG 165, NA.

10. Churchill to Charles H. Studin, June 3, 1918, File 10218-158, RG 165, NA; Studin to Churchill, June 12, 1918, MID File 10218-139, RG 165, NA. Studin was the law partner of Joel Spingarn's brother, Arthur B. Spingarn. See Kellogg, *NAACP,* 61. On Van Deman's removal as MIB director, see Roy Talbert, Jr., *Negative Intelligence: The Army and the American Left, 1917–1941* (Jackson: University Press of Mississippi, 1991), 27–29.

11. *Official Bulletin,* Dec. 4, 1917; *Baltimore Afro-American,* Dec. 8, 1917; Kellogg, *NAACP,* 256–57.

12. Richard B. Sherman, *The Republican Party and Black America from McKinley*

to Hoover, 1896–1933 (Charlottesville: University Press of Virginia, 1973), 117–18; Kellogg, *NAACP,* 190–93.

13. C. D. Gensch to chief, MIB, Jan. 10, 1918, MID File 10218-76, RG 165, NA.

14. Spingarn to Parsons, Aug. 25, 1917, MID File 10218-7, RG 165, NA.

15. Churchill to J. L. Chamberlain, June 19, 1918, MID File 10218-154, RG 165, NA; *Baltimore Afro-American,* May 31, July 12, 1918; J. M. Waldron and T. M. Gregory to Woodrow Wilson, May 11, 1918, *Papers of Woodrow Wilson,* vol. 42, ed. Arthur S. Link (Princeton: Princeton University Press, 1983), 321–32. Gregory was active in the Harlem Renaissance of the 1920s. See Alain Locke and Montgomery Gregory, eds. *Plays of Negro Life* (New York: Harper and Brothers, 1927); Bruce Kellner, ed., *The Harlem Renaissance: A Historical Dictionary for the Era* (New York: Methuen, 1987), 144.

16. R. F. Britton to chief, MIB, July 9, 1918, MID File 10218-60, -154, RG 165, NA; Scott to Spingarn, July 13, July 25, August 1, 1918, ibid.; Spingarn to Scott, July 27, 1918, ibid.; J. J. Gleason to Spingarn, n.d., MID File 10218-196, RG 165, NA; Churchill to IO, Southeastern Dept., June 5, 1918, MID File 10218-160, RG 165, NA; Churchill to IO, Fort Sam Houston, June 8, 1918, MID File 10218-164, RG 165, NA. On the controversy surrounding *The Birth of a Nation,* see Thomas R. Cripps, "The Reaction of the Negro to the Motion Picture *Birth of a Nation*," *Historian* 25 (1962–63), 344–62; Kellogg, *NAACP,* 142–45. See also Carolyn Wedin, *Inheritors of the Spirit: Mary White Ovington and the Founding of the NAACP* (New York: John Wiley, 1998), 148–55. Emmett Scott founded a film company to produce a response to Griffith. Titled *The Birth of a Race,* it was released soon after the Armistice. See Marshall Hyatt, ed., *The Afro-American Cinematic Experience: An Annotated Bibliography and Filmography* (Wilmington, Del.: Scholarly Resources, Inc., 1983), 188; Thomas R. Cripps, "The Making of *The Birth of a Race:* The Emerging Politics of Identity in Silent Movies," in *The Birth of Whiteness: Race and the Emergence of U.S. Cinema,* ed. Daniel Bernardi (New Brunswick, N.J.: Rutgers University Press, 1996), 38–55.

17. Peyton C. March to Pershing, cablegram 1523, June 14, 1918, MID File 10218-154, RG 165, NA; Pershing to adjutant general, D. C., cablegram 1335, June 20, 1918, ibid.; War Dept. press release, June 20, 1918, ibid.; *Washington Post* clipping, n.d., ibid. See also *Official Bulletin,* July 22, 1918.

18. Spingarn to Churchill, June 10, 1918, MID File 10218-154, RG 165, NA; *Chicago Tribune,* April 15, 1918, headlined "Creel Lulls U.S. as Foe within Helps Germany"; *New York Independent,* n.d., reprinted in *Crisis* 16 (May 1918), 24; *Christian Science Monitor,* May 31, 1918. See also Jane Lang Scheiber and Harry N. Scheiber, "The Wilson Administration and the Wartime Mobilization of Black Americans, 1917–1918," *Labor History* 10 (Summer 1969), 437–38; George Creel to Wilson, June 17, 1918, case file 152, Series 4, Woodrow Wilson Papers, LC; Wilson to Creel, June 18, 1918, ibid. That Wilson found black lobbying an unwelcome intrusion is suggested by Robert Russa Moton's wish that he could "relieve the President of any embarrassment which might be occasioned by so many delegations of colored people calling at the White House." Moton to Joseph Tumulty, March 6, 1918, case file 575, series 4, Woodrow Wilson Papers, LC.

19. On Trotter's meetings with Wilson, see Christine A. Lunardini, "Standing Firm: William Monroe Trotter's Meetings with Woodrow Wilson, 1913–14," *Journal of Negro History* 64 (Summer 1979), 244–64; *Papers of Woodrow Wilson,* vol. 31, ed. Link (1979), 298–329.

20. Fred W. Moore to Churchill, June 5, 19, July 15, 1918, MID File 10218-153, RG 165, NA; Churchill to Moore, June 13, 1918, ibid.

21. "Conference of Colored Editors, June 19–21: List of Conferees," compiled by Spingarn, n.d., MID File 10218-154, RG 165, NA. The two absentees were Kelly Miller of Howard University and former Assistant Attorney General William H. Lewis of Boston. The most prominent editors were Du Bois (*Crisis*), Fred R. Moore (*New York Age*), Robert S. Abbott (*Chicago Defender*), Robert L. Vann (*Pittsburgh Courier*), J. H. Murphy (*Baltimore Afro-American*), Ed Warren (*Amsterdam News*), and J. Finley Wilson (*Washington Eagle*). The churchmen were led by John R. Hawkins (AME Church). The educators included Major Allen W. Washington (Booker T. Washington's son, from Hampton), Robert Russa Moton (Tuskegee), and George W. Cook (Howard), who was a director of the NAACP. The office-holders included George E. Haynes (director of the Division of Negro Economics, Department of Labor) and Charles W. Anderson (assistant New York State commissioner for agriculture). The disproportionately large group from the capital included Hawkins, Cook, Assistant District Attorney James A. Cobb, NAACP branch president Archibald H. Grimké, Assistant Superintendent of Schools Roscoe Conkling Bruce, and former Lieutenant Governor of Louisiana P. B. S. Pinchback.

22. *New York Times,* July 7, 1918.

23. Spingarn to Churchill, June 22, 1918, MID File 10218-154, RG 165, NA; *Washington Bee,* July 13, 1918. Arthur Spingarn sat on the NAACP board and was interested in venereal-disease prevention. See A. B. Spingarn, *Laws Relating to Sex Morality in New York City* (New York: Century, 1915); *The War and Venereal Diseases among Negroes* (New York: American Social Hygiene Association, 1918).

24. "Conference of Colored Editors, June 19 to 21, 1918. Address to the Committee of Public Information," MID File 10218-154, RG 165, NA. See also draft of this document in Papers of W. E. B. Du Bois, reel 7, UML. For Du Bois's views on the war, see *Crisis* 9 (Nov. 1914), 28–30; ibid. 14, (Aug. 1917), 165; ibid. 16, (June 1918), 60. See also Elliott M. Rudwick, *W. E. B. Du Bois: Propagandist of the Negro Protest,* 2nd ed. (Philadelphia: University of Pennsylvania Press, 1968), 193–203; Arnold Rampersad, *The Art and Imagination of W. E. B. Du Bois* (Cambridge: Harvard University Press, 1976), 143, 161, 201.

25. "Conference of Colored Editors, June 19 to 21, 1918. Address to the Committee of Public Information," MID File 10218-154, RG 165, NA.

26. "Conference of Colored Editors, June 19 to 21, 1918. Bill of Particulars . . . ," ibid. The list included a federal anti-lynching law, unhindered entrance into government service, abolition of Jim Crow railroad cars, better treatment for black soldiers, and clemency for the remaining men of the 24th Infantry under sentence of death. On the question of nurses, see Darlene Clark Hine, "The Call That Never Came: Black Women Nurses and World War I, an Historical Note," *Indiana Military History Journal* (Jan. 1983), 23–27.

27. Spingarn to Churchill, June 22, 1918, MID File 10218-154, RG 165, NA.

28. Churchill to chief of staff, July 2, 1918, ibid.

29. Creel to Wilson, July 5, 1918, case file 152, series 4, Woodrow Wilson Papers, LC. Creel sent Wilson a fuller account of the conference by Emmett Scott, which included excerpts from the resolutions. See Scott to Wilson, June 26, 1918, ibid. It took an approach from Newton D. Baker to secure a reply from Wilson to Scott. See Baker to Wilson, July 14, 1918, ibid.; Wilson to Scott, July 31, 1918, ibid.

30. Scheiber and Scheiber, "The Wilson Administration," 450. Tyler was a former auditor of the navy, who lost his job when Wilson succeeded Taft in 1913. He peddled the War Department line while in France, where three of his sons were serving, but later he denounced the army's treatment of black troops. See *Chicago Defender,* March 8, 1919; *Cleveland Advocate,* June 14, 1919. On his Tuskegee links, see Louis R. Harlan, *Booker T. Washington: The Wizard of Tuskegee, 1901–1915* (New York: Oxford University Press, 1983), 324, 329, 365.

31. *Baltimore Afro-American,* July 5, 1918; *Indianapolis Freeman,* July 6, 1918; *St. Louis Argus,* July 5, 1918; Britton to chief, MIB, July 9, 1918, MID File 10218-144, RG 165, NA. By agreement, coverage of the conference was held up until Scott issued an official press release through the Committee on Public Information. On John E. Mitchell's editorship of the *St. Louis Argus,* see George E. Slavens, "Missouri," in *The Black Press in the South, 1865–1979,* ed. Henry L. Suggs (Westport, Conn.: Greenwood, 1983), 215–44.

32. IO, Northeastern Dept., to Churchill, July 15, 1918, MID File 10218-154, RG 165, NA; Addresses at Colored Liberty Congress, June 24–27, 1918, ibid.

33. H. R. 11279, H. R. 11554, 65 Cong., 2 sess.; Zangrando, *NAACP Crusade,* 43–44, 54–61; Sherman, *Republican Party and Black America,* 179–95.

34. I. A. Newby, *Jim Crow's Defense: Anti-Negro Thought in America, 1900–1930* (Baton Rouge: Louisiana State University Press, 1965), 138–40; Kellogg, *NAACP,* 231; Ralph Ginzburg, *100 Years of Lynchings* (New York: Lancer, 1962), 94, 244; Sherman, *Republican Party and Black America,* 181, 184–85; Neil R. McMillen, *Dark Journey: Black Mississippians in the Age of Jim Crow* (Urbana: University of Illinois Press, 1990), 234–35. See also Claudine L. Ferrell, *Nightmare and Dream: Antilynching in Congress, 1917–1922* (New York: Garland, 1986), 89–149, 345–428.

35. J. R. Shillady to J. P. Tumulty, Feb. 18, 1918, in *Papers of Woodrow Wilson,* vol. 46, ed. Link (1984), 380–81; *Norfolk Journal and Guide,* Aug. 25, 1917.

36. New England Baptist Missionary Convention leaflet, Feb. 1918, in BI File OG 311587, RG 65, NA; Zangrando, *NAACP Crusade,* 45.

37. "Lynching," *Outlook* 119 (June 5, 1918), 214. See also "Lynching: A National Disgrace," ibid. (June 26, 1918), 339.

38. G. S. Hornblower to Spingarn, May 31, 1918, MID File 10996-36, RG 165, NA. The Legislative Branch sent many recommendations to Congress relating to the war, including a detailed discussion of possible laws to tackle subversion, radicalism, and Bolshevism, prior to the passage of the Sedition Act. This role was agreed on at one of the twice-weekly joint conferences of the federal intelligence agencies. See Memo to Col. Van Deman, "Subject: Counter-Espionage Legislation Suggested," April 17, 1918, MID File 10996-41, RG 165, NA.

39. Moorfield Storey to Walter F. White, July 11, 1918, J. E. Spingarn Papers, M-SRC. On Storey's later decision to support the Dyer bill, see W. B. Hixson, Jr., "Moorfield Storey and the Defense of the Dyer Anti-Lynching Bill," *New England Quarterly* 42 (1969), 65–81. Article I of the Constitution empowers Congress "to declare war," "to raise and support armies," and "to make all laws which shall be necessary and proper for carrying into execution the foregoing powers."

40. House Committee on the Judiciary, *To Protect Citizens against Lynching,* hearing on HR 11279, Serial 66: statements of Maj. J. E. Spingarn and Capt. G. S. Hornblower, 65 Cong., 2 sess., June 6, 1918, 3–4.

41. Ibid., 4, 11, 13. The NAACP's demand for federal investigation of the East St. Louis race riot was made partly on the grounds that it had caused draft registration of black residents to become "confused and aborted." See Elliott M. Rudwick, *Race Riot at East St. Louis, July 2, 1917* (New York: Atheneum, 1972) 262.

42. *To Protect Citizens against Lynching,* 4–6, 8, 9, 12–13. Kellogg calls Hornblower's draft "the Gard bill," after its sponsor, Rep. Warren Gard (D-Ohio). It was made obsolete by the Armistice (Kellogg, *NAACP,* 232).

43. Joel E. Spingarn to Amy Spingarn, June 9, 1918, folder 580, box 95-15, Joel E. Spingarn Papers, M-SRC.

44. House Committee on the Judiciary, *To Protect Citizens against Lynching,* part 2, "Brief of Capt. G. S. Hornblower," 65 Cong., 2 sess., July 12, 1918.

45. Bolton Smith to Spingarn, July 3, 1918, MID File 10996-36, RG 165, NA; Spingarn to Smith, July 12, 1918, ibid.; W. M. Lewis to Spingarn, July 22, 1918, ibid.; Spingarn to Lewis, July 23, 1918, ibid.

46. Spingarn to Churchill, June 24, July 22, 1918, MID File 10996-36, RG 165, NA; Churchill to chief of staff, June 27, July 5, 1918, ibid.; Clifford Jones to chief, MIB, June 28, 1918, ibid.; Churchill to Edwin Y. Webb, July 12, 1918, ibid.

47. Moton to Spingarn, July 13, 1918, enc. copies of Moton to Wilson, June 15, 1918, and Wilson to Moton, June 25, 1918, MID File 10218-154, RG 165, NA. Moton confidentially sent copies of his correspondence with Wilson to other equal rights campaigners. For example, see Moton to A. H. Grimké, July 12, 1918, A. H. Grimké Papers, M-SRC.

48. Spingarn to Churchill, July 22, 1918, MID File 10996-36, RG 165, NA. For example, Spingarn quoted the declaration of the Tennessee Conference of Charities in May 1918:

> The excitement connected with this stupendous war appears to have undermined the self-control of some of the American people to such an extent that lynchings seem to be occurring with increasing frequency; and [this] . . . strikes at the very root of our national solidarity and efficiency, by raising issues of race and of blood among our own people and will inevitably increase the length of the war and the cost in dead and wounded we will have to pay for victory and thus give aid and comfort to the enemy.

See also *Outlook* 119 (June 5, 1918), 214–16.

49. Spingarn to Churchill, July 22, 1918, MID File 10996-36, RG 165, NA; *Amsterdam News,* May 29, 1918.

50. Spingarn to Churchill, July 2, 1918, MID File 10996-36, RG 165, NA.

51. Ibid.

52. Michael I. Handel, *War, Strategy and Intelligence* (London: Frank Cass, 1989), 208–209.

53. Wilson to Moton, Dec. 4, 1918, in *Papers of Woodrow Wilson*, vol. 40, ed. Link (1982), 218. For examples of the pressures on Wilson to speak out on lynching, see M. Storey, J. E. Spingarn, W. E. B. Du Bois, O. G. Villard, et al. to Wilson, Feb. 13, 1918, ibid., vol. 41, ed. Link (1983), 217–18; petition presented by James Weldon Johnson et al., Feb. 19, 1918, ibid., vol. 46, ed. Link (1984), 383–85; J. M. Waldron and J. MacMurray to Wilson, May 25, 1918, Moton to Wilson, June 15, 1918, J. R. Shillady to Wilson, July 25, 1918, ibid., vol. 49, ed. Link (1985), 61–62, 88–89; James Weldon Johnson, *Along This Way: The Autobiography of James Weldon Johnson* (New York: Penguin, 1990, first published 1933), 323–25.

54. Baker to Wilson, July 1, 1918, in *Papers of Woodrow Wilson*, vol. 48, ed. Link (1985), 475–76.

55. *Official Bulletin,* July 26, 1918, 1–2.

56. George Creel, *Rebel at Large: Recollections of Fifty Crowded Years* (New York: G. P. Putnam's Sons, 1947), 199. On the lynching of Robert Praeger, see H. C. Petersen and Gilbert C. Fite, *Opponents of War, 1917–1918* (Seattle: University of Washington Press, 1968), 202–207.

57. Moton to Wilson, July 27, 1918, *Papers of Woodrow Wilson*, vol. 48, ed. Link (1985), 475–76.

58. "The Massacre of East St. Louis," *Crisis* 14 (Sept. 1917), 219–38; "Thirteen," ibid. 15 (Jan. 1918), 114.

59. "The Negro and the War Department," ibid. 16 (May 1918), 7.

60. Du Bois to Emmett J. Scott, April 24, 1918, MID File 10218-129, RG 165, NA; Scott to chief, MIB, April 25, 1918, ibid.

61. Spingarn to Du Bois, June 4, 1918, MID File 10996-36, RG 165, NA.

62. Bielaski to De Woody, June 4, 1918, MID File 10218-139, RG 165, NA; Alfred Bettman to Bielaski, June 1, 5, 1918, BI File OG 17011, RG 65, NA.

63. Spingarn to Amy Spingarn, June 9, 1918, folder 580, box 95-15, Joel E. Spingarn Papers, M-SRC.

64. Manning Marable, *W. E. B. Du Bois: Black Radical Democrat* (Boston: Twayne, 1986), 66–74, 136–43; David Levering Lewis, *W. E. B. Du Bois: Biography of a Race, 1868–1919* (New York: Henry Holt, 1993), 379, 386–87; Du Bois to Archibald Grimké, July 1, 1918, A. H. Grimké Papers, M-SRC. On Du Bois's often poor relations with some members of the NAACP board, especially Oswald Garrison Villard, see Kellogg, *NAACP,* 94–115; *The Correspondence of W. E. B. Du Bois,* ed. Herbert Aptheker, 3 vols. (Amherst: University of Massachusetts Press, 1973–78), vol. 1, 153–64; Lewis, *W. E. B. Du Bois,* 491–99. See also Villard to Mary White Ovington, Nov. 19, 1913, Aug. 11, 1915, Oct. 6, 1917, folder 1, box 120, Papers of Oswald Garrison Villard, HL; Villard to Roscoe Conkling Bruce, Jan. 6, 1916, folder 409, ibid.; Villard to Jessie Fauset, Feb. 24, 1920, folder 946.2, ibid. See also Wedin, *Inheritors of the Spirit,* 137–48.

65. Spingarn to Churchill, June 10, 1918, MID File 10218-154, RG 165, NA.

66. W. E. B. Du Bois, *The Autobiography of W. E. B. Du Bois: A Soliloquy on Viewing My Life from the Last Decade of Its First Century* (New York: International Publishers, 1968), 410; W. E. B. Du Bois Record Card, File 9961-3851, RG 165, NA. (The file summarized on the record card was destroyed with seven thousand other inactive applications in the 1940s.) Churchill to Du Bois, July 30, 1918, folder 5, box 7, Papers of Joel E. Spingarn, NYPL; U.S. Congress, *Biographical Directory of the American Congress, 1774–1971* (Washington, D.C.: U.S. Government Printing Office, 1971), 820. Wendell Phillips Stafford came from an abolitionist family and knew the NAACP through Oswald Garrison Villard. See Kellogg, *NAACP,* 17, 305. In 1913, in congressional debates, Wesley L. Jones sought fairer funding for black colleges. In 1917 he presented the third Spingarn medal for achievement by a black American. See Dewey W. Grantham, Jr., *Hoke Smith and the Politics of the New South* (Baton Rouge: Louisiana State University Press, 1958), 261–62; *Norfolk Journal and Guide,* May 12, 1917. On Du Bois's illness, see ibid., Jan. 6, Jan. 13, 1917.

67. Spingarn to Amy Spingarn, June 18, 1918, folder 583, box 95-15, Joel E. Spingarn Papers, M-SRC; Churchill to J. L. Chamberlain, June 19, 1918, MID File 10218-154, RG 165, NA; Spingarn to Churchill, June 22, 1918, ibid.; W. E. B. Du Bois Record Card, File 9961-3851, RG 165, NA.

68. "Close Ranks," *Crisis* 16 (July 1918), 111.

69. Spingarn to Amy Spingarn, June 26, 1918, folder 583, box 95-15, Joel E. Spingarn Papers, M-SRC.

70. Scott to Spingarn, June 26, 1918, folder 392, box 95-5, ibid.; Spingarn to Churchill, July 6, 1918, MID File 10218-154, RG 165, NA; Churchill, note written on Spingarn's memorandum of July 6, 1918, ibid.

71. William H. Wilson to Du Bois, June 25, 1918, Papers of W. E. B. Du Bois, reel 7, UML.

72. Studin to Du Bois, May 1, 1918, ibid.

73. Du Bois to Grimké, July 1, 1918, A. H. Grimké Papers, M-SRC; Du Bois to Arthur B. Spingarn, July 1, 1918, folder 443, box 94-20, Arthur B. Spingarn Papers, M-SRC; G. W. Cook to Du Bois, July 3, 1918, George W. Cook Papers, M-SRC.

74. Hutchins C. Bishop to Du Bois, July 3, 1918, Papers of W. E. B. Du Bois, reel 6, UML; George W. Crawford to Du Bois, July 3, 1918, ibid.; John Hurst to Du Bois, July 3, 1918, ibid.; Verina Morton Jones to Du Bois, July 3, 1918, ibid.; Arthur B. Spingarn to Du Bois, July 3, 1918, ibid.; Morefield Storey to Du Bois, July 3, 1918, ibid.; Charles Young to Du Bois, July 3, 1918, ibid.; Charles Nagel to Du Bois, July 5, 1918, ibid.; Garnett R. Waller to Du Bois, July 5, 1918, ibid.; C. E. Bentley to Du Bois, July 6, 1918, ibid.; "[Paul] Kennady votes in favor . . . " (handwritten note), July 5, 1918, ibid.

75. Du Bois to Spingarn, July 9, 1918, Joel E. Spingarn Papers, JWJC; NAACP board minutes, July 8, 1918, box A-8, Board of Directors File, NAACP Papers, LC. NAACP Secretary John R. Shillady later told Joel Spingarn that the pacifist/pro-war split at the meeting was not decisive. See Kellogg, *NAACP,* 272.

76. NAACP board minutes, July 8, 1918, box A-8, Board of Directors File, NAACP Papers, LC. On the Washington branch, see Shillady to Grimké, May 6,

1918, A. H. Grimké Papers, M-SRC; Eugene D. Levy, *James Weldon Johnson: Black Voice, Black Leader* (Chicago: University of Chicago Press, 1973), 194.

77. Du Bois to Spingarn, July 9, 1918, Joel E. Spingarn Papers, JWJC.

78. Spingarn to Amy Spingarn, July 10, 1918, folder 580, box 95-15, Joel E. Spingarn Papers, M-SRC; Spingarn to Studin, July 10, 1918, Papers of W. E. B. Du Bois, reel 6, UML.

79. Mary White Ovington to Du Bois, July 10, 1918, Papers of W. E. B. Du Bois, reel 6, UML; Du Bois to Ovington, July 11, 1918, ibid.

80. *New York News,* July 18, 1918, clipping in folder 538, box 95-6, Joel E. Spingarn Papers, M-SRC; *Washington Eagle,* July 13, 1918, clipping in BI File OG 311587, RG 65, NA.

81. *Washington Bee,* July 13, 1918; *New York News,* July 18, 1918. Du Bois also gained support from the *Norfolk Journal and Guide.* See Henry Lewis Suggs, *P. B. Young, Newspaperman: Race, Politics, and Journalism in the New South, 1910–1962* (Charlottesville: University Press of Virginia, 1988), 37. Walter White, the NAACP's assistant secretary, wrote Spingarn that "all of the people here [in Washington] have not lost their heads" over the commission. Walter White to Joel E. Spingarn, July 18, 1918, folder 5, box 7, Papers of Joel E. Spingarn, NYPL. The earliest reports about Du Bois joining the army assumed that he would give up his *Crisis* editorship. See *Washington Bee,* July 6, 1918.

82. Du Bois to Spingarn, July 12, 1918, Papers of W. E. B. Du Bois, reel 6, UML; Du Bois to John Hope, July 12, 1918, ibid.; Hope to Du Bois, July 22, 1918, ibid. See also Leroy Davis, *A Clashing of the Soul: John Hope and the Dilemma of African American Leadership and Black Higher Education in the Early Twentieth Century* (Athens: University of Georgia Press, 1998), 238–39, 389 n59.

83. J. W. E. Bowen to Du Bois, Aug. 8, 1918, Papers of W. E. B. Du Bois, reel 6, UML; Robert Russa Moton to Du Bois, July 17, 1918, ibid.; George C. Bradford to Du Bois, July 13, 1918. ibid.; Henry Lincoln Johnson to Du Bois, July 18, 1918, ibid.; W. H. Bentley to Du Bois, Aug. 10, 1918, ibid.

84. Byron Gunner to Du Bois, July 16, 1918, ibid.; Gunner to Du Bois, July 25, 1918, reel 7, ibid.

85. Spingarn to Amy Spingarn, July 14, July 16, 1918, folder 580, box 95-15, Joel E. Spingarn Papers, M-SRC.

86. Spingarn to Du Bois, July 16, 1918, Papers of W. E. B. Du Bois, reel 6, UML. For an example of the spreading news of Du Bois's enlistment, see Bettman to Bielaski, July 9, 1918, BI File OG 17011, RG 65, NA.

87. Du Bois to Spingarn, July 19, 1918, Joel E. Spingarn Papers, JWJC. On Johnson's journalistic activities and his identification with Tuskegee prior to 1917, see Kellogg, *NAACP,* 133–34; Levy, *James Weldon Johnson,* 167–70, 189; Harlan, *Booker T. Washington,* 18–19. On the low pay of newly commissioned army officers serving in the U.S., the Canal Zone, Puerto Rico, and Hawaii, see "Uncle Sam as Army Paymaster," *New York Times Magazine,* Sept. 9, 1917, 5.

88. *New York News,* July 18, 1918; *Boston Guardian,* July 20, 1918. On Du Bois's criticism of the black press, see Kellogg, *NAACP,* 98–99; Lewis, *W. E. B. Du Bois,* 416–17.

89. *Baltimore Afro-American*, July 26, 1918; *Washington Bee*, July 27, 1918.

90. Talbert, *Negative Intelligence*, 88–89, 145. For examples of anti-Semitism in military intelligence reports, see ibid., 87–88, 205–206. On the virtual absence of Jews from the staff ranks of the United States Army, see Hilaire Belloc, *The Contrast* (London: J. W. Arrowsmith, 1923), 197–98.

91. James A. Bruff, "Memorandum re. Officers and Directors of the National Association for the Advancement of Colored People," July 13, 1918, MID File 10218-158, RG 165, NA.

92. Harry A. Taylor to Alexander B. Coxe, July 19, 1918, MID File 10218-139, RG 165, NA.

93. Churchill to Chief of Staff, Aug. 20, 1919, MID File 10218-361, RG 165, NA; Walter H. Loving memo, Feb. ?, 1918, MID File 10218-109, RG 165, NA.

94. Loving to chief, MIB, July 15, 1918, enc. *New York Voice* clipping, July 11, 1918, MID File 10218-185, RG 165, NA. Hubert Harrison recycled his report for the MIB as a *Voice* editorial on July 25, 1918. See Hubert H. Harrison, *When Africa Awakes: The 'Inside Story' of the Stirrings and Strivings of the New Negro in the Western World* (New York: Porro Press, 1920), 66–70. On Harrison's career, see Theodore G. Vincent, *Black Power and the Garvey Movement* (Berkeley: Ramparts Press, n.d.), 39–42, 78, 79; Kellner, *The Harlem Renaissance*, 158–59; Wilfred D. Samuels, "Hubert H. Harrison and 'The New Negro Manhood Movement,'" *Afro-Americans in New York Life and History* 5 (Jan. 1981), 29–41; *American National Biography*, ed. John A. Garraty and Mark C. Carnes (New York: Oxford University Press, 1999), vol. 10, s.v. "Harrison, Hubert Henry." See also Kevin K. Gaines, *Uplifting the Race: Black Leadership, Politics, and Culture in the Twentieth Century* (Chapel Hill: University of North Carolina Press, 1996), 238–46.

95. Harrison, *When Africa Awakes*, 68, 70.

96. Loving to Nicholas Biddle, July 22, 1918, folder 10, box 113-1, Papers of Walter H. Loving, M-SRC. Loving never suggested that Du Bois was disloyal and he had assured Van Deman that Spingarn "would not allow his name to be connected with any publication that the government would brand as being possible [*sic*] pro-German." Loving to chief, MIB, May 30, 1918, File 10218-139, RG 165, NA. In 1916, Du Bois had unsuccessfully nominated Loving as the recipient of the 1917 Spingarn medal because of his achievements as a musical director in the Philippines. See "Digest of Recommendations for the Spingarn Medal (1917)," folder 1, box 120, Papers of Oswald Garrison Villard, HL.

97. Biddle to Churchill, July 22, 1918, folder 10, box 113-1, Papers of Walter H. Loving, M-SRC.

98. Spingarn to Hunt, July 20, 1918, folder 5, box 7, Papers of Joel E. Spingarn, NYPL.

99. Spingarn to Studin, July 30, 1918, MID File 10218-139, RG 165, NA; Churchill to MI-4, July 29, 1918, MID File 10218-154, RG 165, NA; Churchill to Hunt, July 30, 1918, folder 5, box 7, Papers of Joel E. Spingarn, NYPL.

100. Churchill to Spingarn, July 30, 1918, ibid.; Churchill to Du Bois, July 30, 1918, ibid.; Spingarn to Du Bois, July 30, 1918, Papers of W. E. B. Du Bois, reel 6, UML. The agency Churchill had in mind was probably the Bureau of Investigation,

but he may have meant Emmett Scott's office or that of George E. Haynes, the Division of Negro Economics in the Department of Labor.

101. Van Deman to IO, YMCA, New York, May 6, 1918, MID File 10218-139, RG 165, NA.

102. Hunt to Du Bois, July 30, 1918, Papers of W. E. B. Du Bois, reel 7, UML.

103. Spingarn to Scott, Aug. 1, 1918, MID File 10218-154, RG 165, NA; Scott to Spingarn, Aug. 1, 1918, ibid. See also Scott to Du Bois, Aug. 13, 1918, Papers of W. E. B. Du Bois, reel 7, UML.

104. Lewis, *W. E. B. Du Bois,* 560.

105. Thomas Jesse Jones to Churchill, July 24, 1918, MID File 10218-154, RG 165, NA; Jones to F. P. Keppel, July 27, 1918, MID File 10218-190, RG 165, NA; Hunt to Scott, Aug. 6, 1918, MID File 10218-60, RG 165, NA; Churchill to Scott, Aug. 8, 1918, MID File 10218-196, RG 165, NA; E. L. Munson to J. J. Gleason, Oct. 21, 1918, ibid. On the Morale Section, see Thomas Camfield, "'Will to Win'—The U.S. Army Troop Morale Program of World War I," *Military Affairs* 41 (Oct. 1977), 125–28.

106. Newton D. Baker to William F. Kirby, July 16, 1919, MID File 10218-343, RG 165, NA. Spingarn served with distinction in France as a corps commander, staff officer, and special intelligence gatherer for General Pershing. See Ross, *J. E. Spingarn,* 101–102.

107. Du Bois, *Dusk of Dawn,* 257; Kellogg, *NAACP,* 274–75; Rudwick, *W. E. B. Du Bois,* 345; Spingarn to Shillady, Aug. 2, 1918, MID File 10218-158, RG 165, NA; Shillady to NAACP board of directors, Aug. 6, 1918, NAACP File, Papers of Joel E. Spingarn, NYPL.

108. "A Philosophy in Time of War," *Crisis* 16 (Aug. 1918), 164; "A Momentous Proposal," ibid. (Sept. 1918), 215–16; "Our Special Grievances," ibid., 216–17.

109. "Dr. Du Bois as Chauvinist and Sophist" and "Is Dr. Du Bois a Leader or a Follower?" *Negro World,* Aug. 29, 1918, 2, clipping in MID File 10675-31, RG 165, NA.

110. Lafayette M. Hershaw to Du Bois, July 30, 1918, Papers of W. E. B. Du Bois, reel 6, UML; Du Bois to Hershaw, Aug. 5, 1918, ibid.

111. *Crisis* 16 (Sept. 1918), 215–16; Du Bois, *Dusk of Dawn,* 256. The 24th Infantry executions took place on December 11, 1917, whereupon Du Bois attacked them in the January *Crisis.* See "Thirteen," *Crisis* 15 (Jan. 1918), 114. The "Close Ranks" affair was not the first time he had used the excuse of printing deadlines to deflect criticism. See William Toll, *The Resurgence of Race: Black Social Theory from Reconstruction to the Pan-African Conferences* (Philadelphia: Temple University Press, 1979), 165–66.

112. *Crisis* 16 (Sept. 1918), 216.

113. On the Amenia conference, see Kellogg, *NAACP,* 87–88; Ross, *J. E. Spingarn,* 47–48; Lewis, *W. E. B. Du Bois,* 517–22.

114. For a discussion of these options, see E. Franklin Frazier, "The American Negro's New Leaders," *Current History* 28 (Sept. 1928), 56–59.

115. Neval Thomas to Villard, Sept. 3, 1918, folder 2, box 120, Papers of Oswald Garrison Villard, HL; Thomas to Villard, May 2, 1919, ibid.; Villard to Thomas,

May 7, 1919, ibid. Thomas told Villard in the Sept. 3, 1918, letter that African Americans in Washington knew all about the commission in May 1918, but this was almost certainly untrue. It is clear from this letter that Thomas, at least, believed that Villard was going to try to use the "Close Ranks" episode to oust both Du Bois and Spingarn from the NAACP and fill their positions with James Weldon Johnson and Villard, himself.

116. Thomas to Scott, May 3, 1919, copied by Du Bois to Spingarn, June 18, 1919, folder 141, box 95-2, Joel E. Spingarn Papers, M-SRC; Du Bois to John Haynes Holmes, April 24, 1919, box A-19, Board of Directors File, NAACP Papers, LC; Du Bois to nominating committee, June 19, 1919, ibid.; Thomas to Grimké, July 28, 1919, A. H. Grimké Papers, M-SRC. On Thomas's career, see Marshall Hyatt, "Neval H. Thomas and Federal Segregation," *Negro History Bulletin* 42 (Oct.–Dec. 1979), 96–97, 100–102. On Thomas's clash with Du Bois in 1928, see Levy, *James Weldon Johnson,* 226–27.

117. H. A. Phelps, "Selling Out the Race," *Half-Century Magazine* 6 (Feb. 1919), 9; *The Marcus Garvey and Universal Negro Improvement Association Papers,* ed. Robert A. Hill (Berkeley: University of California Press, 1983), vol. 1, 399, vol. 2, 525–26; Marcus Garvey, "W. E. Burghardt Du Bois as a Hater of Dark People," reprinted from *Negro World,* Feb. 13, 1923, in *The Philosophy and Opinions of Marcus Garvey, or Africa for the Africans,* ed. Amy Jacques Garvey (London: Frank Cass, 1977), 2nd ed., part 2, 313. By "dark water," Garvey was referring to Du Bois's collection of essays, *Darkwater,* published in 1920. On W. A. Domingo, see *Marcus Garvey Papers,* ed. Hill, vol. 1, 527–31.

118. *Crusader* 1 (Sept. 1918), 8; ibid. (Oct. 1918), 13–14. Garvey was exploiting a long-established, if erroneous, view among many African Americans that the NAACP was the preserve of light-skinned people. See Willard B. Gatewood, *Aristocrats of Color: The Black Elite, 1890–1920* (Bloomington: Indiana University Press, 1990), 314–22.

119. Carl S. Matthews, "After Booker T. Washington: The Search for a New Negro Leadership, 1915–1920" (Ph.d. diss., University of Virginia, 1971), 114, 120; "New Leadership for the Negro," *Messenger* 2 (May–June 1918), 9–10. See also Chandler Owen, "The Failure of the Negro Leaders," ibid. (Jan. 1918), 23; "The Crisis of the Crisis," ibid. 3 (July 1919), 10–12; "A Reply to Congressman James F. Byrnes of South Carolina," ibid. (Oct. 1919), 11–14; "Du Bois Fails as a Theorist," ibid. (Dec. 1919), 7–8. Chandler Owen chaired the April 1919 UNIA meeting at which Du Bois was criticized. On Du Bois's relations with other black radicals, see Marable, *W. E. B. Du Bois,* 109–20. On the damage done by "Close Ranks" to Du Bois's standing among black radicals, see also William H. Ferris, "Darkwater," *Africa and Orient Review,* June 1920, reprinted in *Voices of a Black Nation: Political Journalism in the Harlem Renaissance* (San Francisco: Ramparts Press, 1973), ed. Theodore G. Vincent, 242–48. Looking back on the war years, the poet and novelist Claude McKay thought the editorial standards and opinions of the *Messenger* "had the *Crisis* licked miles and miles." See Claude McKay to James Ivy, May 20, 1928, in *The Passion of Claude McKay: Selected Prose and Poetry, 1912–1948,* ed. Wayne F. Cooper (New York: Schocken Books, 1973), 145–47. On persistent ill feeling between Du

Bois and other black leaders following the publication of "Close Ranks," see also Dickson D. Bruce, Jr., *Archibald Grimké: Portrait of a Black Independent* (Baton Rouge: Louisiana State University Press, 1993), 226–53.

120. See, for examples of the uses to which "Close Ranks" has been put by historians, Rudwick, *W. E. B. Du Bois*, 202–203, 306–307; Francis L. Broderick, *W. E. B. Du Bois: Negro Leader in a Time of Crisis* (Stanford: Stanford University Press, 1959), 108–109, 121; August Meier and Elliott M. Rudwick, *From Plantation to Ghetto: An Interpretive History of American Negroes* (New York: Hill & Wang, 1966), 193–94; Ross, *J. E. Spingarn*, 98–101, 271–72; John Hope Franklin, *From Slavery to Freedom: A History of Negro Americans*, 5th ed. (New York: Alfred A. Knopf, 1980), 342; Ernest Allen, Jr., "'Close Ranks': Major Joel E. Springarn [*sic*] and the Two Souls of Dr. W. E. B. Du Bois," *Contributions in Black Studies* 3 (1979–80), 25–35; Mary Frances Berry and John W. Blassingame, *Long Memory: The Black Experience in America* (New York: Oxford University Press, 1982), 314; Marable, *W. E. B. Du Bois*, 96–97, 109; Carole Marks, *Farewell—We're Good and Gone: The Great Black Migration* (Bloomington: Indiana University Press, 1989), 95; McMillen, *Dark Journey*, 303; Judith Stein, *The World of Marcus Garvey: Race and Class in Modern Society* (Baton Rouge: Louisiana State University Press, 1986), 39–40; David M. Kennedy, *Over Here: The First World War and American Society* (New York: Oxford University Press, 1980), 279; Wynn, *From Progressivism to Prosperity*, 175. For an essay that employs "Close Ranks" as a summary of black leaders' responses to World War I, while arguing persuasively that the attitude of the black population at large was more complex, see Theodore Kornweibel, Jr., "Apathy and Dissent: Black America's Negative Responses to World War I," *South Atlantic Quarterly* 80 (Summer 1981), 322–38. On the effect of the controversy on the NAACP, see Kellogg, *NAACP*, 271–74. In a multi-faceted biography, Lewis, *W. E. B. Du Bois*, 553–60, concurs with some of the interpretations in this chapter. For further discussions, see William Jordan, "'The Damnable Dilemma': African-American Accommodation and Protest in World War I," *Journal of American History* 81 (March 1995), 1562–83; Mark Ellis, "W. E. B. Du Bois and the Formation of Black Opinion in World War I: A Commentary on 'The Damnable Dilemma,'" ibid., 1584–90.

6. Diplomacy and Demobilization, 1918–1919

1. Edward M. Coffman, *The Hilt of the Sword: The Career of Peyton C. March* (Madison: University of Wisconsin Press, 1966), 53.

2. Peyton C. March, *A Nation at War* (Garden City: Doubleday, Doran, 1932), 40–41.

3. Marc B. Powe, *The Emergence of the War Department Intelligence Agency: 1885–1918* (Manhattan: Kansas State University Press, 1975), 102; Walter C. Sweeney, *Military Intelligence: A New Weapon in War* (New York: Frederick A. Stokes, 1924), 87. By the Armistice, the MID in Washington consisted of 282 officers, 29 NCOs, and 948 civilian employees, housed in a seven-story apartment. March, *Nation at War*, 226; Marc B. Powe and Ed E. Wilson, *The Evolution of American Military Intelligence* (Fort Huachuca, Ariz.: U.S. Army Intelligence Center & School, 1973), 19.

4. Churchill took twenty MID officers with him to Paris. *Who Was Who in America*, vol. 2 (Chicago: Marquis–Who's Who, 1950), 115; March, *Nation at War*, 229.

5. March, *Nation at War*, 215; Marlborough Churchill, "The Military Intelligence Division, General Staff," *Journal of the United States Artillery* 52 (April 1920), diagram following p. 296.

6. J. E. Cutler to chief, Morale Branch, Dec. 9, 1918, MID File 10218-289, RG 165, NA.

7. Joan Jensen, *The Price of Vigilance* (Chicago: Rand McNally, 1968), 243; March, *Nation at War*, 228. Jensen gives November 20 as the date of this order; March gives November 30.

8. Robert Justin Goldstein, *Political Repression in Modern America, from 1870 to the Present* (Boston: G. K. Hall, 1978), 140; Jensen, *Price of Vigilance*, 246, 248.

9. Norman G. Thwaites, *Velvet and Vinegar* (London: Grayson and Grayson, 1932), 119–20, 131, 144, 222, 258; John B. Trevor to director, MID, Feb. 21, 1919, MID File 10218-158, RG 165, NA; Nathan Isaacs to Hayes, March 16, 1919, ibid.

10. Postal Censorship report, March 8, 1919, re Edgar McCarthy (secretary, Colon branch, UNIA) to Cecil Hope (secretary-general, UNIA, New York), Feb. 18, 1919, New York, MID File 10218-261, RG 165, NA.

11. J. M. Dunn to W. E. Allen, March 15, 1919, BI File OG 5911, RG 65, NA.

12. Rhodri Jeffreys-Jones, *American Espionage from Secret Service to CIA* (New York: The Free Press, 1977), 121.

13. *"Military Surveillance,"* Hearings before the Subcommittee on Constitutional Rights of the Committee on the Judiciary, U.S. Senate, 93 Cong., 2 sess., S2318, April 9, 10, 1974 (Washington, D.C.: U.S. Government Printing Office, 1974), testimony of Joan Jensen, 172; Goldstein, *Political Repression in Modern America*, 149.

14. Richard D. Challener, ed., *United States Military Intelligence, 1917–1927* (New York: Garland, 1978), vol. 1, ix.

15. Churchill, "Military Intelligence Division," 295, 312–13.

16. Ibid., 313, diagram.

17. Challener, *United States Military Intelligence*, vol. 1, vi; *"Military Surveillance,"* Hearings, 173. Churchill contracted sleeping sickness in 1924 and retired aged forty-six. He died in 1942. Powe, *Emergence*, 109; *Who Was Who*, vol. 2, 115. The Office of Naval Intelligence suffered far worse in the post-war cuts than the MID. At the Armistice, the ONI employed 381 people; by June 1919, this had fallen to 109, of whom only 13 were naval officers. Of the remaining 96, 73 were yeowomen and 23 were navy men. Of these navy men, 12 were yeomen and the other 11 were mess attendants and messengers. See "Enlisted Personnel," Naval Intelligence File, June–Dec. 1919, Papers of Josephus Daniels, LC.

18. Sylvia M. Jacobs, *The African Nexus: Black American Perspectives on the European Partitioning of Africa* (Westport, Conn.: Greenwood Press, 1981), 239, 247–48.

19. *Messenger* 2 (Jan. 1918), 6. The first issue of the *Messenger*, vol. 1 (Nov. 1917), 35, and subsequent numbers, carried an advertisement for a booklet by Randolph and Owen titled *Terms of Peace and the Darker Races*.

20. Harrison, *Voice* editorial, July 1918, in Hubert H. Harrison, *When Africa*

Awakes: The 'Inside Story' of the Stirrings and Strivings of the New Negro in the Western World (New York: Porro Press, 1920), 30–32.

21. Reuben Fink, "Visas, Immigration and Official Anti-Semitism," *Nation* 112 (June 22, 1921), 870–72. There was a good deal of annoyance at the post-war insistence that travelers obtain passports. See Anne Herendeen, "Bon Voyage—If Any," *Everybody's Magazine* 51 (Sept. 1919), 29, 79; "Passports and How to Secure Them," *Travel* 35 (May 1920), 44; Kenneth L. Roberts, "Trial by Travel," *Saturday Evening Post* 93 (Sept. 4, 1920), 18–19, 67, 69–70, 73–74, 76; "Passports Passé," *Nation* 112 (Jan. 19, 1921), 75.

22. Robert Russa Moton, *Finding a Way Out: An Autobiography* (London: T. Fisher Unwin, 1920), 250–53; *Crisis* 17 (Feb. 1919), 164; ibid. 18 (May 1919), 9–10. (David Levering Lewis, *W. E. B. Du Bois: Biography of a Race, 1868–1919* [New York: Henry Holt, 1993], 561, mistakenly has the *Orizaba* sailing four days after Wilson's ship.)

23. *Crisis* 18 (May 1919), 11; report of the director of publications and research, Dec. 1, 1918–April 1, 1919, *Crisis* file, NAACP Papers, LC.

24. Loving to Masteller, April 28, 1919, MID File 10218-279, RG 165, NA. After the Brownsville affair of 1906, Scott and Booker T. Washington worked to improve the welfare of black troops. Loving's volunteer regiment had been mustered out of the army in 1901, and when his application for assignment as bandmaster to a regular regiment was rejected (on the grounds that the bandmaster in black regiments was always white), he stayed in Manila and organized the Philippine Constabulary Band. In December 1906, Scott wrote on his behalf to Taft, who remembered Loving as "an admirable leader" and investigated the possibility of giving him a post. In the event, Loving chose not to rejoin the army, because it would have meant a drop in pay from captain to bandmaster, but he appreciated Scott's efforts, writing to Scott in April and May 1907. See Louis R. Harlan, *Booker T. Washington: The Wizard of Tuskegee, 1901–1915* (New York: Oxford University Press, 1983), 313–14, 316–17.

25. Du Bois memo, Nov. ?, 1918, Papers of W. E. B. Du Bois, reel 6, UML; Du Bois to Scott, Nov. 8, 1918, ibid.; Scott to Du Bois, Nov. 10, 1918, ibid.

26. Scott affidavit, Nov. 30, 1918, filed with passport application no. 49576 (1918), Records of the State Department (RG 59), NRC; Harvey O'Higgins to Richard W. Flournoy, Bureau of Citizenship, Nov. 30, 1918, ibid.; Gerald W. Patton, *War and Race: The Black Officer in the American Military, 1915–1941* (Westport, Conn.: Greenwood Press, 1981), 114.

27. *Crisis* 17 (Feb. 1919), 163.

28. Du Bois to J. P. Tumulty, Nov. 27, 1918; "Memoranda on the Future of Africa," file 324C ("Peace Conference"), series 4, Papers of Woodrow Wilson, LC.

29. Tumulty to Du Bois, Nov. 29, 1918, in *Correspondence of W. E. B. Du Bois*, vol. 1, ed. Herbert Aptheker (Amherst: University of Massachusetts Press, 1973), 232; report of the director of publications and research, Dec. 1, 1918–April 1, 1919, *Crisis* file, NAACP Papers, LC.

30. *Crisis* 17 (Jan. 1919), 111–12; ibid. 18 (May 1919), 7; Elliott P. Skinner, *African Americans and U.S. Policy toward Africa, 1850–1924* (Washington: Howard University Press, 1992), 391–94.

31. *Chicago Defender,* Sept. 28, 1918; report of J. G. C. Corcoran, Washington, Oct. 1, 1918, BI File OG 369936, RG 65, NA.

32. Stephen R. Fox, *The Guardian of Boston: William Monroe Trotter* (New York: Atheneum, 1970), 221–22; Corcoran to A. H. Pike, Dec. 3, 1918, BI File OG 49899, RG 65, NA.

33. Corcoran to Alfred Bettman, Dec. 3, 1918, BI File OG 17011, RG 65, NA.

34. Corcoran to Pike, Dec. 3, 1918, BI File OG 49899, RG 65, NA.

35. Report of John E. Bowles, Dec. 19, 1918, BI File OG 369936, RG 65, NA.

36. Ibid.

37. Ibid.; leaflet re Elder R. D. Jonas, MID File 10218-302, RG 165, NA. On Rupert Devereux Jonas, alias Griffith, see BI Files OG 44062, OG 355683, OG 374217, OG 377483, OG 385559, OG 388462, BS 202600-805, BS 202600-1778, BS 208369, BS 215985-15, BS 258421; MID Files 10218-77, -133, -296, -302, -309, -324, -345, -364, -388, -400, -402, -407. See also House Committee on the Judiciary, *"Segregation and Anti-Lynching": Hearings before the Committee on the Judiciary,* on H. J. Res. 75; H. R. 259, 4123, 11873, Serial 14, 66 Cong., 2 sess., Jan. 15, 29, 1920; Allan H. Spear, *Black Chicago: The Making of a Negro Ghetto, 1890–1920* (Chicago: University of Chicago Press, 1967), 193, 195; Arna Bontemps and Jack Conroy, *Any Place but Here* (New York: Hill & Wang, 1966), 204–205; Harrison, *When Africa Awakes,* 61–63; *Crusader* 2 (July 1920), 8; *The Marcus Garvey and Universal Negro Improvement Association Papers,* ed. Robert A. Hill, vol. 1 (Berkeley: University of California Press, 1983), 531–32.

38. Loving to DMI, Dec. 20, 1918, MID File 10218-302, RG 165, NA; Loving to DMI, Dec. 23, 1918, MID File 10218-274, RG 165, NA.

39. Alfreda Duster, ed., *Crusade for Justice: The Autobiography of Ida B. Wells* (Chicago: University of Chicago Press, 1970), 379; Linda O. McMurry, *To Keep the Waters Troubled: The Life of Ida B. Wells* (New York: Oxford University Press, 1998), 321–25.

40. *New York Times,* Nov. 11, 1918; *New York Call,* Nov. 16, 1918; report of D. Davidson, New York, Nov. 12, 1918, BI File OG 329359, consolidated with File BS 198940, RG 65, NA, also in State Dept. File 000.612, ROC, RG 59, NA; *Negro World,* Nov. 9, 1918, quoted in report of R. W. Finch, New York, Nov. 1, 1918, BI File OG 208369, RG 65, NA.

41. Report of D. Davidson, New York, Nov. 12, 1918, BI File OG 329359, consolidated with File BS 198940, RG 65, NA.

42. *Negro World,* Nov. 30, 1918, in MID File 10218, RG 165, NA.

43. *New York Times,* Dec. 3, 1918; *Crusader* 1 (Jan. 1919), 7–14; report of R. W. Finch, Dec. 3, 1918, BI File OG 329359, consolidated with File BS 198940, RG 65, NA; report of D. Davidson, Dec. 5, 1918, MID File 10218-261, RG 165, NA; Skinner, *African Americans and U.S. Policy,* 394–96. Randolph's colleague on the *Messenger,* Chandler Owen, was still confined to an army camp at this time.

44. Du Bois's round-trip passage, rent, and board in Paris from December 10, 1918, to March 22, 1919, amounted to $899. Report of the director of publications and research, Dec. 1, 1918–April 1, 1919, *Crisis* file, NAACP Papers, LC.

45. Report of D. Davidson, Dec. 5, 1918, MID File 10218-261, RG 165, NA; Postal Censorship report, New York, Dec. 11, 1918, re E. Cadet to Marcel Herard,

Port-au-Prince, Dec. 2, 1918, ibid.; Postal Censorship report, New York, Jan. 16, 1919, re Cadet to H. Dorsinville, Port-au-Prince, Jan. 13, 1918, ibid.

46. J. M. Dunn (acting DMI), to Loving, Dec. 17, 1918, ibid.; report of Woolsey W. Hall, Dec. 18, 1918, ibid., extracts in BI File OG 186646, RG 65, NA. Hall's name and his undercover work on behalf of the government were made public in January 1921, when the chairman of a House of Representatives subcommittee on appropriations questioned a claim by the Justice Department for $48 which was owed to Hall for covering meetings in Washington on four days in 1920. See transcripts of hearings before the subcommittee of the House Committee on Appropriations, First Deficiency Appropriations Bill for 1921, Jan. 10, 1921, 630, in MID File 10218-261, RG 165, NA, and DJ Central File 198940-291, RG 60, NA.

47. Loving to DMI, Dec. 20, 1918, MID File 10218-261, RG 165, NA.

48. Dunn to Scott, Dec. 21, 1918, MID File 10218-261, RG 165, NA.

49. Passport application no. 60329 (1918), RG 59, NRC.

50. Statement of W. H. Jernagin, Dec. 17, 1918, ibid.; Albert G. Lawson, Federal Council of Churches, to Jernagin, Dec. 19, 1918, ibid.

51. J. Milton Waldron to Chodi Palda [sic], Indian Freedom Committee, Stockholm, Dec. 14, 1918, MID File 10218-302, RG 165, NA; J. A. Merton to H. T. Jones, March 8, 1919, ibid. The intended recipient of Waldron's letter was Indian socialist V. Chattopadhyaya, who returned to Berlin after the war and later worked for the League against Imperialism. See *The Indian Nationalist Movement, 1885–1947, Selected Documents,* ed. B. N. Pandey (London: Macmillan, 1979), 98. On investigation of Indian nationalists in the United States during the war, see, for example, "The Hindu Conspiracy, The Ghadr Society, and Indian Revolutionary Propaganda," report by Western Dept., Military Intelligence, n.d., MID File 10560-152/115, RG 165, NA; "List of Persons Suspected, c. 1917–19, of Being Foreign Agents," Entry 107, Records of the Office of Naval Intelligence, RG 38, NA. Also Joan M. Jensen, *Passage from India: Asian Indian Immigrants in North America* (New Haven: Yale University Press, 1988), chapters 8–11; Thomas J. Tunney, *Throttled! The Detection of the German and Anarchist Bomb Plotters* (Boston: Small, Maynard, 1919), 69–107.

52. C. S. Macfarland, Federal Council of Churches, to Jernagin, Dec. 31, 1918, filed with passport application no. 60329, RG 59 NRC; G. B. Darby, *Pittsburgh American,* to Jernagin, Jan. 24, 1919, ibid.; Jernagin affidavit, Jan. 27, 1918, ibid.

53. Note by R. W. Flournoy, ibid. Confusion over the National Race Congress and Trotter's activities persisted throughout 1919. See material in MID File 10218-302, RG 165, NA, and BI Files OG 359413 and OG 369936, RG 65, NA. The latter concerned the attempt by Jernagin's National Race Congress colleague, J. Milton Waldron, to obtain a passport in the name of the Cape Verde Missionary Society.

54. Harrison, *When Africa Awakes,* 35–36.

55. *Baltimore Daily Herald,* Feb. 5, 1919; *New York Times,* Feb. 2, 1919. On the same day, the State Department stated that the passports of two white Women's Party members had been canceled just prior to their departure, to stop them demonstrating at the peace conference—or, as the *New York Times* put it, "Militant Women Barred from Going to France to Annoy Wilson."

56. Alvey A. Ada [sic] to W. T. Johnson, Feb. 10, 1919, reprinted in *Richmond*

Planet, Feb. 15, 1919; L. W. Kyles to Alvey A. Ada [*sic*], May 6, 1919, filed with passport application no. 83779 (1919), RG 59, NA.

57. *Baltimore Daily Herald,* Feb. 5, 1919; *Crisis* 17 (March, 1919), 224–25; *New York Call,* n.d., quoted in ibid., 237–38.

58. Maldwyn Allen Jones, *American Immigration* (Chicago: University of Chicago Press, 1960), 264–65; Akira Iriye, *Across the Pacific: An Inner History of American–East Asian Relations* (New York: Harcourt, Brace, 1967), 139–45; Robert H. Wiebe, *The Search for Order, 1877–1920* (New York: Hill & Wang, 1967), 251–54; Russell H. Fifield, *Woodrow Wilson and the Far East: The Diplomacy of the Shantung Question* (Hamden: Archon Books, 1965), 158.

59. *World Forum* 1 (Jan. 1919), 1–3, forwarded by Loving to DMI, Jan. 15, 1919, MID File 10218-296, RG 165, NA. One of those who attended the ILDP's founding meeting was Lewis Garnett Jordan, the foreign mission secretary of the National Baptist Convention and mentor of John Chilembwe, the leader of the Nyasaland Native Rising of 1915. George Shepperson, "Notes on Negro American Influences on the Emergence of African Nationalism," *Journal of African History* 1, no. 2 (1960), 306.

60. Report of R. W. Finch, March 5, 1918, MID File 10218-296, RG 165, NA; *World Forum* 1, (Jan. 1919), 1, 3–4. The address of the *World Forum* and the Messenger Publishing Company were the same (2305 7th Avenue, New York). The first issue of *World Forum* listed ILDP meetings to be held in New York and Newark, N.J., in January 1919. No further issues of this supposedly bimonthly journal appear to have been produced.

61. Report of Finch, March 5, 1919, in MID File 10218-296, RG 165, NA; J. B. Trevor to DMI, April 5, 1919, in MID File 10218-324, RG 165, NA.

62. Fifield, *Woodrow Wilson and the Far East,* 160–69.

63. *New York Age,* Dec. 12, 1918, quoted in Fox, *Guardian of Boston,* 223–24.

64. *Baltimore Daily Herald,* Feb. 5, 1919.

65. *Chicago Defender,* Feb. 8, 1919.

66. *Messenger* 2 (March 1919), 4. Later, when he and Garvey were in dispute, Randolph seemed to blame the Jamaican for the failure of the UNIA delegates to reach France, and implied that Garvey had pocketed the money raised for their journey. Randolph claimed that he "didn't know then that Mr. Garvey was untrustworthy." *Messenger* 4 (Aug. 1922), 470.

67. *Crusader* 1 (Jan. 1919), 7, 14. Briggs also fell out with Garvey. See ibid. 2 (May 1920), 6; ibid. (July 1920), 8–9.

68. *Crisis* 17 (April 1919), 271–74; ibid. (May 1919), 9; report of the director of publications and research, Dec. 1, 1918–April 1, 1919, *Crisis* file, NAACP Papers, LC; *Richmond Planet,* Feb. 15, 1919. The white NAACP directors who attended sessions of the Pan-African Congress were Charles Edward Russell, William English Walling, and Joel Spingarn.

69. Jacobs, *The African Nexus,* 258; C. G. Contee, "The Worley Report on the Pan-African Congress of 1919," *Journal of Negro History* 55 (April 1970), 141; W. E. B. Du Bois, *Dusk of Dawn: An Essay toward an Autobiography of a Race Concept* (New York: Harcourt, Brace, 1940), 261–62; Charles Flint Kellogg, *NAACP: A History*

of the National Association for the Advancement of Colored People, Volume 1: 1909–1920 (Baltimore: Johns Hopkins University Press, 1967), 283. On the Pan-African Congress, see also Elliott M. Rudwick, *W. E. B. Du Bois: Propagandist of the Negro Protest,* 2nd ed. (Philadelphia: University of Pennsylvania Press, 1968), 211–16; Lewis, *W. E. B. Du Bois,* 574–78.

70. John D. Hargreaves, "Maurice Delafosse on the Pan-African Congress of 1919," *African Historical Studies* 1, no. 2 (1968), 233–41 (my translation from the French); *Crisis* 17 (April 1919), 271–74.

71. Hargreaves, "Maurice Delafosse," 235 (my translation).

72. *Crisis* 17 (April 1919), 271–74.

73. Report of the director of publications and research, Dec. 1, 1918–April 1, 1919, *Crisis* file, NAACP Papers, LC; Du Bois, *Dusk of Dawn,* 262; Kellogg, *NAACP,* 283; Skinner, *African Americans and U.S. Policy,* 396–422. Du Bois was introduced to George Beer by Joel Spingarn. Spingarn to Du Bois, Feb. 26, 1919, Papers of W. E. B. Du Bois, reel 9, UML. On Beer's work in Paris, during which Du Bois seems to have made little impression on him, see William Roger Louis, "The United States and the African Peace Settlement of 1919: The Pilgrimage of George Louis Beer," *Journal of African History* 4, no. 3 (1963), 413–33. In 1919–20, the Pan-African Congress was debunked by Garvey and his supporters as having been unrepresentative in its make-up and plagiaristic in its resolutions. Tony Martin, *Race First: The Ideological and Organizational Struggles of Marcus Garvey and the Universal Negro Improvement Association* (Westport, Conn.: Greenwood Press, 1976), 289–93; Elliott M. Rudwick, "Du Bois versus Garvey: Race Propagandists at War," *Journal of Negro Education* 28 (Fall 1959), 423–24.

74. *Pittsburgh Courier,* March 1, 1919.

75. Contee, "The Worley Report," 140–41; W. E. B. Du Bois, "Documents of the War," *Crisis* 18 (May 1919), 16–20.

76. *Christian Science Monitor,* July 25, 1919; Fox, *Guardian of Boston,* 224–32; "A Negro Delegate Who Managed to Reach the Peace Conference," *Literary Digest* 62 (Aug. 16, 1919), 42, 45; *Baltimore Afro-American,* June 20, Aug. 1, 1919; *Chicago Defender,* July 12, 1919; *Chicago Whip,* July 9, 1919. See also *New York Sun,* June 24, 1919, filed with A. P. Niblack, director, ONI, to J. T. Suter, acting director and chief, BI, June 30, 1919, BI File OG 3057, RG 65, NA. When Garvey's Black Star Line purchased its first ship, the S. S. *Yarmouth,* in September 1919, the *Negro World* claimed that it was the ship on which Trotter had sailed to France. Martin, *Race First,* 153. However, in his own accounts of his exploits, Trotter stated that he had sailed on a French vessel, *L'Ancore. Boston Post,* July 24, 1919, quoted in *Baltimore Afro-American,* Aug. 8, 1919; report of H. A. Lewis, Boston, July 25, 1919, BI File OG 49899, RG 65, NA. Trotter clearly succeeded in keeping his intention to sail to France a secret. In April and May, a BI agent looking for him in Boston interviewed a number of potential black informants with regard to the "Bolshevism in his addresses," but could find no trace of him. Reports of H. A. Lewis, April 8, May 8, 1919, BI File OG 49899, RG 65, NA.

77. Passport application no. 83779 (1919), RG 59, NRC; L. W. Kyles to Alvey A. Ada [*sic*], May 6, 1919, ibid.

78. Passport application no. 73446 (1919), RG 59, NRC; Jane Addams and Alice Thacher Post to Mrs. Robert Terrell, March 10, 1919, ibid.; Mary Church Terrell, *A Colored Woman in a White World* (New York: Arno, 1980), 329–32. The ICWPP delegation was reduced from thirty women to fifteen, at State Department insistence, but Terrell was retained. She saw William Monroe Trotter at work in Paris. Ibid., 330, 341. Like all female passport applicants, she had to sign a declaration that she had no near male relative in the AEF or working as a civilian with the AEF. Affidavit of Mary C. Terrell, April 2, 1919, passport application no. 73446, RG 59, NRC. On this rule, see Herendeen, "Bon Voyage—If Any," 29.

79. Passport application no. 93065 (1919), RG 59, NRC; Scott to R. R. Wright, June 17, 1919, ibid.; memo from the office of the assistant secretary of state to Mr. Merryman, July 1, 1919, ibid.; additional note written on a memo from Frank Burke, assistant director and chief, BI, to L. Lanier Winslow, Aug. 7, 1919, File 000.966, ROC, RG 59, NA; report of M. J. Davis, New York, July 15, 1919, BI File OG 359099, RG 65, NA. Born in Virginia in 1855, Wright was educated at Atlanta University, the University of Chicago, and Harvard. During the Spanish-American War, he was a major in the Pay Corps. Robert Ewell Greene, *Black Defenders of America, 1775–1973* (Chicago: Johnson Publishing, 1974), 156.

80. "Chicago's Negro Problem," *City Club of Chicago Bulletin* 12 (March 17, 1919), 75. The speaker was Alexander L. Jackson, soon to be appointed professor of sociology at Howard University and secretary for educational work of the National Urban League. *Baltimore Afro-American*, Aug. 1, 1919. Harvard-educated, Jackson was a founding member with Carter G. Woodson of the Association for the Study of Negro Life and History, publisher of the *Journal of Negro History*. William M. Tuttle, *Race Riot: Chicago in the Red Summer of 1919* (New York: Atheneum, 1978), 223. He was said to be on the payroll of various packing companies that preferred their black workers to join the Wabash Avenue YMCA, rather than trade unions. Spear, *Black Chicago*, 162; Tuttle, *Race Riot,* 101, 151.

81. *Washington(?) Evening Star,* Jan. 25(?), 1919, clipping in MID File 10218-301, RG 165, NA.

82. Memorandum by French Military Mission with U.S. Army, Aug. 7, 1919, reprinted in *Crisis* 18 (May, 1919), 16–18; *Blacks in the Military: Essential Documents,* ed. Bernard C. Nalty and Morris J. McGregor (Wilmington, Del.: Scholarly Resources, 1981), 87–88.

83. Edward A. Stillman, HQ, Advanced Section, Services of Supply, Office of Provost Marshall, to Newton D. Baker, Nov. 7, 1918, General Correspondence, 1918, Papers of Newton D. Baker, LC.

84. Sharp to Secretary of State, cable 5941, Nov. 20, 1918, MID File 10218-256, RG 165, NA. This agent was probably R. S. Sharp, who later served as special-agent-in-charge for the New York district, under R. C. Bannerman, the State Department's chief special agent. See Sharp to Bannerman, Dec. 17, 29, 1920; Bannerman to Sharp, Dec. 13, 1920, File 000.612, ROC, RG 59, NA.

85. Bernard C. Nalty, *Strength For the Fight: A History of Black Americans in the Military* (New York: Free Press, 1986), 123; Mary White Ovington, *The Walls Came Tumbling Down* (New York: Arno Press, 1969), 143–44; Moton, *Finding A Way Out,*

251–56; W. E. B. Du Bois, "Documents of the War," *Crisis* 18 (May 1919), 18–20. See also Du Bois, "Rape," ibid., 12–13.

86. Loving to Churchill, Nov. 18, 1918, MID File 10218-256, RG 165, NA.

87. Ibid.

88. Ibid.

89. Churchill to chief of staff, Nov 19, 1919, ibid.

90. Baker to Woodrow Wilson, June 26, 1918, Dec. 20, 1918, Papers of Newton D. Baker, reel 6, LC. Although he was sure the Rockford crime had been committed, Baker was unable to recommend to Wilson that the death sentences of the court-martial be carried out, because of the unsatisfactory way in which the trials had been conducted. In the other case, involving three soldiers, Baker suggested that Wilson might wish to commute the death sentences because of their "low-grade mentality." After the Houston riot executions, Wilson and Baker had agreed to review carefully every death sentence handed down by courts-martial in the United States. See reply drafted for Wilson by Baker to P. L. Hawkins, Jan. 13, 1918, reel 5, Papers of Newton D. Baker, LC. It is not clear that this process was always effective. Jakob Waldner, a Hutterite conscientious objector, recorded in his diary the execution at either Fort Des Moines, Iowa, or Camp Funston, Kan., on July 5, 1918, of three black soldiers for the rape of a white woman. (These may have been the men about whom Baker wrote to Wilson.) Unarmed black troops were forced by armed white soldiers to watch the executions. Theron Schlabach, ed., "*An Account, by Jakob Waldner: Diary of a Conscientious Objector in World War I*," *Mennonite Quarterly Review* 48 (1974), 104–105.

91. Laurence C. Jones, *Piney Woods and Its Story* (New York: Fleming H. Revell, 1922), 118, 123; George Brown Tindall, *The Emergence of the New South, 1913–1945* (Baton Rouge: Louisiana State University Press, 1967), 24. Bilbo called Sullens a "degenerate by birth, a carpetbagger by inheritance, a liar by instinct, a slanderer and assassin of character by practice, and a coward by nature." Sullens replied that if Bilbo was elected governor the golden eagle on the dome of the capitol should be replaced by "a puking buzzard." Dan Carter, "Southern Political Style," in *The Age of Segregation: Race Relations in the South, 1890–1945*, ed. Robert Haws (Jackson: University Press of Mississippi, 1978), 51, 147. See also Albert D. Kirwan, *Revolt of the Rednecks: Mississippi Politics, 1876–1925* (New York: Harper, 1965, first published 1951), 207–208, 257–58.

92. *Jackson Daily News*, n.d., cited in I. A. Newby, *Jim Crow's Defense: Anti-Negro Thought in America, 1900–1930* (Baton Rouge: Louisiana State University Press, 1965), 172. See also Neil R. McMillen, *Dark Journey: Black Mississippians in the Age of Jim Crow* (Urbana: University of Illinois Press, 1990), 67, 177, 240, 248.

93. G. H. Mattis to Baker, Nov. 21, 1918, MID File 10218-326, RG 165, NA.

94. F. Sullens to Wrisley Brown, Nov. 30, 1918, MID File 10218-289, RG 165, NA.

95. Cutler to chief, Morale Branch, Dec. 9, 1918, ibid.

96. Kellogg, *NAACP*, 234.

97. Arthur E. Barbeau and Florette Henri, *The Unknown Soldiers: Black American Troops in World War I* (Philadelphia: Temple University Press, 1974), 164–66; Addie W. Hunton and Kathryn M. Johnson, *Two Colored Women with the U.S. Expedi-*

tionary Forces (New York: Brooklyn Eagle Press, 1920), 31; Henry Hugh Proctor, *Between Black and White: Autobiographical Sketches* (Boston: Pilgrim Press, 1925), 164. In December 1918, Britain decided to repatriate West Indian troops as soon as possible, after lapses of discipline following discriminatory treatment. C. L. Joseph, "The British West Indies Regiment, 1914–1918," *Journal of Caribbean History* 2 (May 1971), 118.

98. Cutler to chief, Morale Branch, Dec. 9, 1918, MID File 10218-289, RG 165, NA. Cutler added that Thomas Jesse Jones's journey to France had been in order to look out for agitation among black troops.

99. Wilson to Moton, Jan. 1, 1919, Peace Conference Correspondence, 1918–20, Papers of Woodrow Wilson, LC; Baker to Moton, March 3, 1919, General Correspondence, 1919, Papers of Newton D. Baker, LC; Moton to Baker, March 13, 18, 1919, ibid.; Stanley King to Moton, March 21, 1919, ibid.; Moton, *Finding a Way Out*, 262–65; W. E. B. Du Bois, "Robert Russa Moton," *Crisis* 18 (May 1919), 9–10; *Messenger* 2 (Sept. 1919), 16–17. Other conservative blacks who were sent to France to mollify the troops included Moton's half-brother, James E. Blanton, a musician, and Henry Hugh Proctor, a preacher. Proctor, *Between Black and White*, 157–59.

100. *Crusader* 1 (March 1919), 5.

101. Quoted in Hunton and Johnson, *Two Colored Women*, 53–54; Charles H. Williams, *Sidelights on Negro Soldiers* (Boston: B. J. Brimmer, 1923), 70; Barbeau and Henri, *Unknown Soldiers*, 148.

102. Lee Kennett, "The Camp Wadsworth Affair," *South Atlantic Quarterly* 74 (Spring 1975), 210.

103. D. E. Nolan, assistant chief of staff, G-2, GHQ, AEF, to acting DMI, Jan. 30, 1919, MID File 10218-311, RG 165, NA.

104. Nolan to C. E. Officers, Jan. 31, 1919, ibid.; Nolan to acting DMI, Feb 18, 1919, ibid.; F. P. Schoonmaker, HQ, 92nd Division, Camp Meade, to DMI, Feb. 25, 1919, ibid. Nolan's pre-war career had largely paralleled that of the first chief of the Military Intelligence Branch, Ralph Van Deman: Philippines, 1901–02; General Staff, 1903–06; Philippines, 1906–11. *Who Was Who in America*, vol. 3 (Chicago: Marquis–Who's Who, 1960), 642.

105. Dunn to DMI, April 25, 1919, MID File 10218-329, RG 165, NA.

106. C. S. Gordon, statement, April 29, 1919, ibid.

107. Churchill memo, April 26, 1919, ibid.; Churchill to military attaché, U.S. Embassy, Paris, April 26, 1919, ibid.; Churchill to IO, Newport News, April 28, 1919, ibid.; Nolan to DMI, May 24, 1919, ibid.; L. B. Dunham to DMI, April 30, 1919, ibid.

108. Edwin S. Ross, Newport News, to DMI, May 3, 1919, ibid.; CO, Camp Stuart, to CO, Port of Embarkation (PE), Newport News, May 26, 1919, ibid.; CO, Casual HQ, Camp Alexander, to CO, Camp Alexander, June 1, 1919, ibid.; CO, Camp Hill, to CO, PE, Newport News, June 7, 1919, ibid.; CO, Air Service Depot, Camp Morrison, to CO, PE, Newport News, June 10, 1919, ibid.; IO, Newport News, to DMI, June 13, 1919, ibid. Just thirty-one handguns were found on the nine thousand men who passed through Camp Morrison in May 1919. A further twenty-nine

pistols were detected in mail forwarded from France. The CO at Camp Morrison found no spirit of revolution among the returning soldiers; only a wish to return to civilian life. Two pistols were found at Camp Hill and none at Camps Stuart and Alexander.

109. Nolan to acting DMI, Feb. 25, March 7, 1919, MID File 10218-311, RG 165, NA; Loving to DMI, March 1, 1919, ibid.; Cutler to chief, Negative Branch, March 22, 1919, MID File 10218-315, RG 165, NA; Cutler to R. E. B. McKenny, IO, 371st Infantry, Camp Jackson, S.C., March 20, 1919, ibid. (Masteller's opinion was written on Cutler's March 22 memo); Dunn to McKenny, March 3, 1919, ibid.

110. Barbeau and Henri, *Unknown Soldiers,* 173.

111. Nolan to DMI, April 9, 22, 1919, MID File 10218-311, RG 165, NA. One of the letters intercepted was from the historian and Pan-Africanist Rayford W. Logan, then a first lieutenant, to a fellow officer in Washington, D.C., in whom he confided that his army experiences left him convinced that there was now "more race hatred than before." R. W. Logan, Camp Ancona, to Campbell C. Johnson, Howard University, n.d., ibid.

112. Nolan to acting DMI, Jan. 30, Feb. 18, 1919, ibid.

113. Loving to DMI, April 25, 1919, MID File 10218-337, RG 165, NA; Cutler to A. B. Coxe, June 18, 1919, ibid.; note with list of National Liberty Congress delegates, July 13, 1918, filed with unnumbered items in MID File 10218, RG 165, NA.

114. Loving to DMI, March 17, 1919, MID File 10218, RG 165, NA.

115. *Crisis* 18 (May 1919), 14–15.

116. Loving to DMI, April 25, 1919, MID File 10218-337, RG 165, NA; Osceola E. McKaine, "The Buffaloes: A First Class Colored Fighting Regiment," *Outlook* 119 (May 22, 1918), 145. On Osceola McKaine, see also Miles S. Richards, "The Eminent Lieutenant McKaine," *Carologue* (Autumn 1991), 6–7, 14–17.

117. Osceolo [*sic*] E. McKaine, "With the Buffaloes in France," *Independent* 97 (Jan. 11, 1919), 50, 64; and reprinted in *Crusader* 1 (Feb. 1919), 3–4.

118. League for Democracy handbook and application blank, MID File 10218-337, RG 165, NA; Loving to DMI, April 25, 1919, ibid.; *New York News,* April 10, 1919.

119. Barbeau and Henri, *Unknown Soldiers,* 111–63; Harry Haywood, *Black Bolshevik: An Autobiography of an Afro-American Communist* (Chicago: Liberator Press, 1978), 54–64.

120. See, for example, "Our Negro Soldiers Brilliant Record," *New York Times* Feb. 9, 1919, which was compiled from data provided by Scott's office. Scott to Cutler, Feb. 13, 1919, MID File 10218-298, RG 165, NA.

121. On this rumor-mongering, see "The Colored Soldier in France," stenographic report of speech by J. E. Spingarn at the Tenth Anniversary Conference of the NAACP, June 23, 1919, National Conference file, NAACP Papers, LC. See also *Crisis* 19 (Dec. 1919), 45, re a *Harper's Weekly* story. See also Gary Mead, *The Doughboys* (London: Penguin, 2000), 345–46, 415.

122. John Sharp Williams to R. L. Anderson, Jr., Oct. 5, 1919, Papers of John Sharp Williams, LC.

123. Notebook 25, Papers of Ray Stannard Baker, LC.

124. Thomas J. Woofter, *Southern Race Progress: The Wavering Color Line* (Washington, D.C.: Public Affairs Press, 1957), 98–99.

125. Hunton and Johnson, *Two Colored Women*, 59–61; Schoonmaker to IOs, Jan. 1, 1919, Papers of W. E. B. Du Bois, reel 9, UML; Du Bois, *Dusk of Dawn*, 262.

126. *Crisis* 18 (May 1919), 19–20. Du Bois's easy acquisition of army documents made the MID nervous. When an aide to the chief of staff requested details of Greer's letter, the Negative Branch agreed only on condition that "should he desire to exhibit them to other officers in the War Department, he do so in person and not through the medium of enlisted or civilian messengers." William Osgood Field to Campbell, May 3, 1919, MID File 10218-139, RG 165, NA; Churchill to Field, May 5, 1919, ibid.

127. Patton, *War and Race*, 135; proceedings of a board of officers, Feb. 26, 1919, Admin. File, NAACP Papers, LC; Bishop C. S. Smith to John Shillady, May 10, 1919, ibid. See also *New York Age*, May 10, 1919, clipping, General Correspondence, 1919, Papers of Newton D. Baker, LC; *New York Evening Post*, n.d., clipping, ibid.

128. Loving to Masteller, April 28, 1919, MID File 10218-279, RG 165, NA; Loving to DMI, May 6, 1919, ibid. Loving identified the black officer who accompanied Du Bois on visits to the troops in France as Capt. Virgil M. Boutte of the 92nd Division. Loving also claimed to recognize Boutte in a photograph of the Pan-African Congress. Loving to Masteller, May 2, 1919, MID File 10218-139, RG 165, NA. During the Armistice, Boutte, from Louisiana, was attached to the Visitors' Bureau; among the black public figures for whom he acted as a guide and interpreter was Mary Church Terrell. Terrell, *Colored Woman in a White World*, 346. A graduate of Fisk University and the University of Illinois, he had been arrested in July 1918 and charged with twenty-three petty breaches of army regulations, such as the failure of his mess sergeant to display a menu. He returned to duty when it became clear that he was the victim of his battalion commander's extreme malice toward black officers. Hunton and Johnson, *Two Colored Women*, 57–61.

129. Cutler to Churchill, May 9, 1919, MID File 10218-279, RG 165, NA; Churchill to chief of staff, May 9, 1919, ibid. Cutler asked intelligence officers in the camps to report all they knew about grievances of black soldiers in the 92nd Division. Cutler to IO, Camp Dix, N.J., May 12, 1919, MID File 10218-139, RG 165, NA.

130. Newton D. Baker to George Foster Peabody, June 18, 1919, General Correspondence, 1919, Papers of Newton D. Baker, LC; *Baltimore Afro-American*, May 16, 1919.

131. Cutler to Coxe, July 1, 1919, MID File 10218-296, RG 165, NA. Cutler cited, as an example of the "attitude toward the Army of a large proportion of the more intelligent negroes who have been in military service," a highly critical article by William N. Colson, a former 367th Infantry officer, titled "Propaganda and the American Negro Soldier," *Messenger* 2 [July 1919], 24–25. See also William N. Colson, "The Social Experience of the Negro Soldier Abroad," *Messenger* 2 (Oct. 1919), 26–27; Colson and A. B. Nutt, "The Failure of the Ninety-Second Division," *Messenger* 2 (Sept. 1919), 22–25.

132. Loving to DMI, May 19, 1919, MID File 10218-337, RG 165, NA.

133. Cutler to Masteller, May 21, 1919, MID File 10218-279, RG 165, NA; Maj. Edward J. Turgeon, acting adjutant, HQ, 92nd Division, to CO, 367th Infantry, Nov. 1, 1918, ibid. Loving also acquired the name and address of Colonel Greer's stenographer, who had retained a number of the Georgian's letters and memorandums on the subject of blacks. Loving to Cutler, June 12, 1919, MID File 10218-337, RG 165, NA.

134. *Washington Eagle,* May 10, June 14, 1919; O. E. McKaine to Secretary of War, May 24, 1919, MID File 10218-337, RG 165, NA; Ralph Hayes to Cutler, May 29, 1919, ibid.; Cutler to Hayes, June 3, 1919, ibid.; Loving to DMI, June 11, 1919, ibid.; LFD leaflet, ibid.

135. *Denver Star,* May 31, 1919; *New York News,* June 12, 1919; *Washington Eagle,* June 14, 1919; *Chicago Defender,* June 14, 1919; Loving to Cutler, June 11, 1919, MID File 10218-279, RG 165, NA; Adjutant general to McKaine, June 11, 1919, ibid.; Loving to Cutler, June 12, 1919, ibid.; League for Democracy to adjutant general, July 3, 1919, ibid.; Adjutant general to LFD, July 2, 1919, ibid. Capt. Samuel F. Sewall, promoter of the Grand Army of Americans, called at Cutler's office to complain that the LFD, with which he had considered a merger, was too radical. Asked by Cutler about a number of black officers from Washington, Sewall said they were unfit to hold commissions. Cutler to Coxe, June 18, 1919, MID File 10218-337, RG 165, NA.

136. Loving to DMI, June 17, 1919, MID File 10218-337, RG 165, NA.

137. Patton, *War and Race,* 95; Barbeau and Henri, *Unknown Soldiers,* 155–57.

138. Cutler to DMI, June 20, 1919, MID File 10218-279, RG 165, NA; Baker to Peabody, June 18, 1919, General Correspondence, 1919, Papers of Newton D. Baker, LC.

139. Baker to Wilson, Oct. 1, 1917, in *Papers of Woodrow Wilson,* vol. 44, ed. Link, 288–89.

140. Cutler to DMI, June 20, 1919, MID File 10218-279, RG 165, NA; *Cleveland Advocate,* June 14, 1919, clipping, ibid.

141. Barbeau and Henri, *Unknown Soldiers,* 389. Scott had agreed to be held responsible for Tyler's output. Churchill to assistant chief of staff, G-2, AEF, Oct. 22, 1918, MID File 10218-88, RG 165, NA. Loving alleged that Scott had helped Tyler to get press credentials in September 1918, so that he could collect material for Scott's book on the war. Loving to Masteller, April 28, 1919. MID File 10218-279, RG 165, NA. On Tyler's post-war speeches and writings on the ill-treatment of black troops, see also *New York Age,* Dec. 28, 1918, cited in Patton, *War and Race,* 111, 115; *Chicago Defender,* March 8, 1919.

142. *New York Times,* Nov. 8, 1919; *Crisis* 19 (Dec. 1919), 45–46; "Newton D. Baker Official Statement about Negro Troops," *Southern Workman* 48 (Dec. 1919), 636–39; Barbeau and Henri, *Unknown Soldiers,* 155; Patton, *War and Race,* 95.

143. Herbert J. Seligmann, *The Negro Faces America* (New York: Harper and Bros., 1920), 58, 151.

144. Frank S. Dickason, 50th Artillery, to S. A. Cash, Tuscaloosa, Ala., n.d., MID

File 10218-300, RG 165, NA. For examples of black press comment about the Klan, see *Crisis* 17 (March 1919), 229–31; *Baltimore Afro-American,* July 11, 1919; *Houston Informer,* July 12, 1919.

145. John Hope Franklin, *From Slavery to Freedom: A History of Negro Americans,* 5th ed. (New York: Alfred A. Knopf, 1980), 346–47; Barbeau and Henri, *Unknown Soldiers,* 307; John Dittmer, *Black Georgia in the Progressive Era, 1900–1920* (Urbana: University of Illinois Press, 1977), 204; Leon F. Litwack, *Trouble in Mind: Black Southerners in the Age of Jim Crow* (New York: Alfred A. Knopf, 1998), 331; McMillen, *Dark Journey,* 304–306; Loving to DMI, Dec. 23, 1918, MID File 10218-274, RG 165, NA; *Baltimore Afro-American,* April 11, May 23, 1919; *Cleveland Gazette,* May 17, 1919; *Crisis* 19 (Nov. 1919), 346.

146. *Baltimore Afro-American,* Aug. 29, 1919.

147. Philip S. Foner, *Organized Labor and the Black Worker, 1619–1973* (New York: Praeger, 1974), 131, 132, 134.

148. Jerrell H. Shofner, "Florida and the Black Migration," *Florida Historical Quarterly* 57 (Jan. 1979), 276; *New Orleans Times-Picayune,* Aug. 15, 1919. Loving reported that some veterans' organizations were advising their members to move to the North. Loving to DMI, March 1, 1919, MID File 10218-311, RG 165, NA.

149. Foner, *Organized Labor and the Black Worker,* 132. See also *Half-Century Magazine* 6 (March 1919), 10.

150. Edward Easton, Jr., BRSS, to Elliot P. Frost, March 10, 1919, MID File 10218-319, RG 165, NA; Scott to Frost, March 13, 1919, ibid.

151. Dunn to Frost, March 30, 1919, ibid.

152. Ralston Flemming, Camp Wheeler, Ga., to acting DMI, March 11, 1919, ibid.; Dunn to Flemming, March 14, 1919, ibid.

153. Forrester B. Washington, supervisor of Negro Economics in Illinois, to John Fitzpatrick, Chicago Federation of Labor, Jan. 25, 1919, Papers of John Fitzpatrick, Chicago Historical Society; George E. Haynes to Fitzpatrick, Feb. 12, 1919, ibid.; minutes of executive committee, BRSS, Chicago, Feb. 17, May 1, 1919, ibid. See also *Crisis* 18 (Sept. 1919), 236–38.

154. *Baltimore Afro-American,* May 16, 1919; *New Orleans Times-Picayune,* Aug. 5, 14, 15, 16, Sept 3, 1919. See also Chicago Commission on Race Relations, *The Negro in Chicago: A Study of Race Relations and a Race Riot* (Chicago: University of Chicago Press, 1922), 103–105; Spear, *Black Chicago,* 203; *Half-Century Magazine* 7 (Sept. 1919), 18.

155. James Weldon Johnson, *Along This Way: The Autobiography of James Weldon Johnson* (New York: Penguin, 1990, first published 1933), 341.

156. *Commoner,* June 28, 1919, in MID File 10218-337, RG 165, NA.

157. *Veteran,* June 28, 1919, File B-397, Entry 40, Records of the Post Office Dept., RG 28, NA. A semi-monthly paper, the *Veteran* began publication on April 19, 1919.

158. Ibid.

159. *The Passion of Claude McKay: Selected Prose and Poetry, 1912–1948,* ed. Wayne F. Cooper (New York: Schocken Books, 1973), 124.

7. Conclusion

1. Senate Subcommittee on the Judiciary, *Brewing and Liquor Interests, and German and Bolshevik Propaganda*, 66 Cong., 1 Sess., Sen. Doc. 62, 1574, 1784–86. See also *Chicago Evening Post*, Dec. 14, 1918.

2. W. E. B. Du Bois, *Dusk of Dawn: An Essay toward an Autobiography of a Race Concept* (New York: Harcourt, Brace, 1940), 249.

3. See H. C. Petersen and Gilbert C. Fite, *Opponents of War, 1917–1918* (Seattle: University of Washington Press, 1968); William Preston, Jr., *Aliens and Dissenters: Federal Suppression of Radicals, 1903–1933* (New York: Harper & Row, 1966); Harry N. Scheiber, *The Wilson Administration and Civil Liberties, 1917–1921* (Ithaca: Cornell University Press, 1960); Donald Johnson, *The Challenge to American Freedoms: World War I and the Rise of the American Civil Liberties Union* (Lexington: University of Kentucky Press, 1963); Charles Chatfield, *For Peace and Justice: Pacifism in America, 1914–1941* (Knoxville: University of Tennessee Press, 1971), 62–76; Robert H. Ferrell, *Woodrow Wilson and World War I, 1917–1921* (New York: Harper & Row, 1985), 200–18; Ronald Schaffer, *America in the Great War: The Rise of the War Welfare State* (New York: Oxford University Press, 1991), 13–30; John Sayer, "Art and Politics, Dissent and Repression: The *Masses* Magazine versus the Government, 1917–1918," *American Journal of Legal History* 32 (Jan. 1988), 42–78.

4. Paul A. C. Koistinen, *Mobilizing for Modern War: The Political Economy of American Warfare, 1865–1919* (Lawrence, Kans.: University Press of Kansas, 1997), passim.

5. Jane Lang Scheiber and Harry N. Scheiber, "The Wilson Administration and the Wartime Mobilization of Black Americans, 1917–1918," *Labor History* 10 (Summer 1969), 433–58.

6. Robert Russa Moton, "The South and the Lynching Evil," *South Atlantic Quarterly* 18 (July 1919), 193–96; James Weldon Johnson, "Lynching—America's National Disgrace," *Current History* 20 (Jan. 1924), 596–601. See also Robert Higgs's suggestion that African-American migration resulted over time in periods of "labor market disequilibrium" and that consequent adjustments included a decline in lynching and rising wage rates for black workers. Robert Higgs, "Race and Economy in the South, 1890–1950," in *The Age of Segregation: Race Relations in the South, 1890–1945*, ed. Robert Haws (Jackson: University Press of Mississippi, 1978), 89–116.

7. Neil R. McMillen, "The Migration and Black Protest in Jim Crow Mississippi," in *Black Exodus: The Great Migration from the American South*, ed. Alferdteen Harrison (Jackson: University Press of Mississippi, 1991), 83–99, esp. 95–97. See also Neil R. McMillen, *Dark Journey: Black Mississippians in the Age of Jim Crow* (Urbana: University of Illinois Press, 1990), xv, 302–307, 316–17.

8. See Nelson Blackstock, *COINTELPRO: The FBI's Secret War on Political Freedom* (New York: Vintage, 1976); Patrick S. Washburn, *A Question of Sedition: The Federal Government's Investigation of the Black Press during World War II* (New York: Oxford University Press, 1986); Kenneth O'Reilly, *"Racial Matters": The FBI's Secret*

File on Black America, 1960–72 (New York: Free Press, 1989); Robert A. Hill, ed., *The FBI's RACON: Racial Conditions in the United States during World War II* (Boston: Northeastern University Press, 1995); Theodore Kornweibel, Jr., *"Seeing Red": Federal Campaigns against Black Militancy, 1919–1925* (Bloomington: Indiana University Press, 1998); Mark Ellis, "J. Edgar Hoover and the 'Red Summer' of 1919," *Journal of American Studies* 28 (1994), 39–59.

Selected Bibliography

Manuscript and Archive Collections

National Archives of the United States

Records of the Military Intelligence Division, General Staff (Record Group [RG]165)
Records of the Bureau of Investigation, Justice Department (RG 65)
Records of the Justice Department (RG 60)
Records of the Office of Naval Intelligence (RG 38)
Records of the Office of the Counsellor, State Department (RG 59)
Records of the Post Office Department (RG 28)
Records of the Department of Labor (RG 174)
Records of the Secretary of War (RG 107)

Library of Congress

Papers of Newton D. Baker
Papers of Ray Stannard Baker
Papers of Albert Sidney Burleson
Papers of Josephus Daniels
Papers of John Sharp Williams
Papers of Woodrow Wilson
Papers of the NAACP

Harvard University, Houghton Library

Papers of Oswald Garrison Villard

Howard University, Moorland-Spingarn Research Center

Papers of Archibald H. Grimké
Papers of Walter Howard Loving
Papers of Joel E. Spingarn

New York Public Library

Papers of Joel E. Spingarn

University of Massachusetts Library, Amherst

Papers of W. E. B. Du Bois

Yale University, Beinecke Rare Book and Manuscript Library

(James Weldon Johnson Collection)

Selected Bibliography

Papers of Joel E. Spingarn
Papers of James Weldon Johnson

Published Collections

Blacks in the Military: Essential Documents (Wilmington, Del.: Scholarly Resources, 1981), ed. Bernard C. Nalty and Morris J. McGregor.

The Marcus Garvey and Universal Negro Improvement Association Papers (Berkeley: University of California Press, 1983–1990), ed. Robert A. Hill.

Papers of Woodrow Wilson (Princeton: Princeton University Press, 1966–1994), ed. Arthur S. Link et al.

Official Documents and Reports

House Committee on the Judiciary. *To Protect Citizens Against Lynching, Hearing on HR11279,* 65 Cong., 2 sess., June 6, 1918 (Washington: U.S. Government Printing Office, 1918).

Senate Foreign Relations Committee. *Investigations of Mexican Affairs, Report and Hearings,* 2 vols., 66 Cong., 2 sess., Sen. Doc. 285 (Washington: U.S. Government Printing Office, 1920).

Senate Judiciary Committee. *Brewing and Liquor Interests, and German and Bolshevik Propaganda, Report and Hearings of a Subcommittee,* 3 vols., 66 Cong., 1 sess., Sen. Doc. 62 (Washington: U.S. Government Printing Office, 1919).

Congressional Record. 1917–1919. Washington, D.C.

Newspapers and Magazines

Amsterdam News
Baltimore Afro-American
Boston Guardian
Chicago Defender
Cleveland Gazette
Crisis
Crusader
Current Opinion
Half-Century Magazine
Literary Digest
Messenger
Negro World
New Republic
New York Age
New York News
New York Times
New York Tribune

Selected Bibliography

Norfolk Journal and Guide
Outlook
Southern Workman
Survey
Washington Bee

Books and Articles

Asher, Robert, ed. "Documents of the Race Riot at East St. Louis." *Journal of the Illinois State Historical Society* 65 (Autumn 1972): 327–36.

Ayers, Edward L. *The Promise of the New South: Life after Reconstruction*. New York: Oxford University Press, 1992.

Baker, Ray Stannard. *Following the Color Line: An Account of the Negro Citizenship in the American Democracy*. New York: Doubleday, Page, 1908.

Barbeau, Arthur E., and Florette Henri. *The Unknown Soldiers: Black American Troops in World War I*. Philadelphia: Temple University Press, 1974.

Bardolph, Richard. *The Negro Vanguard*. New York: Rinehart, 1959.

Broderick, Francis L. *W. E. B. Du Bois: Negro Leader in a Time of Crisis*. Stanford: Stanford University Press, 1959.

Bruce, Dickson D., Jr. *Archibald Grimké: Portrait of a Black Independent*. Baton Rouge: Louisiana State University Press, 1993.

Chase, Hal S. "Struggle for Equality: Fort Des Moines Training Camp for Colored Officers, 1917." *Phylon* 39 (Dec. 1978): 297–310.

Churchill, Marlborough. "The Military Intelligence Division, General Staff." *Journal of the United States Artillery* 52 (April 1920): 293–315.

Cobb, James C. *The Most Southern Place on Earth: The Mississippi Delta and the Roots of Regional Identity*. New York: Oxford University Press, 1992.

Cripps, Thomas R. "The Making of *The Birth of a Race:* The Emerging Politics of Identity in Silent Movies." In *The Birth of Whiteness: Race and the Emergence of U.S. Cinema*, ed. Daniel Bernardi, 38–55. New Brunswick: Rutgers University Press, 1996.

———. "The Reaction of the Negro to the Motion Picture *Birth of a Nation*." *Historian* 25 (1962–63): 344–62.

Cummings, Homer S., and Carl McFarland. *Federal Justice: Chapters in the History of Justice and the Federal Executive*. New York: Macmillan, 1937.

Cutler, James Elbert. *Lynch-Law: An Investigation into the History of Lynching in the United States*. New York: Longmans Green, 1905.

Davis, Leroy. *A Clashing of the Soul: John Hope and the Dilemma of African American Leadership and Black Higher Education in the Early Twentieth Century*. Athens: University of Georgia Press, 1998.

Detweiler, Frederick. *The Negro Press in the United States*. Chicago: University of Chicago Press, 1922.

Dittmer, John. *Black Georgia in the Progressive Era, 1900–1920*. Urbana: University of Illinois Press, 1977.

Selected Bibliography

Du Bois, W. E. B. "The African Roots of War." *Atlantic Monthly* 115 (May 1915): 707–14.

——. *The Autobiography of W. E. B. Du Bois: A Soliloquy on Viewing My Life from the Last Decade of Its First Century.* New York: International Publishers, 1968.

——. *Dusk of Dawn: An Essay toward an Autobiography of a Race Concept.* New York: Harcourt, Brace, 1940.

Ellis, Mark. "Federal Surveillance of Black Americans during the First World War." *Immigrants & Minorities* 12 (March 1993): 1–20.

Ferrell, Claudine L. *Nightmare and Dream: Antilynching in Congress, 1917–1922.* New York: Garland, 1986.

Ferrell, Robert H. *Woodrow Wilson and World War I, 1917–1921.* New York: Harper & Row, 1985.

Ferry, Henry Justin. "Patriotism and Prejudice: Francis James Grimke on World War I." *Journal of Religious Thought* 32 (Spring–Summer 1975): 86–94.

Fox, Stephen R. *The Guardian of Boston: William Monroe Trotter.* New York: Atheneum, 1970.

Gaines, Kevin K. *Uplifting the Race: Black Leadership, Politics, and Culture in the Twentieth Century.* Chapel Hill: University of North Carolina Press, 1996.

Gatewood, Willard B. *Aristocrats of Color: The Black Elite, 1890–1920.* Bloomington: Indiana University Press, 1990.

Ginzburg, Ralph. *100 Years of Lynching.* New York: Lancer, 1962.

Goings, Kenneth W., and Gerald L. Smith. "'Unhidden' Transcripts: Memphis and African American Agency, 1862–1920." In *The New African American Urban History,* ed. Kenneth W. Goings and Raymond A. Mohl, 142–66. Thousand Oaks, Calif.: Sage, 1996.

Grossman, James R. *Land of Hope: Chicago, Black Southerners, and the Great Migration.* Chicago: University of Chicago Press, 1989.

Harlan, Louis R. *Booker T. Washington: The Wizard of Tuskegee, 1901–1915.* New York: Oxford University Press, 1983.

Harrison, Alferdteen, ed. *Black Exodus: The Great Migration from the American South.* Jackson: University Press of Mississippi, 1991.

Harrison, Hubert H. *When Africa Awakes: The 'Inside Story' of the Stirrings and Strivings of the New Negro in the Western World.* New York: Porro Press, 1920.

Haynes, Robert V. *A Night of Violence: The Houston Riot of 1917.* Baton Rouge: Louisiana State University Press, 1976.

Heinl, Nancy Gordon. "Colonel Charles Young." *Army Magazine,* March 1977, 30–33.

Hill, Robert A. "Introduction. Racial and Radical: Cyril V. Briggs, THE CRUSADER Magazine, and the African Blood Brotherhood, 1918–1922." In *The Crusader,* ed. Robert A. Hill, vol. 1, v–lxvi. New York: Garland, 1987.

Hunter, Tera W. "Domination and Resistance: The Politics of Wage Household Labor in New South Atlanta." In *The New African American Urban History,* ed. Kenneth W. Goings and Raymond A. Mohl, 167–86. Thousand Oaks, Calif.: Sage, 1996.

Jensen, Joan. *The Price of Vigilance.* Chicago: Rand McNally, 1968.

Selected Bibliography

Johnson, James Weldon. *Along This Way: The Autobiography of James Weldon Johnson.* New York: Penguin, 1990 (first published 1933).

Jordan, William. "'The Damnable Dilemma': African-American Accommodation and Protest in World War I." *Journal of American History* 81 (March 1995): 1562–83.

Kelley, Robin D. G. "'We Are Not What We Seem': Rethinking Black Working-Class Opposition in the Jim Crow South." *Journal of American History* 80 (June 1993): 75–112.

Kellogg, Charles Flint. *NAACP: A History of the National Association for the Advancement of Colored People, Volume 1: 1909–1920.* Baltimore: Johns Hopkins University Press, 1967.

Kennedy, David M. *Over Here: The First World War and American Society.* New York: Oxford University Press, 1980.

Kennett, Lee. "The Camp Wadsworth Affair." *South Atlantic Quarterly* 74 (Spring 1975): 197–211.

Koistinen, Paul A. C. *Mobilizing for Modern War: The Political Economy of American Warfare, 1865–1919.* Lawrence, Kans.: University Press of Kansas, 1997.

Kornweibel, Theodore, Jr. "Apathy and Dissent: Black America's Negative Responses to World War I." *South Atlantic Quarterly* 80 (Summer 1981): 322–38.

———. *"No Crystal Stair": Black Life and the Messenger, 1917–1928.* Westport, Conn.: Greenwood Press, 1975.

———. *"Seeing Red": Federal Campaigns against Black Militancy, 1919–1925.* Bloomington: Indiana University Press, 1998.

Levy, Eugene D. *James Weldon Johnson: Black Leader, Black Voice.* Chicago: University of Chicago Press, 1973.

Lewis, David Levering. *W. E. B. Du Bois: Biography of a Race, 1868–1919.* New York: Henry Holt, 1993.

Link, William A. *The Paradox of Southern Progressivism, 1880–1930.* Chapel Hill: University of North Carolina Press, 1992.

Litwack, Leon F. *Trouble in Mind: Black Southerners in the Age of Jim Crow.* New York: Alfred A. Knopf, 1998.

Logan, Rayford W., and Michael R. Winston, eds. *Dictionary of American Negro Biography.* New York: W. W. Norton, 1982.

Luker, Ralph E. *The Social Gospel in Black and White: American Racial Reform, 1885–1912.* Chapel Hill: University of North Carolina Press, 1991.

Lunardini, Christine A. "Standing Firm: William Monroe Trotter's Meetings with Woodrow Wilson, 1913–14." *Journal of Negro History* 64 (Summer 1979): 244–64.

March, Peyton C. *A Nation at War.* Garden City: Doubleday, Doran, 1932.

McMillen, Neil R. *Dark Journey: Black Mississippians in the Age of Jim Crow.* Urbana: University of Illinois Press, 1990.

Moton, Robert Russa. *Finding a Way Out: An Autobiography.* London: T. Fisher Unwin, 1920.

———. "The South and the Lynching Evil." *South Atlantic Quarterly* 18 (July 1919): 191–96.

Selected Bibliography

——. "Status of the Negro in America." *Current History* 16 (May 1922): 221–36.

Newby, I. A. *Jim Crow's Defense: Anti-Negro Thought in America, 1900–1930.* Baton Rouge: Louisiana State University Press, 1965.

Ottley, Roi. *The Lonely Warrior: The Life and Times of Robert S. Abbott.* Chicago: Regnery, 1955.

Petersen, H. C., and Gilbert C. Fite. *Opponents of War, 1917–1918.* Seattle: University of Washington Press, 1968.

Platt, Anthony, ed. *The Politics of Riot Commissions, 1917–1970: A Collection of Official Reports and Critical Essays.* New York: Macmillan, 1971.

Powe, Marc B. *The Emergence of the War Department Intelligence Agency: 1885–1918.* Manhattan: Kansas State University Press, 1975.

Preston, William, Jr. *Aliens and Dissenters: Federal Suppression of Radicals, 1903–1933.* New York: Harper & Row, 1966.

Reich, Steven A. "Soldiers of Democracy: Black Texans and the Fight for Citizenship, 1917–1921." *Journal of American History* 82 (March 1996): 1478–504.

Ross, B. Joyce. *J. E. Spingarn and the Rise of the NAACP, 1911–1939.* New York: Atheneum, 1972.

Rudwick, Elliott M. *Race Riot at East St. Louis, July 2, 1917.* New York: Atheneum, 1972.

——. *W. E. B. Du Bois: Propagandist of the Negro Protest.* 2nd ed. Philadelphia: University of Pennsylvania Press, 1968.

Schaffer, Ronald. *America in the Great War: The Rise of the War Welfare State.* New York: Oxford University Press, 1991.

Scheiber, Jane Lang, and Harry N. Scheiber. "The Wilson Administration and the Wartime Mobilization of Black Americans, 1917–1918." *Labor History* 10 (Summer 1969): 433–58.

Schuyler, George S. *Black and Conservative.* New Rochelle, N.Y.: Arlington House, 1966.

——. "Our White Folks." *American Mercury* 12 (Dec. 1927): 385–92.

Scott, Emmett J. *Negro Migration during the Great War.* New York: Oxford University Press, 1920.

——. *The American Negro in the World War.* Chicago: Homewood Press, 1919.

Seligmann, Herbert J., Jr. *The Negro Faces America.* New York: Harper and Bros., 1920.

Shapiro, Herbert. *White Violence and Black Response: From Reconstruction to Montgomery.* Amherst: University of Massachusetts Press, 1988.

Sherman, Richard B. *The Republican Party and Black America from McKinley to Hoover, 1896–1933.* Charlottesville: University Press of Virginia, 1973.

Skinner, Elliott P. *African Americans and U.S. Policy toward Africa, 1850–1924.* Washington: Howard University Press, 1992.

Spear, Allan H. *Black Chicago: The Making of a Negro Ghetto, 1890–1920.* Chicago: University of Chicago Press, 1967.

Sweeney, W. Allison. *History of the American Negro in the Great World War.* Chicago: G. G. Sapp, 1919.

Selected Bibliography

Talbert, Roy, Jr. *Negative Intelligence: The Army and the American Left, 1917–1941.* Jackson: University Press of Mississippi, 1991.

Terrell, Mary Church. *A Colored Woman in a White World.* New York: Arno, 1980.

Thwaites, Norman G. *Velvet and Vinegar.* London: Grayson and Grayson, 1932.

Toll, William. *The Resurgence of Race: Black Social Theory from Reconstruction to the Pan-African Conferences.* Philadelphia: Temple University Press, 1979.

Tolnay, Stewart E., and E. M. Beck. *A Festival of Violence: An Analysis of Southern Lynchings, 1882–1930.* Urbana: University of Illinois Press, 1995.

Villard, Oswald Garrison. *Fighting Years: Memoirs of a Liberal Editor.* New York: Harcourt, Brace and World, 1939.

Vincent, Theodore G., ed. *Voices of a Black Nation: Political Journalism in the Harlem Renaissance.* San Francisco: Ramparts Press, 1973.

Wedin, Carolyn. *Inheritors of the Spirit: Mary White Ovington and the Founding of the NAACP.* New York: John Wiley, 1998.

Weiss, Nancy J. *The National Urban League, 1910–1940.* New York: Oxford University Press, 1974.

———. "The Negro and the New Freedom: Fighting Wilsonian Segregation." *Political Science Quarterly* 84 (March 1969): 61–79.

Williams, Charles H. *Sidelights on Negro Soldiers.* Boston: B. J. Brimmer, 1923.

Williamson, Joel. *The Crucible of Race: Black-White Relations in the American South since Emancipation.* New York: Oxford University Press, 1984.

Woofter, Thomas J. *Southern Race Progress: The Wavering Color Line.* Washington, D.C.: Public Affairs Press, 1957.

Wynn, Neil A. *From Progressivism to Prosperity: World War I and American Society.* New York: Holmes and Meier, 1986.

Zangrando, Robert L. *The NAACP Crusade against Lynching, 1909–1950.* Philadelphia: Temple University Press, 1980.

Index

Abbott, Lyman: on East St. Louis riot, 40; and access to Wilson administration, 230–31
Abbott, Robert S., 280n21; investigation of, 23–24, 113–18; on East St. Louis riot, 40. *See also Chicago Defender*
Addams, Jane, 10, 202–203
Adee, Alvey A., 195, 202
African Americans: impact of American war aims on black discourse, 1–2, 4–5, 13–17, 27, 38–40, 41–42, 43–44, 45–47, 54–55, 62, 64–65, 99–100, 106–107, 109–110, 118, 121, 123, 125–26, 136–37, 149–50, 163, 181, 189, 191–92, 196–97, 199, 200, 203, 209, 213–15, 222–23, 225–26, 228–29; and officer training, 2–4, 50–51, 73, 144, 146, 238n8; white criticism of black draft, 11, 75; as soldiers, 55–57, 74–100 passim; and draft, 76–79, 258n14, 260n20; and army camps, 85–92, 262nn41,46, 263nn48,58, 265n76; domestic servants, 25, 67, 69, 80; and East St. Louis riot, 38–40, 41–42, 43–46; and rumor, 68–70, 80–84, 261n26; and migration, 18–25, 32–33, 117, 223–24, 242nn57,58, 303n6; editors' conference, 147–52, 280nn21,26, 281nn29,31; and Versailles conference, 186–87, 189–203 passim; and passports, 187–88, 190, 191–203 passim; army veterans, 203–26 passim, 298n108; post-war unemployment, 223–25
Albert, H. F., 120
Aluminum Ore Company, 31, 36
Amenia Conference (1916), 178
American Legion, 213
American Mercury, 16
American Protective League (APL), xvii, 82, 184, 208, 276n126; on *Chicago Defender,* 24, 114–15; on NAACP, 134–37; on black press, 271n51; membership, 236n22

American Steel Company: and post-war unemployment, 223
Amsterdam News, 157, 180; on a proposed black republic, 15, 106; on rumor, 82; on patriotism, 106–107; investigation of, 107–108
Anderson, Charles W., 280n21
Anderson, James H.: and rumor in Harlem, 82; on Briggs's editorials in *Amsterdam News,* 106, 107–108
Army Reorganization Act (1920), 186
Atlanta Constitution: on East St. Louis riot and migration, 40

Baker, Newton D., xvii, 88, 131, 145, 149, 151, 230; and military intelligence, xix, 62; on Charles Young, 51–52; and Emmett Scott's appointment, 54–57; on use of black troops, 4, 74; and lynching, 159; and Du Bois's commission, 164, 181; and black veterans, 204–209, 219–22; on army death sentences, 297n90
Baker, Ray Stannard, xii; on southern racial attitudes, 10; on white ignorance of black radicalism, 105; on black troops, 216
Baldwin, Roger, 102
Ballou, Charles C., 218; and "Bulletin 35," 79–80, 260nn22,24; refers to "rapist" division, 205
Baltimore Afro-American, 44, 45, 93; on East St. Louis riot, 39–40; on Mason, 66–67; on Loving, 70; reports rumors, 83; on editors' conference, 151; on Du Bois's commission, 170–71; on lynching, 223
Baltimore Daily Herald, 198
Barnes, Earl B.: warning to *Crisis,* 131–32
Barnett, Ferdinand L.: on East St. Louis riot, 38–39
Barry, Thomas H.: and East St. Louis riot, 35–36

Beer, George, 200
Bernstorff, Johann von, 48
Bettman, Alfred, 190; and investigation of *Crisis,* 132–39, 161; application of Espionage Act, 275n115
Biddle, Nicholas, 71, 82; on New York race relations, 53–54; on Joel Spingarn and Du Bois, 174
Bielaski, A. Bruce, xvii, 236nn20,23; and suspected black disloyalty 17, 241n53; and East St. Louis riot, 33, 36, 39; and investigation of Henderson, 44; and collaboration with military intelligence, 53, 82, 126; and investigation of NERL, 121; and investigation of Harrison, 124; and investigation of Kelly Miller, 126–27; and investigation of *Crisis,* 133, 161
Bilbo, Theodore G., 207, 303n91
Birth of a Nation (film), 147, 176, 266n88, 279n16
Bliss, Tasker H., 52; on deployment of drafted black men, 74
Bontemps, Arna, xi
Boston Guardian, 57, 104, 120, 148, 170
Bouldin, G. W.: prosecution under Espionage Act, 108–109
Boutte, Virgil M.: service in army and Visitors' Bureau, 300n128
Bowen, J. W. E.: on Du Bois's commission, 168
Bowen, Robert Adger: on black press, 117–18
Bowles, John E.: as Justice Department informant, 124, 190–91
Bradford, George C.: on Du Bois's commission, 168
Brennan, E. J.: and investigation of East St. Louis riot, 35–37
Briggs, Cyril V.: on black self-determination, 15, 105–106, 241n46; on black loyalty, 106–107; resignation from *Amsterdam News,* 108; on Du Bois's commission, 179–80; on visit of Du Bois and Moton to France, 199, 209
Britton, Roy F.: and investigation of *St. Louis Argus,* 118–20
Brown, Larmon J.: funeral of, 71
Brownsville, Tex., riot (1906), 75, 84–85

Bruce, Roscoe Conkling, 280n21
Bruff, James L., 207; files critical memorandum on NAACP, 171, 181
"Bulletin No. 35," 81, 93; criticism of, 79–80
Bureau of Investigation (BI), 101; activities and growth, xvi–xvii; and alleged German racial propaganda, xx, 17–18, 26–30, 65, 228; and black informants, 124–25, 189–91, 256n71; and black migration, 21–23; and East St. Louis riot, 33–38, 44–45
Bureau of Returning Soldiers and Sailors (BRSS): and employment of black veterans, 224–25
Burleson, Albert Sidney, 112; and wartime powers of Post Office, 101–103; and *Chicago Defender,* 116–17
"Burnt Offering to Democracy, A" (poem), 223
Burroughs, Nannie: investigation of, 61

Cadet, Eliezer: election as UNIA delegate to Versailles, 192–93; attendance at Pan-African Congress, 200
Carothers, W. T.: and investigation of NAACP, 134–35
Cavanaugh, R. W.: and East St. Louis riot, 35–36
Central Trades and Labor Union (CTLU): and racial tension in East St. Louis, 31–32
Chase, Calvin, 272n72; on black loyalty, 12
Chase, Wilson: on effect of NAACP literature on black troops, 130
Chattopadhyaya, V.: and intercepted letter from Waldron, 194, 293n51
Chicago Defender, 130, 147; and migration, 23–25; investigation of, 24–25, 113–18; on East St. Louis riot, 40; carries extracts from Simmons's speeches, 62, 113; on "Bulletin No. 35," 79–80; on black delegates to Versailles, 198
Chicago Tribune: on federal investigation of black migration and voting, 32
Christian Science Monitor: on enemy conspiracy as a cause of East St. Louis riot, 40–41

Church, Robert R., Jr., 253*n*40; assists military intelligence, 60, 63, 254*n*49

Church of God and Saints of Christ, 255*n*64; and opposition to draft, 67

Church of God in Christ, 78; and opposition to draft, 66–67

Churchill, Marlborough, 144, 151, 156, 161, 183, 290*nn*4,17; on German racial propaganda in Washington, 69; and Du Bois's commission, 161–64, 172–75; on Joel Spingarn's service in military intelligence, 176; and military intelligence in peacetime, 185–86; on black veterans, 206, 211; on black officer training, 218

Clabaugh, Hinton G.: and East St. Louis riot, 35–36; and investigation of Ferdinand Barnett, 39; and investigation of *Chicago Defender,* 114

Clark, Champ, 69; seeks federal investigation of East St. Louis riot, 41

Cleveland Advocate, 151, 221

Cleveland Gazette, 14–15; on black officers' training camp, 3

"Close Ranks." *See Crisis;* Du Bois, W. E. B.

Cobb, James A., 280*n*21

Columbia (S.C.) State: on lynching and migration, 19; demands no blacks be trained in South, 75

Committee on Public Information (CPI), 122; produces material for black audiences, 71–73, 257*n*81; contradicts allegations concerning black troops, 82; sponsors black editors' conference, 147–51; hires Ralph Tyler as war correspondent, 151

Commoner: LFD publication of, 225

Cook, George W., 166, 280*n*21

Cooper, William Knowles: on loyalty of black YMCA staff, 98

Corcoran, J. G. C.: and investigation of National Liberty Congress, 123–24; and investigation of NERL, 124–25; and investigation of National Race Congress (conference, 1918), 190; on Du Bois's visit to France, 190

Coxe, A. B., 185

Craig, Arthur U., 273*n*87; as Justice Department informant, 124–25, 189–90

Crawford, D. D.: on black morale, 156

Creel, George: attempts to influence black opinion, 71–73; organizes black editors' conference, 147–51; on Woodrow Wilson's denunciation of lynching, 159; assists Du Bois's passage to France, 187–88

Crisis, 1, 2, 3, 13, 142, 160; circulation, xv; and East St. Louis riot, 37; denounced to military intelligence, 57; investigated by YMCA Intelligence Division, 93–94; influence of, 104, 139; Charles Studin asserts loyalty of, 145; disliked by military intelligence officers, 146; and Post Office, 129–31, 275*n*108; investigated by Justice Department, 129–38, 161, 162; "Close Ranks" editorial, 163–82 passim, 288*nn*115, 119; on black troops, 216–17, 221; "Returning Soldiers" editorial, 214, 225

Crispus Attucks Circle for War Relief (CACWR), 267*n*94

Crowdy, William S.: and Church of God and Saints of Christ, 67

Crusader, 105, 108, 180, 199

Curtis, Helen Noble, 266*n*88; investigation of, 95–98

Cutler, James E., 183; on causes of racial tension in army, 87, 91–92; on loyalty of black YMCA staff, 98–99; on black veterans, 208, 218–21, 223; on migration, 224

Dailey, Frank C.: and investigation of black migration and voting, 32

Dallas Morning News: on need to improve life in South for blacks, 40

Dallinger, Frederick W., 162

Darrow, Clarence: opposes mail ban on anti-war journals, 102

Davidson, James B.: cartoon in *Washington Eagle,* 120

Davis, William H.: assists Emmett Scott, 56

De Frantz, Robert B.: and alleged agitation in YMCA, 93–95, 97–99, 265*n*73

Delafosse, Maurice: on Pan-African Congress, 200

Democratic Party, xii; and black migration, 32; Gunner on, 121

Dent, Thomas M.: denied post-war commission, 217–20

Diagne, Blaise: and Pan-African Congress, 199–200

Dickason, Frank S.: seeks Klan membership, 222

Dill, Augustus G., 170; denies *Crisis* is disloyal, 129, 135

Disgrace of Democracy (pamphlet): investigation concerning, 125–28

Division of Negro Economics (DNE): and problem of post-war unemployment, 223–24

Dockery, Albert: refusal to serve under Charles Young, 51–52

Domingo, Wilfred A.: on "Close Ranks" editorial, 179

Dorsey, Hugh M., 203

Du Bois, W. E. B., xii, 96, 122, 143, 145, 192; prominence in equal rights campaign, xiv, 104, 110, 144; on World War I, 1–3, 237*n*2; and his black critics, 3, 109, 113, 167–69, 170–71, 173, 177–80, 181, 287*n*111, 288*n*119; on spy scares, 11–13; and East St. Louis riot, 37, 41, 246*n*97; on patriotism, 50; and appointment of Emmett Scott, 54–57; and federal investigators, 129–35; relationship with Joel Spingarn, 142, 169; and editors' conference, 150, 280*n*21; and application for commission, 152, 159–81 passim, 285*n*81; and "Close Ranks" editorial, 163–65, 167–71, 172–81; and proposed history of war, 187–88; secures passport visit to France, 188–89, 216; and Pan-African Congress, 189, 195–96, 199–201, 292*n*44; acquires army documents in France, 201, 216–17; Sullens on, 207; on black veterans, 214, 220

Dudley, James B.: denies connection between migration and spies, 12

Dunham, Lawrence B.: on racial conflict in army, 86–87; on black veterans, 212

Dunn, John M., 183; on black veterans, 211

Dyer, Leonidas C.: seeks federal investigation of East St. Louis riot, 37, 42; and anti-lynching bills, 49, 118, 152, 153, 154; and National Liberty Congress, 123

East St. Louis, Ill., riot (1917), 73, 81; causes and outbreak, 31–33, 246*n*97; government inquiries into grounds for full federal investigation, 33–38; black reaction to, 38–40, 42, 43–46; white reaction to, 40–41; activists' attempts to see Woodrow Wilson about, 41–42; Gompers on, 42; Theodore Roosevelt on, 42; congressional reaction to, 42–43, 246*n*104; silent protest marches in New York and Providence, R.I., 43, 129; Baker on, 56; fear of repetition in 1918, 67; Ballou on, 80; Spingarn on, 156; grounds claimed by NAACP for full federal investigation, 282*n*41

Eastman, Max, 105, 226

Edson, J. S.: and investigation of Robinson, 137–38

Elaine, Ark., riot (1919), 30, 245*n*82

Ellis, J. H., 78

Espionage Act (1917), 17, 39 111, 113, 115, 164, 126–27; interpretation within Post Office, 101–105, 130; interpretation within Justice Department, 130–39, 275*n*115

Europe, James Reese: false rumor about, 84

Federal Council of Churches, 98, 194

Florence (S.C.) Daily Times: on spy scare, 7

Fosdick, Raymond B.: on rumor in Harlem, 81–82

Francis, Floyd Delos: questions blind patriotism, 65

Frankfurter, Felix: warned by Van Deman about black rebelliousness, 54

Frissell, Hollis B.: urges blind patriotism, 14

Galveston Daily News: on need to improve life in South for blacks, 40

Garvey, Marcus, 165, 199, 240*n*29, 288*n*118; suspicion aroused by street meetings of, 82; and Harrison, 121; on Du Bois's "Close Ranks" editorial, 177, 179, 288*n*117; investigation of, 184,

192–93; and Versailles conference, 191–92, 294n66; and ILDP, 196

German agents, allegations about: government reaction to, xvii, 236n23; white press and, 5–9; denied by black leaders, 11–12, 66–67; and African Americans, 23, 25–26, 48, 65–66, 67–69, 71, 72, 84, 127, 128–29, 142, 147, 154, 155, 157–58, 182, 228, 262n36

"Get Off the Earth" (leaflet), 44–45, 248n131. *See also* Henderson, James E.

Gompers, Samuel, 103; on East St. Louis riot, 42

Grand Army of Americans, 213

Greer, Allen J.: and "Bulletin No. 35," 79; writes letter to McKellar on black veterans, 205, 217–18, 300n126; LFD campaign against, 219–22, 301n133

Gregory, T. Montgomery, 279n15; assists Joel Spingarn in military intelligence, 146

Gregory, Thomas Watt, 12; and efforts to counter subversion, xvii–xviii; and East St. Louis riot, 35–37

Grimké, Archibald H., 280n21; relations with Du Bois, 132; on Du Bois's commission, 165–68

Grimké, Francis J.: on patriotic hypocrisy, 17

Gruening, Martha: investigates East St. Louis riot for NAACP, 37

Gunner, Byron: Justice Department on, 121; criticizes Du Bois's "Close Ranks" editorial, 168–69

Half-Century Magazine, 96; criticizes Du Bois, 179; urges migrants not to return to South, 225

Hall, Woolsey W.: and investigation of Wells-Barnett, 193; identity exposed in 1921, 293n46

Harlem Neighborhood Organization, 48

Harris, George W.: and allegations about German propaganda, 6, 8; and rumor in Harlem, 82

Harrison, Hubert, 174, 199; on East St. Louis riot, 40, 43; cooperates with Trotter, 121; and National Liberty Congress, 121–25; on "Close Ranks" editorial and Du Bois's commission, 172–73, 181, 286n94; on Versailles conference delegates, 186–87, 194–95

Hawkins, John E.: and investigation of *Chicago Defender,* 24

Hawkins, John R., 194, 280n21; defends black YMCA staff, 98

Hawkins, W. L.: and investigation of NAACP, 137

Haynes, George E., 144, 280n21

Hays, Will: on Albert Burleson as postmaster general, 104

Henderson, James E.: investigation of, 44–45

Hennacy, Ammon: on black religious objectors, 78

Herron, William: on grounds for full federal investigation of East St. Louis riot, 34–35

Hershaw, Lafayette: and "Close Ranks" editorial, 178

Hope, John, xiv; advises Du Bois regarding commission, 168

Hornblower, George Sanford: assists Joel Spingarn with anti-lynching bill, 153–56

Horton, James A.: and investigation of *Chicago Defender,* 117

House, Edward M., 75, 200; on Albert Burleson, 101

Houston Mutiny (1917), 46, 86, 131; execution of mutineers, 46, 57, 61–62, 81, 85–86, 130, 132, 249n135, 297n90; Parsons on, 50; Baker on, 56–57; and funeral of Brown, 71; effect on army policy, 74, 84–85, 129; effect on southern views of black troops, 75; Ballou on, 80; Threadgill-Dennis on, 108; prosecution of Bouldin and, 108–109; Joel Spingarn on executions, 156; Du Bois on executions, 160

Houston Post: on need to improve life in South for blacks, 40

Howe, Frederic C.: carries army documents for Du Bois, 216–17

Hulson, F. E.: and East St. Louis riot, 35–36

Hunt, Henry T.: expresses regret regarding withdrawal of Du Bois's commission, 175–76

Hunt, Nathan, 187
Hunton, Addie W.: employed by YMCA in France, 96; attends Pan-African Congresses, 199, 266n88

"If We Must Die" (poem), 226
Igoe, William L.: questions origins of Joel Spingarn's anti-lynching bill, 155
International Committee of Women for Permanent Peace (ICWPP): mission to Berne, 202–203, 296n78
International League of Darker Peoples (ILDP): bids to send delegates to Versailles, 196–97; meeting with Shuroku Kuroiwa, 197; dissolution of, 197–98

Jackson, Alexander L., 296n80
Jackson Daily News, 207
Jenks, Jeremiah W.: liaison with military intelligence, 49, 57, 249n3
Jernagin, William H., 136; leadership of NRC, 125; passport application of, 193–94; attendance at Pan-African Congress, 199
Johnson, Henry Lincoln: opposes Du Bois's acceptance of commission, 168
Johnson, James Weldon, 41; on German spy scare, 12–13; on patriotism, 15, 50, 79; and lynching, 60; Du Bois's opposition to proposed *Crisis* editorship of, 170
Johnson, Kathryn M.: employed by YMCA in France, 96; pickets *Birth of a Nation,* 266n88
Jonas, Rupert D.: participates in National Race Congress (conference, 1918), 190–91; and creation of ILDP, 196–97
Jones, Thomas Jesse, 272n81; advises military intelligence, 122–23, 176; accompanies Robert Moton to France, 187, 298n98
Jones, Wesley L., 162, 284n66
Jordan, D. J.: on black loyalty, 45–46
Jordan, Lewis Garnett, 294n59

K. *Lamity's Harpoon,* 147; objects to black conscription, 75

Karch, Charles: recommends full federal investigation of East St. Louis riot, 35
Kelley, Florence, 10, 165
Keppel, Frederick P.: and rumors in Harlem, 81–82; and investigation of YMCA Colored Men's Branch, 99
Ku Klux Klan: post-war growth, 222
Kuhn, Loeb and Company, 48
Kuroiwa, Shuroku: meets ILDP representatives, 197
Kyles, Lynnwood W.: secures passport, 202

Labor's National Peace Council, 120. *See also* Rintelen, Franz von
Lamar, William H.: interpretation of Espionage Act, 102–104; declares one issue of *Amsterdam News* non-mailable, 107; allows mailing of *Messenger,* 112, 270n44; receives complaints about *Chicago Defender,* 116–17; allows mailing of *Chicago Defender,* 117; allows mailing of *Disgrace of Democracy,* 127; monitors *Crisis,* 129; allows mailing of *Crisis,* 130–31
League for Democracy (LFD): formation and purpose of, 214–15; campaigns for dismissal of Greer, 218–21; publishes *Commoner,* 225
Lehman, Charles: and East St. Louis riot, 37
Lew, Gerard M.: investigation of, 95, 97–99
Lewis, William H., 280n21; defends Kelly Miller, 127
Lewis, William Mather, 155–56
Lexington Herald: on German propaganda regarding East St. Louis riot, 41; and "Get Off the Earth" leaflet, 44
Liberator, 226
Liberty League: formation and purpose, 121–22; collaborates with NERL, 148
Logan, Rayford W., 261n32; on army experience, 299n111
Loud, Joseph Prince, 165
Louisiana, State Negro Civic League of: calls for black people to enjoy same rights as aliens, 65
Loving, Walter Howard, 73, 110, 229, 253nn34,37, 291n24; work in military

intelligence, 57–59, 176, 184–85; relations with Queen, 59; relations with Parsons, 59–60; and nationwide tour, 60–64; and investigation of Simpson, 70; and funeral of Brown, 71; on "Bulletin No. 35," 79; on rumor in Harlem, 82–83, 261n30; on disturbance at Camp Merritt, 87; on conditions of blacks in training camps, 88, 91; and investigation of *Chicago Defender*, 115–16, 118; and investigation of *St. Louis Argus,* 119–20; and Joel Spingarn, 144, 286n96; and Du Bois's commission, 172–74, 181; on Du Bois's attempted deal with Scott on publishing a history of war, 187–88, 301n141; on delegates to Versailles conference, 191–93; on black veterans, 205–206, 212–13, 217–20
Low, William Gilman: and investigation of black YMCA staff, 92–99
Lynching, 78, 81; characteristics and frequency of, xiii, 159, 245n83; and migration, 19; and white fear of black uprisings, 29–31; in Tennessee, 60; linked to allegations of German plots, 67; military intelligence views on, 71; antilynching petition to federal government 72; Post Office views on, 117; wartime anti-lynching bill, 144, 152–58, 182, 282nn42,48; Joel Spingarn's call for Woodrow Wilson to speak out on, 144; Woodrow Wilson on, 148, 158–59; Du Bois's call for Woodrow Wilson to speak out on, 150; Baker's call for Woodrow Wilson to speak out on, 159; of veterans, 222–23
Lynching and the Negro in the South, The Truth about: defends lynching, 30

Macon (Ga.) Telegraph: on spy scare, 9
McGlynn, Dan: and East St. Louis riot, 35–36, 246n104
McIllheron, Jim: lynched at Estill Springs, Tenn., 152
McKaine, Osceola E.: on blacks' willingness to join army, 78–79; and LFD, 214–15, 219–21
McKay, Claude, 226, 288n119

McKellar, Kenneth D.: and letter from Greer regarding black troops, 205, 217–18, 220
Madden, Martin B.: and National Liberty Congress, 123
Manning, Richard I.: objects to training of black Puerto Ricans in South Carolina, 75
March, Peyton C.: and staffing of military intelligence, 143, 144; and Joel Spingarn's program, 151, 156; reorganization of military intelligence under, 183; and post-war retention of black officers, 218–19
Marshall, Thomas R., 41
Mason, Charles Harrison, 78; investigation of, 66–67
Masteller, K. C.: observes limits on post-war military intelligence work, 185, 212, 224
Meadows, Herbert: warned by military intelligence, 118–19
Messenger, 104, 132, 135, 180; and World War I, 109; and Houston mutiny, 109–10; and patriotism, 110; and arrest of Randolph and Owen, 110–12; and Post Office, 112, 270n44; suspension of publication, 112–13; and peace conference, 186, 290n19; circulation, 269n35
Mexican plots, allegations about: 18, 22–23, 24, 259n17, 267n94; and Plan of San Diego, 7–8, 239n20
Migration. *See* African Americans: and migration
Military Intelligence Branch (MIB). *See* Military Intelligence Division (MID)
Military Intelligence Division (MID): origins and military response to wartime subversion, xviii–xx, 236nn24,26, 281n38; growing interest in "Negro Subversion," 48, 65, 101, 141–43; reorganization of, 183; and army demobilization, 184–86, 289n3; and black veterans, 204–14, 217–19, 224, 298n108, 300nn129,131; and post-war attempt to connect black opinion and German propaganda, 228

Miller, George Frazier, 41, 196, 199, 267n94; on "Bulletin No. 35," 79

Miller, Kelly, 273n90, 280n21; on black indifference to world war, 1; speeches monitored by military intelligence, 94–95; attempted entrapment regarding *Disgrace of Democracy,* 273n95; investigation stemming from *Disgrace of Democracy,* 125–28

Miner, Uzziah: denies black duty to fight, 45–46

Missouri Malleable Iron Co., 35

Mitchell, J. E.: and investigation of *St. Louis Argus,* 118–20; and editors' conference, 151–52

Mitchell, John, Jr.: on benefits for blacks in world war, 15; gets mail bar on *Richmond Planet* lifted, 45

Moens, Herman M. B.: causes scandal in Washington, D.C., 68; attends National Liberty Congress, 124

Mollman, Fred, 32, 35

Montgomery (Ala.) Advertiser: on spy scare, 9; on draft, 76

Moore, Fred R., 41, 280n21

Moores, Merrill: introduces anti-lynching bill, 152, 154

Moorland, Jesse E.: and investigation of black YMCA staff, 93–99

Morale Branch. *See* Morale Section

Morale Section: and investigation of training camps disturbances, 86–87; and investigation of Sidney Wilson, 90; and investigation of YMCA staff, 92, 94; and surveillance of Moorland, 98, 99; reorganization of, 183–84; and Moton's visit to France, 209; and employment of black veterans, 224

Morton, Ferdinand Q.: on "Bulletin No. 35," 79

Moton, Robert Russa, 73, 144, 189, 203, 231, 280n21; on spy scare, 14; and retirement of Charles Young, 52; and appointment of Emmett Scott, 54; cited by Joel Spingarn on lynching, 156; presses Woodrow Wilson to condemn lynching, 158–59; on Du Bois's commission, 168, 180; encouraged by Wilson

administration to visit France, 187; criticized by black radicals, 195, 199, 209; misses Pan-African Congress, 199–200; exposes lies about black troops, 205; addresses black troops, 208–209; regrets frequency of black delegations to White House, 279n18

Munson, Edward L., 183

Murphy, J. H., 280n21; on effect of East St. Louis riot on black morale, 39–40

Nail, John E.: and rumor in Harlem, 82

Nash, Royal (Roy) F., 58; on blacks' reluctance to volunteer, 6

Nation: one issue declared non-mailable, 103

National Association for the Advancement of Colored People (NAACP), 142; origins and purpose, xiii–xv; holds conference on black Americans and the war (1917), 15–16, 147; and East St. Louis riot, 43; investigation of, 128–38 passim; and Progressive movement 141, 277n1; and Joel Spingarn's military intelligence work, 144–46; and Du Bois's commission, 165–70, 178–79

National Colored Soldiers and Citizens Council: publishes *Veteran,* 225–26

National Colored Soldiers Comfort Committee, 151; investigation of, 267n94

National Committee of Patriotic Societies (NCPS), 155; criticizes Creel, 72, 148

National Equal Rights League (NERL), xiv, 125; wartime stance and affiliations of, 120–21; Tenth Annual Convention of (1917), 121–22; Eleventh Annual Convention of (1918), 124–25; calls for "a National Race Congress," 189–90, 272n74; and National Race Congress (conference, 1918), 190–94, 201, 202. *See also* Trotter, William Monroe

National Liberty Congress (1918): planned by Harrison and Trotter, 121; proceedings and investigation of, 122–24; Joel Spingarn attempts to delay meeting of, 148; speeches attacking

Spingarn and Scott at, 152; Loving on black perceptions of, 174; military intelligence secures list of delegates to, 122–23, 213

National Race Congress (conference, 1918), 189–91, 201, 202

National Race Congress (NRC) (association): origins and support of, 125; meeting with Woodrow Wilson of, 125, 136; nominates delegates to peace conference, 193–94; and Asian Indian nationalists, 194, 293n51

Negro American Alliance, 65; membership drive, 255n57; attempt by black informant to infiltrate, 274n96

Negro World, 82, 177, 191; copies distributed at Pan-African Congress, 200

New England Baptist Missionary Convention: condemns lynching in wartime, 153

New Republic: on world war, 1; on training of blacks in South, 75

New York Age, 41, 170, 180, 187; on black loyalty, 4–5; on black delegates to Versailles, 198

New York Evening Post: carries Du Bois's denial of black disloyalty, 11–12; on black migration, 40

New York News, 6, 82; on black officers' training camp, 3; on Plan of San Diego, 8; on "Bulletin No. 35," 79; on Du Bois's commission and "Close Ranks" editorial 167, 170

New York Sun: carries letter questioning black obligation to fight, 4

New York Times: on spy scare, 6–7, 22

New York Tribune: on spy scare, 5–6, 22; black leaders deny spy scare reports in, 11–12

New York Voice: published by Harrison, 122; editorial regarding Du Bois's commission and "Close Ranks," 172

New York World, 79

Niagara Movement, 170; objectives of, xii, xiv

Nolan, Dennis E., 298n104; on black veterans, 210

Norfolk Journal and Guide, 39; derides spy scare, 12; on migration, 20, 104; on Uzziah Miner's protest, 46. *See also* Young, P. B.

Norfolk Ledger-Dispatch: on East St. Louis riot and migration, 40

Norfolk Virginian-Pilot: on East St. Louis riot and migration, 40

O'Brian, John Lord, 132; on subversiveness of black press, 130; on interpretation of the Espionage Act, 275n115

Odum, Howard: on southern race relations, xi

Office of Naval Intelligence (ONI), 76; post-war relationship with postal censorship, 184; post-war reduction of, 290n17

Outlook: on East St. Louis riot, 40; on lynching in wartime, 153

Ovington, Mary White, xii; asks Chandler Owen about his army service, 113; surveillance of, 136; on Du Bois's commission, 166

Owen, Chandler, 104; response to APL inquiries, 135; on Du Bois's "Close Ranks" editorial, 180, 288n119; on peace conference, 186; is arrested and drafted, 109–13, 292n43

Page, William: lynching of, 153

Pan-African Congress (1919): conceived by Du Bois, 189; State Department opposition to, 195–96, 202; activities of, 199–201; criticized by Garvey, 295n73

Parsons, Herbert, 143, 249n3; works for military intelligence in 1917, 49–50, 57, 58–60; liaises with Joel Spingarn, 49–50, 146

Passport Control Act (1918), 187

Payton, Philip A.: alleged to be connected with German agents, 48; mistaken report on, 59

Peabody, George Foster, 189, 208

Pershing, John J., 251n16; and deployment of black combat regiments, 74; on black casualties, 147

Persons, Ell: lynching of, 60, 90

Phillips, William A.: issues passport

to Jernagin, 194; issues passport to Richard R. Wright, Sr., 203

Pickens, William: on racial discrimination at Camp Lee, 93, 133

Pike, A. H., 190; on applicability of federal law to black agitators, 18; and investigation of NAACP, 131–38; differences with Bettman and O'Brian, 132–34, 138, 275*n*115

Pinchback, P. B. S., 280*n*21

Pisgah Forest Mutiny (1918), 88

Post, Alice Thacher: and ICWPP delegation, 203

Post Office Department: application of wartime powers, 101–104; attitudes toward black press, 105; and *Amsterdam News,* 107; and *Messenger,* 112; and *Chicago Defender,* 116–118; and *Disgrace of Democracy,* 127; and *Crisis,* 129, 130–31; Translation Bureau of, 117–18

Pou, Edward: on black loyalty, 8

Powell, Adam Clayton, Sr., 41; applauds Theodore Roosevelt's condemnation of East St. Louis riot, 42; and ILDP, 196

Praeger, Robert: lynching of, 159

Press, black: on black participation in war, 3–5, 240*n*45; on spy scare, 12–15; on migration, 20; on East St. Louis riot, 39–40, 45–46; on "Bulletin No. 35," 79–80; and rumors about black casualties, 82–83; investigations of, 104–20 passim, 229; suggested prosecutions of, 130; white officials and, 139; editors' conference (1918), 147–52, 182, 280*n*21, 281*nn*29,31; on Du Bois's commission and "Close Ranks" editorial, 167, 170–71, 179–80; and efforts of black leaders to lobby peace conference, 198–99; and post-war radicalism, 225

Queen, Hallie E., 61, 249*n*3; becomes military intelligence informant, 49; criticizes black press, 57; differences with Walter Loving, 59; exposed as informant in Washington, 70; on rumors of black casualties, 82–84; on enemy propaganda and black soldiers, 85; on YMCA, 97–98

Race relations, xi, xv–xvi, 9–11, 232; Wilson administration and, 37–38, 46–47, 52–57, 73, 74–75, 127, 139–40, 141, 229–32

Randolph, A. Philip, 104, 199; arrest of, 109–13; response to APL inquiries, 135; on Du Bois's commission and "Close Ranks" editorial, 165, 180; on black representation at peace conference, 186; elected delegate to Versailles conference, 192, 193, 294*n*66; and ILDP, 196–97

Republican party: and race, xi–xii; and migration, 21, 32

Richmond Planet, 15; and Uzziah Miner's protest, 45–46

Rintelen, Franz von: and German propaganda in 1915, 120

Robinson, J. G., 276*nn*128,129; investigation of, 136–38

Rodenburg, William: seeks congressional investigation of East St. Louis riot, 42

Roosevelt, Franklin D., 2; addresses black editors' conference, 149

Roosevelt, Theodore, 2, 32, 54; condemns East St. Louis rioters, 42, 159

Rowan, Eugene C.: refuses to draw up white soldiers with blacks, 88

Ruckman, John: calls for suppression of NAACP literature, 130

St. Louis Argus: investigation of, 118–20; and black editors' conference, 151–52

San Antonio Inquirer, 108. *See also* Bouldin, G. W.

Savannah Morning News: on need to improve life in South for blacks, 40

Savory, P. M. H., 105

Schoonmaker, F. P.: on secret black soldiers' organization, 210–11, 215; orders watch kept on Du Bois's activities in France, 216

Schuyler, George S.: on black loyalty, 16–17; on Charles Young's retirement, 251*n*16

Scott, Emmett J., 58, 80, 119, 144, 145, 156, 160, 215; and appointment to War Department, 54–57, 59, 73; and attempt to counteract rumor in Harlem, 82; and conditions in army camps, 85, 87, 91; and investigation of YMCA staff, 94; supports call for more black YMCA staff in France, 96; and Joel Spingarn's work, 143, 146; and editors' conference, 147, 149, 151; criticized at National Liberty Congress, 152; helps persuade Baker to approve Du Bois's commission, 163–64, 180–81; post-war retaliation against Du Bois, 179; asks Moton to visit France on behalf of government, 187; and intention to publish history of war, 187–88, 301n141; and Du Bois's visit to France, 187–89; and passport applications of black radicals, 193; Harrison on, 195; supports Richard R. Wright, Sr.'s passport application, 203; on black veterans, 204, 224; produces *Birth of a Race* (film), 279n16; assists Loving in 1906, 291n24

Scott, Hugh L., 50

Scott, Ligon (or Lation): lynching of, 60, 114

Sedition Act (1918), 120, 131, 164; passage of, 103; and powers of Post Office, 103–104; application in Cleveland, Ohio, 270n39

Selective Service Act (1917), 75–76

Sewall, Samuel F.: heads Grand Army of Americans, 213; gives information to military intelligence, 301n135

Shillady, John R.: and Du Bois's commission, 166, 284n75; releases cablegram from Du Bois about Pan-African Congress, 195–96

Simmons, Roscoe Conkling: on black loyalty, 4; undertakes speaking tour for military intelligence, 61–64; frequently quoted by *Chicago Defender,* 113

Simpson, Georgiana: threatened with dismissal for teaching pro-Germanism, 70

Sims, W. T.: lynched for allegedly opposing draft, 78

Smith, Bolton: and Tennessee Law and Order League, 128; sparks investigation of NAACP, 128–29; his support for anti-lynching bill sought by Joel Spingarn, 155–56

Smith, Ellison: objects to training of black Puerto Ricans in South Carolina, 75

Smith, Harry C.: and black officers' camp, 3; on benefits of war service, 14–15. *See also Cleveland Gazette*

Soldiers' Association for the Fight for a True Democracy: investigation of, 212–13

Spingarn, Amy E., 161, 162, 163, 166, 169

Spingarn, Arthur B., 166, 169, 280n23; addresses editors' conference, 149; on Du Bois's commission, 176

Spingarn, Joel E., 94, 229; and black officers' training camp, 2–4; views sought by military intelligence in 1917, 49–50, 57; persuades Bettman not to prosecute *Crisis,* 134; and work in military intelligence, 141–82 passim; aims as an intelligence officer, 141, 143–45, 146; relationship with Du Bois, 142, 169; academic career, 141–42, 278n2; posted to Washington, 142–43; encounters obstacles in government circles, 145–46, 171–72; creation of "Negro Subversion" subsection, 146; and editors' conference, 147–51, 158; criticized at National Liberty Congress, 152; and wartime anti-lynching bill, 152–58; helps persuade Wilson to condemn lynching, 158–59; attempts to secure commission for Du Bois, 159–67, 169, 175, 178; and Du Bois's "Close Ranks" editorial, 164, 180–81; faces criticism over Du Bois's commission, 167, 170; Biddle on, 174; posted to France, 176; Churchill on, 176; results of his work in military intelligence, 182; military service in France, 287n106; attends Pan-African Congress, 294n68

Stafford, Wendell Phillips, 162, 284n66

State Department, 204–205; and passport applications, 187–203 passim, 293n55

Stedman, Seymour: represents Randolph and Owen in court, 111, 270n40

Stevenson, Archibald, 184

Stewart, Joseph: alleged connection with enemy propaganda in Washington, 124

Stoddard, Lothrop, 10

Storey, Moorfield: endorses Joel Spingarn's anti-lynching bill, 154

Studin, Charles, 278n10; warned by New York assistant U.S. attorney about *Crisis,* 131–32, 133; gives commitment to Joel Spingarn regarding *Crisis,* 145; scrutinizes content of *Crisis,* 162; and Du Bois's commission, 166

Sullens, Frederick, 297n91; on Du Bois, 207; on black veterans, 207–208

Survey: on East St. Louis riot, 40

Taft, William Howard, 32, 54; lobbied by Emmett Scott on behalf of Loving in 1906, 188, 291n24

Taylor, Harry A.: files critical memorandum on *Crisis,* 171–72, 181

Tennessee Law and Order League, 128, 155

Terrell, Mary Church: as ICWPP delegate, 202–203, 296n78

Thomas, James: speech on democracy, 106–107

Thomas, Neval H.: prolongs criticism of Du Bois over commission and "Close Ranks" editorial, 178–79, 181, 288n115

Thomas, Robert Y.: defends lynching, 155

Threadgill-Dennis, C. L.: on Houston riot, 108

Thwaites, Norman, 184

Tillman, Ben, 10; objects to training of black Puerto Ricans in South Carolina, 75

Trading with the Enemy Act (1917), 117, 267n2

Trotter, William Monroe, 104, 174, 199; protests against segregation of federal employees, xiv; allegations made to military intelligence about, 57; feud with Washington, 59, 148; and NERL, 120–25, 148; cooperates with Harrison, 121; and National Liberty Congress, 121–23, 125, 148–49; criticizes Joel Spingarn, 148–49, 152; on Du Bois's commission and "Close Ranks" editorial, 170; and National Race Congress (conference, 1918), 189–91; travels secretly to Paris, 201–203, 295n76, 296n78

Truth about Lynching and the Negro in the South, The, 30

Tumulty, Joseph P., 126; prevents black delegations reaching Wilson, 41, 42, 189

Tyler, Ralph W., 267n94, 281n30, 301n141; hired by CPI as war correspondent, 151; writes critical stories about army on return to America, 221. *See also* National Colored Soldiers Comfort Committee

Universal Negro Improvement Association (UNIA), 121, 179; and Versailles conference, 191–93

Van Deman, Ralph H., 62, 63, 72, 88, 126; and expansion of military intelligence, xviii–xx; becomes concerned about "Negro Subversion," 48, 50, 53–54; liaises with Bielaski on black radicalism, 53; and appointment of Emmett Scott, 54; recruits Loving, 58–59; and network of black volunteers, 60; receives reports of Loving's tour with Simmons, 63–64; supports Loving, 70–71; and rumor in Harlem, 82; recruits Joel Spingarn, 143; posted to France, 144, 183

Vann, Robert L., 280n21

Vardaman, James K., 207; opposes black enlistment, 11, 75; defends Rowan, 88; on black veterans, 222

Veteran, 302n157; advises readers to retaliate to violence, 225–26

Vicksburg Herald: on effects of war on black expectations, 11

Villa, Pancho, 86

Villard, Oswald Garrison, 169; on Washington, xiv; on East St. Louis riot, 40; suggests silent protest parade, 43; and treatment of black troops, 57; and postal censorship, 103–104; and Du Bois's commission, 165, 170, 178–79, 288n115; and access to Wilson administration, 230–31

Waldron, J. Milton: writes intercepted letter to Asian Indian nationalist, 194,

293*n*51; attempts to secure passport, 293*n*53

Walker, C. J., 41; and ILDP, 196–98

Walker, James E.: rumor surrounding death of, 83

Walling, William English, 166; attends Pan-African Congress, 294*n*68

Walton, Lester A.: accompanies Moton to France, 187

Warren, Edward, 280*n*21; on Briggs's editorials in *Amsterdam News,* 106, 107–108

Washington, Allen W., 280*n*21

Washington, Booker T., 4, 59, 96, 158; and black leadership, xiv; and Emmett Scott, 54; Trotter's antipathy toward, 121; Atlanta Compromise address of (1895), 180

Washington Bee: on black patriotism, 12; on editors' conference, 151; on Du Bois's commission, 167, 171; suspected of disloyalty, 271*n*72

Washington Eagle: possible German financial support of, 120

Wells-Barnett, Ida B., 110, 125; and East St. Louis riot, 38–39; and Versailles conference, 190–93

Whaley, Allen: and National Liberty Congress, 122–23

Whaley, Richard S., 13; criticizes black enlistment, 11

Whipple, Durand: suggests *Chicago Defender* is German propaganda, 25

White, Walter: on "Close Ranks" controversy, 285*n*81

Williams, Charles H.: on conditions of black troops in training camps, 91, 264*n*63

Williams, John Sharp: seeks training of blacks in Cuba, 11; seeks action against *Chicago Defender,* 116–17, 128; on Charles Young, 51–52; on black soldiers' service, 216

Wilson, J. Finley, 123, 272*n*72, 280*n*21; investigation of, 120

Wilson, Sidney: court-martialed for writing ill-tempered letters, 89–91

Wilson, William H.: on Du Bois's "Close Ranks" editorial, 164

Wilson, Woodrow, 112, 187, 221; and segregation of federal employees, xiv–xv; on German spies, 8; and investigation of fraudulent voting of migrants 32; on East St. Louis riot, 35, 37, 41; and black delegations, 41, 125, 136, 148, 279*n*18; and appointment of Emmett Scott, 54; on Charles Young, 51–52; and postal censorship, 102–103; declines Creel's invitation to meet participants in editors' conference, 148; encouraged by Moton to speak out on lynching, 156; condemns lynching, 158–59, 182; and Fourteen Points, 186; on equality of races, 198; approves of Moton's activities in France, 209; receptiveness to uncomplimentary stories about black troops, 216; and policy on army death sentences, 297*n*90

Wood, Leonard: and black officers' training camp, 3

Woofter, Thomas J., Jr.: on war and rumor in the South, xv–xvi; and false allegations about 92nd Division, 216

World Forum, 197, 294*n*60

Worley, Harry F.: on Pan-African Congress, 201

Wright, Richard R., Jr., xii, 203

Wright, Richard R., Sr., 296*n*79; secures passport, 203

Young, Charles A., 166; on black officers' training camp, 3; retirement, 51–52, 73, 81, 251*n*16

Young, P. B.: on East St. Louis riot, 39; on migration, 104. *See also Norfolk Journal and Guide*

Young Men's Christian Association (YMCA), 133; provision in army camps, 92–93, 264*n*69; monitoring by YMCA's Intelligence Division (YMCAID) and military intelligence of YMCA's Colored Branch staff, 92–94, 95–99, 213, 266*nn*83,90; YMCAID assists military intelligence with surveillance of Kelly Miller, 94–95

Zimmerman telegram, 7